THE UNDYING PAST
OF
SHENANDOAH NATIONAL PARK

The *UNDYING PAST* of
Shenandoah National Park

DARWIN LAMBERT

foreword by Harry F. Byrd, Jr.

ROBERTS RINEHART, INC. PUBLISHERS
in cooperation with
SHENANDOAH NATURAL HISTORY ASSOCIATION

A Roberts Rinehart Book
A wholly owned subsidiary of The Rowman & Littlefield Publishing Group, Inc.
4501 Forbes Boulevard, Suite 200
Lanham, MD 20706

Distributed by National Book Network

ISBN 13: 978-0-911797-57-2 (pbk : alk. paper)
Library of Congress Catalog Card Number 88-063790
Printed in the United States of America

Frontispiece: Governor Alexander Spotswood led his "Knights of the Golden Horseshoe" across the Blue Ridge section that's now in the national park. Through this expedition and through his policy of granting land in the "west" to planters and others, including himself, he launched a rush for ownership and settlement of piedmont, Blue Ridge, and Shenandoah Valley. (From Hatch's *Alexander Spotswood*)

All photos not otherwise credited are by the author

The Shenandoah Natural History Association

The Shenandoah Natural History Association is a private, non-profit corporation whose purpose is to provide overall support for Shenandoah National Park. We achieve this primarily through the education of the park visitor, because we as visitors learn more about the park, our appreciation of it and involvement with it grows as well. The association provides maps, pamphlets, field guides, trail guides, and books on the human and natural history of the Blue Ridge region. Profits are channeled back into Shenandoah primarily through support of the park's interpretive division. Membership in SNHA is open to the public and offers the opportunity to personally support the park. Information on membership categories and benefits may be obtained by writing to Shenandoah Natural History Association, Rt. 4, Box 348, Luray, VA 22835.

Shenandoah offers much for our enjoyment as park visitors—vistas, hiking trails, plant and animal study, the opportunity to learn about the interrelationships within the natural world, and our place in that world. The stories of man's life in these mountains and Shenandoah's development as a national park are fascinating ones. This book explores those stories and invites the reader to become a participant in them.

It is appropriate that the natural history association initiate the production of this history as part of Shenandoah's 50th anniversary: Darwin Lambert was one of the new park's first employees and has maintained a deep interest in our mountains. The Park itself is entering into a new level in its transition from farmland to forest—as the effects of man's early stewardship fade and forest regrowth proceeds, an important part of Shenandoah's past might easily be forgotten. We hope that this book will help to celebrate that past, and remember it.

An anniversary such as this also provides the park, and those of us as park supporters, an opportunity for a healthy bit of introspection—a chance to examine our past, and perhaps plan our future in light of it.

Lynne Overman, Chairman
Board of Directors

Contents

When the last Red Man shall have perished and the memory of my tribe shall have become a myth among the White Men . . . and when your children's children think themselves alone in the field, the store, the shop, or in the silence of the pathless woods, they will not be alone. . . . When [these places] are silent and you think them deserted, they will throng with the returning hosts that once filled them and still love this beautiful land.

—Chief Seattle

Now when the angels come
To take my soul to rest
  They will find it in the park.

—John T. Nicholson

There on the crest where the strong winds blow,
By the trail that only the trampers know,
Scatter my ash like the driven snow
  On the peak of Marys Rock.
Fear not that I shall haunt the way,
To frighten the tramper at close of day,
For a word of cheer I will bring if I may
  On the peak of Marys Rock.

—L. F. Schmeckebier

Foreword

My grandfather built a cabin at Skyland several decades before that area became a part of Shenandoah National Park. This was Richard Evelyn Byrd, a lawyer and Speaker of the Virginia House of Delegates, 1908-14. He suffered from hayfever and spent each August at his cabin on the Blue Ridge along with his lawbooks. The only way to get there was by horseback or buckboard over a dirt road from the valley below.

When my mother and father were married in 1913, Richard Evelyn Byrd gave them the cabin, which he called Byrd's Nest, as a wedding present. My mother and father spent their honeymoon there in 1913, as did my wife and I in 1941.

As a boy, I went to Skyland frequently with my parents, and through the years I have climbed Old Rag Mountain many times, as have my three children and my nine grandchildren. My father's last climb was at age 74. As a member of the Virginia Senate, 1948-65, I had various legislative colleagues as my guests at Skyland and would test their mountain climbing abilities—which, I might say, were not as formidable as their poker-playing skills.

Through the years Shenandoah National Park has meant much to me and to our entire family, but it was especially dear to the heart of my father, who—along with George Freeman Pollock, William E. Carson, and several others—was instrumental in establishing the park. It was the first national park ever to be formed entirely from land that had all been lived on and used by private owners. My father led the effort to raise a million dollars from private sources to purchase the land, and the Virginia legislature appropriated another million. Harry Flood Byrd, Sr., was then governor of Virginia.

The land-acquisition program for the park—an undertaking over an eight-year period of vast proportions and many difficulties—was launched by a newly established state commission, Conservation and Development, under the able and enthusiastic leadership of its chairman,

William E. Carson of Front Royal, who devoted many years of his life
to the park. Senator Byrd, Sr., encouraged President Franklin D.
Roosevelt to extend and develop the Skyline Drive, which now runs 105
miles through the park along the crest of the mountains. Trails lead from
the Skyline Drive into the mountains. Much of the park is more than
2,000 feet above sea level, and it has about 60 wooded mountain peaks,
the highest being Hawksbill at 4,049 feet. The park was dedicated July
3, 1936, by President Roosevelt. On its 50th anniversary in 1986,
Governor Gerald L. Baliles and I were the principal speakers.

Senator Byrd, Sr., paid for the building of four hiking shelters within
the park. The first, Byrd's Nest Number 1, was at Old Rag in 1961. The
others were Hawksbill, Marys Rock, and Beahms Gap, in 1962, 1963,
and 1965, respectively. The delightful and able Conrad Wirth was
director of the National Park Service when Senator Byrd told him he
would like to pay for the construction of a shelter at Old Rag. Director
Wirth was enthusiastic. A year later, when the work had not been started,
Senator Byrd phoned Wirth to find out the problem. Connie Wirth was
succinct in his reply: "Senator, we haven't got your check yet." My father
sent the check immediately and commended Director Wirth for not
proceeding until he had the funds on hand: pay-before-you-go.

During its 50-year life, Shenandoah National Park has attracted an
estimated 85 million visitors. Annually, now, approximately two million
persons enjoy the beauty, the sereneness, the wildness of this park in the
heart of the Blue Ridge Mountains. It means much to the heavily
populated Washington, D.C., metropolitan area, most of whose residents
are within a two-hour drive of the park. Through the years, the natural
beauty of the park has been preserved. As a United States senator I
authored legislation in 1976 to designate 80,000 acres of the 200,000-acre
total as wilderness area. The legislation specifies that the trails to Old Rag
Mountain be kept open.

This book is a definitive history of Shenandoah National Park. It
traces the history of the area from the Indians 12,000 years ago, as well
as the early settlers of the Piedmont, the Shenandoah Valley, and the Blue
Ridge itself. It is a book a mountain lover can enjoy. It captures the
majesty and the beauty of the mountains. I echo what my father wrote
in 1951:

> There is something in the mountains that brings to one a contentment and
> peace of mind—that gives to every mountain lover a happiness that should
> be treasured.

Harry F. Byrd, Jr.
United States Senator, 1965–83

Ha'nts: Author's Opening Statement

The human story of Shenandoah National Park was in crisis when I became aware of it in 1934. I was an 18-year-old file clerk from the sparsely settled Great Basin, cooped up in a Washington office all day and in university classes at night, feeling desperate to escape the crowded city. One Saturday when the half day of work ended, I fled on my bicycle. I reached Blue Ridge forest as darkness thickened and spent the night rolled in a blanket beside a trickling stream. The place seemed wild and remote, but at dawn I saw smoke rising from a stone chimney. Imagining an angry mountain man, I hurried quietly away.

During the next week I learned the Shenandoah situation. Congress had authorized this national park in 1925 to provide the very escape from crowding that I'd sought. There'd been unending difficulties, and the park still wasn't established. Virginia had finally condemned the all-private land, but the U.S. government couldn't accept it because a resisting landowner had taken his case to the federal courts. This landowner was a mystery, becoming a regional myth. A giant physically and maybe in strategic initiative, he'd come from secret depths of the Blue Ridge, but his puzzling address was a town in Pennsylvania. The U.S. Supreme Court would soon be listening to him.

Though the park-land was thus in uncertain status, the 80-mile-long "park," occupying the Blue Ridge Mountains of Virginia at a width of two to ten miles between Front Royal and Waynesboro, already had 34 miles of Skyline Drive. This drought-and-depression–relief project, ordered by President Herbert Hoover while riding horseback with the National Park Service director near Big Meadows, was being extended in length by President Franklin D. Roosevelt. FDR, after inspecting by car, had further provided a thousand Civilian Conservation Corps boys to prepare the area for visitors.

The 180,000 or so acres were rich in mountain scenery, dashing streams and waterfalls, young forest cover, wildflowers, grassland, and birds. Larger wild mammals were absent, but there were bobcats, foxes,

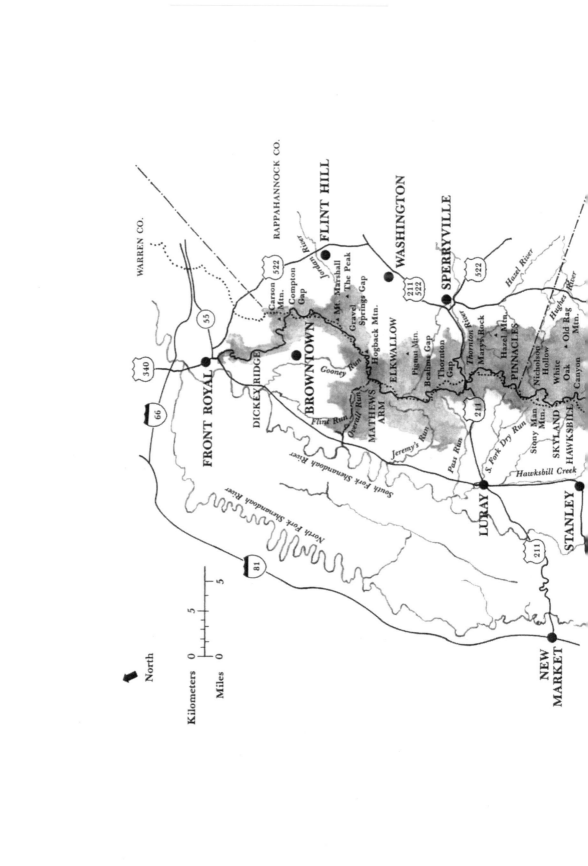

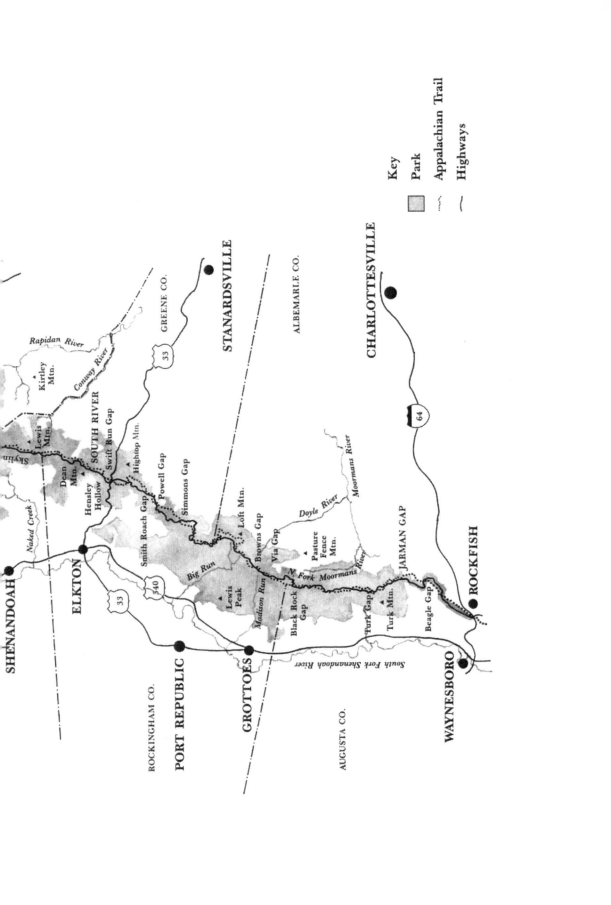

and smaller creatures. The park was to represent the Southern Appalachian Mountains in pristine condition and to offer abundant opportunities for "outdoor life and communion with Nature."

In some views it was falling short. Though incredibly scenic and partly wild, it had been diversely exploited for more than two centuries and still had a year-round population of approximately five hundred families. The forest was anywhere from second-growth to seventh-growth—spindly. The Skyline Drive (only the central section was then open) traversed more pasture than forest, and the animals seen along it in 1934 were nearly all domestic beef cattle. From your car you could easily see log cabins with families living in them.

Leading advocates of the park tended to feel embarrassed by the omnipresent signs of human use. But typical visitors were mesmerized by the tremendous "panoramic views" of valley, piedmont, and mountains from the Skyline Drive in its largely open setting. Far from resenting the human use, most visitors were intrigued by the people of the cabins. There was speculation about which myth of origin to believe. Had there been a mass migration from the highlands of Scotland? Or a mass desertion of soldiers, including Hessians, from the British army during the Revolution? What would these people do if they were ousted from their longtime homes? Nearly everyone supposed the park-land had always been the domain of the mountain residents (who did not mostly originate in either of the ways supposed), but in fact most of the land and resources had been owned and used by piedmont and valley planters, farmers, and businessmen from the beginning of the white era.

The whole situation pulled me. I applied for transfer to the new park—if and when it got established. My study of botany at the university became a spring, summer, and fall of collecting Blue Ridge wildflower specimens while also getting acquainted with mountain people. Weekends and all my annual leave were spent with the Newt Sisk family; the Sisk youngsters were good guides to where flowers were blooming.

Shenandoah National Park was officially established the day after Christmas 1935. National Park Service funds became available March 1, 1936. That morning I woke up in first light at the Sisks' and hurried down to Luray to be sworn in and start setting up the NPS files and accounts. Though I soon resigned to write and sell the park guidebook (1937), I've kept watching the Shenandoah show ever since, mostly from home alongside the boundary or briefly again from the inside as seasonal ranger or as researcher-writer under contract.

Removal of the mountain people, to return the land to nature's ways after more than three hundred years of heavy exploitation by white people, was an episode rare in history. Rare, too, is the half-century

Old-fashioned snowballs go on blooming a century after the people who planted them alongside their log house have gone. Other domestic vegetation surviving at old house sites includes lilacs, day lilies, snowdrops, daffodils, and periwinkle.

regeneration of wilderness. Where else has the supposedly inevitable trend of civilization, toward more and more consumption of earth's resources, been so completely reversed by democratic decision on so large an area? Where else has nature been so protected in re-creating wild forest populated by its native wildlife and rebuilding soil where erosion had destroyed it? The episode has worldwide significance. It shows that civilization can lastingly halt human consumption of some resources. It suggests that earth need not ultimately become a wasteland, as many people have feared, but could be saved forever as a beautiful and productive home for humans and other forms of life.

A hundred graveyards remind us that
these mountains were populated by whites
for more than two centuries. This
gravestone was placed near Overall Run in
1820. (Eileen Lambert)

A patent for park-land issued by Virginia
governor William B. Giles in 1827 to
"James Deen" (usually spelled Dean).
(Courtesy of John W. "Bill" Wilson)

One day in 1935 I asked Winfield Sisk, age 13, to guide me to the
Devil Stairs—the bigger one of the two. He told me the gorges of Little
Devil Stairs and Big Devil Stairs "ain't different in size. It's the devils
that's different!" He thus introduced me to the realm of haunts (locally
pronounced *ha'nts*, rhyming with *pants*), which was an influential part of
life in the Blue Ridge, and the rest of early America, too. I laughed with
Winfield and imagined a giant moonshiner with a long rifle running his
still in one gorge and a dwarfed but oh-so-crafty moonshiner in the other.
Winfield said he didn't know if the devils had been stillers long ago, but
he reckoned they'd been some kind of humans.

Recent-growth forest camouflages signs of human occupation and use.

The Corbin cabin as it was before park establishment, when George T. Corbin and family lived here. The gracefully tall white pine on the left and the cabin (saved as a hikers' shelter) seem little changed to this day, but the root cellar (roof on right) is gone and most boulders are hidden now by vegetation. (Anonymous)

After researching and writing a detailed administrative history of the park (1979) for policy and management purposes, I started digging deeper into the prepark past. It soon appeared likely that Shenandoah has more human history—in both variety and years—than any other national park. In cooperation with Shenandoah Natural History Association, my goal became an integrated telling of the whole human story here, beginning with the very first people. The tough problem was how to experience deeply what had happened before I came in—that far past, that old living and changing reality. In a section on Sources and Helpers I credit old documents, secondary studies, and living helpers. I can't similarly credit the haunts; many of them have been nameless anyhow.

Time and again, though, when I might have trimmed the story to a narrow line, the haunts have reminded me that people did just about everything in the park-land that people have done anywhere. They loved and raised families, prayed and played, hunted and gathered, knapped flint and mined minerals, deadened and felled trees and burned forests and meadows, made pottery, produced lumber and charcoal and other wood products, raised and processed crops and livestock, built wigwams and cabins and roads, founded missions and schools, fought battles, tried to govern themselves, felt longings and fears, pleasures and pains, and developed individual personalities.

Haunts of the most ancient people have been hard to stir up, but living intermediaries have helped. So, too, has standing where the spearpoints were found, holding a handful of jasper chips and maybe a broken point in my hand, and knowing that a pattern of posthole stains testifies to a structure many thousand years old. I tried this method successfully several times.

The haunts and myths of later Indians come more easily. Quite a few of us have found projectile points in and around the park. From childhood on we've heard of whites captured by Indians or living with Indians as traders. There are local myths of white families with Indian blood. We can accept tales of Indian hunters encircling elk herds with flames in the grass and brush, thus concentrating them for easier killing. The difference between fact and myth becomes not "true or false," but "habitually or rarely."

Indians who had Shenandoah villages before the white settlers came left before there could be acquaintance with individual personalities. Anonymous haunts have tended to come in the quiet forest—particularly when I've sat for a while among the small boulders of a burial mound. Our last Indians come to life much more strongly, though, in a remarkable individual. The story of the Medicine Man of Stony Face Mountain (Stony Man) is preserved in the lore of four families. I believe it is based on fact, though the details seem embroidered.

A different myth involving Indians—that some Manahoacs and Monacans living in headwaters of rivers rising in the Blue Ridge had rich mines of gold and silver—was never proved, or totally forgotten. It has meaning in our story because it influenced the attitudes and behavior of explorers and settlers. One of my most vigorous haunts, Isaac Overall, owner of 28,000 acres that now make one-seventh of the entire park, could never stop dreaming of a secret silver mine with no end of riches. He kept prospecting for silver and finding copper instead, but not enough in any one place to justify the cost of mining. I've studied documentary evidence of his obsession and its persistence almost through the 19th century among his descendants.

Among other haunts who've helped me is Lord Fairfax, who once had a slightly unsure grip on five million acres of Virginia, including more than half the park-land. He haunts Blue Ridge places where I've roamed, especially around Mount Marshall and along Gooney Run. He drew my wife and me to remains of the old Fairfax headquarters, Greenway Court, north of the park. Fairfax seems not a stuffy lord to me now, but a warmly human fellow. I regret I can't say quite the same of Virginia governors Spotswood and Gooch, who quarreled with Fairfax over the land, though in my reading of the facts they were as justified in their behavior as Fairfax was in his.

Other haunts I have feelings from include the mythical-typical planter (establishment gentry) in relation to the mythical-typical German farmer (nonestablishment). Somehow I draw satisfaction from the 19th-century trend that took much rich mountain land from gentry and put it into the ownership of nonestablishment farmers. Another haunt I feel sympathetic with, though reason doesn't altogether approve, is "the King of Free State Hollow," Aaron Nicholson. He may actually have been a near-dictator, reigning so strongly in his territory around the end of the 19th and beginning of the 20th centuries that—so the myth says—neither sheriff nor revenue officer dared venture in.

The past keeps calling to the present out of the earth itself and through local or family myths and haunts and the living old-timers and from the heavy old books kept in the court houses of eight park counties. The past speaks from stone walls and chimneys now crumbling and from Indian burial mounds and a hundred cemeteries of whites and at least a few of blacks. It survives in the makeup of the forest and as scratches or dimples on the land. The park's past reaches far beyond the boundary. Bits of it survive in all the lives that ever intertwined with park region lives, in old newspapers and clippings, in regional or family history books, in libraries and the files and displays accumulated by historical societies.

You consider all these things. You study old maps along with not-so-old maps. Indian place names in the park vicinity have faded out, except for a few such as the word *Shenandoah* itself, and *Massanutten*, maybe *Pocosin* and one or two more. The names on maps now usually tell who owned and used the land in the 1700s or early 1800s—Compton Gap, Overall Run, Beahms Gap, Thornton Gap, Hazel Mountain (not hazelnut or witch hazel but a human Hazel), Milam Gap (original site of the small but ultratasty Milam apple), Dean Mountain, Simmons Gap, Browns Gap, Via Gap, two Lewis Runs (one on each side of Lewis Peak, all once part of a plantation), Moormans River, Turk Mountain, and on and on. Most of the names are of British gentry, the big owners for a century or more, though Beahm is German, Brown may be Welsh, Via is French-Huguenot, Turk is Scotch-Irish, and Lewis may be mixed Scotch-Irish and French.

As if playing solitaire, you sort by origins of immigrants or routes they followed to get here, by counties or neighborhoods, by primary occupations, by different periods of time. Then you might shuffle and try different patterns. You go out onto the land again and again and look and listen and imagine. You may hear bits of old blues rising from basic failures of one culture to understand another culture—Indians pushed out by whites, masters and slaves pushing and pulling, the north-south war,

A ghost chestnut tree launches new life in a decaying crotch. The American chestnut, once dominant here, was wiped out by an oriental fungus blight, mostly in the 1920s. Chestnut wood has survived half a century but is now decaying. Persistent roots still send up new sprouts. (Eileen Lambert)

the rural and mountain peoples being ousted by urbanites bent on holiday escapes. You catch all the facts and feelings you can and weave them into a pattern.

Sometimes whole situations come together, complete with the characters of the drama doing what they wanted to do or what they couldn't avoid doing, or both. Other times every effort fails to clear your confusion. You know that never in a whole lifetime can you have wholly complete and perfect information, so you go ahead as best you can at last and sometimes make mistakes. If you're lucky, then, a haunt might come in the night and set you straight, or a well-informed reader of your typescript might save you from red-faced apology.

I hope this book will feel haunted—a little—as it tells the unique human story of Shenandoah National Park.

Darwin Lambert
Shaver Hollow
March 8, 1988

CHAPTER I

Spear Hunters

The people that Columbus mistakenly named for India, and that English adventurers dreamed would make them rich from gold and silver mines in the mountains, have never fully emerged from myth. But the pace of our learning has stepped up. Recent archeological work in and near Shenandoah National Park—and throughout the East—has shown that descendants of immigrants from northeast Asia used the Blue Ridge 30 times longer than have people of European and African origins in the centuries since Columbus.

The original Americans hunted with spears and ingenious traps to bring in the animals they needed for food, clothing, and shelter. They used trees for housing and fuel and other plants for food, medicines, and ceremonial purposes. Though little is known about the beliefs of these early people, or their languages or social customs, the lasting things they left behind tell us much about the material aspects of their lives. These aspects developed and changed over some ten millenniums before these people hunted with bows and arrows, made clay pots, or raised Indian corn.

The early people came at a time not yet agreed upon but more ancient than 11,500 years ago and possibly as far back as 20,000 or even 35,000 years. They crossed shallow Bering Strait between Siberia and Alaska when a "land bridge" was exposed because so much water was locked up in glacial ice. Many generations must have passed while the people found their ways farther and farther south, through an ice-free corridor in Canada or down the current-warmed Pacific Coast. Ultimately, and perhaps simultaneously, they spread into the western and eastern parts of what is now the United States.

The oldest date with possibly solid evidence of their presence in the mid-Atlantic region—but not yet backed by a consensus of archeologists—is from Meadowcroft Rockshelter in southwestern Pennsylvania. Organic material found in direct association with broken fragments from stone-knapping in the making of projectile points and tools, gave a radiocarbon date of around 18,950 B.P. (Before Present). Meadowcroft is thus one of the oldest dated stone-tool assemblages in the Western Hemisphere.

If the first humans were here that long ago, they confronted the Wisconsin Ice Age in all its frigid fury. The continental glacier had thrust southward deep into Pennsylvania. The Shenandoah–Blue Ridge may have had an isolated mountain glacier. All the higher mountains and the plateaus such as Big Meadows would have resembled the above-timber-line country of today—no trees, just lichens, moss, grass, and other small plants characteristic of tundra. Valley and piedmont would have had extensive grasslands and brushlands, with maybe a scattering of evergreen trees and birches.

Giant animals grazed and browsed. Among those challenging the early hunters were the woolly mammoth, 10 to 15 feet tall at the shoulders; the American mastodon, smaller than the mammoth but much larger than today's elephant; a ground sloth that could stand on two legs and reach tree vegetation 20 feet above the ground; and an immense bison with a horn-spread four times that of the bison found here much later by Europeans.

These giant animals, especially the species that lived in large herds, were once thought to have been confined to the midcontinental plains, but in fact they frequented the East as well. Mammoths ranged from the icecap to Florida. Though weapons weren't yet adequate to cope with mammoths, early hunters must have at least tried. Virginia archeologist Floyd Painter wrote of one that got away. Among its bones, which showed no signs of butchering by humans, were "more than eighty bone and ivory projectile points."

Remains of mammoth and mastodon have been found in the vicinity of the park. Thomas Jefferson collected some of the giant bones and puzzled over them. Shenandoah Valley historian John W. Wayland wrote, "In 1891 parts of the skeleton of a mastodon were found one mile north of Singer's Glen, by Henry Frank, while digging out an old pond." On July 25, 1912, Wayland "saw parts of one of the great teeth, preserved by Mr. Edward Funk."

In the 1960s, Virginia archeologist Elizabeth M. Wilkison studied a jasper quarry and stone-knapping sites along Flint Run, a stream that flows northward from the park's Gimlet Ridge and Mathews Arm to join the Shenandoah River. She found crude tools of the Flint Run jasper with "heavy patination," indicating "ages far greater than Paleo-Indian." At that unknown time—the date may correspond to that at Meadowcroft—the continental glacier's front was "only about 180 miles north" and giant mammals were still here in Shenandoah. Among the herd animals were

Jasper handax-chopper-scraper, found near Flint Run and the South Fork of the Shenandoah River just west of the park, is one of the tools described by Elizabeth Wilkison as heavily patinated and far more ancient than Clovis points. (Wilkison collection, reproduced from *Chesopiean* 24, no. 3 [Summer 1986])

caribou and musk-ox, found at least as far south as Saltville, Virginia. Wilkison believed caribou were the most frequent prey of the earliest hunters. The crude spearpoints in use at that time could hardly have coped with mammoths or mastodons.

In the 1970s and 1980s the Flint Run complex, now called Thunderbird, was studied by William M. Gardner of Catholic University, Washington, D.C., and his associates. They focused most compellingly on 11,500 B.P., when the remarkable invention known as the Clovis point was spreading quickly over both eastern and western North America. This exquisitely crafted spearpoint was sharp enough to penetrate the thick hide of a giant mammal. Many impressive weapons and tools on display at Thunderbird in the mid-1980s were knapped from Flint Run jasper.

The climate had warmed considerably by Clovis (or Paleo) time. Pollen studies show that the Shenandoah Valley had more and bigger trees. There were hemlock and pine in addition to spruce and fir. There were deciduous trees such as cottonwood, aspen, birch, alder, ironwood, blue beech, and already, it seems, a few oak, ash, and hickory trees. Yet extensive grasslands remained, in some places fairly dry, in other places marshy.

The Clovis point was a technological marvel enabling early people to kill giant, tough-hided mammals of 11,500 years ago. Clovis points are believed to have been used on strong wooden spears that were thrown at close range or thrust directly into the giant beast immobilized in a bog or surprised by hidden hunters. (From *Chesopiean* 24, no. 3 [Summer 1986])

Though the people used Flint Run primarily because of the jasper, there were other attractions, including good hunting. The Shenandoah River here was shallow, with winding streamlets and numerous islands. There were bogs that might help hold the animals for killing. The weather was least severe in the valley bottom, and campsites could face the sun. The contact among different groups at this attractive location must have approximated a regional congress, with much exchange of information and the year's best chance for young people to find mates not too close kin to marry.

I like to imagine highly skilled knappers working near the river. They'd use hammerstones to shape the top-quality jasper, then softer instruments of antler or wood to complete and sharpen the improved spearpoints that were being recognized across the land as excellent for bringing down mammoths and mastodons. When the knappers glanced up from their work, they'd watch the women in nearby open places gathering vegetable foods and plants. Or maybe the women would be at the base camp, looking after the children while scraping flesh from hides, making skin bags, or cooking by putting fire-heated rocks inside the skin bags.

Or the knappers' eyes may have rested on the nearby Blue Ridge that would have more trees now than during the height of the ice age. There would be clusters of pointed spruce, with dark green spires reaching skyward, and areas of dark pines. Yet most of the land was open, unforested still. Perhaps the knappers couldn't help searching for game animals on the grassy slopes that would become almost endless forest as the climate continued to warm.

Gardner and his associates suggest that the giant mammals were already far along toward extinction, too scarce to serve as a main support for the people of Clovis time. The principal game may have been moose, elk, or deer, and for these animals, too, Clovis points served well. Yet a mastodon or two might still have shaken up the groves and brush patches, or a few long-horned bison might have grazed the open slopes. If either were sighted, there must have been an all-out effort, for such a large animal would support families for a long time, especially over the nine-month winter when meat would stay frozen.

Some of the people may have spent all winter at Flint Run, probably sleeping in the large, skin-covered dome structure indicated by a post-hole pattern in the ground that was one of Gardner's first discoveries. This structure was rebuilt in 1986, using the kinds of tools and materials the ancients may have used to create this building, possibly the first structure in North America.

Remains of the oldest dwelling known to have existed in North America, perhaps in all America, were discovered in the early 1970s just west of the park near Shenandoah River, a location easily seen from Gooney Run Overlook on Skyline Drive. The discovery was the first of many significant findings on the Thunderbird site by William M. Gardner and associates. This drawing shows the likely appearance of the structure when it was used by Paleo people between 11,000 and 12,000 years ago. The framework of locust saplings anchored in the ground was probably covered with deerskins in the old days, as Thunderbird archeologists and helpers began covering a rebuilt framework in the 1980s. (Drawing by Steve Bair)

In the 1980s an eruption of scientific studies linked the Clovis people and mastodons in the eastern third of the United States. Articles published during 1984 in *Nature* (London) and *Paleobiology* came to grips with the reluctance of some archeologists to believe that Clovis people in the East actually killed and butchered mastodons. Evidence of mastodon butchering—beyond the now-doubted evidence of bone scratching that could have happened when the bones were trampled in sand by later animals—was also presented at the 1985 meeting of the Ohio Academy of Science.

After much study and conversation with archeologists, I find it easier to believe that there was mastodon hunting and butchering in the Shenandoah region than that there was not. *I can imagine a whole hunt—without, I think, contradicting known facts. People here must have had plans ready. When news came of a sighting—possibly near Flint Run—everyone was alerted. Mothers would gather their children in the safest places. All the men, including bold teenagers and probably the strongest women, would take up their spears and diverse noisemakers but keep quiet until just the right time.*

If the massive creature, towering so much higher than a human, was anywhere near a bog, there would be a stealthy effort to encircle it, leaving an opening on the side toward the bog. At a signal there would be a burst of noise, of leaping and shouting, of waving showy objects, of rushing toward the beast (yet with a readiness to retreat). If the beast fled toward the bog, there would be a fast closing in to keep it from changing course. If it moved in any other direction, a massed effort would be made to turn it.

Quite often, I fear, the mastodon would break through the line and avoid the bog. Maybe it would head for the mountains. The hunt would become a long one, maybe days and nights of following. The mastodon, unless grievously

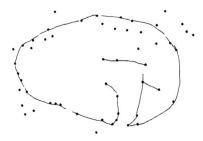

The pattern of the ancient dwelling of Paleo people was preserved through the millenniums as posthole stains (or postmolds) in the ground at the base of the plow zone. The new framework was erected at a different location so as not to disturb the postmolds that are the scientific evidence. Tools of the ancient style, used in the reconstruction, are shown interspersed with text below. The handles of antler or wood were held on with beeswax or rawhide or both. (Drawings reproduced from *Thunderbird News*, 1985, nos. 2, 3, 4)

wounded, was unlikely to charge and use its tusks on anyone, or trample the hunters. Probably it would move away from the people, toward the wildest place in sight. But this movement would be anticipated. The hunters would slowly push toward a gorge with cliff walls, perhaps toward a canyon that narrowed like a funnel and was finally blocked by a headwall. The high waterfall of what's now called Overall Run, halfway up the Blue Ridge inside the park, might do.

The swiftest hunters hurried ahead and hid in handy crevices or behind immense fallen blocks of rock. Or they stationed themselves on ledges higher than the tall beast's long tusks could reach. The rest of the party kept pushing from behind. As the canyon's sides got steeper, the mastodon was less likely to turn. Soon it was moving between cliffs it could not climb.

Suddenly it must have seen the headwall and felt trapped. It whirled, but before it could dash back to attack its pursuers the first spear from overhead penetrated its hide. As it swung toward that assailant, another spear struck, and another. Hunters rushed out from hiding places on both sides and thrust their spears into the thrashing mastodon. The risk of being gored or trampled was feared, of course, but the fear got lost in the surging excitement. The beast was bleeding heavily now, and one Clovis point, at least, had reached a vital place.

The mastodon collapsed. There were shouts of victory. Almost immediately the butchering began. The meat had to be cut up with stone knives into sizes that could be carried all the way back to the mouth of Flint Run. The people were so few that several trips would be needed.

Many archeologists are no longer comfortable with the notion of a clear end to the Paleo period of American Indians followed by a clear beginning of an Archaic period. They tend to see gradual change rather than out-migration of one group and in-migration of another. A few

Clovis families could have moved northward, of course, and some new families could have arrived from the south or the west. In this region a smooth shift to a more typical hunter-gatherer lifeway would have been easy enough. Gradually, as the environment became richer with warming weather, more and smaller species of game animals were hunted and more numerous and diverse species of plants were used.

Perhaps with scarcity and eventual extinction of giant mammals and the development of the spearthrower called the atlatl, the superbly crafted Clovis point was no longer needed. In 1986, during rebuilding of Skyline Drive in the park's south district, National Park Service archeologist Paul Y. Inashima found Palmer Corner-Notched points, evidence that people were there "at least 10,000 years ago." Kirk Corner-Notched points followed the Palmer points within a few centuries. Analysis of blood residues on both kinds of points showed they were used for hunting animals of the family Cervidae—elk and deer.

About 7500 B.P. the population began growing rapidly, and the people used the mountains more heavily than before. Differences in seasons became marked, so the seasonal movements of the small bands became more definite. Though the quality of stone workmanship declined, with

Paleo people here probably depended mostly on species of the deer family for their livelihood, but almost certainly they sometimes tried to bring down the giant mastodons. Evidence is strong that the people were here long before the mastodon became extinct in the park region. Some scientists believe human hunters caused the extinction of the great mammals of the glacial era. (Drawing by Steve Bair)

coarser materials such as quartzite more generally used than jasper, the variety and abundance of tools increased almost to affluence. Discarding worn or damaged points and tools and quickly making new ones from common kinds of rock became the normal way—easy come, easy go.

There was no agriculture, but hundreds of wild species of plants and animals were helping the people toward environmental and cultural stability. Food-grinding equipment like mortars and pestles came into use. Wild crops ripened over longer periods. When berries were gone in the lowlands, they ripened in the foothills and still later in the mountains. It was similar with acorns and other nuts, and with greens, roots, and seeds. As time went on, some people preferred higher land, while others clung to the rivers for their fish and waterfowl. The abhorrence of incest persisted, making frequent meetings of bands necessary for approved matings. Partly for this social reason—and partly, of course, for economic reasons—networks of trade and technology exchange became more widespread.

Based partly on the extensive archeological studies conducted in the 1970s by Michael A. Hoffman of the University of Virginia, *I'm imagining a day in 5500 B.C. near the middle of the park's south district. The chestnut burrs had split open. Many nuts had dropped, and the women, wearing only moccasins and wraparound deerskin skirts, were bending over, picking them up, and putting them in their baskets. The chestnut leaves had turned yellow, then bright brown. The great trees were still covered with them, though many were drifting down now and looking dull as soon as they touched the ground. A few whole burrs thumped down, and the shiny red-brown nuts teased through half-open cracks. One woman couldn't resist trying to extract them. The stiff points pricked her fingers and she laughed. The others, hearing, seeing, laughed too.*

The laughter stopped abruptly, and the six women—varying from teenage to almost elderly, yet each graceful and healthy looking—stood straight with ears testing. They'd heard something, but none could tell just what. The children had stayed in camp on the black terrace with the elderly women. Had a child screamed? The men had gone hunting, perhaps toward a range-crest meadow, but whether north or south, who could tell? Had a wounded bear attacked them? Or had a tree, uprooted on a distant slope, scraped and screeched against another in falling?

The black terrace is near the site of long-gone Black Rock Springs Hotel, the first commercial recreational development in what's now the national park. The place attracted people because it was good for warm-season living, offered berries in summer and nuts in fall, had excellent hardwood for spear shafts and tool handles, and was close to brook trout and, most of the time, many elk, deer, bear, and smaller animals. It was cooler than the summer-hot lowlands, yet within easy distance of both valley and piedmont.

The oldest spearpoint found at the terrace is described as "St. Albans-like," dated about 5500 B.C. Different kinds of stone artifacts found here were butchering tools (scrapers, knives, sharp flakes) and tools for working wood, bone, and antlers (axes, spokeshaves, denticulates). All these tools showed wear, indicating the terrace was a multiple-use center with diverse resources. At least seven of the knives had been hafted—that is, equipped with handles. The stone axes might also have had handles; they weren't heavy and were probably used to girdle trees and cut sticks.

Hoffman and his associates studied 66 other Archaic sites inside the park, which they located through a survey that covered almost one-third of the park's acreage. Several sites appeared to have been used for quarrying quartzite for knapping. The sites most favored as warm-season bases were near streams in hollows. Next in preference were flattish uplands. The gaps (or passes) all had campsites used for short stays by small groups throughout many millenniums; they told of a great many crossings of the Blue Ridge.

Hoffman concluded that the highest density of Indian population in the park's mountains was during the Late Archaic, 2500–1000 B.C. The people had achieved "primary forest efficiency"—that is, they made excellent use of the greatest variety of wild animal and plant species. They had reached "a stable economic adaptation" to the eastern hardwood forest and the open areas within it, which were maintained by the grazing of herds, the cutting and dragging of beaver, and deliberate burning by humans.

The people lived mostly in bands of 20 or 30. They ranged limited territories, moving seasonally. Their dressed-skin garments were prepared with the aid of scrapers, smoke treatments, awls, and needles (of bone?). They probably made some clothing and baskets of plant fibers, but in this climate such items were likely to decay within a few centuries, and samples haven't yet been found here by archeologists. By 2000 B.C., Inashima says, the users of the uplands were processing nuts and seeds by grinding. Around 1000 B.C. or before, the people acquired a few steatite (soapstone) bowls. Very likely they played a variety of games, chanted, and danced, had puberty rites for boys and girls separately, and sometimes smoked tobacco in pipes.

Burials were often in round graves that may have first been dug as food-storage pits. Occasionally there were bone-bundle burials (more than one skeleton in a bundle); sometimes there were cremations. Archeological digs have disclosed shell beads and bone ornaments with incised designs and sometimes paint. Bannerstones and boatstones,

Palmer points have recently been found on the main crest of the Blue Ridge near Skyline Drive by a National Park Service archeologist. (Drawing by Steve Bair)

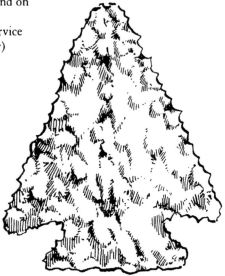

probably used with the spearthrower, have also been found, as well as antler headdresses and other showy accoutrements probably used by medicine men in religious or healing ceremonies. Most of the people were near-perfect physical specimens, strong and graceful. The hunting-gathering lifeway provided healthful diet and exercise.

When our women had filled their baskets and were walking back toward the black terrace, they could hear occasional shouts from children playing and the sharp cracks of quartzite knapping. Another family group had arrived. Already a temporary shelter of poles and numerous twigs had been erected. An elderly man near it looked up briefly from his knapping, and the women recognized him. He went on working, almost soundlessly now, using an antler for pressure-flaking to perfect the roughed-out tool. The new group must have come with broken tools and few supplies. While the hunters had gone for meat and the women for plant foods, the elderly man was hurrying to complete an urgently needed implement. There'd be talk later.

The old dog and most of the children came running to greet the women with the chestnuts. Water was boiling at the established fire, tended by two women too old to walk far from camp unless absolutely necessary. The younger women took over and boiled a skin bag of the nuts, while everyone tried to get into the chatter. The nuts were spread out on fallen leaves to cool before shelling. Later the nutmeats would be cooked further, along with venison or whatever the men might bring.

The Hoffman team studied grassy areas in the park as well as forests. Big Meadows—unusual in having both a reliable water supply and wide, flattish land as high as 3,500 feet above sea level—was found to have been occupied by people during warm weather for some four thousand years, beginning about 3000 B.C. Rings of stones suggest Archaic dwellings. Perhaps the stones weighted down "tents" or helped anchor huts where the wind blew so hard.

Big Meadows artifacts included axes made of Blue Ridge lava rock, soapstone bowls, a few tools of jasper and chert, and a great many tools and debris of quartzite (the blanks probably carried from the Koontz Farm site just outside the western boundary of the park). An art object of slate was found, cut into on both sides by a sharp implement to make a chevron design. Perhaps it was imported from North Carolina, where similar objects have been found.

Big Meadows and some other places in the park may have been kept as open land since the early people-time of mountain tundra. Tree sprouts could have been killed each fall by Indians burning the grass to maintain grazing areas for their "livestock" (which would eat any sprouts that survived the fire), and later by whites who burned and cut brush to maintain grazing for *their* livestock. These open places with fertile lava soil produced hundreds of different species of plants, adding essentials to the food and medicine supply. One of the products now is blueberries, and it's likely such berries have been picked by humans at Big Meadows for, say, up to ten thousand summers.

Our women processing chestnuts looked up through the forest canopy of the black terrace—the trees thinned by human use—and saw smoke rising above and to the right of Black Rock Mountain. It boiled higher into the sky. They told each other their men must have found a herd of elk, maybe on grassland near the head of the fall-fall stream—which had one waterfall after another—and were trying to use fire to drive or encircle or at least confuse the animals. Quickly the women gathered the sharpest knives. One with strong muscles and some experience in hunting found her own atlatl and spear.

The woman with the spear dreamed a lot about hunting. Now she remembered an old grandfathers' story. There'd been a different kind of big deer long ago—caribou—which moved in endless herds along the frigid, near-naked mountain range, eating lichens and moss and the sparse grass. A gathering of hunters had found a massive herd of caribou. Somehow, maybe accidentally, a grass fire started from the cooking fire. The medicine man said the Spirit had made it happen, to provide meat and skins.

A half-circle of flames drove the herd toward the fall-fall canyon. The hunters ran to keep the animals from escaping the trap. Yet hundreds did escape, the story said, because some of the hunters hadn't been paying enough respect to the Spirit. Other hunters were in good standing, though, so a dozen caribou were killed as they plunged over the first waterfall, and half as many lay beneath the second waterfall, ready for butchering. The Spirit sent cold weather quickly after that, and the people had more meat than they could eat all winter long.

The woman with the spear looked up and saw the smoke much nearer now, billowing from the grassland. She told the other women what she'd been remembering, and they all laughed because they couldn't believe their men were smart enough or good enough for the Spirit to kill a winter's supply of meat and skins for them. But still they hurried on to help with the butchering and the carrying. Even if no elk fell over the waterfall, the spearwoman thought, the animals would be confused by the smoke, so at least one spear would fly true and hard from the atlatl. Maybe her own. She'd be thankful for a share of one elk—and for escaping the moons of unending work that went into saving a surplus as large as that of the grandfathers' tale.

I pull back a little from the imagined people. Let's say they're haunts from half-conscious depths, doing what they used to do so long ago and thus giving life to the multiplying data of archeology. A moving picture, even if only in words, may integrate and enliven a thousand dry facts. Though reason may tell us these people are gone forever, we still may feel their presence—and each of the successive ways of life in the long story here—as glow-and-shadow background for the later chapters.

CHAPTER II

The Last Indians

The Woodland woman dug where reddish soil had been uncovered by heavy rain. She thrust the sharpened stick deeper, then pulled and jerked to get it out of the clinging clay. It came suddenly, and she almost fell. A yellowish red blob clung to the stick. Maybe it was what she needed.

There'd been talk of baskets that wouldn't burn. She'd heard it at camp in the mountains where people from foothill or riverside base camps had come to hunt deer, elk, turkey, and grouse and to gather nuts. Nobody there had actually seen a fireproof basket, but a stranger showed a piece from a broken one. The fragment was reddish tan—as this clay might become when dried.

The woman thought a clay basket would be handier in cooking than a skin bag or a tight fiber basket daubed with resin, which did well enough with cold water but leaked hot water. With digging stick in one hand and a flat stone in the other, she scooped at the clay. Then, impatiently, she dropped the tools. With both hands she clawed directly into the sticky mass. It clung powerfully. She didn't know whether she had the clay or it had her. It oozed between her fingers but wouldn't drop. A clay basket—or pot—might be possible.

Archeologists consider pottery the most obvious beginning of the Woodland period—which followed the Archaic, which followed the Paleo-Clovis and whatever was here still earlier. The first pot style in the park vicinity was trough shaped, resembling the soapstone bowl that had penetrated in small numbers but maybe more as a status symbol or for ceremony than for practical use. Shenandoah potting probably started with red clay, the pots sun dried, scratchable with a fingernail, softening when wet, breaking from slight pressure.

About 1200 B.C. there were Marcey Creek Plain pots in the Shenandoah Valley. The clay had been dug and dried, beaten to powder and cleaned of impurities, tempered with ground up soapstone, and only then dampened and kneaded. The early pots—or bowls or pans—were molded of flattened clay sheets. A century or so later pots were more shapely, only the bottoms being molded flat. The sides were formed of clay rolled

Indians called Monacans and Manahoacs lived where the Rappahannock and James rivers head in and near the Blue Ridge mountains, now Shenandoah National Park. Many of the colonists at "James towne" expected to get rich on gold and silver, which these Indians were rumored to mine in large amounts. The ocean and Chesapeak Bay are near the bottom of the map, the mountains at the top, and north to the right. The map shows Virginia as "Discovered and Described by Captayn John Smith," 1607–10. (From John Smith, *The True Travels, Adventures and Observations*, 1629)

between the hands, coiled in spirals, and smoothed with a roundish rock held inside and a wooden paddle striking and stroking outside. Baked in a quick fire, the pots got quite hard. Rounded bottoms proved better than flat bottoms for cooking directly in hot coals. Sometimes the wooden paddle was wrapped tightly with cord to roughen the pot's exterior. These pots were easier to handle, having shallow ridge-and-valley designs that distinguished pots of different times and places.

A type called Accokeek Cord-Marked became common here. Still later, styles were produced that archeologists gave local names, like Page Cord-Marked for a national park county, Keyser Cord-Marked for a nearby farm, and Rappahannock Fabric-Impressed for the river if not the park county. The Page style was tempered with ground limestone. The Keyser was tempered with crushed mussel shells from the Shenandoah River. These round-based pots had somewhat narrowed necks, wide mouths, and slightly flared rims. They were decorated with a cord-marked stick and by incised or punctate designs.

This rock shelter in the Park's south district is one of many sites used by Indians for millenniums before Virginia colonists came from Europe. As former park ranger Roy Sullivan shows, a person could sit or lie down here but not stand up.

Styles of pots, as well as styles of stone points, distinguish centuries when different archeological sites had been occupied. The Hoffman group studied 26 Early Woodland sites inside the park, finding no evidence of abrupt change from Archaic customs except in the pottery sherds. Big Meadows on top of the range continued in use, but most of the hunting-gathering camps were in the larger hollows—some of which would later be occupied by Caucasians.

A rockshelter in the park's south district linked Archaic and Woodland periods in successive layers, showing continual use from about 2000 B.C. to about 1600 A.D. Quartzite boulders deposited by floodwaters just outside the shelter were cracked and shaped into stone tools. The people hunted and gathered nearby. The differing artifacts of three strata strengthen the picture, poorly documented elsewhere in Virginia, of the millenniums-long change from hunting and gathering to a more sedentary life based partly on agriculture. Here, as elsewhere, pottery indicates that people were settling down in villages, as pots, being fragile, don't travel well. Most of the 112 sherds found in the rockshelter had cord or fabric markings of styles indicating use of these mountains by both valley and piedmont people.

Capt. John Smith of the Jamestown colony identified the Indians of the east slope, at least, of Shenandoah park-land. What he called "Powhatan flu"—now James River—"is navigable 150 myles," he wrote. "It falleth from Rockes farre west in a Country inhabited by a nation they call *Monacans*." Further, the Rappahannock "is navigable some 130 myles. At the top of it inhabit the people called *Mannahoacks* amongst the mountaines." Smith's information came from Indians nearer the coast, probably Powhatans. They reported that a confederacy of upper piedmont and Blue Ridge Indians was frequently at war with the coastal Indians. The Powhatans apparently played war games, dividing into groups called Monacans and Powhatans and practicing for the next real encounter.

A German scholar named John Lederer (whose explorations will be described in Chapter 3) actually visited these Indians of the upper piedmont and received impressions different from Smith's. Lederer found the Indians peaceable and surprisingly intelligent. "The faculties of the minde and body they commonly express by Emblemes," he wrote. "By the figure of a Stag, they imply swiftness; by that of a Serpent, wrath; of a Lion, courage; of a Dog, fidelity; by a Swan, they signifie the English, alluding to their complexion, and flight over the Sea." Lederer said the Indians had a kind of calendar arranged on a string or leather thong with knots of varying colors, the string being wrapped on "small Wheels." They worshiped "one God, Creator of all things." They believed the first humans were four women, who gave rise to four tribes. Marriages must be between members of two different tribes—"for two of the same Tribe to match, is abhorred as Incest, and punished with great severity." Lederer continued:

Though they want those means of improving Humane Reason, which the use of Letters affords us; let us not therefore conclude them wholly destitute of Learning and Sciences: for by these little helps which they have found, many of them advance their natural understandings to great knowledge in Physick, Rhetorick, and Policie of Government: for I have been present at several of their Consultations and Debates, and to my admiration have heard some of their Seniors deliver themselves with as much Judgement and Eloquence as I should have expected from men of Civil education and Literature.

Skeleton of Indian woman found by Archeological Society of Virginia excavators in the Shenandoah region about 1969.

Woodland Indians of the East used an astonishing number of wild plant species—at least 130 for food, 275 for medicine, 31 in rites of magic, 27 for smoking, 25 for dyes, 18 in beverages or to flavor food, and 52 for other purposes. Among those found in the park were gooseberries, black-gum berries, crabapples, onions, moss, mulberries, wild peas and hog peanuts, persimmons, grapes, prickly pears (yes, this cactus is native here), many kinds of mushrooms, smilax or greenbrier roots, strawberries, wild sweet potatoes, haw-apples. The Indians used several tree species, not only sugar maple, to make sugar and syrup. They used reeds, grasses, and other fiber plants for baskets and mats, fish traps, and nets.

The native tobacco (*Nicotiana rustica*) was used throughout the East for ceremonial smoking, often mixed with other plants including sumac. Tobacco wasn't just smoked but was cast upon the waters or the ground or elsewhere to show respect to the Great Spirit or some lesser spirit such as that of a tree, a peak, or a stream. Medicine men were priests and conjurers as well as herb doctors.

Woodlanders—and most likely their predecessors, too—sometimes used mountain laurel to commit suicide. Hepatica, which produces early wildflowers in the park, was a treatment for coughs; the roots, combined with maidenhair-fern roots, were taken for women's ailments including leukorrhea. Pipsissewa and its near-relative, spotted wintergreen, had many medicinal uses—to relieve dropsy, rheumatism, female troubles, internal ulcers, and external wounds. Skunk cabbage leaves made bandages for wounds, or the root was powdered and applied to wounds or used against colds and headaches.

Deer was the most important wild animal in the Woodland lifeway, providing most of the meat and clothing. Parts of antler were used as tools in fine-flaking stone points, and antler tips themselves might serve as projectile points. Deerskin might be stretched over a pot or section of hollow log to make a drum. Deer hoofs might become rattles in dances or be boiled to make glue. Sinews and other fibers from deer became thread or cord, sometimes fishnets, sometimes bowstrings. Parts of antlers or bones were made into needles.

Bear fats and oils were used in cooking; the whole hide with fur left on made a good robe or bedding. Thongs of bear innards became bowstrings. Bear claws were ornaments. Beavers were eaten. The skins could make clothing or pouches. A tree-cutting tooth from a beaver could be fastened onto a handle and do cutting for humans. Elk was good food, and the hides made clothes, including moccasins. Most other mammals were also hunted. Raccoon meat was tasty and nourishing, and other parts were useful. Squirrels and rabbits were pleasing food. Turkey was the main bird hunted in the mountains. One big turkey made a feast, and its feathers would be used to wear or to stabilize arrows in flight. Grouse and quail were hunted. Bird eggs were eaten. Wasp larvae, cicadas, beetles, grubs, and wood borers proved tasty.

It's not known exactly when the bow and arrow replaced the spear for hunting in the park region. Some archeologists say the time of Christ; others, not until after 800 A.D. Perhaps for a long time both spears and arrows were used, depending on what creature was being hunted. The small points, usually triangular, that are most easily identified as Woodland arrowheads are reliably dated around 1400 A.D., but other arrowheads preceded them.

Many boys have pretended to be Indians. I once made a bow of a green branch about an inch in diameter and four feet long. I peeled off the bark and tapered the ends, bent the bow slightly and tied on a bowstring of hard cord. I made a few simple arrows and once hit a bull's-eye painted on a pasteboard box. But when I tried for rabbits I got skunked—always zero score.

The making of good bows and arrows by real Indians was different. Here's how archeologist-scholar M. R. Harrington says to proceed: Choose a tree three handspans around without branches near the base. Scatter tobacco around the trunk, then speak respectfully to the tree.

When you sense permission, grasp your flint knife (with buckskin to protect your hand) and saw into the tree a foot from the bottom, making a horizontal, inch-deep groove. Make a similar groove five feet above, then two vertical grooves three fingers apart connecting the horizontal grooves. This will take hours. Maybe you'll need to come back tomorrow. Use a stone wedge to split off a piece an inch by an inch and one-half by five feet. This must season, maybe for months, even a year. Then, with your flint scraper, shave the piece down to two fingers wide in the middle and one finger wide at the ends. Leave it flat on the back where the bark was; round it on the belly. Smooth it well. Notch the ends for the bowstring. Grease with bear grease.

The most obvious signs of Woodlanders in the park's region—after the Indians themselves and their wigwams were gone—are burial mounds. The Middle Woodland mounds are on the valley side only. They are small and scattered, made for several centuries beginning about 430 A.D. Joan Walker of Thunderbird reported 16 such mounds of cobbles "on bluff tops overlooking broad floodplains." Pits under the cobbles contained no more than five skeletons each. The charred appearance suggests use of ceremonial fire when human remains were buried.

Later and larger burial mounds, dating from shortly before the white people came, have been found on both sides of the park but no farther east than the upper piedmont. Several were inside the park (see Appendix 1, Cemeteries in the Park), but most were on lower land, near the good-sized streams where most families lived. They've been reported as big as 40 feet in diameter and 10 feet high, but most were smaller. Nearly all have been reduced or obliterated by plowing or "pot hunters." Along with human bones, many had projectile points, pipes, beads, axes, and other artifacts. The bringing together of numerous bodies at one site indicates a social-political organization larger than the family or small band, likely a cohesive though scattered cluster of hamlets.

Three sizable mounds (known to Thomas Jefferson) near Jarman Gap suggest home hamlets inside the park boundary. The two I visited had been plundered, but the raised areas of smallish boulders remained noticeable in the forest. The burial mound below and to the west of Stony Man, visited by archeologist Gerard Fowke, must have been inside the park. The Virginia State Library has an unpublished record of four "Indian cairns," one 20 by 20 feet, "on the farm of Captain Simpson" south of Front Royal. Part of this old Simpson plantation is in the park.

Woodland Indians in some locations raised crops as early as 1000 B.C., but archeologists doubt there was significant agriculture in the park region until 900 A.D. Whenever cultivation did get going, the wooden digging stick was the main tool, though on the looser soils of floodplains hoes made of deer shoulder blades mounted on wooden handles were often used. The possibility of accumulating surpluses beyond immediate needs necessitated the digging of pits for storage and increased the size and permanence of villages. Agriculture here seldom provided more than 25 percent of the Indians' nutrition; the men still hunted and the women still gathered.

Fire was used in village agriculture—as, according to Fowke, it was used on a much larger scale "to prevent timber from growing and thus diminishing the area of their hunting grounds." The Indians here used fire in spring to sweep dried weeds and other debris off the cropland. New ground was cleared for cultivation every few years, and the old gardens were allowed to go back to forest. Corn hills were about four feet apart. With a stick a hole was punched in each and about five seeds dropped in, after which a heel thrust closed the hole. When the corn came up, vine beans were planted to spread between corn hills. Tall-growing sunflowers lined the northern edge where they'd cast no shadows on other crops. Wild creatures raided corn just as they do still; a boy was often assigned to sleep in the corn patch to chase raiders out.

At least five kinds of corn were raised, some maturing early, others late. Hard corn might be made into hominy. Soft white corn might make flour—and bread. The shelled corn was first boiled to loosen the hulls, after which the soft parts were ground with mortar and pestle. Bread was usually baked in hot ashes. All parts of the corn plants might be used; dried leaves, for instance, could be woven as mats or rugs.

Village ceremonies thanked the Spirit for the harvest, perhaps with dancing accompanied by the rhythmic rattle of beans or pebbles in a dry gourd. The children played games, some organized with rules, other rough and tumble—swimming, running, tag. Boys often wrestled—as white boys do.

The method used in constructing homes resulted in rounded sides and roofs. Trees three or four inches thick in the trunk, often black locust, were cut green, peeled, and charred a bit. The big ends were put into the ground, about four feet apart in the circle, and the limber tops were bent over and tied together to make a dome. Thinner poles lashed horizontally reinforced the verticals. The structure was then covered with big pieces of bark, or sometimes with skins, except for a hole at the top to let out the smoke from the fire in the center of the earthen floor.

Clothing was generally made of skins well scraped on the inside, soft tanned with a paste of deer brains and wood ashes, and dried in smoke from burning corncobs. Men and boys wore breechclouts and, when weather got cold, shirts and maybe large skins tied over one shoulder and

Shapes and sizes of Woodland Indians' dwellings varied widely, but most in the park region were dome-shaped by the custom of thrusting lightly charred locust saplings into the ground and tying the limber branches and twigs together overhead. The homes were covered with pieces of bark or with skins. The door opening could be closed with large skins, such as of elk or bison. Corn, beans, and squash grew in the garden. (Drawing by Steve Bair)

possibly around the waist. Women wore skirts reaching from the waist almost to the knees, sometimes fringed. In cold weather they covered the upper part of their bodies with a mantle of skins and added leggings. They often wore ornaments of shells or beads. Most women had long, black hair, but most men had their hair cut short. Men might be painted colorfully. Most women weren't painted, though a few had diverse designs tatooed on their bodies.

The Indians began disappearing even before white settlement in the park region, though disorganized groups continued to move through or even camp a while. Fact is, the white people's influences had been damaging the Indians indirectly for at least a century. Iroquoian aggression had been strengthened by French and Dutch fur traders. More Virginia Indians had been dying of white people's diseases—smallpox, measles, tuberculosis—than from guns, somewhat as more Europeans in Virginia had been dying of Indian diseases—"swamp fevers" including malaria and yellow fever—than from tomahawks and arrows. But

Europeans were being replaced in Virginia by long-continued immigration, while Indians simply dwindled and disappeared.

John R. Swanton of the Smithsonian's Bureau of American Ethnology, who weighed the words of explorers along with archeological data, concluded the park region was peopled in 1650 by Sioux-speaking groups. There were about one thousand Manahoac and a similar scattering of Monacan. Before 1700 most of them had died or moved out of the region, joining other groups offering temporary reinforcement. Some remnants may later have lived with the powerful Iroquois and been absorbed. No descendants are now known. Though rumors of rich gold and silver mines that spread in colonial Virginia are matched by rumors around these mountains today, the Monacans and Manahoacs never revealed any such mines. An Indian copper mine was, however, found on Mount Marshall in the park's north district.

Nothing seems to be known for sure about who lived on the parkland's west slope and in the valley before the Europeans came to Virginia. Somebody was surely here in substantial numbers, however, during the 1400s and 1500s. They used a lot of Keyser-type pottery tempered with mussel shells, but their villages were deserted when the quarrel of the northern and southern Indians intensified over the fur trade. A great warpath traversed the valley, with a branch along both Shenandoah forks and a less-used branch along the eastern foothills of the Blue Ridge. The north-south conflict continued until about 1722, keeping the region a no-man's-land.

The end of Indian independence in the park region—and by implication all around the East—can be dramatized through the oral tradition of four Page County families that, though mythlike now, fits in with findings of archeologist Fowke and was recorded half a century ago by park-purchase engineer Fred T. Amiss.

Keyser Cord-Marked pot, a style used by Woodland Indians of the Shenandoah region, was named for the Keyser Farm archeological site near Luray beside the park. The round bottom of the pot wouldn't do well on a stove but was excellent for cooking in hot coals. (Drawing from Griffin, *Archeology of Eastern United States*, 1952)

Pottery pipe smoked by woodland Indians
of the eastern United States. (Drawing
from Griffin, *Archeology of Eastern United
States*, 1952)

*The medicine man of a Sioux-speaking village east of the Blue Ridge, almost
certainly Manahoac, smoked the pipe in the council with the other elders, and
a voice sounded within him. He spoke aloud as he listened. "The Spirit tells us,"
he said, "that we must move again as we did centuries ago—but not to the
southward with our cousins the Tutelo who, not knowing, go deeper into the
foul air that has already taken half our people. We cannot remain here. We can
only go westward to the Spirit's dwelling in the mountains. There we will
receive further directions."*

*The council agreed. The people took their seeds of squashes and beans and
corn, their best bows and arrows, all the essentials they could carry. They
climbed to places where they had hunted and gathered in summer and fall. Then
they climbed higher. The medicine man saw the great peak with cliffs like a
chin, a nose, and a brow—a massive face looking into the sky—and felt the Spirit
there. Alone, he went to the cliffs and listened. The Spirit seemed almost as
confused as the people were. "You must aim to go far, far," the Spirit said, "to
where your ancestors lived long ago. But first you must escape the grasping arms
of the whiteman, one of which is now covered in an Iroquoian robe. Spring is
almost here. You must plant and grow much food. I will tell you when the time
to travel farther has come."*

*They built their new wigwams below Stony Man Mountain on a natural
terrace in a canyon that was hidden from the deadly valley and the warring
Iroquois and Catawba. With stone axes they cut rings around tree trunks,
deadening the trees so leaves would not come out and shade their crops, and they
planted while listening to the cascades called Talking Waters. The Spirit could
not tell them a time and a way to travel, so they planted and harvested through
many cycles of the sun.*

*The medicine man grew old and took an apprentice to learn healing and
perhaps the fading art of sustaining the faith of the ancestors. Then fur-greedy
white bandits raided the Talking Waters hamlet, capturing everyone but the
medicine man and apprentice, who were out gathering herbs. From the ruins
of the wigwams that night, the old man blew tobacco smoke toward Stony Man
and appealed to the Spirit. Soon he spoke to the apprentice. "Our people are held
as slaves to get skins for selling across the ocean," he explained, "but the Spirit
promises they will escape and return to us." Yet days and moons passed, and the
people did not return. "The whiteman's Spirit is stronger than our Spirit," the
old man said one day. And that night he died.*

The apprentice, alone, unable now even to get a response from the Spirit, climbed a pinnacle and looked into the valley. At its nearest edge a whiteman, helped only by a woman and a girl, was trying to build a cabin. All three seemed ill. Stealthily, he went closer—and closer. He learned that the family, traveling to make a home, had lost their son and only gun and all their food to a war party— but still had seeds to plant. He shared his food with them, healed their scurvy, helped them build their cabin, and, in spring, taught them how to raise crops in the forest by girdling trees to let the life-giving sun shine through.

The apprentice communicated again with the Spirit and thus gained strength, but the Spirit could not tell him where to find his people. The white family fondly called the apprentice Bright Stony Face all the rest of his life. He healed and helped peaceful farmers of German stock—Somerses, Comers, Millers, and Varners—whose descendants still live beside the park. They invited him to live with them, but he clung to the Talking Waters ruins, visiting the farms only when someone needed him.

A day came in 1790 when he was needed and wasn't at his wigwam. Knowing his habits, the families searched farther. High on Stony Man he lay with recently gathered baskets of herbs, at peace forever, having lived, so the families calculated, 105 years—his people in the park region, I calculate, more than 105 centuries.

CHAPTER III

Fur Trader–Explorers

L ong before 1607, when the English founded Jamestown—their first permanent settlement in America—high-value furs from what's now Shenandoah National Park were available in Europe. These furs were harvested, or taken from other Indians, by the Iroquois and traded to the French and, later, the Dutch. The Iroquois political-military league began about 1570 and prospered. It came to dominate or eliminate other Indians in a vast region, ultimately including the Shenandoah Valley and adjacent mountains, which became, in effect, an Iroquois game reserve and fur plantation.

An economic report from Jamestown to the king in 1628 failed to mention furs but said, "There is great hope of the ritchness of the Mountains . . . certain assurance of a silver mine." Obscure Virginians, not officially authorized, must have been traveling as far as Shenandoah if not farther, guided by an Indian or two, and trading varied trinkets and metal tools for furs. But the English leaders were slow to explore far, even for precious metals.

Into this situation, in 1669, came John Lederer, a 25-year-old German scholar who'd studied medicine. He seemed to have antagonized the colonists by saying cockily that he would explore farther into the American interior than had any known Englishman. Veteran governor William Berkeley, however, encouraged him. Berkeley had repeatedly planned to lead an expedition himself—to find a passage to the sea that bathed the Orient, to promote the Indian trade, to seek valuable minerals and to limit French influence. One cause and another had prevented his going, and he couldn't go now, so he commissioned Lederer to go instead.

Lederer disappeared into the wilderness and was gone seven months, starting early in March 1669 and, by the old calendar then in use, slipping into 1670 on March 25. When he returned at the end of September and tried to tell what he'd seen, he met doubt and derision, or perhaps jealousy. Angry, he left Virginia. Pausing in Maryland, he was encouraged to complete his report there. It was the first written account of a

John Lederer was the first European to report climbing the Blue Ridge where Shenandoah National Park is now situated. He saw mountains and wilderness, such as in this view, blocking the way westward. Such views, plus bad weather and other hazards, discouraged him at two different places here, and both times he "returned back" the way he came. (Eileen Lambert)

white person visiting the Shenandoah park-land. Written in Latin, it was translated into English and published in London in 1671.

Some people have questioned whether Lederer really made the wilderness trips. Geographic names were scarce out there, and it's almost impossible to tell from his map exactly where he went. But he told so many new facts that have proved authentic, not only about the forest and wildlife and mountains but also about the Indians and the art of trading with them, that it's evident he went beyond the paths most whites knew.

With a small party I tried to follow Lederer's route in the upper piedmont and Blue Ridge three hundred years after his exploit. He left the York River fall line on March 9, riding horseback, guided by three Indians walking. En route toward the high range (then called Quirauk or Ricahecrian or Apalatæan), he saw a rattlesnake "as big as a man's arm," "a Doe seized by a wild Cat," a deposit of "Isinglas," wolves, herds of both "Red" and "Fallow" deer, bears, gray foxes, otters and beavers, and many other remarkable things. Here are more of his own words:

> The fourteenth of March, from the top of an eminent hill, I first descried the Apalatæn Mountains, bearing due West to the place I stood upon: their distance from me was so great, that I could hardly discern whether they were Mountains or Clouds, until my Indian fellow travellers prostrating themselves in Adoration, howled out after a barbarous manner, Okeepoeze, i.e. God is nigh.

We who were trying to follow think we found and climbed Lederer's "eminent hill" (Peter's Mountain). We studied the Blue Ridge as he had and chose the peak that looked highest (Hightop), though others are actually higher. He may have judged better than we did and gone to the real highest (Hawksbill). He continued:

> The eighteenth of March, after I had in vain assayed to ride up, I alighted, and left my horse with one of the Indians, whilst with the other two I climbed up the Rocks, which were so incumbred with bushes and brambles, that the ascent proved very difficult. . . . The height of this Mountain was very extraordinary: for notwithstanding I set out with the first appearance of light, it was late in the evening before I gained the top.

Lederer spent the night on the mountaintop. As day dawned he was dismayed by wild mountains at a distance blocking the way both northward and westward. He walked on the Blue Ridge for several days, failing to find any encouragement toward a Northwest Passage, so "returned back by the same way that I went."

Lederer made a second trip—quite long, farther south, not touching the park-land—then a third that climaxed in the park's north district. The third expedition, starting August 20, 1670, consisted of 11 whitemen on horses, including owners of plantations along the Rappahannock, and five Indians on foot. The starting point was the house of Robert Talifer (Taliaferro) on the Rappahannock below the fall line. They went upriver, taking the north and largest branch, and were much impressed by extensive open meadows. Lederer says:

> These Savanae are low grounds at the foot of the Apalatæans, which all the Winter, Spring, and part of the Summer, lie under snow, or water when the snow is dissolved, which falls down from the Mountains commonly about the beginning of June; and then their verdure is wonderful pleasant to the eye, especially of such as having traveled through the shade of the vast Forest, come out of a melancholy darkness of a sudden, into a clear and open skie.

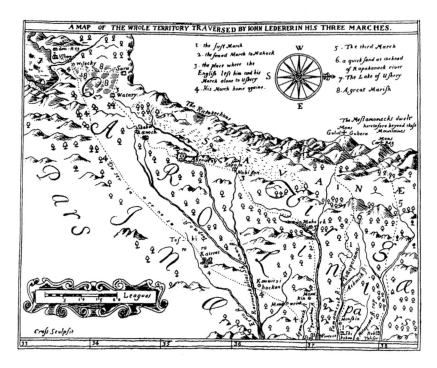

Lederer drew this rough map of his three different expeditions, only two of which reached the park-land. See dotted lines on right side, leading to high points. Geographic names weren't settled then. "Mons Guliel Gubern" could be Hightop in the park's south district or Hawksbill in the central district. "Mons Car Reg" could be Compton Peak in the park's north district. (From Charles E. Hatch, Jr., *Alexander Spotswood Crosses the Blue Ridge*, 1968, reproducing Alvord and Bidgood, *The First Exploration*)

On August 26 the explorers left their horses and walked up what was probably Compton Peak. Again the view ahead gave little hope of a Northwest Passage. Col. John Catlett, a plantation owner–mathematician–surveyor, and others of the party agreed with Lederer that they might as well turn back.

In discussing his various discoveries, Lederer said he no longer believed that great and navigable rivers, resembling those that reach the Chesapeake and Atlantic, would be found on the far side of the Appalachians leading into the Indian Ocean. He did believe, though, that passes would be found leading into western parts of North America. He considered his most significant accomplishment to be an understanding of the Indians he had visited on his three trips. He advised European colonists to explore "in company" but not more than ten together, including Indian guides, as larger groups would be interpreted as threatening. He said "neighbor-Indians" were eager to trade skins of deer, beaver, otter, wildcat, fox, and raccoon for coarse cloth, axes, hoes, knives, scissors, guns, powder, and shot. To trade with remoter Indians, he recommended

> small Looking-glasses, Pictures, Beads and Bracelets of glass . . . and all manner of gaudy toys and knacks for children. . . . For they are apt to admire such trinkets, and will purchase them at any rate, either with their current Coyn of small shells, which they call Roanoack or Peack, or perhaps with Pearl, Vermilion, pieces of Christal.

The Indian way was fading. The white people had the technology, the power, and the dream, though little conscious control of it all. The Europeans were a tide rising, and nobody knew just where or how high the tide would go. The Spirit of Stony Face—the nonmaterial embodiment, say, of the park region's Indians—would have watched the horsemen coming, dismounting perhaps to climb the steeper slopes and peaks, and would have watched, too, and just as sadly, the Iroquois who were stimulated by Europeans to loot fellow Indians.

A few of the whites were official, commercially or governmentally, and would report to someone, perhaps orally or in writing soon lost or misplaced. But most were self-motivated, reporting to nobody except at random through tall tales that couldn't be believed yet carried elements of fact. Many would load their horses with what "truck" they could gather and travel the wilderness for weeks or months alone or with one or two Indian helpers or guides, most likely of tidewater tribes already dominated by the English. Some whitemen married Indian women, lived in far-off hamlets, and had papooses of their own. Through inside-track trading they might become prosperous and have a dozen or more Indian hunter-trappers bringing them furs. They might visit "civilization" only once a year, with bundles of furs piled high on their packhorses, and return with guns and blankets and whatever their families and friends might want or need. The rewards might be high, or somewhere along the way they might lose everything, including their lives.

Quite a few were hunters more than traders. They carried little truck. Hunting partners might pick a site where animals were abundant and build themselves a "half-faced cabin" if not an "Indian cabin." Back and side walls might be of logs, chinked to keep wind from blowing through. The roof might be poles covered with pieces of bark or skins. The front would be open, and a fire there would heat the interior, supposedly without much smoke coming in. Such structures were probably the first in the park area that didn't completely imitate Indian structures. The hunters, if diligent and lucky, might earn enough to acquire bits of land, in isolation or back at the edge of settlement.

The colonial government tried to control far travel and trading. All who traded with Indians were supposed to be licensed and to obey regulations—such as to trade only at official posts that were leap-frogging up the rivers to the Blue Ridge, for instance, up the Rappahannock to the site that would later be Washington, Virginia, beside the park. But such control was far from possible. The people, some of them plantation owners, others owners of nothing except maybe a horse and a gun, were dreaming of wealth in one form or another and following their dreams. If a small group traveled and traded all the way to the Ohio River and back—or even to the Mississippi—or if men lived with Indians in secret places far away, they might brag a bit on occasion, but who would believe them?

There was Col. Cadwallader Jones, for instance—plantation owner, Indian fighter, Indian trader. Quite possibly he was with Lederer and Colonel Catlett at Compton Peak in 1670. Twelve years later he explored the headwaters of the Rappahannock and probably descended into the Shenandoah Valley. Maybe he explored much farther. There's a historical tidbit saying he sent the governor of Virginia a map of wilderness camps he'd used between 1677 and 1686. The upper reaches of six Virginia rivers were included, with maybe the first Virginia knowledge that the Shenandoah was a branch of the Potomac.

In 1706 a Louis Michel (Michelle?) from Berne, Switzerland, explored up the Shenandoah to the vicinity of present-day Front Royal and Massanutten Mountain. He was seeking land where Swiss might settle and apparently had applied to Queen Anne of England for land grants. He was aided by Indians; some showed him a silver mine that couldn't be found by anyone later.

There was spreading hope for cooperation between Indians and whites. Virginia historian Robert Beverley, in the 1600s, and Thomas Jefferson, a century later, are said to have advocated intermarriage, linking families of both races, as a means of strengthening and prolonging peace— somewhat as had the marriage of Pocahontas and John Rolfe. There might have been lasting cooperation in the fur trade, even in finding and mining minerals. But there could be no cooperation over land. Whites sought to own and to use (exploit) land, and their aggressive movement up the piedmont into the mountains and up the Shenandoah Valley doomed the Indian way of life.

If any one man fired a starting gun for the land race toward the Shenandoah–Blue Ridge, it was Alexander Spotswood, titled "lieutenant-governor" but in effect governor of the Virginia colony. Spotswood came

Spotswood's expedition westward started at Germanna, near present-day Fredericksburg. It was long supposed he crossed Swift Run Gap in the park-land, but recent studies suggest he may have crossed at Milam Gap. Both routes are shown here, based on opinions of leading investigators. (From *Journal of John Fontaine*, ed. Edward Porter Alexander, with permission from the publisher, The Colonial Williamsburg Foundation)

from Britain in the spring of 1710. He worried about the French reach down from the St. Lawrence and the Great Lakes along the Mississippi and its tributaries. He wanted to increase Virginia's share of the Indian trade and beyond that to push English settlement up to and over the Blue Ridge and farther to discourage the French. This Spotswood was accustomed to wealth and power. He was a great-grandson of John Spotswood, archbishop of St. Andrews and author of the *History of the Church of Scotland*. In his younger years Alexander had served as a colonel under the duke of Marlboro and been severely wounded in action.

Spotswood got off to a fast start in Virginia, authorizing a "Company of Adverturers" to explore westward. In December 1710 he reported they'd climbed "the highest mountain with their horses," a hundred miles beyond the present edge of English settlement, and they would have ridden down into the valley if there hadn't been danger of getting caught by winter. The Blue Ridge, which had been considered impassable, was proving to be not much of a barrier after all. Spotswood encouraged "the Rangers" to make further discoveries. They did, and the barrier became still less fearsome.

Spotswood was now living in a palace at Williamsburg. He was a versatile man, credited with designing fine buildings in Virginia's impressive capital. As customary among the colonial elite, he wore a powdered wig and the best of clothes, and he traveled in an elaborate carriage. It seems "conflict of interest" wasn't much frowned upon in those days. Spotswood was acquiring land personally through his own government. About 30 miles above the nearest settlement at the fall line of the Rappahannock, up the Rapidan branch, he established what was probably at first a military fort and trading post. Iron deposits had been discovered nearby. He invited German-Swiss miners and ironworkers to settle there, on 1,300 acres of land he'd acquired. Soon the population was 40, and growing.

With this fortified village, named Germanna, as a convenient launching pad, Spotswood decided to make a grand gesture by personally leading an expedition across the Blue Ridge. The party was mostly "gentlemen" but also included servants, "Rangers," Indian guides, a few piedmont "pioneers," some hunting dogs, and 74 horses—mostly for riding but some to carry food, drink, and ammunition. One of the two score or so gentlemen was Robert Beverley, prominent plantation owner and historian.

The first and second days' rides (August 29-30, 1716) covered only three miles each. There were tents to sleep in and plenty of good food to eat, including venison killed along the way. The third day's ride covered 14 miles up the Rapidan River. A bear as well as more deer were killed. The "Appalachian Hills" were now in plain sight.

On up the piedmont they went, a horse party in a long line, 13 miles the fourth day, 5 of them on a "pleasant plain" where the horses would have spread out a bit, then into forest with unusually large trees, yet scattered enough for grass to grow lushly as well. A horse must have stepped on a yellow jacket nest. According to diarist John Fontaine, only horses were stung, but there was "some commotion" and a delay to put the baggage in order. Three bears and three deer were killed. Where there was a major fork of the river, they followed the north fork (Robinson River).

The next two days were hard going—difficult terrain, many small but deep streams, trouble staying on the horses, then "a thicket, so tightly laced together that we had a great deal of trouble to get through." Clothes were "torn all to rags, and the saddles and holsters also torn." On the seventh day, at the edge of the mountains, two men became sick with the measles and a horse was bitten by a rattlesnake. The disabled were made as comfortable as possible and left behind. As Lederer had reported earlier, the mountainsides were dense with vines and briers. "We were forced," wrote Fontaine, "to clear most of the way before us." They got a fine view of the plains below, then came to a slope so steep and so covered with loose stones that the men dismounted and led their horses.

September 5 was a day of success. The party reached the crest of the Blue Ridge—perhaps not at Swift Run Gap as had been supposed until recent decades but at or near Big Meadows, the approximate center of today's park. In celebration they drank King George's health "and all the Royal Family's." When they tried to descend into the Shenandoah Valley (via Lewis Spring?), they were forced back by "prodigious precipices." But soon, a bit further southward (Milam Gap and along Tanners Ridge?) they found human marks on trees and guessed the route was used "by the Northern Indians." It was an easy way to ride down. They reached the valley floor with much daylight left, and some of the gentlemen urged turning back, but Spotswood insisted on going farther.

The explorers came at last to a river they named Euphrates—the present Shenandoah, South Fork. It was very deep, Fontaine wrote, 80 yards wide at the narrowest place, flowing northward. They spent September 6 along the river, finding a convenient ford and riding across. They did ceremonial drinking on both sides of the river, the supply of liquors being ample and diverse. Some men fished; others went hunting and got both deer and turkey. Spotswood "buried a bottle with a paper inclosed, on which he writ that he took possession of this place in the name and for King George the First of England."

The return to Germanna, thence to Williamsburg, went smoothly. Spotswood dubbed those who had made the trip "Knights of the Golden Horseshoe." He is said to have presented each "Knight" with a gem-studded golden horseshoe. The great expedition might seem a mere lark. We moderns might equate it with a "television event" and realize, at the same time, that such events sometimes touch the public mind and emotion and thus have powerful effects on the future.

CHAPTER IV

The Powdered Wigs

As Britain's feudalistic land policy encountered the seemingly endless acreage of America, confusion and conflict surged. In Virginia, Gov. Alexander Spotswood and his Cavalier friends, pushing westward, collided with Lord Fairfax, the feudal proprietor of the Northern Neck domain. Fairfax was determined to take and hold land the Spotswood people wanted, including three-fifths of the Shenandoah park-land.

The Northern Neck Proprietary had been granted by kings Charles I and II, along in the mid-1600s, to seven court favorites. It was supposed to take in everything "within the heads of the rivers Tappahannock, alias Rappahannock, and Quirough or Patawomack, the courses of those rivers, and the Bay of Chespayoak, &c." Lord Culpeper got enough control of the proprietary in the 1670s to start granting patents. The first one became the Mount Vernon estate on the Potomac.

His daughter Catherine married the Fifth Lord Fairfax, who thus became proprietor of the Northern Neck.

The couple's son and heir would become a Virginia citizen. Thomas, Sixth Lord Fairfax, was born at Leeds Castle, County Kent, England, in 1693. The ways of British nobility must have become second nature to him there. He attended Oxford. When he was 26, after his parents had died and he was head of the family, he began a career close to King George I. But he didn't thrive at court or as an officer of the Horse Guards. He got jilted in love; the bride-to-be attracted a duke and decided to be duchess instead of merely lady.

While young Fairfax was in England wondering if his Virginia land might be worth his attention, he was visited—so wrote Shenandoah Valley historian Samuel Kercheval in the early 1800s—by a John Howard and son. They had explored westward through Virginia, passing just south of the proprietary's Rappahannock River line and on into the Shenandoah Valley. They told Fairfax that much of the land they'd seen was wonderfully fertile, with grass so tall the tops could be tied together

Lord Fairfax's land office, still standing at old Greenway Court near White Post, about
ten miles from the park's north entrance, was headquarters for surveys and records.
George Washington, Fairfax's friend (when very young employed by Fairfax as a
surveyor) worked here as well as far afield in mountains and valley. Gooney Run
Manor, in the park's north district now, was managed from Greenway Court until
Fairfax died in 1781. (Eileen Lambert)

in front of their chests as they sat in their saddles. They also hinted slyly
that the head of the Rappahannock River might be farther south than
anyone had yet supposed. Land that had been considered to belong to the
Colony of Virginia might actually belong to the Proprietary of the
Northern Neck.

Fairfax told his agent in Virginia, Robert "King" Carter, what the
Howards had reported. The next time Spotswood granted land north of
the Rappahannock's large southern tributary (now called Rapidan River),
Carter called foul. The Council of Virginia made some gesture toward
studying conflicting claims but delayed and maybe conveniently forgot.
Spotswood created the new county of Spotsylvania (a fancy word for
Spot's wood or *forest*) just south of what's now called the Rappahannock.
It was the first county above tidewater and possibly the largest in world
history, in theory extending to the Great Lakes and the Pacific. It
included, of course, Spotswood's Germanna village, plantations, and iron
industry.

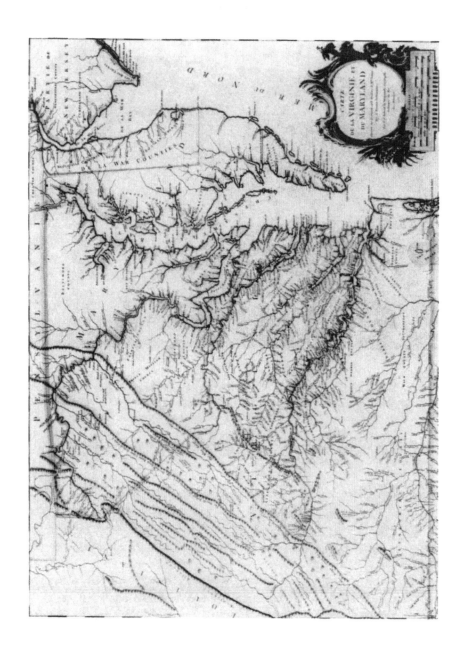

The extent of Lord Fairfax's victory shows on this map by Joshua Fry and Peter Jefferson that was printed with a French title in 1755. The Potomac is the broad river branching left from Chesapeake Bay halfway up the map and forming the much-curved Maryland-Virginia boundary all the way to the headwaters, upper left. The Rappahannock is the narrower river just below the Potomac. The Fairfax view, which prevailed, made the main Rappahannock follow the Rapidan in a great swing to the southwest. The notorious Fairfax Line shows faintly but perfectly straight—from the Blue Ridge across half a dozen other ranges to the Potomac's headspring at the sharp corner of Maryland. (Courtesy of James R. "Bob" Johnson)

The land rush to the mountains gained momentum. The colony determined that enough people were involved to warrant creation of vast St. Mark's Parish, which extended all the way to the Blue Ridge crest. Spotswood was the dominant force and personal owner of the largest acreages. The pattern of the colony's advance would repeat itself: first, the boldest and best-financed Cavaliers with working servants; second, the Anglican parish to keep them coordinated (there was a fine for not attending services); and, third, when numbers and problems demanded, formation of a new county (in which the Anglican vestrymen were a majority of the gentlemen-justices sitting in a court with both executive and judicial authority).

Fairfax was slow to apply his weight. In 1733, though, he made a strong complaint to London that the colony was granting land which was the proprietary's, and in 1735 he came to Virginia to see that the situation got straightened out. The king ordered a commission—three representatives of the Virginia colony, three of Fairfax—to set a dividing line, a definite southern and western boundary of the Fairfax domain. The six men met and arranged for measurement and mapping of the Rappahannock's south fork "and all the runs and creeks." They also took testimony on the ground.

Col. William Byrd, a Virginia representative, reported:

> We . . . went to the fork of the river, and found the North branch to be wider by three poles and nine links, though it was objected by my Lord's Commissioners that the South was made narrower by an island that runs along the south shore. We carried a surloin of beef from Col. Carter's, and picked it as clean as a pack of wolves would . . . a wounded deer. The same gentleman furnished us with strong beer, but forgot to bring a vessel to drink it from. However, we supplied that want with the shell of a poor terrapin, which we destroyed, as Henry VIII did Cardinal Wolsey, for the sake of his house. We then proceeded to Germantown, where Governor Spotswood received us very courteously.

Which stream did the royal charter for the Northern Neck mean when it said Rappahannock? The first principal witness, Francis Thornton, gentleman, "aged 53 years and upwards," said he'd been acquainted with the forks of the river about 27 years, and one was called the South Branch and the other the North Branch. Diplomatic neutrality, I think. The second, William Russell, aged 56, a high sheriff, a hunter, and, like Thornton, an owner of much land, shrugged off diplomacy. He said he'd been acquainted with the forks for 35 years. One branch (the south) was always called South River until Spotswood named it Rapidan and the other branch (the north) had always been called Rappahannock.

To the Virginia commissioners it seemed clear that Rappahannock meant the North Branch. They met at Williamsburg in August 1736, having an "elegant map, delineating clearly the branches of the Rappahannock up to their sources." They thought the colonial government had every right to issue patents for land anywhere south of the North Branch, the real Rappahannock. At stake were approximately two million acres of rich land.

But Lord Fairfax took his commissioners' report to England, and the eminent Lords of the Committee of Council accepted its view and declared the South Branch, what Spotswood called the Rapidan, to be the Rappahannock. In order to implement the decision, however, there'd have to be a survey from the head of Conway River, southernmost branch of the Rapidan, to the head of the Potomac, a long-accepted cluster of springs where the point of western Mayland now juts into Tucker County, West Virginia. Somehow, with Fairfax staying in England and Spotswood and his friends active in Virginia, that survey kept getting delayed.

Spotswood exploited his holdings at Germanna and on up the Rapidan. When landowner-settlers, mostly sons of wealthy tidewater planters whose soil was nearing exhaustion, got numerous upriver, Spotswood helped organize Orange County. He rented one of his plantations for operation of a ferry—at 630 pounds of tobacco a year— but debarred "the keeping of a tipling house or hoggs running at large at the Ferry Plantation." Spotswood died in 1740, leaving a widow and a son John, perhaps others. The widow married a Rev. Mr. Thompson of the official church. John lived on and prospered in Orange County, owning 39 blacks.

William Russell, a Spotswood "Knight" and anti-Fairfax witness, patented 20,000 acres alongside the present national park in Warren County, where Paleo people had made Clovis points 11,500 years before. Another "Knight," Robert Beverley, whose history of Virginia had been published in 1705, got a 15,000-acre patent (along with two associates). Robert's son, William, soon patented more than 100,000 acres. We can't trace all the "Knights"—not even a reliable list of them survives today— but it's likely most of them patented big tracts of piedmont, mountain, or valley.

Francis Thornton, a possible "Knight," lived in lower Spotsylvania. He was related by marriage to the Washingtons and played a major role in the park's past. Thornton Gap, Francis Thornton Valley (also called F.T. Valley), and Thornton River were named for him, and it's said he named Marys Rock for his daughter. Even before the ride of 1716 he was acquiring and selling piedmont land. Two years later, together with Anthony Thornton and William Strother, he got additional acreage described as in the "Great Mountains." He acquired and sold land in what's now Madison, Page, and Rappahannock counties but held onto enough for family plantations in and beside the Blue Ridge. A neighbor in Rappahannock was Samuel Kennerley, whose "Great Kennerley's Mountaine Wilderness," backcountry of his plantation, included much park-land.

Capt. Thomas Chester, another possible "Knight," was an early landowner in what's become Warren County. In 1736 the Orange court licensed his ferry from the mouth of Happy Creek across the Shenandoah River. Chester Gap is on the maps today, and an important road toward Orange Court House was called Chester's for a long time.

Kin groups of gentry soon straddled the Blue Ridge, almost commuting between piedmont and valley. John Madison was ancestor of both a U.S. president, raised on the piedmont, and an eminent bishop, raised in the valley—both named James. Madison Run in the park was named for the bishop's branch. The mother of President Madison was Nelly Conway. The Conways had park-land; they were related to the Washingtons, the Taylors (who also produced a U.S. president), the Catletts, the Strothers, and the Willises (a Willis was an owner-resident of land when it was bought for the park). Anthony Strother was an early landowner under Doubletop Mountain in the park. Three Strother sisters of tidewater-piedmont origin married three prominent landowners on the western edge of what's now the park's south district. Many of the "big" landowners were soon kin.

Indian rights were sometimes the subject of negotiation—mostly with the Iroquois, who themselves were usurpers in many areas—but weren't seen by the British gentry as a real obstacle. Each county had a militia to remove or subdue Indians who gave trouble. When the land rush had reached park-land and speeded westward, a prominent Virginian named Benjamin Harrison put this comment on record: "I confess my feelings are hurt and my humanity shocked" by "the unbounded thirst of our people after Lands that they cannot cultivate, and the means they use to possess themselves of those that belong to others. An Indian has his National rights as well as a White man."

The survey to determine the southwestern boundary of Lord Fairfax's domain finally got started in September 1746. Peter Jefferson (Thomas's father) and Robert Brooke were surveyors for the Virginia colony; Thomas Lewis and a Captain Winslow, for Fairfax. Lewis wrote a journal, starting with his horseback ride across the park-land from his father's home near Staunton, via Jarman (then called Woods) Gap. He met high-ranking representatives of king, colony, and lord proprietor on the piedmont. By September 18 all the baggage was packed—food and drink, instruments, lots of powder and shot. There were 40 men, all with riding horses, and 14 packhorses besides. Part of the group rode across Swift Run Gap and would rejoin on the west side. The others went up the Conway River.

The Conway branched, and it took the surveyors and commissioners a week, up there south of Big Meadows, to agree on the correct branch. Lewis reports they surveyed three different ones. I see on my map now that a likely branch (Devils Ditch) heads near Lewis Mountain, and I suspect this Lewis Mountain in addition to one in the park's south district was named for Thomas Lewis. These surveyors were making history, and Lewis probably argued for that branch which would give his patron the most acreage. Why not? If the head of the Rappahannock was the Rapidan and the head of the Rapidan was the Conway, why shouldn't the head of the Conway be Devils Ditch?

But the commissioners agreed on a spring a bit farther north. Bearings were taken on prominent peaks. The line was run over the Blue Ridge, down the west slope, and into the valley. It had to be undeviatingly straight regardless of highly uneven topography. Somewhere in the seemingly unending wilderness the men came to a stream they called Styx (in Hades?). Lewis, not noted for spelling and punctuation, wrote:

> ye Lorals Ivey & Spruce pine so Extremly thick in ye Swamp through which this River Runs that one Cannot have the Least prospect Except they look upwards the Water of the River of Dark Brownish Color & its motion So Slow that it can hardly be Said to move its Depth about 4 feet the Bottom muddy & Banks high. . . most of the horses when they attemp'd to asend the farthest Bank tumbling with their loads Back in the River.

The survey party endured such adventures through worsening cold until completion of the line—76 miles and 138 poles long—in mid-November. The Fairfax empire proved to have a total of 5,282,000 acres—to have had, rather, as by this time much land had been granted in huge estates.

Thomas Lord Fairfax, now 53 years old and destined to remain a British lord, made his home in the Shenandoah Valley beside the Blue Ridge (today near White Post in Clarke County) and took direct hold of his domain. He met screened resentment. It wasn't easy for a lord to fit into wild America. He built modest buildings (three of them still standing in the 1980s) and later a comfortable but unpretentious house, Greenway Court. Of course he had to have helpers, white servants as well as Negro slaves, skilled surveyors and other associates, map makers, record keepers. Though he had fancy clothes, he almost never wore them but dressed plainly.

People soon realized that Fairfax wasn't arrogant as they'd expected. He was fairly accessible personally at home or around his buildings and fields. He employed hunters, hound trainers, foresters, and so on, but he liked to ride out himself, sometimes alone, and look at forests and fields. He enjoyed hunting, especially when wolves or bears were scaring his tenants or damaging property.

Fairfax's land-leasing system might not be a pioneer's ideal, but, if you had little or nothing, you could get started easier with Fairfax than without him. He offered leases that would run 21 years at one shilling a year for each hundred acres, or longer leases for "three lives," meaning possession could be held for the longest lifetime of the three. These were usually husband, wife, and youngest son (who would have the most life expectancy). You didn't have to pay anything for a year, and annual quitrents after that were small. You were expected to build a cabin with a masonry chimney, to fence and cultivate at least some land, and to plant a few fruit trees—but you'd want to do all that anyway. If you ran low on food or other essentials before you were producing, Fairfax might lend you what you needed, sometimes even money, interest free. He wasn't aiming for quick wealth, but for annual incomes that would go on benefiting Fairfaxes forever.

A very early patent from Fairfax in what would be Page County— part of the enlargement he'd won—was four hundred acres of rich land near present-day Leaksville to Jacob Rothgeb and his bride, free, on September 15, 1749. Rothgeb had served a seven-year indenture to a settler beside the Shenandoah River to pay his ocean passage, then seven years to pay passage for his bride. How could Fairfax not have reached out for citizens of this quality?

But Fairfax wasn't so friendly with neighbor Jost Heydt, a wealthy German baron who'd obtained Shenandoah land in the 1730s, without authorization by Fairfax, and founded splendid plantations. Fairfax resented the prosperity of the Heydt people on, perhaps, the very meadows that Howard and son had told him about and he'd struggled so long to win. He knew the colonial government had granted 100,000 acres to Heydt and a Quaker named Robert McKay, but Gov. William Gooch, who had succeeded Spotswood, had had no right. It was Spotswood who'd encouraged such overstepping of authority. But Spotswood was dead now, in 1749, so Fairfax moved against Heydt, and soon they were antagonists in a seemingly endless court case. Fairfax and Heydt would glare at each other in the courtroom at Winchester, or salute each other coldly if they met on roads they both sometimes used. A decision in 1771 favored Heydt, after he was dead, and the aging Fairfax appealed to a higher court. The final verdict again favored Heydt, after Fairfax, too, was dead.

An excellent historical novel, *Long Meadows* (1941), by Minnie Hite Moody, a descendant of Jost Heydt, gives a touching glimpse that's probably based on fact. Heydt's funeral was held in a valley church. Fairfax didn't consider it fitting actually to attend; the family wouldn't like it. He came on his horse to the edge of the churchyard, got off the horse, took off his hat, and stood there alone, motionless, all through the service, but leaving before the people came out.

Fairfax made 160,000 acres his personal domain (as separate from His Lordship's domain). In addition to Greenway Court Manor, he held the Manor of Leeds, named for the family's Leeds Castle, and Gooney Run Manor, which included much land now inside Shenandoah National Park. From the front windows at Greenway Court, Fairfax could look south-ward at the heights of his park-land manor—Dickey Ridge and Mount Marshall—and beyond them in blue haze to Hogback. Gooney is a name of uncertain origin, yet there's a likely story that Fairfax went hunting along the stream and Gooney, one of his best hunting hounds, drowned there while tangling with a bear, wolf, or raccoon—so, Gooney Run.

This park-land manor might have developed faster, with larger estates maybe and more lasting structures, if the settlers could have owned the land outright. But once the system got going it did well under the Lord Proprietor. Many leases were for a hundred acres or more, and most of the families lived up to the terms. Good-sized cabins were built of broad-ax-faced logs, chestnut-shingled roofs, and stone chimneys with fireplaces—solid structures typical of early plantations in and around the Blue Ridge.

Fairfax did his work, gave time and energy in service to the govern-ment of his home county (Old Frederick), including service in the militia, and prospered almost smoothly until 1776, when he was 83 years old. During the Revolution the Virginia legislature enacted laws that would have wiped out his remaining empire if he hadn't been a Virginia citizen. He worried, behaved as the good Virginian he'd become, and got by. But in December 1781 he died, two months after Lord Cornwallis surren-dered to George Washington at Yorktown. His main Virginia lands were inherited by his nephew, Rev. Denny Martin—who was *not* a citizen!

A Pandora's box opened. The Virginia government, long impatient with Northern Neck feudalism, started selling Fairfax-Martin lands in the personal manors to the leaseholders—at a price it arbitrarily set. Denny

Gooney Run Manor, in the park, along with additional vast lands nearby, was managed from this mansion for many years after Fairfax's death. John Marshall, eminent chief justice, was part owner, along with his brother James Markham Marshall. James was in charge on the ground. The ruins of his Happy Creek House, near Front Royal, are still impressive but not habitable after a disastrous fire about 1921. (Courtesy of Mrs. E. Keith Monnington)

Martin sought advice from aging "Valley Lawyer" Gabriel Jones and younger John Marshall, who would become the famous chief justice. When Marshall filed suit to stop the selling, Virginia proved stubborn. Leaseholders reacted to the confusion by ceasing to pay quitrents. They formed a "Free State" and refused to deal with Martin or Virginia or any authority whatsoever.

John Marshall and his brother James Markham Marshall, along with their brother-in-law Rawleigh Colston and Harry "Light Horse" Lee, thought they saw a way to settle the dangerous conflict out of court while making a profit for themselves. They offered to buy the disintegrating Fairfax domain. Many factors caused delays. The peace treaty with Britain restored landowning rights for British subjects, but Virginia was too deeply in to draw back. It expanded its selling of Fairfax-Martin lands even beyond the personal manors. In 1795 James Barbour, a 20-year-old powdered wig of Orange County, grandson of a James Barbour who'd learned real estate maneuvering with Spotswood, moved to escalate the antifeudal drama. He grabbed Fairfax-Martin land in great chunks, including two "Big Surveys" in what's now the national park—a 42,000-acre tract in the central district and a 28,000-acre tract in the north district.

Moving fast, he soon bounced off the spectacular ownership to win greater wealth, power, and fame—as governor 1812-14, U.S. senator 1815-25, secretary of war 1825-28, and so on.

Barbour's biggest Big Survey in the park-land enclosed 66 square miles of what's now the central district. Thirty-three tracts inside the surveyor's line, claimed by persons in possession, added up to nearly 20 square miles. Barbour was thus left with 46 square miles, which soon turned up in the ownership of Thomas Shirley, Gent. Barbour's smaller Big Survey on Fairfax (and park-) land was 44 square miles in the north district, which sold to a man in Baltimore, then to powdered wig Isaac Overall, and stayed largely in Overall family hands until the park was established. Barbour had a still smaller Big Survey in the park's south district, but that wasn't Fairfax land.

Barbour has haunted park-land people for nearly two centuries. The Big Surveys encouraged the contrary independence of Americans—thus: Much of the land wasn't noticeably used by owners, so to the public it was pie-in-the-sky, a vast "common." If people needed logs, they simply went up there and got them. They turned cattle loose to browse and hogs to root. They might settle up there, blazing trees around the land, building a cabin, raising a family. It had become an unwritten rule in limitless America that every family deserved enough land to support itself. If your big acreage was idle, and you failed for years to protect it, the county courts just might decide ownership disputes in favor of squatters actually in possession. (Later chapters include examples.)

Denny Martin and the Marshall group struggled through complexities. Virginia offered at last to allow clear title to the personal manors, in and near the park-land, if Martin would relinquish all other claims in the Northern Neck. He agreed. James Markham Marshall paid £7,700 to Martin and got a deed for 55,000 acres near the Shenandoah River. In 1806 the Marshall group, apparently without Lee now, paid Martin £14,000 and got deeds for 160,382 acres. Colston took 40,000 acres in Fauquier County; the Marshall brothers, 120,000 acres in and west of the Blue Ridge, including Gooney Run Manor park-land.

Marshalls were old-timers here. John's and James's father, Thomas Marshall, who'd helped George Washington survey Fairfax lands, had acquired large acreages in the Blue Ridge and nearby piedmont. He and his wife raised 15 children and gave Mount Marshall its name. James married a daughter of Robert Morris, a leading patriot and financier of the Revolution. Family tradition says James had financial backing from Morris and had also gained wealth through buying French securities and profiting as France recovered from its revolution. James built a mansion called Happy Creek House, its ruins still impressive, about two miles

north of the park. From there he managed most of the former personal
domain of Lord Fairfax, including much park-land.

U.S. chief justice John Marshall didn't meddle with the land, but he
worried about a court case that wouldn't die. It involved a Fairfax-manor
leaseholder who'd bought his leased land from Virginia and, along with
the "Free State," resented efforts by Denny Martin and the Marshalls to
nullify Virginia's action. Yet it seemed to Martin that whatever justifi-
cation Virginia might have had for selling "his" land had disappeared
with the treaty recognizing the right of Britons to own land in this
country. Martin's effort through the courts to recover ownership reached
the U.S. Supreme Court in 1813. The court ruled in Martin's favor, but
Virginia refused compliance.

The case, rooted in the Shenandoah–Blue Ridge, threatened the very
existence of our new nation. Its name changed as one principal party died,
but at the most crucial time, in 1816, it was *Martin* v. *Hunter's Lessee*. It
is reported to this day in history books, encyclopedias, and lawbooks.
The focus sharpened on this fatal question: Are the U.S. Supreme Court
and the U.S. Constitution really supreme?

Strong, proud, long-established Virginia was in direct confrontation
with the youthful and possibly weak federal government. Marshall, U.S.
chief justice, hadn't been participating in the judicial proceedings because
he was personally involved. Justice Joseph Story handed down the
famous decision that definitely proclaimed the appellate jurisdiction of the
U.S. Supreme Court over the highest court of any state. Both sides must
have blinked a bit. There was no general reversal of Virginia's disputed
land sales, though cases in the lower courts would go on for years. Yet
Virginia stopped antagonizing the federal government by denying the
U.S. Supreme Court the right to overrule any and all state courts. The
deadly quarrel faded; both state and nation lived on.

In the former Fairfax manors many semifeudal proprietor-tenant
relationships continued. Some old three-lives leases went on. Though
leases were being bought and sold in public almost as if they were deeds,
they were still understood to run out upon the death of the last of the three
persons originally tenants.

Soon James Markham Marshall was selling land outright, at first only
to tenants wishing to buy, then to others. He acquired John's share in the
land, then turned the Happy Creek responsibility over to his son Robert.
The baronial mansion survived more than a century in good condition.

In 1837 more than half of Gooney Run Manor was bought by
William Woodward. He built a brick plantation house in Gooney Run
valley (later Browntown Cove), calling it Liberty Hall; it was still solid
in the 1980s. Woodward sold land outright to many leaseholders and

A frontier gristmill, something like this old log ruin that survived into the present century, was established beside the Blue Ridge about 1734 by Francis Thornton, whose name then became attached to the river and the gap. The mill helped this real estate promoter in selling land and starting roads. (NPS)

others, and he bought out the leases of tenants who wanted to sell. His son, William S., continued to sell for decades, reducing the Woodwards' holdings to their eight-hundred-acre home tract.

In all these ways, multiplied by a thousand, the piedmont and Blue Ridge and parts of the valley went into private ownership—a condition foreign to the American Indians, who'd felt the land was everyone's (or the Spirit's), and foreign also to Europeans accustomed to feudal ownership-tenancy from the monarch down through nobles and workers, servants and serfs, each continuing to owe responsibility or duty to the others.

Private ownership—each owner the king—was prevailing, the land simply bought and sold as a commodity. Yet, even as late as park-purchase time in the 1930s, the flavor of feudalism remained in many owner-tenant relationships in and around the park. It might still be found surviving in some piedmont-mountain-valley situations today.

This discussion of the British gentry's acquiring nearly all the land in the Blue Ridge and piedmont, and some parts of the valley, shouldn't end without recognizing that the line between gentry and folk was weakening in America. A yeoman farmer might marry a gentlewoman, buy a slave or two, and call his farm a plantation. Almost any man who could get a little money—through honest effort, or a rich uncle, or skulduggery—could buy five hundred or so acres and start adding "Gent." or "Esq." to his signature. Conversely, members of the gentry, especially younger sons and daughters left with little inheritance, might become "folk."

"Benj. Cave, Gent.," for instance, got a thousand-acre grant on the Rapidan, signed in 1728 by William Gooch, Virginia governor. In 1731 Cave was a founding vestryman of St. Mark's Parish. He prospered and was elected to the House of Burgesses. He got another plantation on the upper Rapidan, at what was soon being called Cave's Ford. One of his descendants, according to Madison County historian Claude Yowell, accepted a job as turnpike gatekeeper at Fishers Gap, now in the park, married a mountain woman, and "produced all the Caves of the Blue Ridge." They were "mountain folk." Some were genuine squatters—successful ones—as a later chapter will show.

CHAPTER V

Nonestablishment Settlers

P eople living in the park mountains filtered in slowly with the complex human currents that were moving in the region after Lederer climbed the Blue Ridge in 1669 and moving a bit faster as the 1700s advanced. Though British powdered wigs were the earliest landowners, there are hints of a few white inhabitants a decade or more before Spotswood and his "Knights" supposedly opened the way.

Samuel Kercheval, a Shenandoah Valley historian old enough to have known Lord Fairfax, mentioned "many instances" of whites living with Indians in the wilderness. Billie Jo Monger, present-day prober into the colonial period, tells me some Englishmen were living in the Blue Ridge before 1700, though she hadn't found documents giving absolute proof. Bernard Bailyn, author of a recent book based on vast research in England and America, tells of many single whitemen in Virginia being displaced by plantations with increasing numbers of slaves and "moving off to frontier lands," especially after about 1697. He speaks of Indian-style "cabins" on frontiers, apparently built of small logs arranged vertically.

Descriptions of land in early patents sometimes mentioned hunters' cabins. They were found in first scoutings of Fairfax lands; a cabin on Gooney Run, for instance, had been bought by "Wm. Owins . . . of Samuel Wilson a Hunter lately a resident thereon." Early Scots settlers east of the Shenandoah River when Augusta County was being formed found families already in the foothills, dressed in deerskins and living from hunting, trapping, foraging, and maybe gardening. The big activity in wilder places was getting animal skins, either directly or by trading with Indians.

Some Europeans came to the foothills or mountains first as servants or employees or tenants at plantations' remote quarters. Many moved on, or back, but some stayed, perhaps pulling loose from the plantations, acquiring land of their own and having children and grandchildren. The early few who became independent in the park-land long before the Revolution were mostly Englishmen from tidewater and piedmont

Rail fences in great variety marked early settlement in Virginia, whether plantations or small homeplaces. Countless trees were split into rails. Chestnut rails would last 50 years or more. Oak rails might rot in less than ten years, but many settlers used them anyway. This old fence was more ambitious than most, apparently intended at first to stop pigs as well as sheep, cattle, and horses.

Virginia. They were yeomen farmers who could no longer compete with slave-rich plantations, younger sons of planters seeking fresh opportunities, artisans tired of working for tiny wages, indentured people who'd completed their mandatory service. Mountain residents not tied to any plantation were seldom commercial farmers, but most of them raised fruit, vegetables, flax, and domestic animals for their own needs. Most of them also sold deerskins or beaver pelts. More than 34,000 deerskins a year were being shipped to Europe from Virginia in the early 1700s. Bounties paid for wolf scalps helped, too.

Nearly all these people were, or quickly became, skilled in homecrafts. Many homes had spinning wheels—small ones for flax, bigger ones for wool. Some had handlooms and wove their own "linsey-woolsey" for clothing when furs and skins felt unsuitable. They had tanning vats and cobblers' lasts. Many had their own small stills. Nearly every family had a smokehouse for preserving meat. Potatoes, apples, and other vegetables and fruits were stored in cellars or other structures. Summer refrigeration was provided by a springhouse. Milk was cooled there, and cream was skimmed off and butter made in a variety of churns, mostly wooden.

Wild plants were sources of dyes and medicines, the knowledge more Indian at first than European. Hickory bark was a source of yellow; black walnut hulls or bark, of brown; oak, of purple; sumac berries, of red. Oak bark, especially chestnut oak, had tannin for making leather. Dozens of different plants were used for treating illnesses. Willow, for instance, was used against fevers, though no one yet knew it contained a substance resembling quinine.

The people in the remoter places, mountain or lowland, would get up early, usually one at a time as they pleased. The first one up would probably wake the fire, then go outside and check on the day, maybe watching the sun rising over the piedmont or the long shadows shrinking on the valley. He or she might dip a gourd into the spring and drink the ever-fresh water and carry a filled wooden bucket into the house. There'd be no privy at the remote homes, though a chamber pot might be hidden somewhere in the house for use when conditions weren't right to go outside into the bushes or forest or to hide behind the cowshed. There'd be many challenges, of course, even what others might call hardships. But there was also the satisfaction of coping on your own, away from unpredictable social-economic complications.

A remote family before the Civil War was likely to be successful in proportion to its knowledge of nature and skills in homecrafts. Those whose primary goal was to accumulate wealth, rather than simply to live, weeded themselves out by fitting into plantation life or moving west. Even in those long-ago days, the "rat race" repelled some and pulled others. Families who continued remote and independent generation after generation, though varying widely in origin, wealth, poverty, self-image or ambition, and preferred location, tended to love their surroundings and the feeling of at least partial separation from "the world" that could be frantic and frustratingly unfulfilling even centuries ago.

Among English families known in the Jamestown vicinity in the 1600s and in what's now the Blue Ridge of east Rockingham County in the 1700s were the Hensleys, Breedens, Meadowses, and Deans. Fonda Breeden (born Hensley) showed my wife and me the impressive ruins of an old log house in Hensley Hollow, just inside the park east of Elkton, and an old Hensley cemetery just outside the park. The oldest part of the house, she thinks, was built by a Benjamin Hensley in 1813. He married Nellie Meadows in August that year.

In 1986 the natural forest growth had taken over. The roof had fallen. Some walls remained intact six to ten feet up from the ground. They were

A mountain home beneath Old Rag Mountain on a site now in wilderness again. The roof is skillfully covered with chestnut shingles. Such roofs—if maintained by replacing occasional shingles that might crack or be loosened in gales—could shed rain and snow for many decades. (NPS)

of tulip-tree logs, many of them 24 inches from round top to round bottom as placed horizontally in the walls but broad-ax–hewn by smooth skill to a thickness of only eight inches. The corners were superbly crafted, neat and tight. The chimney was solid halfway up, then eroded; a pinnacle of sparse stones remained precariously but scenically perched on top. The whole place, I felt, was haunted by Hensleys, and Mrs. Breeden showed me a picture of a hundred of them and their kind, with a proud, white-bearded patriarch, at a family reunion in the hollow in 1902. Such English families were to be found here and there in all sections of the park-land, thriving on Blue Ridge production, from long before the Revolution until long after the Civil War.

Europeans of different origins also came early to the Blue Ridge and adjacent lowlands. German-speaking people from Spotswood's Germanna, in 1722 if not earlier, were exploring upstream along the Rapidan, looking for a place where they might make homes of their own. They reached the Robinson River, and up along it, past what's Madison town today, they liked the land above the mouth of Island Run (later called White Oak Run, but not the same as the park stream noted for waterfalls). They took preliminary steps toward acquiring 75 to 400 acres per family but didn't wait for the patents. The migration probably started in 1724. The next year the Spotsylvania County Court gave permission for opening "the German Mountain Road," and the year after that, in June, about two dozen Germans obtained land patents.

The settlers built a fort but used it as a church since the few Indians that remained, or traveled through, proved harmless. After the settlers had built shelters for themselves and their livestock and cleared enough farmland for survival, they built the "German Chapel" of rough logs. They were Lutherans, a denomination then rare in America, so they had to search far for a pastor. The first one received a salary of 3,000 pounds of tobacco, worth maybe $40. Yet it was a lot for a small congregation in the wilderness, especially since members were required by law to contribute also to vast St. Mark's Parish of the official Anglican church.

Their small chapel became Hebron Church, the first Lutheran church in the South. Some of the funds to complete it were raised in Europe. A hundred specially cut pieces of glass were brought across the ocean for its windows. When the building was finished in 1740, slaves were bought to work church land that—as was the custom of Anglican parishes also— earned money to help pay the pastor. The 685-acre plantation was near the Champlain plantation just below Old Rag Mountain. Hebron Church operated what may have been the first public school in Virginia. It also abolished slavery for itself and as far as its influence could reach—decades before the Civil War.

Germans, somewhat like other European emigrants, left their homeland because wars and religious tensions were sabotaging their peace and contentment, sometimes even their economic existence. The Fischbach family, living in the villages of Ober and Nieder Fischbach,

Sarah Harris Gardner Maiden, an English resident of the Blue Ridge above present-day Elkton, was born in 1798 and died in 1886. This picture was taken when she was in her 80s. Her body was buried at the Maiden family cemetery in the park (see Appendix 1), which she and her husband William David Maiden are credited with starting. (From old 5- by 7-inch tintype, courtesy of Billie Jo Monger)

Seelbach and Truppbach near Siegen, a city in the Prussian province of Westphalia, had felt their European situation would never improve. In the fall of 1713 John and Harmon Fischbach, brothers, having heard of Spotswood's iron plans, joined others to sail from London as indentured servants. During a delay in England, Harmon married a woman named Kathrina. They reached Germanna in April 1714, when Harmon was 21 years old. Harmon and John worked in the iron industry and raised gardens. They weren't among the very earliest settlers on the Robinson, but Harmon moved there about 1728.

Generations later this family line, having joined with the Hoffmans and the Clores, other early Madison County settlers, produced John Fishback. An enterprising craftsman-businessman, John became widely known as a wagonmaker, winning a ribbon for a wagon in a San Francisco Exposition and having a wagon on permanent exhibit in a San Francisco museum. Many Fishback wagons crossed the continent.

This John's doings—gleaned mostly from one of his account books lent to me by descendant Raymond Fishback—give sharp glimpses into the life of piedmont and Blue Ridge. John Fishback bought iron from Henry Miller, who was producing it in Augusta and Rockingham counties and hauling it over Swift Run Gap. John bought two batches of bar iron, for instance, 112 heavy bars, in December 1821, for $702.50 delivered. He must have had both equipment and skills to convert iron into the metal tires of wagon and carriage wheels and to make a variety of other iron things. He used charcoal, partly from mountain forests, and sold quantities to others; the going price in 1829 was only 3¢ a bushel.

Among Fishback's customers I noticed two dozen family names identical with names of owners or residents of land that's now inside the park. He had a running account with William Barbee, for instance, above Sperryville. He did business with Bootons (later spelled Booten) and Bradleys, Graveses and Strothers, Weakleys and Chapmans, Broaduses and Thorntons, Finkses and Thomases.

Long-term credit, often year-long, was customary in the early 1800s. Bills were paid more in commodities than in cash—for instance, "coal" (charcoal), flaxseed, timber, cows, horses, hogs, hemp, scrap iron, chestnut rails and shingles, firewood, furniture, wool, teaching of his children. Most of what Fishback took in he sold or bartered to other customers. He lent money, in some cases charging no interest; in other cases, involving the larger amounts and longer terms, he charged 6 percent.

Fishback made a "riding carriage" for William Twyman, who owned an immense plantation near Syria (partly on park-land, I believe); the price was $205. He sold a Negro woman named Agga in 1825; $200 was paid at the time, with $60 more to be paid the next February. A newly

Seven Hensley brothers of Hensley Hollow near Swift Run Gap. They were of English descent, sons of Benjamin Hensley, Jr. (born 1822) and Rebecca Breeden, who were married in 1846. Seated, left to right, Samuel, Charles, and John. Standing, Thomas, Solomon, Nicholas, and Frank. (Courtesy of Billie Jo Monger)

made gig cost $60. He charged 50¢ for a pair of horseshoes. His shop shoed lots of horses—many, for instance, belonging to a Norborne Spotswood. He bought whiskey at 45¢ a gallon and sold it at 10¢ a pint. He paid $3.50 a cord for tanbark.

At least two German (or German-Swiss) families came up the piedmont, over the Blue Ridge, and into the valley. Adam Mueller (Miller) may have heard about the valley from the Spotswood expedition; he's been called the very first permanent settler in Shenandoah Valley. He settled beside the park-land near present Elkton in 1726, according to hints in the paper work that ultimately gave him Virginia citizenship and land title.

A John Harnsberger was definitely associated with Spotswood's Germanna, arriving in 1717 or 1719 and working there, then moving to Madison in 1725. John's son Stephen moved across the Blue Ridge in 1751 and took up land near Elkton. Stephen's son Henry married Mary Ann Bear, a granddaughter of pioneer Adam Miller. Stephen's son Adam owned land in the Blue Ridge near the park's Swift Run Gap, though it's doubtful he ever lived in the mountains. The family became influential in politics.

Hensley cemetery on ridge above (north of) the park part of Hensley Hollow has the remains of Benjamin Hensley, Jr. (1822–1908), father of the seven Hensley brothers. The site resembles dozens of others where longtime residents of the park-land are buried. (Eileen Lambert)

A larger and longer flow of Germans than that up the piedmont moved into the Shenandoah Valley from Pennsylvania. Hans Jost Heydt (later Hite), who brought many settlers in a wagon-and-carriage caravan on roadway his own party chopped, founded "New Muhlenberg" south of today's Winchester in 1732. He was previously mentioned in relation to his court feud with Fairfax.

A dozen or so families may have actually preceded Heydt and built homes and raised crops before he did, though doing without land titles for some years. Nearly all the Germans and Swiss were genuine farmers. They tended to acquire a hundred or so fertile acres and labor personally in raising grains and livestock. They prospered moderately and enjoyed community life centered around churches, some of which strongly resisted violence, including war. Most of the Germans and Swiss, but not quite all, resisted the melting pot for decades and went on speaking German.

About the same time Adam Miller and family were settling near the river between present Shenandoah and Elkton, a group of German-Swiss families began raising crops along the river a few miles from what would be Luray. The "Page Valley Dutch," augmented by continued immigration, would prosper on the rich limestone soil of the valley. Pioneer families with such German names as Brubaker, Long, Spitler, Gander, Hershberger, Grove, Koontz, Brumback, and Varner would grow strong as the English plantations weakened in the mid-1800s. They would become the primary influence on the Blue Ridge park-land after the Civil War, as they raised thousands of cattle on vast pastures where the Skyline

Drive and Appalachian Trail would later be built. Offenbackers, Beahms, Jolletts, Herrings, among other Germans, would have full-time homes in the Blue Ridge.

The settlers of the 1700s in what would become Page and Rockingham counties were close to 80 percent German. Churches were mostly of German origin—Church of the Brethren (Dunkard), United Brethren, Mennonite, Lutheran, Protestant Reformed—and for many decades sermons were preached in German. Though Rockingham was populated largely by Germans, there were influential Anglicans who kept the German majority from controlling county government. Page, much smaller, was German-dominated governmentally and otherwise for many decades. Not until after 1800 did German start fading as a public language. The first gentlemen-justices, when the county court was set up in 1831, were mostly men with German names—Strickler, Stover, Spitler, and so on.

The Anglicans weren't asleep, however. William A. Harris became clerk of the court. Authorized attorneys included Francis S. Smith (English?), Peachy R. Grattan (Irish?), as well as Jacob Pennybacker (of the Pennsylvania German iron-smelting family). Early constables were Jacob Oferbacker (Offenbacker), Thomas J. Compton (English source of geographic names both inside and outside the park?), and Peter Lauck (your turn to guess origin). Edmund Broadus (a family name associated also with the piedmont and with a mill high in the Blue Ridge) was among those named to arrange for Page County public buildings. Elias Overall

Ruins of a Hensley house, now engulfed in forest, still suggest the high skills and dedication that went into many mountain homes. This house is believed to have been built in what's now the park by Benjamin Hensley, Sr., about 1813, of tulip-tree logs. (Eileen Lambert, 1986)

(of Overall Run, a park stream, the name English but Elias descended also from German baron Jost Heydt) was soon added to the court that administered the county as well as judged its legal cases. Frederick A. Marye (French?) was made county surveyor, a position of strong influence then.

I indulge in this burst of factual detail spiced with bits of guessing partly to emphasize two crucial themes—first, the ethnic melting pot, though slow here and there, really was operating; and, second, life in the lowland and life in the Blue Ridge were intricately intertwined.

The variety of origins must have helped make life lively. Though there may not have been enough Englishmen in Page County to make fox hunting with hounds as popular as it was in plantation country across the Blue Ridge, there were enough to promote a horse race now and then, maybe even some cock fights. The Germans weren't fun-loving people to the same extent, though they had their playful customs. Stealing the bride's shoe, for instance, was an amusing contest between dexterous "thieves" and loyal defenders that might erupt before the wedding guests dispersed. The German-nature of the Page County gentlemen-justices, usually serious and nonviolent, may have had something to do with the prominence of an order in the court's first minute book, started in 1831, that the oath of office of county officials must include allegiance to "political equality for all men before the law," and, further, declaring "that I have not . . . fought in a duel, the issue of which was, or probably might have been, the death of either party . . . and have not been a bearer of any challenge or acceptance to fight a duel actually fought . . . nor will I, during my continuance in office, be so engaged, directly or indirectly. So help me God."

Though the Germans resisted mixing cultures or bloodlines, one of the great families of park-land residents was a complex mix. Jacob Boehm (Beahm, Behan, Beham, Beam) came from the Palatinate in Germany about 1715 and settled in Lancaster, Pennsylvania. His son John Boehm migrated to the Shenandoah Valley about 1750. John was a miller and probably worked and lived at a gristmill. In June 1780 he obtained patents for two tracts of land—90 acres "at a foot of the Naked Mts. on a branch of Pass Run in Shenandoah County" (the part that became Page County) and 179 acres in the counties of Culpeper (later Rappahannock) and Shenandoah, near Thornton Gap, likely where "Beham's Gap" appeared on maps during the Civil War. In 1789 he got a patent for another 276 acres on the Blue Ridge.

John's son John married Nancy Bowen. The Bowens were almost certainly English. Moreover, they had a slave burial ground (now in the park) with approximatley a hundred burials (see Appendix 1, Cemeteries in the Park). John and Nancy had a dozen children, including George Washington Beahm—who, in 1846, married Nancy Bolen. The Bolens were mostly English, but their ancestry included a well-known Indian. A Col. Robert Bolling (Bolen), down in tidewater Virginia, had married a granddaughter of Pocahontas and John Rolfe. Despite these links with plantation-type families, the Beahms went on doing their own farm work, most of them having enough children to make the tasks not too great a burden.

George and Nancy had eight sons and seven daughters. Born in the 1820s, they had 71 years of married life. Around World War I they were known as the oldest living couple in Virginia. George was a real mountain man. Though his income wasn't high in money, his family was well taken care of. His children didn't have to go barefooted. People said that when his female dog was in heat at their isolated home on top of Pickerel Ridge, Rappahannock County, he tied her outside the fence. She attracted no small number of male dogs. George tanned their hides and made especially fine shoes for his children.

Also flowing along the Shenandoah Valley from Pennsylvania, beginning in the 1730s, was a stream of Scotch-Irish. Their ancestors were Scots who had left Scotland in the first half of the 1600s because a new form of land tenure pushed them off their old lands and because the British kings were threatening the Scottish (Presbyterian) church, trying to make it more like the English church. These Scots lived in northern Ireland until about the time of Spotswood's expedition over the Blue Ridge, but they couldn't avoid grievous political and religious pressures. America sounded good to them. Pennsylvania extended a welcome, and many came.

John Lewis—born in County Donegal, Ireland, about 1690, maybe a pure Scot, maybe descended partly from a French Huguenot who fled King Louis XIV—appeared at the southwest corner of the Shenandoah park-land about 1732. Gov. William Gooch of Virginia, continuing the Spotswood-sponsored promotion of western settlement, planned large patents for subdivision, but they hadn't materialized yet. Lewis set up a round-log cabin, as pioneers often did before building something more ambitious. He was a squatter at first and soon had fellow squatters around him. When a 118,491-acre grant to William Beverley came through, Lewis got 2,071 acres. The deed was recorded at Orange County Court House in 1738. In 1745, when Augusta County started functioning, he was the presiding justice, called the Founder of Augusta. He helped settle hundreds of Scotch-Irish nearby.

Beverley, son of "Knight" Robert Beverley, did a "land-office business" beside the Blue Ridge as well as out in the valley. The flow from Pennsylvania gained volume as Presbyterians were assured they wouldn't suffer in Virginia from not belonging to the official church and as they realized they could sell their holdings in Pennsylvania at high enough prices to buy larger holdings in wild Shenandoah and still have money left over.

The Scotch-Irish liked foothills with flowing springs and land partly forested, where cattle could browse and hogs fatten on acorns and other wild nuts, fruit, and roots. High ground, they learned, was most healthful for homes, having much less "swamp fever." Livestock could, with a little help from human cutters of timber trees, create their own pasture. Some family lines—for instance, Patterson—were in the valley-mountain cattle business on park-land from the 1740s to the 1930s.

Beverley sold 1,313 acres to Robert Turk. As a good Scot should, Turk took care of his money. Before he paid his £40 for the land, he required Beverley to post an £80 bond guaranteeing the title. When the Tinkling Spring Presbyterian Church was established, he pledged £1 per year to help support the Rev. Mr. John Craig (also an early landowner). He kept putting off paying from 1741 through 1746, and court records show that in 1747 he was officially forced to pay the £6.

Turk would spend plenty on slaves, though. He and descendants produced many hogsheads of money-equivalent tobacco and expanded their plantation up the Blue Ridge and down on the Albemarle side. Geographic names now in the park include Turk Mountain west of Skyline Drive, Turk Gap on the Drive, and Turk Branch on the eastern slope. Such names, with few exceptions, reflect extended landownership during the 1700s and/or early 1800s. An old map shows "Turk's Path" roughly following Turk Run from up in the Blue Ridge down to the Shenandoah River.

In 1966 a Robert A. Turk wrote to the park superintendent about the older Turks and their neighbors, and I exchanged letters with him in 1986. He lived in Florida and had never lived here. He hoped, as I did, to gain more information about the Turks of long ago. He volunteered that one descendant of old Robert, Rudolph Samuel Turk, born in 1849, had served in the Confederate Army, later studied law at University of Virginia, became a prosecuting attorney and still later editor of a Virginia newspaper called *Staunton Spectator*.

So it went, here as elsewhere. Many people of many kinds came and struggled, achieved and prospered, or slid into poverty, or moved away and vanished or got homesick and came back, and will, in one way or another haunt the park forever.

The Founder of Augusta died in 1762. By that time his son, Thomas Lewis, the Fairfax-line surveyor, was in the prime of life and prosperity. He'd married a daughter of the establishment, Jane Strother, who grew up at Ferry Farm near the fall line on the Rappahannock and was a schoolmate of George Washington. Thomas and Jane created a plantation north of what's now Port Republic, alongside the park's south district, and he became a supporter of the Anglican church, though tradition says he avoided actually joining, as that would be disloyal to his origin.

Thomas Lewis was a serious man, unlike many plantation owners on the east side of the Blue Ridge who were fond of fox hunting, horse racing, party giving, and fancy dressing. Lewis was plainly dressed, a bit taller and heavier than average but not fat. He was so nearsighted he felt unfit for military duty, and this troubled him. In his library he read history, biography, philosophy, theology, government, and law. An excellent mathematician, he enjoyed the details of surveying, buying, subdividing, and selling land.

He carried many public responsibilities—for Augusta County, then for Rockingham after the 1778 revision. He served in the conventions that virtually governed the colony just before the Revolution. In agreement with most Scotch-Irish and German leaders of the Shenandoah region, he wrote and presented to the Fifth Convention in May 1776 a powerful resolution that amounted to a declaration of independence from England and contributed to the famous document of July Fourth. In 1788 Thomas Lewis helped significantly in winning Virginia's ratification of the U.S Constitution—by a narrow margin. He got cancer on his face, and he died in January 1790.

The will of Thomas Lewis helps toward understanding 18th-century situations and attitudes affecting the park region's people. He was leaving the largest landholding in Rockingham County—and trying to leave his heirs imbued with firm morality. Lewis directed that the plantation "whereon is my Houses, together with all my Negroes, Household furniture & Stock of Horses Cattle Sheep & Hogs . . . be appropriated for the Maintainance of my Wife Dureing her Natural Life and the Maintainance" of sons Charles and William Benjamin and daughters Ann and Sophia until they are married. Afterward there's to be a division of land and other property, mostly to the two younger sons but "upon this express Condition that Neither of them take to those Detestable Vices of Immoderate Drinking Gameing or Gambling . . . but on the contrary it is hoped that they and each of them will pay due regard to the Dying request of their ancient Parent and live Soberly honestly & Chastly & Shun those Rocks their unhappy Brothers have Split upon." He firmly disinherited his three oldest sons and one of his daughters because of "Disobedience to parents Drunkeness . . . and concomitant Vices."

The plantation proper included 1,160 acres "of Patented land together with my New unpatented land containing about 1,000 acres." Lewis related the new land to "the Mountain" and to several mountain streams. A sizable tract west of the river, adjacent to Gabriel Jones's land, was to be sold. A substantial homeplace with unspecified but substantial acreage was to go to "my son in law Layton Yancey & my Daughter Franey." Another tract, "now in the Tenure of William Vaters," was to remain Vaters's home until the family could be properly situated elsewhere. A similar arrangement was ordered for "William Campbel my Tennant." He was to keep the place he was on "in Good Tenantable Repair" and pay into the estate "One third of what Crops made thereon annually Flax only excepted."

The Lewis family name began to appear on Blue Ridge maps. Today the park maps show Lewis Peak with Lower Lewis Run on its north and Upper Lewis Run on its south, then Lewis Mountain. Descendants of Thomas and Jane live here at Lynnwood beside the park now (1988).

The basic pattern of the ownership and peopling of the park-land and neighboring territory by whites was in place by the time of Thomas Lewis's death. We can turn next to the diverse occupations of people who lived here.

CHAPTER VI

Planters and Laborers

The planting Browns reached the Blue Ridge in the early surge and were soon extending their ownership and operations toward what's called Browns Gap on the Skyline Drive now. Benjamin Brown of Browns Cove, a Welshman, was patenting land in the 1740s and 1750s, totaling more than six-thousand acres. He was sheriff of Louisa County just before Albemarle County took over here. He and his wife (formerly Sarah Thompson) had vigorous sons and gave them all names beginning with B. The swiftly multiplying family became known as the B. Browns.

Dr. Charles Brown, a grandson of Benjamin, lived until 1879, a few weeks before he would have celebrated his 96th birthday. When he was young at 85, after many years of medical service in Charlottesville, he remembered:

My grandfather, Benjamin Brown, moved from what is Hanover county now, to Brown's Cove in 1745. . . . My grandmother has told me that when she moved to Brown's Cove the top of the Blue Ridge was the boundary between the Whites and Indians. They were friendly, and some of them were at her house nearly every week, and her nearest neighbor was seven miles off. . . .

The people ate very little meat, except pork and bacon, and early in the autumn beef, and when they could kill it, venison and bear, then vegetables, even cabbage, turnips, Irish potatoes; in 1795 my mother introduced asparagus, and about 1800 she raised beets, carrots, parsnips, tomatoes, but few of the neighbors would eat or raise the last four named. I remember one of the neighbors dining with us; we had beets on the table; he tasted the beet as a new vegetable, and pronounced it "The beat of anything he had ever tasted."

. . .February, 1800, my father was killed by the fall of a tree.

Dr. Brown's father, Bernard, and other B.B. brothers, sons of old Benjamin, built eight big homes. Brightberry Brown's was a brick structure first called Mountain View, later Headquarters, near the headwaters of the Doyle River, on a 740-acre tract patented in 1750. The bricks were made on the plantation. The slaves and other helpers of the B.B. brothers, on one or another of their nearby plantations, made almost everything any of them needed—strong but not fancy cloth and clothing, leather and shoes and harness, horseshoes and other ironwork, barrels and hogsheads. There weren't any towns, and transportation was difficult and slow. The plantations were the centers of supply, information, commerce, defense, political influence—just about everything.

Brightberry was an officer in the Revolution. In addition to fields lower down, he maintained a quarter at Browns Gap. His workers cut timber up there and cleared ground for tobacco and cattle where the basaltic soil was fertile. An old map shows a tobacco house well inside the park in that vicinity, and there's a family tradition that Brightberry had an overseer or tenant there, whose descendants were mountain residents for generations.

Brightberry invented and patented a loom run by waterpower, and he designed and built a water system. It had pipes made of hollowed-out logs, with ten-foot lengths joined by threading tight enough to prevent leaks. The spring was distant, yet the plantation headquarters had running water for many years before that service was to be expected. According to Vera Via, a researcher-writer of another northwest Albemarle pioneer family, the 12-foot-long auger used to bore the holes through the centers of the logs was owned in the 1950s by John R. Brown of Proffit, Virginia. The auger cut a hole two and one-half inches in diameter, and the boring was done by three or four men—all but one slaves if we judge by custom on similar plantations then.

Brightberry's son Thomas succeeded him at Headquarters. There may have been a fire, and about 1818 Thomas built a frame structure onto the surviving brick part—or, according to historian Nathaniel Mason Pawlett, who was intimately familiar with the old structure not so many years ago, Thomas may simply have added to the original part, which appears to have been about 14 by 28 feet. There are reports of building dates in the attic of the brick structure—1769, 1782, 1785—and there may have been additions since those early in the 1800s. Thomas made clocks and carved wood, including the trimming and mantels at Headquarters. He also made artificial arms and legs for soldiers who'd had amputations, working along with Bernard H. Brown—who, I'm guessing, was a brother of Dr. Charles, son of Bernard who was killed by the tree in 1800.

A Benjamin Brown paid Albemarle personal property taxes in 1782 on 16 slaves, 5 horses, and 28 "neat cattle." Benejah Brown paid on 10 slaves, 4 horses, and 18 cattle. Another B.B. was a Methodist minister in Albemarle; this Bernis and other preachers sometimes gathered at Headquarters. I don't believe there were many Methodists in this region before 1800, so Bernis must have been one of the younger brothers, or a pioneer Methodist.

There's need for many patient person-years of research into plantations that operated partly on land now in the park. My sampling indicates there could have been a hundred or more. Even if we had full information—which we never will—the exact number would depend on how we define *plantation*. For the present purpose I'll say a plantation was an estate of four hundred acres or more on which agricultural commodities were produced for commerce, with most of the manual labor done by slaves, servants, or employees, not by the owner or his family. It probably didn't have an especially impressive house or mansion. Early plantation houses here were most likely to be two-story log structures with four to eight rooms.

The park part of the Blue Ridge—except the western boundary area from Rocky Branch, just north of U.S. 211, south to Gap Run beyond Elkton—was dominated by the plantation system from about 1740 until the War Between the States. German farmers, who did most of their own work—manual or mental, with the help of their children—dominated the valley-and-foothill area. Some of these Germans did have a slave or two, though their farms were seldom plantations by my definition. A slave auction block used at Luray before the Civil War was preserved by the town as a relic, being put on a concrete foundation at the Inn Park in 1936. It was of native sandstone, 17 by 20 inches, 58 inches high; slaves were required to exhibit themselves by standing on it while being auctioned.

The plantation system won out over most farmer-owners for more than a century because of a combination of vast "empty" land, inexpensive labor, the seemingly unlimited European market for American commodities, and the domineering ambition and financial strength of aristocrats and prosperous merchants, almost all of one kind or another of British stock. Though "small" owner-operators, also largely British, had gained footholds in eastern Virginia, few of them could compete for the market or the new land after slaves became easily available in large numbers.

The inexpensive labor in Virginia had been more white than black in the 1600s. Agricultural and other workers in the British Isles, and to some extent on the European continent, were in surplus and miserable. Many were accustomed to short migrations in pursuit of jobs; they longed to

Flax fiber was broken from the other parts of the harvested and retted stems by crushing in slatted frames (left). The remaining nonfibrous material, called shives, was combed out, and the fibers were then twisted into yarn on a spinning wheel (below). Every plantation and most smaller homeplaces raised flax for fiber and linseed oil. Some older people interviewed here at park-establishment time remembered wearing linsey-woolsey— part flax, part wool. (Photos taken in 1969 at craft demonstrations, Belle Grove Plantation, founded in the 1700s by a close descendant of valley pioneer Jost Heydt, see chapters 4 and 5)

escape. They could get to America by trading parts of their lives—four years or more—for passage across the ocean. Those put under contract before sailing were indentured servants. Those who had no contract beforehand might be accepted by ship captains as redemptioners; on landing in America they had to find someone to pay their passage or the captain could sell them to the highest bidder. Workers from Britain were mostly indentured servants; those from Germany, mostly redemptioners.

Quite a few white workers were actually kidnapped, though this was illegal. There was also legal provision for transporting vagrants and criminals, often "political," to America; a common term of servitude for such people was seven years. By far the majority, however, entered indenture voluntarily, knowing more or less what they were getting into. Terms ran out in due course; some servants, not wanting to confront the fierce world on their own, contracted renewal. Others boldly became freemen and adjusted, getting a little land for themselves, or working for hire as craftsmen or overseers, or hurrying to the frontier and becoming hunter-trapper-herder-traders.

In 1670 Virginia had about six thousand white servants and two thousand black. When Spotswood led the famous expedition and the plantation system began spreading toward the Blue Ridge, white servants

The "mammy" was important at plantations. (Drawing by Edith V. Cowles, from Thomas Nelson Page, *Social Life in Old Virginia*, 1897)

were about 20 percent of the population. Their proportion was declining, while blacks were increasing fast. Around 1725 Virginians were importing 1,200 slaves a year, many taken into the Northern Neck and on up the piedmont. By the time the Browns were settling along the Doyle River, black slaves were becoming more numerous than white servants and would soon be about 40 percent of the whole Virginia population.

Partly by plantations directly, partly by their sharecropping tenants, partly by freeholders nearby, tobacco was farmed on much of the Blue Ridge. It was planted where the volcanic and granitic rock weathered into fertile soil that wasn't too terribly steep, but seldom where the base rock was quartzite, sandstone, or shale, which made poorer soil. Tobacco was usually grown in hills among tree stumps or deadened trees, as many Indians had grown their corn, beans, and squash. All the work was done by hand anyway, so the dead wood didn't hurt as long as sunshine reached the plants. The paying fertility of tobacco land normally lasted only three or four years. New ground was continually being opened. After tobacco came corn, perhaps, for another three or four years. When corn wouldn't produce well, something else might be tried. When no crop paid for itself, the field was left to livestock that could eat weeds, some of which proved to be grasses. Where enough manure was dropped, certain grass species might continue to grow. In most fields, though, the broom sedge and brambles would take over, then the juniper and scrub pine pioneering a new forest—which might be cut after several decades and another cycle launched.

Tobacco persisted as a cash crop, though not necessarily utilizing the most acreage, as it was highly labor intensive. The tobacco seeds were planted in well-prepared beds. When the plants were big enough, about May 1, they were transplanted to prepared hills four feet apart. When plants gained sufficient strength, the tops were cut off; thereafter the suckers were removed to keep the leaves few enough to reach substantial size and weight. Weeds had to be hoed frequently. In August, usually, the plants were cut, left a few hours on the ground to wilt, then taken to a tobacco house, or barn, where they were hung up barely touching each other. They had to dry five or six weeks, till the big vein in a leaf would snap when bent. When the air was moist enough that the leaves could be handled without crumbling, they'd be stripped off the stalk, bound into bundles, and packed into hogsheads for transportation to market.

This crucial industry was much regulated by law—grade standards, rules for packing in big hogsheads, inspections. Properly certified tobacco in storage was like money in the bank. The plantations had the land, the financing, and the labor to get top prices; they had the coopers to make the hogsheads that would roll to market or to shipping points with oxen pulling them. The small operator could seldom compete. Yet there was upward mobility as people moved "up the country," clearing, selling for a profit, and moving on to do the same again. Energetic, persistent men might win through and become slaveholding plantation owners themselves.

Wheat came in strongly as a commercial crop in the late 1700s and kept on—sometimes up, sometimes down, as was the pattern with tobacco, too. Cattle and corn were almost universal but not always commercial. Hemp was generally grown to make rope and coarse fabric for sacks, and it could be marketed. Some plantations had hemp mills and bartered the products with others of the region.

All the plantations had to be multicapable. They had to fill their own internal needs as well as produce a marketable crop. The first mills and stills in the park region were on the plantations, as were the first tanners, cobblers, harness makers, blacksmiths, weavers, and the first of almost every kind of development beside or on the Blue Ridge.

Plantations fed, clothed, and housed lots of people. *Let's imagine a B. Brown plantation in action. B.B. and his wife have eight children. There are ten blacks, mostly field hands but some household workers and craftsmen. There's a black crew foreman; B.B. couldn't direct all the work all the time. A detached quarter at Browns Gap has no resident white people. There are two white indentured servants with some years left to serve, one of them a miller. Some of the personnel have youngsters too young to work. There's a widowed aunt— and a homeless uncle of Mrs. B.B. The population of the whole plantation exceeds 30. Nearly all, of course, help somehow with the work.*

Harvesting wheat using scythes to cut and cradles to catch and hold the stalks with heads. Wheat replaced tobacco as major crop on some plantations in the park region. (Drawing by M. Cowles, from Page, *Social Life in Old Virginia*)

There's a large volume of plantation crops to plant and tend and harvest. Mrs. B.B. has wool and flax to spin and weave and sew, and she's responsible for the kitchen, which is separate from the house, and the kitchen garden. Slaves and her own children help her, but she's responsible. Just think of the amount of cooking and sewing for 30 active people! And don't forget there's an orchard and fruit to pick and process and hogs to butcher and process and store. There are cows to milk and poultry to take care of. And travelers often ride in, needing food and lodging for themselves and horses. Neighbors drop by and want to sit on the porch a while and visit—or the wife visits, while the husband barters home-grown tobacco or corn or deerskins for salt or sugar or brandy or shoes for his horse or himself.

Life is endlessly complicated here. Can B.B. and his wife afford imported cloth and an expert dressmaker and tailor? Or is one of the black or white artisans at the place skillful enough to duplicate current fashions? There are standards to maintain, after all. Perhaps B.B. will have business down in tidewater soon and can pick up a few things, maybe even a book or two recently from London. A family ought to have books in sight when other planters and wives and young beaus and belles come to your parties. Your own daughter might have a beau— and that could launch a whole new series of complications. What fabric will be good enough for a wedding gown? What financial and land arrangements will

Well water was used on many plantations to supplement the original springs that characterized most sites chosen for homes in early times. Some hand-dug wells were 50 feet deep or more. The wooden structure and the concrete gave protection from surface contamination or collapse.

have to be made to give the new couple a proper start in family life? Maybe a B.B. can't match, say, Thomas Walker of Castle Hill, Albemarle, who in 1764 offered £4,000 in money or land to establish his son John in a new life with Elizabeth, daughter of Bernard Moore, while Moore promised £500 the next spring and more quite soon. But you'll have to do something substantial of that sort if you're to go on holding your head up.

I've mentioned quite a few plantations earlier, in connection with the land rush and other matters. Though present knowledge has more blanks than visible details, let me try to suggest an overall picture by making a circuit around the park. West of the ridgetop—in Augusta, some of which soon became southeast Rockingham—there'd be Kirtleys, Lewises, Madisons, Pattersons, Turks, Jarmans, Harnsbergers, certainly a Yardley plantation in 1778 as it held the beginning point of the dividing line at "South Mountain" (Blue Ridge) when Rockingham County was created off Augusta. We might ride back to Albemarle over Jarman Gap and stop at Michael Woods's, as Thomas Lewis did, and maybe gossip about neighboring plantations, Moormans, Doyles, just about all the same family names as we found in Augusta-Rockingham, and some others.

You can read plantation names from geographic features all over the park. North of the Browns in Greene County now there'd be Powells and maybe Bacons. We find several Kirtley plantations and their detached quarters. In 1851 a Milton Kirtley had 5,933 acres in Madison County alone, probably just north of the Conway River around Kirtley Mountain. There'd just about have to be a Conway plantation or two—and

Graveses and Stauntons, Chapmans and Strothers, Bootons (later spelled Booten), and more. Thomas Graves "and his oldest children owned upwards of fifty slaves" at the height of their plantation operations in the Jones Mountain vicinity during the late 1700s, according to author Tom Floyd.

The Kirtleys might have had even more. They were at work on both sides of the park-land and inside the present boundary, too. When Francis Kirtley, Sr., died in 1763, he left land on the Staunton River to son Thomas, land "at the head of South River" to son Francis, along with land in Augusta, and 310 acres "on the branches of Conway" to daughter Mary. Son-in-law Jonathan Cowherd got to keep the Swift Run Gap plantation "whereon he now lives." Most of the property, land, slaves, equipment, livestock, would remain with his widow, living on the undivided main plantation. Property appraised at about £1,000, including 15 slaves, would be sold at auction. At one time or another Francis Sr. had had 20,000 or more acres in the park vicinity.

The Kirtleys had connections with other park region plantations. Francis Jr. married Elizabeth, daughter of Honorias Powell (of the park's Powell Gap and Powell Mountain; old Honorias was buried in the park). William Kirtley married Sarah, daughter of Jeremiah Early, or Yearley. There's a story that George Washington and small group on horseback, crossing Swift Run Gap in 1784, were refused lodging at a Kirtley plantation. After they'd left a servant identified them to Kirtley—or would it have been Jonathan Cowherd?—and he sent a rider inviting them to return. Washington refused, however, and was soon welcomed at the plantation of "the Widow Yeardley" (Early).

By far the biggest park-land plantation I've learned about was Thomas Shirley's. His home base was above Syria, maybe a mile from the present park line. Apparently he'd owned about six thousand acres of foothills and lowland, then acquired Barbour's biggest Big Survey. Madison County records show he was paying taxes on 48,933 acres around 1850, and some of his land at one time or another was in Page and Rappahannock counties as well. There were lots of slaves, tobacco fields and other crops, at least one mill, probably extensive timber cutting, and distilleries scattered all around the Blue Ridge—the historian Ann Brush Miller says even out into West Virginia—making excellent and legal liquor. Much could be learned about Shirley and his domain, but at present myth and fact are tangled together. His three and one-half-story house just south of Old Rag Mountain still stands solidly beside the Rose (Row's) River; it is now a Christian counseling center. Thomas Shirley died about 1851, and his grave, in accordance with his will, was marked only by a pile of stones.

Thornton's Montpelier, a plantation house much larger than was typical in the park region, was built about 1745 by land-magnate Francis Thornton for his son William. The Thorntons had many thousands of acres on the piedmont and up to the Blue Ridge crest, including 1,300 acres along Hawksbill Creek near present-day Luray. (Eileen Lambert, 1987)

Scouting on north into Rappahannock County, we find Thornton country. Old Francis, whom we've met, kept living near Fredericksburg but gave plantations out here to his children, who liked mountains better than lowlands. Caravans of oxcarts came from Francis's plantation with slaves, carpenters, blacksmiths, and stonemasons, glass and nails, to help build two mansions. One was Montpelier (not to be confused with President Madison's home), for son William; the other was Thornton Hill, for son John. Daughter Mary (according to one legend, the Mary of Marys Rock) wed William Champe, and they built another mansion—Champeplain, soon shortened to Champlain, beside Old Rag Mountain.

George Washington liked to visit these Thorntons, his second cousins. He was at Mary's one Christmas when the house caught fire and burned. The people barely escaped. Washington mounted Buckskin, his favorite horse, and rode five miles to Montpelier. This mansion and Thornton Hill survive today (1988).

Thorntons and Kennerleys and Bryans (ancestors of William Jennings Bryan) had plantation backcountry in what's now the park. There were

The most prosperous planters might travel in horse-drawn carriages. Such vehicles, some fancy, were made by piedmont and valley craftsmen, including the Fishbacks of Madison County, who also made transcontinental wagons. (Drawing by Cowles, from Page, *Social Life in Old Virginia*)

Keysers, Jenkinses, Harrises, Rushes, Comptons, Marshalls, and others. Rounding the north end of the park, we'd find the name Chester, for Thomas Chester, who had a long road and a Shenandoah plantation and ferry. But here in Warren County no place names are on park maps for Bucks—though they were long prominent around Front Royal and one of them, Marcus Blakemore Buck, had a plantation with the mansion itself inside the park—or for Simpsons or Woodwards or even old Fairfax. In southern Warren and northern Page County we traverse 12 miles or so of the great Overall plantation (see Chapter 10), then leap from Neighbor Mountain, once Overall's, over the rest of Page and much of east Rockingham County—German country—and land in another vast tract of the park, Gambill-Alexander land, where Rockingham took over from Augusta, thus completing our park circuit.

The plantation system was giving way to other lifeways some while before the Civil War. Soil fertility was dwindling almost everywhere, and though manuring and other forms of fertilizing were known, they weren't being used enough to save the system. Streams of people were leaving for places farther west and south. Slavery didn't pay so well any more in this region, and some of the plantation owners, partly on moral grounds, wanted to terminate it. Albert Early of Madison County wrote thus in his will in 1839:

I give and bequeath unto my above named executors all the negro slaves I own or may own. I do most solemnly and seriously request and exhort them to do with my said negro slaves as I now prescribe, that it is my wish that they should be liberated so that they may enjoy all the liberties and blessings of a free and independent people and not approving the custom of liberating slaves to remain in the United States, I would recommend to my executors to select for their residence some section . . . which may supply them . . . with all the comforts and necessities.

Early provided that money enough to resettle the slaves be raised from selling as much of his land or other property as necessary. Joseph Early put a similar plan into his will in 1852, wanting his former slaves sent to Liberia, each given $50, "and Verindy and all her children, one hundred dollars, to take with them besides getting them out, and bacon enough to last them six months after they get to Liberia."

In Augusta County, many years before the Civil War, 215 ladies signed a petition for emancipation. The planter-slave system was sickening toward death, and farmer-grazers, mostly German, would soon own much of its park-land.

CHAPTER VII

Miners and Charcoal Makers

W hen George Washington was clinching victory at Yorktown, Dirck Pennybacker, who'd helped make iron for
Revolutionary cannons and cannonballs, was seeking a
site for an iron furnace of his own. He knew where the ore was—at the
foot of Neighbor Mountain in the Blue Ridge. Neighbor and Jeremys
Run forests (on park-land) might be vast enough to furnish the unending
loads of charcoal he'd need. The haul should be downhill and, if possible,
less than five miles. There had to be limestone, too, and much water.

Pennybacker was prepared to solve the problems. A wagon master in
Berks County, Pennsylvania, he'd worked at Hopewell Furnace with
ironmaster Mark Bird—who'd just gone into partnership with Henry
Miller in Augusta County, Virginia, ironworks. Bird had been encouraging Pennybacker. So had Isaac Zane, a wealthy Quaker of Pennsylvania
who had iron furnaces and foundries at several places in the mid-Atlantic
region and owned land near Neighbor.

Pennybacker found his site beside Hawksbill Creek. It was in working
distance from Neighbor, at a spring considered bottomless with steady
flow of eight million gallons a day—later called Yager Spring. The deal
with Zane for about two thousand acres went on record in 1785, but
Pennybacker must have been at work here earlier. It would have taken
more than two years to get everything functioning, not only to be mining
and smelting iron but to be manufacturing designed stoves. On the front
plate of a six-plate stove these words were cast: "D. Pennebacker His
Redwil Furnace Septe 21, 1787." The proof of this surprisingly early
start is from H. E. Comstock of Winchester, who researched these
ironworks deeply.

Charcoal blast furnaces of the Redwell type, built of native stone, were
15–20 feet square and 30–40 feet tall. The inner chamber, where smelting

Cast-iron stove panels, many of which survive at old home sites in the park, remind us that large quantities of iron ore and charcoal were taken from the parkland between 1785 and 1905. In addition to stoves, furnaces and foundries here sold iron kettles, grave markers, and other locally useful iron things. The main sales for many years, though, were in the form of "pigs" shipped down the Shenandoah River in gundalows.

took place, was lined with firebrick. It widened upward to ten feet diameter, then tapered toward the smoke outlet to three feet. Water-powered bellows blew air into the chamber. The hearth at the bottom, where molten iron collected, was about 30 inches in diameter and twice that high. The iron was drawn off and cast into "pigs," not too heavy for workmen to load for transport.

It took 180 bushels of charcoal, 1,600 pounds of limestone, and about three tons of ore to produce one ton of pig iron. Once started, the furnace operated day and night. Pennybacker had more than a hundred workers, including slaves. Much of the work away from the central plant was contracted out—digging, hauling, wood cutting, charcoal burning—so this iron operation furnished as many as two hundred jobs for three-quarters of a century.

There were two ore banks of considerable size. One iron mine was in what became national park. Another, which became a pond after being abandoned, was outside the park boundary. There may have been other mines in the same general area. Mining was mostly open cutting with pick and shovel. The heavy brown lumps were selected to the extent possible but were always dirty. The ore was hauled in wagons, each pulled by four horses, a distance of four miles to the furnace. At the crossing of Pass Run, about halfway, the loose dirt was washed out by the stream; there might be further washing in the Hawksbill.

Wooden shedding sheltered the furnace, and there were structures and different grade levels to ease feeding in of the materials. Nearby were storage buildings, dwellings for the personnel, kitchen and dining facilities, a commissary, smokehouse, dairy, shelters for horses and oxen, a blacksmith shop, gristmill, sawmill, waterwheel, millrace, and so on and

Charcoal to operate just one early-day iron furnace required at least eight thousand acres of forest. Many square miles of mountain thus became "naked" at intervals. To "burn" the charcoal, four-foot lengths of wood no more than five inches thick were stacked as shown above. (Drawing from "The Iron Industry in Land Between the Lakes," Tennessee Valley Authority)

on—for half a century or more the largest concentration of population and development in what would become Page County.

Total production of iron at Redwell could have been as much as 50,000 tons. In 1808 the business was sold to Benjamin Blackford and John Arthur. They changed the furnace name to Isabella, for Blackford's daughter. There was production and prosperity for more than three decades. Then in 1841, because of debt, the whole "plantation" was sold to Nicholas Yager—who'd married Christina Overall, whose half-brother Isaac owned 28,000 acres of the Blue Ridge park-land nearest the furnace, almost certainly the main source of charcoal. The deal included 3,189 acres, 33 adult Negroes with 10 children, 70 horses, 26 mules, 4,000 cords of wood, 800 loads of charcoal, 300 tons of pig iron, 80 tons of castings, 50 cattle, 1,000 barrels of corn, 25,000 pounds of beef, 6,000 pounds of bacon, and numerous other items.

The Yagers built a big new home on the furnace property for their son William Overall Yager. Nicholas Yager had a home and merchandising business in Luray. It's hard to be sure now just when the Yagers stopped smelting iron—maybe as late as 1860, when a four-story woolen mill was built on the foundation of the furnace.

Mining, though nowhere near as big economically as agricultural production in the valley, was larger at various times on the western foothills of all three park districts than any other activity in the mountains. There's a generally accepted estimate that it took 8,000 acres of forest to support one charcoal blast furnace. As I'll show, there were three other furnaces getting charcoal from the park's mountains, so it's evident that 32,000 or more park acres were heavily and repeatedly cut over for iron smelting.

To produce 50,000 tons of iron, Redwell-Isabella would have consumed 9.5 million bushels of charcoal. It also burned cordwood directly in ore preparation. Pennybacker, owning little forest himself, preferred either to buy timber rights from landowners and contract out the cutting and hauling of cordwood or to buy cordwood at so much per load from any and all persons who delivered it. His own crews of colliers—some white, some black—took over from there, supposedly producing a better quality and consistency of "coal." The total cost was high, however, and Redwell operators were soon buying many loads of charcoal from contractors who'd "burned" it in the mountains. Good charcoal weighs only about one-fifth of the weight of the wood from which it's made, though it preserves the shape of the wood, is hard and black, and doesn't easily dirty the hands. If it's burned close to where it's cut, the hauling cost is greatly reduced.

The men with axes, carts, wagons, oxen, and mules went out into the forest, cut trees into four-foot lengths, split as necessary to thicknesses of no more than five inches, and brought the cordwood to the "pit" or "hearth." Trees no more than five inches thick to start with didn't have to be split, so forests were worked over often to get the trees while they were small. Some old-timers say their forebears mentioned "coaling pits" on lands now in the park, but the sites are hard to pin down. Returning forest and falling leaves erase them, or fragments of charcoal uncovered on the ground might be attributed to an old forest fire. The method didn't require any actual pit or structure, just a flattish open area large enough for a circular pile of wood 30 feet in diameter, plus working space around it.

About 50 cords of wood were needed for a burning, each cord expected to produce about 30 bushels of charcoal. A three-cornered "chimney" was made by crossing lengths of wood. Then cordwood standing on end but leaning slightly inward was stacked around and around the chimney as densely as possible. A second layer of cordwood on end was added on top of the first until the whole circle 30 feet across had two dense stories 8 feet tall. Leaves were then hauled in from the forest floor and placed thickly all around and over the woodpile. The leaf layer was dampened and packed, then plastered with clay to a thickness of about five inches around the sides and eight inches or more on top. It was a tedious and delicate process, but necessary for controlling the burning. Any failure could lose the whole batch to roaring flames.

Fire was kindled in the central "chimney." A cover could be put over the chimney to smother the fire, and small holes or pipes were opened or closed around the outside to admit or stop the air. The master collier had to be experienced, cautious, and always alert. A pile was burned as evenly as feasible 24 hours a day for one week or even two. The idea was to get all impurities out, including the high water content, and leave the carbon. The slowest burning made the highest-quality product. A crew of six colliers might have several hearths operating at once, and they had to stay watchful the whole time. Food had to be brought. The master collier could judge the rate and stage of burning by color of smoke.

When the job was done and the fire smothered, the pile was opened on the side, and hot "coal" was taken out with long-handled tools. This, too, was a slow process. Water was poured on the coal to be sure the fire was out. Even so, sometimes it ignited again. You had to keep water handy to douse it, even barrels along the haul route. Fire could escape into the forest. Records suggest that forest fires were a serious menace far more often then than now.

Another iron operation along the Blue Ridge east of Shenandoah and Elkton was started by Daniel and Henry Forrer, brothers, also from Pennsylvania, with construction of Furnace No. 1 in 1836. Most of the ore came from the vicinity of Naked Creek. The first Forrer furnace had capabilities similar to Redwell's. It was built where Shenandoah town is now. Furnace No. 2 was built in 1857 about four miles to the southeast, on the south bank of Naked Creek near Fox Mountain, a prolific source of the brown ore. It was a steam hot-blast furnace, an advance over No. 1 and Redwell, and could turn out 3,000 tons of iron a year, using about 540,000 bushels of charcoal.

Shenandoah Iron Works included forges and all related facilities and developments, and another furnace called Catherine on Massanutten Mountain that didn't depend on Blue Ridge resources. Unlike Penny-backer, who dealt with many landowners, the Forrers owned plenty— 31,483 acres—mostly mountain forests but some lowland. In 1866 they sold the works to other Pennsylvanians—William Milnes, Jr., and Thomas Johns—who introduced newer techniques and equipment. In 1871 the Milnes firm built a big forge or bloomery with a 20-ton steam hammer; in 1883, the Big Gem Furnace at Shenandoah. The railroad had come, and coke from mined coal was brought in for use in Big Gem. Diverse forms of iron were shipped.

Early in the 1890s the works were sold to Allegheny Ore and Iron Company of Pennsylvania, which operated until about 1905 and still had large holdings of mineral and charcoal lands in the Blue Ridge when

Mt. Vernon Furnace, inside the park beside Madison Run, survives as a massive ruin. Much of the stonework is intact, as seen here, but dense vegetation interferes with showing the third dimension. Both ore and charcoal came from the park-land. Iron was loaded on the flatboats at Port Republic.

Virginia bought the mountains to create the national park in the mid-1930s. (Owners of land at park establishment time are listed in Appendix 3 and Appendix 4.) The appraisers found the forest depleted. Low prices ($1.50 to $2.50 an acre) were paid, plus 25¢ an acre for "mineral," which was also depleted. Another Pennsylvania mining firm, Madeira Hill and Company, had park-lands nearby and was paid similar rates.

There's disagreement as to just when the Mt. Vernon Furnace, on the south bank of Madison Run inside the park above the present town of Grottoes, entered the Blue Ridge iron industry. I accept the findings of historian Edward Steere, who scouted the area's past when the park was being established and learned too much from family papers and pictures and interviews around Grottoes to have been far wrong. He reported that the furnace was built by Col. John Miller about 1830 and was operated by the Millers until the Civil War. One of the managing ironworkers in the 1850s was Marassa Blackburn, a great-grandfather of John W. "Bill"

Wilson, who has many old land patents and other documents and has helped me learn about the past of east Rockingham County. The ore first came from the Miller Run area, south of the furnace. This geographic name and quite a few others in the park came from the mineral industry—Furnace Mountain, for instance.

The Miller family had been making iron in Augusta County for many years. Henry Miller, in the 1820s, was selling Augusta iron regularly to John Fishback, wagonmaker in Madison County. As early as 1795, Millers owned Blue Ridge land along or near Madison Run. R. T. Miller of Grottoes, a descendant of Col. John, told historian Steere that after the first mine was exhausted a rich surface deposit was found about five miles northeast of the furnace. Other sources pinpoint iron ore beds on the south side of Big Run just above its emergence from the park. R.T. said Big Run ore was mined by open-cut methods and hauled on a tram line.

The idea of a five-mile tram line to the furnace intrigues me. It must have been a mine-tunnel-type tram, not aerial. But what would power the little cars on the little rails: mules? oxen? miners? slaves? Then, studying my topographic map, I notice a sort of bench along the foot of the Blue Ridge. You could start in Big Run at the 1,400-foot level and descend gradually in a line that's almost straight, except for smallish curves, and ease down to the furnace at or near the 1,300-foot level. Gravity could be the main power.

There's scientific authority for what six separate Mt. Vernon Furnace mines looked like in 1931. William M. McGill, then assistant state geologist, studied them in evaluating land proposed for the park. He found the Big Run mine "chiefly iron, some manganese. . . . Operations consist of two open cuts, a caved-in shaft and two or more shallow trenches, all in a rotten (decomposed) clay from Shady dolomite in upper part of Erwin quartzite. . . . There are not sufficient showings of either manganese or iron in any of the old workings to justify further exploration." He found extensive workings at all but one of the other five sites, including the first-used "Miller Bank." He agreed with those who'd ceased work—no values left—and the land was bought for park.

R. T. Miller said the hired labor, mostly white but including some free blacks, had done the mining. Crews of slaves cut cordwood in the mountains for making charcoal. Hearths for charcoal burning were on flattish places in mountain hollows. R.T. showed Steere photographs of the old ironworks, remnants of wooden structures that had included office, superintendent's house, and seven cabins for white workers. The pig iron was hauled in wagons pulled by six-mule teams to a foundry, where a power plant was later built at Port Republic. The iron was cast into three-hundred-pound blooms there and shipped downriver.

Though the "Iron Millers" lost control of the property after the Civil War, there were efforts to revive the industry. John F. Lewis (of the old Thomas Lewis family) and others operated the furnace at intervals until 1878. Many people have expressed a hope that the stone remains of Mt. Vernon Furnace can be stabilized as a historic exhibit in the national park before they're too far gone to evoke the extensive and powerfully haunting iron operations.

Iron wasn't the only mineral in the park-land. At several places the old lava (greenstone, Catoctin formation) carried teasingly colorful copper ores—green or blue or bronze compounds with sulphur and other elements—and even bits of native copper. A showing on Stony Man peak teased J. B. Gray, A. G. Grinnan, and David S. Jones into patenting 63 acres there in 1849 and 2,308 acres in 1850, and a Stony Man Mining Company to buy 3,000 acres from A. N. Smith in 1858. Ore was dug and some copper melted out, but the best thing these deposits ever did may have been bringing George Freeman Pollock, pioneer of Skyland, to look at the property. Later, in 1935, he explained away the copper efforts: "The name Furnace Spring was given to the spring where the smelting plant was located. To this day considerable slag and other materials can be found there. . . . The ore was carried on mule-back from the mine around back of the peak. . . . This copper mine proved to be worthless."

Hope didn't die easily, though. In the 1880s an Alexander Cristadoro (the name is spelled Christadora in park-land purchase records of 1934) acquired 10,455 acres of "copper land" in the Stony Man vicinity, and a Joseph Cristadoro got 5,757 acres. Richards Mining Company went to work under the management of B. P. Stebbins. Nuggets of native copper were reported, along with ore assaying 55 percent copper in a four-inch thickness of a green vein—so company officials said. The newly completed railroad that went along the valley contracted to haul ore to Baltimore at $2.50 a ton. In February 1882 an assay showed 46 percent copper and .5 percent silver. Some ore was shipped. "Booten mine" was opened 12 miles south of Stony Man. By June 1883 the Stony Man shaft was "100 feet deep." Then, without explanation, the work stopped. The encouraging reports may have been invented to sell stock. Still another flurry, in 1903, involved a Blue Ridge Copper Mining Company. Geological researchers in 1905 and 1911 found an old shaft, maybe 60 feet deep but crumbling, and half a mile west an open cut 50 feet long, 15 feet wide, and 30 feet deep.

The Dark Hollow Mine—on Rose River Loop Trail east of Fishers Gap—had a similar history. Rhesa M. Allen, Jr., reported in 1963 that this mine had been "a well developed operation" and continued:

Remnants of the old workings include a caved adit, several partially filled open pits or trenches, and a dump, well overgrown with brush and trees. . . . Concrete bases for mine equipment such as draw works and boiler are present. The operation was opened before the Civil War, was dormant for many years, and was reopened by the Blue Ridge Copper Mining Co. about 1902.

Some ore was certainly shipped from three shafts of unknown depth—but briefly.

The Stony Man and Dark Hollow mines are near trails and findable still. Several similar mines outside the park boundary, such as on Hightop in Greene County, might also be found with determined effort. I'm not sure anybody now could find the Mount Marshall Mine ("Indian Copper Mine") that's inside the park, but it was on the 6,666-acre John J. Miller tract in Rappahannock County in 1907. A company was incorporated then to work it. Miller was one of the directors. The vein was examined by experts and found genuine but too low-grade to make the project practical. So it was forgotten again—yet not totally forgotten. Who can totally forget buried treasure? Some people around the park carry on the myth of precious metals. The version I picked up in 1987 has a rich but lost bonanza in the park somewhere between the Rose River and Cedar Run. It's sometimes called "the Chief's Mine."

Most renowned in mining and metallurgical circles of all park region minerals was manganese—almost all along the west foot of the Blue Ridge from Front Royal to Waynesboro. Manganese is used mainly in making alloys of iron, aluminum, and copper. Manganese steel is about 12 percent manganese; it is tough yet malleable, the material of drill bits, some military hardware, and rock crushers. The name the steel people still remember is Crimora; the location, ten miles northeast of Waynesboro, between the park's Turk Mountain and Davis Mountain–Wildcat Ridge. When the park was being established, the boundary was pulled sharply back to leave out this historic source of manganese.

From Crimora Lake Overlook on the Skyline Drive, you can see the lake that was created to supply water for washing the clay and other dirt off the ore. About a mile to its left are other "lakes"—powdery green—which are flooded pits once mined. The richest deposit was about 3,000 feet long, 500 feet wide, and 200 feet deep. Waste is piled about—yellow-red-white-brown clay, shale, sandstone, and quartzite, long inhospitable to vegetative cover. Much information about Crimora's mine and ore mill is to be found in technical journals and books, including reports by Dr. Thomas Leonard Watson, professor of economic geology at the University of Virginia in the early twentieth century.

Manganese ore was found along the west foot of the Blue Ridge the full length of the park. In some places it was commercially mined for decades.

Crimora Lake, prominent from Crimora Lake Overlook on the Skyline Drive (south district, Milepost 92.6), supplied water for cleaning ore from the Crimora manganese mine. This mine was world-champion producer for some years in the 1880s and remained a major source on into the 1900s. Other "lakes" a mile farther south, not easily visible from the drive, represent open pits once heavily mined. (NPS)

The Virginia Manganese Company began producing here in 1867, taking ore from both shafts and open pits and shipping mostly to European steel plants. For a time, beginning in 1880, Crimora was said to be producing more manganese than any other single mine in the world. The 21st Annual Report of the U.S. Geological Survey (1901) says, "Prior to 1894 when the Crimora mine was producing liberally, Virginia annually contributed the major portion of the manganese ores mined in the United States." From 1882 to 1892 the mine was leased to American Manganese Company, a subsidiary of the great Andrew Carnegie Steel Works of Pittsburgh. During World War I the Crimora Manganese Corporation installed new equipment and introduced advanced excavating methods to mine and process the remaining ore-bearing clay through inexpensive mass production. Crimora shut down, finally perhaps, in 1957, the ore no longer economic.

Though Crimora had dominated, there were other manganese producers alongside the park and teasing ore-showings inside the boundary. J. Blake Kendall of Washington, D.C., mined just south and east of Elkton between 1891 and 1902. American Manganese of Pittsburgh and New York, apparently the same firm that had done so well earlier at Crimora, was producing from the Elkton mines, low on Hanse Mountain, during World War I.

Old miners never stop dreaming of bonanzas. Their haunts are probably prospecting after every thunderstorm that might have washed the cover off rich deposits, maybe even the gold that the gentlemen of the Jamestown colony never stopped believing was hidden in the Great Mountains of the Manahoac and Monacan Indians.

CHAPTER VIII

Roadmen and Boatmen

The Blue Ridge was never the impenetrable barrier the early Englishmen feared it was, and crossing it became easier and easier. For almost two centuries, more than a dozen gaps or passes of the park-land had roads that followed packhorse trails, which followed Indian paths, which followed elk and bison, which followed mastodons. An unforgettable river route also linked the park-land to the world.

On June 26, 1740, the gentlemen-justices who were the Orange County Court ordered that "Abraham Strickler & Phillip Lung lay off ye sd road"—from the Shenandoah Valley through the Blue Ridge to Thornton's Mill—"and that all the Male laboring tithables . . . work on ye sd road under the said Strickler & Lung who are hereby appointed Overseers." It was further ordered that the "said Overseers"—among the earliest settlers at "Massinuttin" by the Shenandoah River west of present-day Luray, "cause the Same to be cleared & Bridges to be made where necessary & keep ye Same in repair according to Law."

Though roads might develop from paths through repeated use, they came into official existence by such actions of the county courts. The law required each male tithable to give six days of roadwork a year. When the surveyor or overseer called them, they had to come or send slaves, employees, or indentured servants. No governmental funds were involved, except that the county court might contract bridges of special difficulty to persons with special skills and pay them. If a structure was too big or difficult for a county's resources, an appeal might be made to the Virginia Assembly.

The system evolved, of course, and the road through Thornton Gap (U.S. 211 now) reached a new phase in 1786. Though the tithables and often-changing overseers had been doing their jobs, traffic increased, as traffic does. Sometimes after spring melting or heavy rains many vehicles might be mired to the axles in mud. People howled. Young Andrew Russell Barbee and Enos McKay must have heard. They formed a

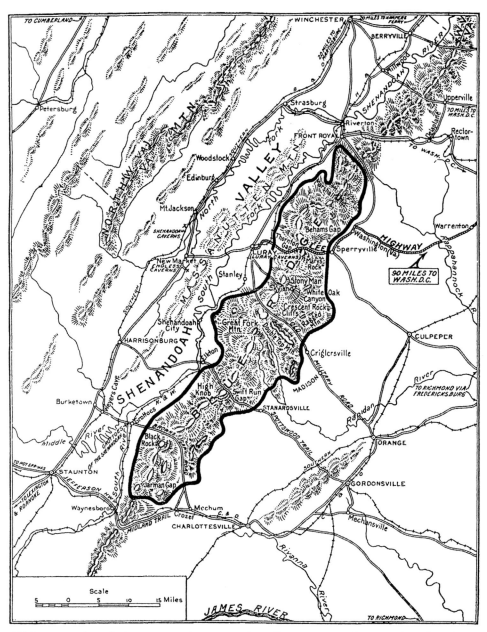

This map—though from an early proposal outlining a possible boundary for the prospective Shenandoah National Park—graphically depicts the important roads that crossed the Blue Ridge. (*National Parks Bulletin, Dec. 25, 1924, National Parks Association, Wash., D.C.*)

A stage coach of the type that crossed the Blue Ridge on turnpikes through major passes such as Thornton and Swift Run. (From Edward Steere, "The Shenandoah National Park," 1935)

partnership and built what a descendant would call a "macadam road," though John L. McAdam was only beginning in 1786 to experiment with his crushed stone pavements in Scotland. The new Thornton Gap road had sledge-cracked stone and was graded. Andrew Barbee was responsible for the Blue Ridge section. His slaves did the labor. Tollgates were installed, and the Barbees collected 25¢ for each stagecoach or wagon with driver and horses or oxen going through a gate, 12¢ for smaller vehicles, and lesser sums for individual travelers. Fees for livestock were 1¢ to 3¢ per head. Supposedly Andrew made a profit, and the road over Thornton Gap would be intertwined with the careers of three generations of Barbees, including two men whom many consider the most famous persons of the park-land.

Barbour's biggest Big Survey on park-land used as one anchor point a place in Page County, "on top of the Blue Ridge Mountains" near Marys Rock, where Barbees "formerly lived"—as though their home was a long-established landmark. They were certainly there long enough to have a family cemetery (see Appendix 1), quite possibly a generation or two before Andrew. Lower down eastward in Rappahannock County they soon had two additional bases. At about 1,400-feet elevation on the turnpike was Hawsberry (sometimes called Hawsbury or Hawsburg), a combination inn, post station, and tollgate. It had a U.S. post office long before the Civil War. Still farther down, comfortably distant from the turnpike, Andrew bought a stone house that had been built before the

Revolution by a John Skinner as a hunting lodge. The Barbees named this house The Bower and lived in it a long time. It was still standing in the 1930s and might have been the oldest house left in the park. Ruins are still impressive as I write, but crumbling.

William Randolph Barbee, born in 1818 at one of the three locations, turned out to be a prodigy. He loitered along the way to and from school, which was near present-day Sperryville, and carved images on trees and stones. His schoolwork was excellent despite the distraction, and he was sent off for higher education. At age 25 he was admitted to the bar. He became a successful Virginia lawyer while also helping his aging father with the turnpike business. He married at age 29, and, I think, took his bride, Mary Jane McKay, to the old Barbee home at Panorama alongside the turnpike. They had four children. The oldest, Herbert, was born in 1848.

That same year, influenced by William the lawyer as well as by elderly Andrew, a third phase in the Thornton Gap road was launched by the Virginia Assembly. There would be major improvement of the New Market and Sperryville Turnpike by a newly organized company with Andrew on its board of directors. The company would issue $100,000 of stock at $25 a share. The Virginia Board of Public Works—created in 1816 by the General Assembly along with a Fund for Internal Improvement that together inaugurated state support of the road system—would buy $60,000 worth. The rebuilt road would have a right-of-way 40 feet wide. An 18-foot width would be macadamized—this time in the genuine McAdam way. Some relocation would bring the maximum grade down to "four degrees."

Construction, including bridges, started in July 1849 with a crew of about two hundred men. With the expenditure of $103,437.35 in one year, the job was virtually completed. Company president was Samuel T. Gibbons, paid $420 a year. Directors besides Andrew Barbee (Scottish descent?) were two valley men of German descent and two piedmont men from English gentry. (The mixing pot was mixing in many different ways.) Toll receipts for the year ending September 1851 were $1,821.91—and rapidly rising.

Continued success of the new turnpike regime, in which Barbees now held substantial stock but carried no direct responsibility, soon gave William a feeling of release. At age 38, in 1856, he left his law practice and took his family to Florence, Italy, where he set up a studio and began carving marble. Soon he was selling life-sized statues to wealthy people at high prices—*Fisher Girl*, $10,000; *The Coquette*, $7,500, vast amounts in those days. He was offered a studio in the Capitol at Washington and commissioned to complete the frieze on the west wing. But the Civil War

William Randolph Barbee, internationally
known sculptor who was also a roadman
born and raised where Shenandoah park is
now, is immortalized by this marble bust
by his son Herbert Barbee. Herbert placed
it on the father's grave site beside U.S. 211
at Panorama in 1930. Some years after the
Skyline Drive was built close by, the
family repossessed the bust for
safekeeping. (NPS)

broke into his work; several Barbee houses in Virginia burned, apparently
including old Panorama and Hawsberry. William's morale and health
deteriorated, and he died at The Bower in 1868, age 50, leaving much
of his sculpture unfinished.

Herbert, who'd worked with his father in Florence, dedicated himself
to sculpture. He opened a studio in New York, then returned to Florence.
He completed some of his father's projects, including *Star of the West*,
which was bought by a noted bridge builder in St. Louis and given top
award at the World Exposition in 1892. Though Herbert continued in
his father's shadow, he did highly praised work of his own, including
many monuments representing Virginia. His statue of a Confederate
soldier on picket duty, of heroic size, ten feet tall, white marble, on an
already high pedestal with Robert E. Lee in bas-relief, continues
prominent in east Luray.

In 1930 Herbert erected a marble bust of his famous father in the old
Barbee cemetery where his father was buried in 1868. The remains had
been moved to Green Hill, Luray, perhaps when Herbert's mother died
in 1908. The bust showed William looking up at Marys Rock—which
Herbert said his father named long ago for his bride Mary McKay.
Herbert in 1930 was working on a companion bust of his mother to go
on Marys Rock, looking toward William at Panorama. He kept working

Ruins of the Barbee family's beautiful stone house, The Bower, a mile from the busy
Barbee Turnpike that's become U.S. 211, haunt the returning wilderness. The most
famous Barbee died here after suffering serious losses in the War Between the States.

on it at intervals but was an octogenarian-plus and couldn't satisfy himself
with the likeness and the expression.

Herbert's emotions reached back toward the turnpike of his boyhood,
and he prepared glimpses for historian Steere, who'd been asking him
questions. He sketched the old Hawsberry Inn—a frame building with a
veranda 60 feet long. Coaches stopping overnight drove through a
tunnel-like entrance into the basement. Passengers went upstairs from
there to the rooms. In excavations behind the inn, wagoners were accommodated for the first night's rest of their three-day trip from the valley
to Fredericksburg. Some vehicles made the briefest of stops:

> Crack coaches, with red bodies and yellow wheels, carried the mails and
> passengers from New Market through the gap to the railroad at Warrenton.
> As stage time arrived, a fresh four-horse team in full harness was brought
> out by the roadside. The clattering express arrived at a full trot and stopped
> with a final lurch of the strap-hung body. The driver tossed his reins down
> to an attendant while others unhooked the steaming horses. With a quick
> rattle of chains and swingle-trees, the fresh four were hooked in and the
> reins passed to the driver. A crack of the whip and the Warrenton Express
> was off down the mountain grade to the next post station.

The motor of the buckboard seems about to get a drink of water. Traffic was likely to be light on most of the park-land's roads during the 19th century. (Stereoscopic photo, courtesy of Dr. and Mrs. Eric Rhodes)

I'll give glimpses, beginning at the north, of all park region routes that attracted more than local traffic. Manassas Gap just north of the park has the easiest grade, may have been visited by Lederer in 1670; it now carries both a railway and Interstate 66. Chester Gap, nearer the park, was easy and early, too, having the old Chester Road (roughly U.S. 522 now) from the piedmont to Chester Ferry across Shenandoah River. In the park's north district, Gravel Springs Gap and Beahms gap had cross-mountain roads. Rappahannock people especially used them for access to the railroad in Warren and Page after it was built along the valley. Cattlemen, timber cutters, tanbark peelers, and mountain residents used these roads—and others not widely known to exist.

In the central district, south of Thornton, Hughes River Gap had a recognized horseback trail before the Civil War and a wagon road, mostly used in hauling tanbark, after the war. Fishers Gap entered the road derby strongly in 1850. A company was formed for this Blue Ridge Turnpike (also known as the Gordonsville-New Market Turnpike or Red Gate Road), and the work proceeded somewhat as had that on Thornton Gap after 1848. Officers and directors were nearly all piedmont gentry. There were 3,300 shares at $50; 2,000 of them were bought by the state and the rest by 320 individuals. The labor in the Blue Ridge itself was nearly all by Irishmen who'd fled the potato famine in the old country. They were supervised by Paschal Graves of Page County, the first president of the turnpike company and later, I've been told, a contractor.

The 56-mile turnpike connecting Virginia Central Railroad and the markets of eastern Virginia with the Shenandoah Valley via Fishers Gap was completed in 1853. Total construction cost was $176,044. One of the many bridges—over Rapidan River with lattice and arch—cost $7,113. The road went through private lands, and people using it had to open and close gates at property lines. In 1862, with pocket-size money scarce in small denominations, the company issued script-currency for paying fees—3¢, 5¢, 10¢, 25¢; it circulated for a time in nonturnpike transactions as well. While the company controled the road, before the Civil War, a total of $22,659 in tolls was collected along the whole route. Robert Graves, at east foot of the Blue Ridge, lodged and fed many turnpike travelers. Fishers "stole" traffic that had moved via Milam Gap and Tanners Ridge in the first half of the 1800s.

At Swift Run Gap, now traversed by U.S. 33, we get into-far-back puzzles. We will never be sure that Alexander Spotswood and his "Knights" rode through this pass—instead of farther north—in 1716, or positive that John Lederer did not follow the Indian path at Swift Run and climb Hightop as I think he might have. The road history followed a pattern resembling that of Thornton Gap (now U.S. 211). By 1740 a wagon road via Lydia was in use, connecting on the west with Port Republic, then across the river and on to Staunton. In 1765 Augusta County put a levy on tithable inhabitants to pay for repairing the old road up to the Blue Ridge crest, and there were further levies authorized by the General Assembly. In 1809 the assembly chartered Swift Run Gap Turnpike Company. After making improvements, it collected tolls. In 1849 there was another surge of improvement, financed by $120,000 worth of stock—$70,000 sold to individuals, $50,000 to the state.

Moving into the park's south district, we find Civil War maps showing cross-mountain roads at Powell and Simmons gaps and an excellent turnpike over Browns Gap, apparently built with slave labor between 1805 and 1810. Tradition says Brightberry Brown's crews working up from the piedmont and William Jarman's up from the valley were consciously competing in both speed and quality. Serviceability of different shipping points carrying freight on the James River and the advance of the railroad up the piedmont deeply affected the competition of Browns Gap with roads over Jarman, Swift Run, and even Rockfish gaps. The Browns Gap Turnpike Company kept promoting its road even after trains started running across Rockfish Gap in 1850 and Shenandoah River flatboats were carrying an increasing volume of cargo down the river. Browns was used during the Civil War—toll free!—and in 1867 Albemarle County took over the eastern Blue Ridge section.

The Jarman Gap road had been one of the earliest; packhorse use went back to 1734 when Michael Woods and his large family planted crops near the summit. The famous old "Three Notch'd Road" or "Three Chopt Road," from Richmond into the valley, went over Jarman. Also in the park's south district, Black Rock Gap had a rather good road, used from 1830 or so for access from the valley to Black Rock Springs. Turk, Beagle, and McCormick gaps were crossings but aren't known to have had much traffic from a distance.

Celebrating roadwork. Businessmen-promoters of tourist travel and the proposed park dress down, ca. 1925, to emphasize the importance of turnpike work. A note on the back of this photo by Rhodes Studio, Luray, records "Will Fitch, Ralph E. Mims with ax, Everett Berrey sitting.." (Zerkel collection, SNP archives)

At the southern terminus of the park is the Rockfish Gap crossing, apparently a slow starter among the major routes. It was the subject of Albemarle County road orders from 1789 on, according to highway historian Nathaniel Mason Pawlett, and presumably the tithables in Augusta as well were doing their legal duty by keeping the road usable from the valley to Warren east of the Blue Ridge. In 1811, though, an effort to raise $60,000 by selling $25 shares to build a turnpike seems to have failed, despite the promoters' insistence that annual dividends would be 15 percent. When Albemarle's Scottsville on the James offered convenient water transportation to Richmond about 1824, however, Rockfish Gap came into prominence. The Staunton and James River Turnpike Company, capital $200,000, built a graded road. This gap's traffic has been growing ever since, soon by rail as well as road. It has been U.S. 250 for many years, and is now Interstate 64 as well.

Despite all the work done on turnpikes in what's now the park, mountain travel and freighting in the old days weren't for the faint-hearted. Horses and oxen toiled slowly up the slopes. Some teamsters were rough in language if not behavior. Wagons were at risk going down with heavy loads, their wooden brakes smoking. Some dragged felled trees to control speed; some had devices forcing wheels to slide instead of turn around. Coaches dashed on tight schedules. Rolling hogsheads could break loose. Herds of livestock moved more easily toward the markets, but in fierce storms or for causes unknown they might stampede and be hard to recover. Vehicle parts were scattered along like debris on a battlefield. Bridges washed out.

Much-used routes pulled different kinds of people into the mountains—innkeepers and their staffs, tollgate keepers, blacksmiths to replace loose horseshoes and improvise or mend iron parts for diverse vehicles, wheelwrights to repair or rebuild them. Some of these people settled and stayed.

Trips with freight took many days. In camps where valley and piedmont teamsters mingled, rowdiness was part of the fun. Piedmonters derided valleymen as "Cohees," and valleymen countered with "Tuckahoes," implying small potatoes. Yet the teamsters carried a romantic aura, and many boys are said to have longed to become such men when they grew up—just as in later years boys envied engineers on trains and drivers on long-distance trucks and, of course, airplane pilots and astronauts.

Early freight in addition to livestock and tobacco included hemp, butter, beeswax, ginseng, cheese, and many animal skins. In 1770, for instance, one Augusta County merchant alone shipped 755 deerskins, and his elkskins were running around 300 a year. As wheat became a major crop and more gristmills were built, flour shipments increased until they made up most of the loads. A four-horse wagon might haul 3,500 pounds of flour; a six-horse wagon, 6,000.

Many turnpike wagons were shaped like boats, higher at bow and stern than in the middle, with hickory bows supporting coarse canvas covers that protected the loads from rain. There were often whole caravans with 20 or so wagons in line, creeping up the mountain, grinding down, threatening to break loose, careen, and crash. Mountain residents might be attracted to the traffic, the strong action, and get work connected with it. Some joined it and never returned. Different mountain residents were repelled, moving away from the noise and bustle that disturbed their peace.

Improving Lee Highway, now U.S. 211, across the Blue Ridge, long after the Barbees and the turnpike company were responsible. The location is a shale bank by park headquarters; the time, 1922, two years before the park promotion started. (SNP archives)

Some travelers were on business; others sought pleasure. From about 1830 on, there was a flow to and from mineral springs. Busy men of busy cities might bring their wives and children to spend the cool summers, staying only a day or two themselves. In 1851 a Mary Jane Boggs crossed Rockfish Gap and was so impressed with the scenery that she wrote, "We were, both literally and figuratively, up in the clouds." She observed "a great many Irish cabins," most of them with "one or two barrels on the top of the chimney." Some of the Irish lingered after completing their work on turnpikes or other construction, and descendants lived in the mountains.

The busier turnpikes had inns such as the Barbees' Hawsberry. The brick Mountain Hotel on the Swift Run Gap road was built about 1832, and the building with its antique furniture was still there in the park after 1936. Funds weren't available to save this inn, and it was lost to fire. The Mountain Top Hotel in Rockfish was a stagecoach stop and summer resort. Fire destroyed it early in the 1900s. Rockfish is also the location of Leakes Tavern, where, in 1818, Thomas Jefferson, James Madison, James Monroe, John Marshall and others gathered to debate where to locate a major university. Jefferson's preference, Charlottesville, prevailed, and University of Virginia resulted.

County courts fixed prices the inns were to charge. I came across these early ones for Augusta: "Hot diet 12½¢, cold diet 8¢, lodging with clean sheets 4¢, stabling and fodder at night 8¢, whiskey gallon $1."

A quite different transportation system ran along the park on the west, using the Shenandoah River's South Fork, the larger and longer of the two. When George Washington visited Thomas Lewis, below the park's Lewis Peak, they talked river transportation. Washington's journal entry for October 1, 1784, reported the Shenandoah near Lewis's "makes a respectable appearance altho' little short of 150 miles from its confluence with Potomack River; and only impeded in its navigation by the rapid water & rocks which are between the old bloomery and Key's Ferry; and a few other Ripples." He said Lewis believed all the impediments could easily be removed and navigation even extended upriver from where he lived.

Some flatboats were already in use on the river. In 1798 the Virginia Assembly discussed continuous freight runs all the way to the Potomac and soon enacted laws designating sections of the stream "a public highway." In 1802 the assembly authorized the town of Port Republic upstream from Lewis's, where a major tributary joins the river.

By 1820 the river was busy whenever the water level was normal or above. The main commodities shipped were iron, flour, and lumber. Most of the iron and lumber loaded between Port Republic and Front Royal came from the Blue Ridge. Among other mountain commodities shipped in quantity were tanbark, fence rails, shingles, posts, apples, and brandy. Tobacco, potatoes, and corn were also shipped, and some of these probably originated on park-land.

The flat-boats (popularly called *gundolas*, the accent on the first syllable, or even *gundalows*), were of diverse designs and sizes—40 to 80 feet long, 9 to 12 feet wide, built of two-inch boards, mostly pine, not planed. Wooden pins (often locust) as well as iron spikes were used to fasten the boards on. Two boatmen operated a gundola, standing on platforms at bow and stern. The platforms extended several feet out beyond the boat's sides to give maximum space for movement and leverage in guiding with the long sweeps. Each boat carried a great horn longer than a man is tall, and its distinctive notes were said to carry five miles.

The boatmen were paid about $15 for the trip of four days from Port Republic to Harpers Ferry, and they had to walk back, the boats being sold for lumber ($18 to $25 each) at the end of the run. The work was dangerous. A boy remembered this incident at a place where the boats were bypassing a dam in a chute of heavy timbers:

We got in sight just in time to see the first boat go through, strike a great rock, split in twain, and the whole cargo of pig iron went to the bottom. When the boat broke, those on it were carried to such water that they had to swim. . . . Soon the men began to wade in and gather the iron together into a pile. The broken boat was then taken to the bank and repaired, reloaded and started on its way again.

The Front Royal newspaper, according to the diary of the editor, S. R. Millar, published an 1870 report from a Charlie Wines who said the boatmen "often did a nice quiet business in moonshine." Once they brought Capt. Samuel J. Simpson (the Simpson plantation house was on Dickey Ridge) a keg of applejack. The captain sent Charlie, age 15½, down to the boat to get it. One boatman said Charlie was too small for such a load, "but if you take a drink of" this good applejack "you can handle it." Charlie did, and it worked.

The boatmen always seemed full of fun, boisterous, and clever. Front Royal editor Millar had boyhood memories of his own reaching back into the 1800s:

> I can remember those boats . . . and still can hear the long-drawn notes of the boatmen's horns or their hallooing and signals on the river. . . . I had a small silver watch which one of the boatmen wanted me to trade for a pet deer he had on his boat, and when I asked him what good the deer would do me, he replied, "You can ride it to school. And if you don't like to go to school, I'll trade you this bear and you can start a circus."

A *gundalow*, a kind of flatboat, in rapids of the Shenandoah River beside the park. Such boats, moving in fleets during the 1800s, hauled vast quantities of iron, lumber, and other Blue Ridge and valley products downstream to Harpers Ferry. (Courtesy of Joseph P. Mills)

The boat freighting dwindled as the railroads came, step by step, until by 1882 the rails paralleled the South Fork all the way. Gundolas were a curiosity by 1900, totally gone long before the park was established. Yet some old-timers insist the sounds of those great horns still echo and reecho along the western slopes of the Blue Ridge.

CHAPTER IX

Warriors and Watchers

Few park region people were isolated from the effects of wars. Members of Blue Ridge plantation families were officers in forces protecting settlements from Indians and the French (Lewises, for instance), in the Revolution (Brown, Jarman, and others), in the War of 1812 (Overall, Barbour), and in the Civil War (Buck, Simpson, many others). Nonplantation people were deeply involved too—Nicholsons, for instance, in both the Civil War and World War I.

George Washington knew the Blue Ridge well and considered it in his planning. Military action of the Revolution merely brushed the park-land, but beef and wild-animal skins from these mountains helped keep our soldiers from starving or freezing. Mountain riflemen were skillful in battling the British, especially in forests. Park region people strongly wanted independence.

British prisoners that had been held since the American victory at Saratoga, New York, in 1777, were brought across the park region from Charlottesville barracks in the fall of 1780. A letter written then by one of the prisoners, a British lieutenant, told of crossing at Jarman (then Woods) Gap and praised the road that, "by its winding," reached a "prodigious height" without as much difficulty as he had experienced crossing lower mountains in Connecticut. He also praised the "delightful" scenery, including "a beautiful river."

In January 1781 about five hundred prisoners, resulting from Tarleton's defeat at Cowpens, South Carolina, by Gen. Daniel Morgan, crossed via Rockfish Gap. Both bands of prisoners were delivered safely to Winchester, apparently with all still present. There is no evidence from these episodes for the popular legend that Hessians, hired as soldiers by the British, escaped into these mountains and founded families.

The Blue Ridge section that would become the park's south district experienced an amusingly serious flurry in June 1781. The month before, feeling endangered in tidewater by the British under Lord Cornwallis, the Virginia legislature and Gov. Thomas Jefferson fled the capital. They

planned to gather in Charlottesville to choose a new governor, as Jefferson's term was expiring. Cornwallis sent dragoons under Banastre Tarleton to capture them here. He also sent five hundred soldiers under Col. John Simcoe to destroy American military supplies stored near Charlottesville. Simcoe succeeded, but Jefferson and others were warned by Jack Jouett after an all-night ride and scattered to meet later at Staunton in the valley. Tarleton caught only seven legislators.

Tarleton and his dragoons were reported, however, to be heading across the Blue Ridge to catch the rest. Acting Gov. Col. William Fleming ordered 50 men to Swift Run Gap and 30 to Jarman Gap to watch for dragoons. The legislature decided to flee still farther. Men and boys of Augusta, bolstered by one legislator with Augusta troops, headed for Rockfish Gap to defend it.

Francis T. Brooke, commanding some American troops in Albemarle, was ordered to Staunton. He crossed south of Rockfish and reported meeting a thousand American riflemen whose general stopped him, saying he had orders to bring all troops to block Rockfish. After discussion, though, Brooke went on to Staunton. Confusion was rampant there. Citizens said Patrick Henry had fled so hurriedly he was wearing only one boot. Brooke received an order to return across the Blue Ridge. Avoiding the high-danger Rockfish, he went via Port Republic toward Swift Run Gap. A horse had shoe trouble, and he stopped at a blacksmith shop. People there spoke only "Dutch." Considering their fancy-uniformed visitor a British officer, they held him prisoner until one of them who spoke English could be found.

Meanwhile at Rockfish, which was crowded with defenders, some having guns but some armed only with stones, several suspicious-acting persons had been captured. One of these "confessed" he was an advance scout for Tarleton. This story multiplied the excitement and brought even more defenders, including Rev. William Graham of Lexington with the Rockbridge militia, some of whom daringly ventured into Albemarle looking for the enemy. No enemy was found. No enemy came to Rockfish. Tarleton and his dragoons, after failing to corner Jefferson at Monticello, had gone eastward, never at all toward Staunton.

The legislators then gathered at Staunton, and on June 12 elected Gen. Thomas Nelson, Jefferson's choice, as governor, 11 days after the scheduled election day. The Virginia government and the Blue Ridge between Swift Run and Rockfish gaps were thus saved. Though the British may have laughed when they heard the details, they also realized more clearly than before how strongly the Blue Ridge and valley people wanted them out of America. I've found no evidence of Tory sympathy in the mountains, or this part of the valley. Even old Lord Fairfax, I understand, avoided opposing his friend George Washington. Cornwallis soon surrendered to Washington at Yorktown, and that war was over.

The War Between the States, unlike the Revolution, surrounded and criss-crossed the park-land continually for years. Some mountain people and some valley Germans favored the Union instead of the South, though I never found evidence of overt rebellion against the Confederacy in the park region. Spies of both sides used high viewpoints and hideaways. People used the mountains to conceal themselves or their property, especially livestock. Some young men hid here from Confederate recruiters. But the hiding was far from sure. This part of the Blue Ridge was definitely in strategic position, sheltering "the breadbasket of the Confederacy" and joining with the valley in producing much meat for the South as well. Both sides scouted and mapped park-land. Mountain roads and gaps were used in communications and maneuverings, sometimes by large armies, and several lively battles spread into the park.

The famous Valley Campaign that distracted the Federals from their drive toward Richmond in the spring of 1862 used Blue Ridge gaps and roads in crucial phases. Early in April the amazing Confederate general Thomas J. "Stonewall" Jackson, with only 6,000 men, was facing the Union general N. P. Banks, with 20,000 men, north of New Market. Banks apparently thought he could drive Jackson out of the valley. He began moving on April 17, apparently planning to cross New Market Gap and hurry up the narrow Luray valley to take Swift Run Gap in the Blue Ridge and prevent Jackson from being reinforced by Gen. Richard S. Ewell, who was near Stanardsville with 8,000 men.

Jackson made one of those long, fast marches that always surprised his enemies. He seemed to read Banks's mind, and he sped up the main valley to Harrisonburg, around the south end of the Massanutten, past Conrad's Store (later Elkton). His army was in possession of Swift Run Gap, ready to defend it, while Banks's force was still short of the goal. Banks apparently saw the futility of attacking there, and Jackson held Swift Run Gap until Ewell replaced him, the new soldiers moving into the same camps.

There'd been much rain, and mud was deep in the roads. Long, fast marches must be considered impossible, so Jackson made another one, disguising his intentions with masterful skill. He organized farmers with oxen and horses to help move his wagons and cannons through the clinging mud to Port Republic and up as far as the firmly macadamized

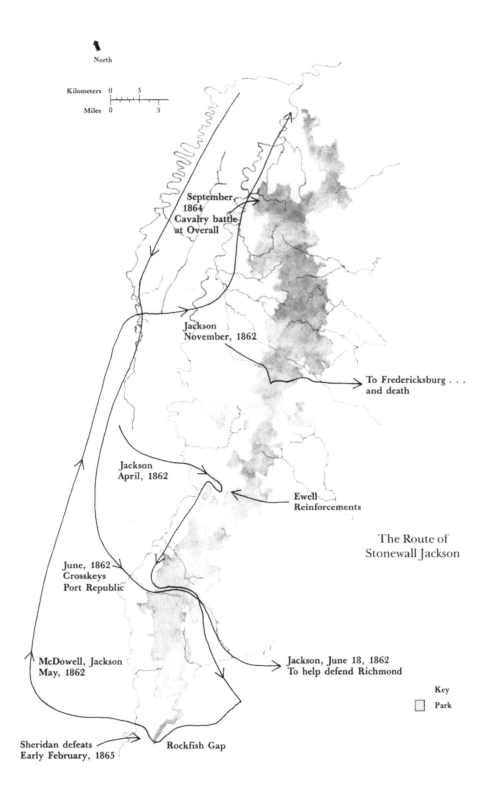

North

Kilometers 0   5
Miles 0   5

September
1864
Cavalry battle
at Overall

Jackson
November, 1862

To Fredericksburg . . .
and death

Jackson
April, 1862

Ewell
Reinforcements

The Route of
Stonewall Jackson

June, 1862
Crosskeys
Port Republic

McDowell, Jackson
May, 1862

Jackson, June 18, 1862
To help defend Richmond

Key

Park

Sheridan defeats
Early February, 1865

Rockfish Gap

Cavalry engagements were swift and fierce in the War Between the States. One such battle was fought in the park, along Overall Run. (From M. Quad, *Field, Fort and Fleet*, 1885)

road in Browns Gap. It's said that when he was riding his horse down the east side of the Blue Ridge through the Browns' plantations, one of the Browns asked him where he was going. "Can you keep a secret?" Jackson asked Brown. "I sure can," Brown replied. "So can I," said Jackson, moving on down the road. He went on to the Virginia Central Railway at Mechum's River Station. By now everyone supposed he was moving to help threatened Confederate forces near Richmond.

Instead, he quickly swung west toward Staunton, the troops going by rail and the artillery and wagons by road back across the Blue Ridge via Rockfish Gap. He joined with Gen. Edward Johnson's brigade, and together on May 8 they trounced Federal forces at McDowell west of Staunton, preventing a Federal linkup that would have been dangerous. He then moved down the wide valley to New Market and over the Massanutten to Luray. Coordinating with him, Ewell had moved to Luray from Swift Run Gap, and they advanced northward together, 17,000 strong. At Front Royal they demolished part of Banks's army. Other parts they put into retreat from Winchester, and they drove Banks north across the Potomac. As a result, a large Federal army moving to help Gen. George B. McClellan take Richmond was divided, with Gen. James Shields being sent instead to help defeat Jackson.

The new Federal plan was to pin Jackson between two armies, either one alone larger than Jackson's and Ewell's forces combined. Gen. John C. Frémont would push Jackson up the wide valley, while Shields would hurry up the narrower valley via Luray. They'd trap him somewhere south of the Massanutten. But Shields was slow and Jackson was fast, despite having to bring along prisoners and plunder from Banks's defeat. Jackson veered eastward again from Harrisonburg, not to Swift Run this time but to Port Republic. He sent the prisoners and plunder eastward over Browns Gap, then arranged his forces to attack the big Federal armies before they could combine and attack him.

Frémont was hot on his trail, so Jackson gave Ewell the task of slowing Frémont while he got set to "welcome" Shields. Ewell took the initiative at Cross Keys, where his smaller force could be fully used, while Frémont could hardly use his full numbers. For hours on June 8 the cannons roared and the rifles chattered. Gradually Frémont's left wing and center gave way. Ewell didn't have enough men to turn his advantage into full victory, but he'd done enough damage to delay Frémont so Shields could be attacked separately. Jackson called Ewell to Port Republic, except for one regiment assigned to block the way and, if pushed to the river, to burn the bridge so Frémont couldn't cross to bolster Shields.

There were skirmishes before dark with advance units of Shields' army, but the main battle started the morning of June 9. At least 60,000 men must have been involved in the Cross Keys–Port Republic battles. There were casualties by the hundreds. A clearing on a foothill of the Blue Ridge, where iron-smelting charcoal had been made, proved crucial. Federal artillery there poured destruction into Jackson's lines. Jackson took the hill at great cost, but the Federals took it back. Then the Confederates won it again and turned the cannons on the Federals. More of Ewell's men arrived, enough to give Jackson the margin of strength needed to prevail. The surviving Federals limped back toward the Potomac. Frémont had pulled his force together at last and reached the river, but Jackson's men had burned the bridge and the Federals couldn't cross, so Frémont, too, began a long retreat from the valley.

Some historians say Jackson was psychic; he seemed to know in advance what would happen. Military writers have called his Valley Campaign the strategic equal of any in history. In approximately a month Jackson's small army had covered almost four hundred miles, taken four thousand prisoners and an immense amount of military supplies including cannons, broken up and discouraged the Federal effort to take the Confederates' rich source of bread and beef, and had scared the Federal government with visions of a long, fast march on Washington itself.

Jackson and his men moved up into the mountains to rest and prepare for the next round of fighting wherever it might be. They camped several days "in the beautiful pasture-saddle of Browns Gap" and stayed in that general area until June 17. Probably during this time they built the Browns Gap breastworks, remnants of which still exist. In 1934 Mrs. Elizabeth Shifflett of Grottoes told Civilian Conservation Corps foremen about them. Her husband, Robert T. Shifflett, had helped build them in 1862. They may have been reconditioned in September 1864 by Gen. Jubal A. Early's forces when they took refuge here. A small shift in alignment of Skyline Drive construction was made to avoid damaging them. Perhaps also in 1862, moving eastward, Jackson's men removed the tollgate that had been operated by Lewis Franklin Crickenberger a few hundred yards downslope.

Stonewall Jackson relaxing on the evening of December 15, 1862, near Fredericksburg, about three weeks after he and his army left the Shenandoah Valley for the last time by crossing the Blue Ridge over Fishers Gap, near the center of the present park. The artist-sculptor, Alexander Galt of Norfolk, wrote in his sketchbook: "Visit to Genl. Jackson's h'qrs—Supper with staff—take a sketch of him—goes to sleep while I read N.Y. Herald." (Courtesy of Mary Pearson)

Death of Stonewall Jackson. Shot accidentally by fellow Confederates, Jackson had his left arm amputated but had lost so much blood he couldn't recover, though he survived eight days. He became unconscious, then waked and said clearly, "Let us cross over the river and rest under the shade of the trees." Perhaps in his mind he did so, and he died. It was May 10, 1863— about 13 months since the beginning of the campaign that made him famous around the world. (From M. Quad, *Field, Fort and Fleet*)

Orders had arrived from Commander in Chief Robert E. Lee for Jackson to come and help defend Richmond but keep his move from the valley secret. There were diversionary maneuvers and different troops moved by different routes, some going eastward by rail through Rockfish Gap, some by the old road over Jarman Gap. Jackson and most of his men moved on over Browns Gap and filtered out through Browns Cove on the east.

Jackson was back in the valley that fall. He took Harpers Ferry from the Federals and maintained headquarters in Winchester. In November he was maneuvering again in the Blue Ridge, alert for any Federal forces, especially in the vicinity of Manassas Gap just north of the park. Then, around Thanksgiving time in 1862, he marched out of his much-defended valley for the last time—via the Gordonsville-New Market Turnpike over Fishers Gap in the middle of what's now the national park. There was snow on the Blue Ridge. Jackson and his army of maybe 20,000 were coming from New Market and had been delayed several days because bridges across the Shenandoah had been destroyed. They went from Fishers Gap on to Orange, toward Fredericksburg and diverse victories on the trail to Chancellorsville, where Jackson would be mortally wounded on May 2, 1863.

Marcus Blakemore Buck, whose plantation house Belmont was still standing on Dickey Ridge when the park was established, wrote a diary before, during, and after the Civil War. His niece Lucy Rebecca Buck, who lived at Bel Air, now part of Front Royal, wrote one also. Together they show the cataclysm in human depth.

Marcus had fertile mountain land on top of, and on both slopes of, Dickey Ridge. In 1856 he sold 450 acres to Thomas Fox, who was becoming a much-liked neighbor. Fox had about 100 cattle and raised sizable farm crops, aided before the war by several slaves. The ridge land around Buck's large brick house was almost all pasture, devoted primarily in spring, summer, and fall to feeding 200 or so beef cattle, of which about 50 would be kept through the winter. Belmont had productive orchards and vineyards and diverse fields, mostly producing grain. The Belmont inventory of January 1, 1861—just before the war—included 10 horses and colts, 4 work oxen, 47 beef cattle, 7 milk cows, 18 hogs, 450 bushels wheat, 300 rye, 2,000 corn, 250 bushels potatoes, 600 shocks corn fodder, 5 tons hay, 2,000 pounds pork and bacon, 200 pounds beef, 500 cans fruit, and 25 gallons wine.

Marcus Buck was 45 years old in 1862. He and his wife, Jane Letitia Bayly Buck, had seven children. The oldest, 19-year-old Walter, was a lieutenant in the Confederate cavalry, commanding a group of mountain scouts assigned to explore "secret" trails. Walter was thus often able to visit home and the town of Front Royal, where he was much admired. The next son in line, Richard or "Dick," age 17 in 1862, was also soon in the Confederate army, a lieutenant in the Warren Rifles.

Before the war Marcus's diary was filled with records of hauling beef and corn to the railroad, hauling up ice to keep through the summer, cutting and hauling wood, sowing clover and timothy seed and "plaster" fertilizer, filling gullies in "King field," plowing in "Claig field," preparing new ground for potatoes and corn, harvesting wheat with two cradles, shucking and housing corn. Marcus sold a black mare to T. Fox

and spent a day assisting Fox to thresh. On December 4, 1858, he wrote, "Mrs. Fox died suddenly yesterday evening." Marcus visited T. Fox and children at intervals, sometimes taking along his daughter Jacquie, age 13 in 1862. Fox completed payment of $5,000 for his 450 acres in 1860.

Early in 1862 the operations of peace were giving ground to war:

Feb. 17. News received tonight of terrible battle. . . . The Federals thus far repulsed with great slaughter. Oh, horrid war!

Feb. 26. Mr. Reinhart commenced trimming vines, assisted by several hands.

March 12. Hauling rails and wood. Plowing in new ground. Trimming vineyard. Tremendous excitement on account of approach of Federal army.

March 15. The railroad bridge and South River bridge burned this morning. . . . Many persons abandoning home and property.

March 18. Heavy and continued firing heard in direction of Strasburg and Winchester. Horrible, horrible, to think of brothers engaged in deadly fighting. My very soul is sick with the idea.

March 27. Hauling out manure on Wilson lot. Commenced plowing same. Working in garden and fencing across upper side of barn field. A troop of Federal horse came into town yesterday, the first there. I started to town and learning they were there, returned home.

March 30. Federals encamped at Mr. Richards' last night. For the first time I saw their banner and their soldiers. O, God, my poor country, my dear family and friends!

Lucy's diary, being written just outside what was then the Front Royal village and branch-railroad stop, was even more filled with soldiers and war. She was 21 years old when on June 22, 1863, she wrote of her shock upon hearing that "dear Walter" had been killed in action at Upperville, Virginia. She couldn't believe it, but it was soon confirmed. A message was sent up to "Uncle Mack" (Marcus, Walter's father) at Belmont, and that afternoon he and Jacquie came to the Bel Air gate. Lucy watched her father tell his brother all that was known. They didn't come into the house. Marcus sent Jacquie home with a message to her mother, and Marcus rode off immediately toward Upperville to learn all he could and if possible to bring home the body. C. T. O'Ferrall, later governor of Virginia, was with Walter when he was shot and later wrote fondly of him, adding that his body was recovered and buried at his home in the mountains.

Uncle Mack's and Aunt Letitia's other military son, Dick, recovered Walter's horse Belle, with a blood-stained saddle that was brought home. Dick was in the Blue Ridge later in 1863 with a group rounding up deserters and draft dodgers. Apparently this was done frequently, as the forested ridges and hollows of Gooney Manor were considered "a favorite hideout for renegades."

Lucy kept worrying about Dick—as did, of course, Marcus and his wife and other children. Lucy was sewing at home when word came that Dick had been "mortally wounded." She mourned much of the day, but Father and Uncle Mack had been investigating. The truth was bad but not irremediable. Dick had been severely wounded and captured by the enemy but would survive.

At Belmont on Dickey Ridge, Marcus heard and watched the war. He had a "glass" (telescope?) and witnessed tremendous battles as far away as Strasburg and Winchester. In September 1864 he witnessed and recorded early stages of the battle of Overall Run, fought mostly in what's now the park:

> We saw the Confederate cavalry drawn up in line of battle. . . . Federal cavalry had come up on a hill one mile distant. . . . A regiment formed in the road and made a charge on the Confederate pickets and drove them in, but when they came to the reserve force on the hill, they were driven back in the greatest disorder, only to rally and make a second attempt, with the same result. . . . It was a very spectacular affair to look down on men riding, charging and firing their carbines and pistols. About dusk the Federals ran up a battery of artillery on a high hill and began to fire at the Confederates, who thereupon brought out their artillery and returned the fire. . . . After dark the passage of the shells through the air could be followed by the streaks of fire that were thrown off. . . . Every discharge could be seen and every report could be heard long after the flash from the cannon's mouth.

The Confederate General Jubal A. Early had sent Gen. W. C. Wickham to delay or stop Federal Gen. A.T.A. Torbert, who'd been ordered by Gen. Philip H. Sheridan to hurry southward, cross New Market Gap, and thus trap Early's army in retreat toward Harrisonburg. Wickham had met the Federals at the river near Front Royal and slowed them down, but he chose Overall, where river and mountain squeeze the valley, for his firmest stand. The main battle lines reached from the river to a "high mountain." Wickham occupied the south bank of Overall Run. Torbert realized the creek banks were so steep his men couldn't cross to attack directly. He made a vigorous attack on the mountain flank. But the Confederates held.

Next day, September 22, Torbert sent two divisions of cavalry into the battle, supported by artillery. The Confederates threw them back, and there were numerous casualties. Two Yankees died on the porch of a farmhouse in Bentonville. A wounded Yankee was carried into the Isaac Overall house on the north side of Overall Run—head of household now, I think, William Overall, but he was off to war himself—and the Overalls tried to treat his wounds, but he died. A lasting spot of blood was left on the floor.

According to Laura Virginia Hale, who researched the Overall battle thoroughly, Sheridan credited the Wickham force with thwarting his plan to capture Early. If Torbert had broken through and reached New Market, Sheridan wrote, "I have no doubt that we would have captured the entire Rebel Army." The crucial point of Torbert's failure and Wickham's victory was at least two miles above the river, deep inside what's now the park.

General Sheridan was burning the valley during this fall of 1864, wiping out barns, mills, crops, and livestock from the Blue Ridge edges westward. He was trying also to wipe out the weakened forces of General Early. In the campaign that included the Overall battle, he failed. Early got past New Market with no trouble and, as Stonewall Jackson had done, veered eastward around the south end of the Massanutten, taking refuge in Browns Gap to await reinforcement—which arrived but proved insufficient to enable him to challenge Sheridan. The Confederate capital was in trouble, and little manpower or material could be spared to save Early.

By late February 1865 Early was near Waynesboro with only about two thousand men. Sheridan attacked there on March 3 with overwhelming force, including cavalry and mounted infantry, and pursued Early's fleeing army up through Rockfish Gap. Early's men and supplies were nearly all lost—1,600 soldiers, 14 artillery pieces, 200 wagons with varied loads including Early's desk and recent records. Sheridan had erased just about all means of sustenance and defense from both valley and mountain. He went on over the Blue Ridge toward Charlottesville, extending his devastation, burning and looting as he'd already done so thoroughly in the valley.

The diaries give revealing sidelights. Marcus Buck wrote of learning "with great pain" that Thomas Fox had been arrested and imprisoned, "probably for aiding his son in escaping to the Yankees." Later, Fox's horses were confiscated. Marcus, loyal to the South, nevertheless got up

Belmont, home of Marcus Blakemore Buck, a plantation house that was in the park, on Dickey Ridge, about 1.6 miles from the north end of Skyline Drive. The house was built in 1845. Front Royal town records were brought here for safekeeping during the Civil War. Marcus Buck lost a son in the war. Another son was wounded. The plantation raised cattle, wheat, rye, corn, and fruit including grapes from which wine and brandy were made on a commercial scale. (NPS, 1933)

a petition for his friend's release. The Bucks and Foxes kept up their close friendship. Marcus continued deeply hurt, however, by the horrible war that turned brother against brother, even son against father, or vice versa. It's not known whether Fox ever tried to explain the incident; most likely father and son disagreed politically but father helped anyhow because a son, after all, is a son. Many families were deeply divided.

The maelstrom swirled even more constantly around the Bel Air Bucks. They hated the Yankees, yet admired some Yankee individuals and tried to feed at their plantation all who were caught without food supplies in the frequent Front Royal confusion. They sent most of their horses into the Blue Ridge to remain hidden from Yankees who might steal them, leaving them so long they ate the bark off trees as high as they could reach. Yet when the plantation slaves ran away, taking the rest of the horses with them—quite likely incited by Yankees—Lucy Rebecca and other women and girls of the Bucks quickly learned cooking personally and went on feeding the hungry, including Yankees.

Lucy felt sorry for her father over the financial loss of a dozen slaves and three horses—estimated at $16,000. Her father and a neighbor, Mr. Beecher, went in pursuit as far as Winchester, hoping to recover at least the horses. They learned that Mahala, their cook, had been one of the leaders. She and her children had reached Greencastle, Pennsylvania, according to a friendly cavalryman, but had no money left and no horses. She wished she was back home. She had no way to feed her children. A later rumor, though, said she'd found responsible work somewhere up north and was doing well. It was also rumored that most of the slave men who ran away in Virginia were captured before they got far and sent to Richmond to work on fortifications. Most of the slaves in Virginia actually stayed with their former owners through the war and maybe worked for them afterward, for wages.

Lucy felt more sorry for the runaway slaves than for the plight of the plantation without them. She adapted well to housework and cooking. Once she wrote proudly, "My biscuits were pronounced faultless tonight." Almost everything was caught in the cataclysm. Livestock were mostly confiscated; fences were torn down or burned; buildings were burned.

After the war Marcus made a long effort to recover prosperity. Adequate labor and other essentials weren't available to restore plantation-type crop production, so he expanded his fruit growing. His diary entry of August 5, 1865, said, "I am compelled, most reluctantly, to commence preparing peaches for the still, another consequence of the War and breaking up of our transportation." He made brandy, and in 1866 he went into the wine business, hauling the product in bottles and hogsheads to Winchester for shipment to Alexandria, Philadelphia, Baltimore, and other cities. Annual production climbed to 25,000 gallons of wine and 8,000 gallons of Catawba brandy. By 1875 he had 500 acres of grapes and 6,000 fruit trees on Dickey Ridge. According to a descendant, Belmont was "acknowledged one of the finest fruit farms in Virginia." But the economics refused to stabilize. The business failed, and so did Marcus's health. He died in 1881 at age 64.

CHAPTER X

Dynasty

T he Overalls of Overall Run span settlement in the park region from its beginnings to its end. They owned one-seventh of the entire park-land, and their lives interwove plantation life with nearly all the other human elements that soared or clashed in these mountains. Descendants have loaned dozens of documents representing two and one-half centuries and have freely discussed the long-continued family traditions. The Overall story might help bring the "overall" picture to life.

The name Overall evolved in the County of York, England, from Adam del Overhalle, whose extensive landholdings and imposing over-hall (almost castle?) were reflected in official records of the 1200s. Encyclopedias show a John Overall as "a learned English prelate" of the 1600s, bishop of Norwich, the author of *The Convocation Book*, which set forth the divine origin of government. This book gained high-placed favor that led, via Gov. Alexander Spotswood, to a large land patent in tidewater-piedmont Virginia for an adventurous John Overall of the early 1700s.

This John had a son who, before 1740, became the first Shenandoah John Overall. He married Maria Christina Frohman, granddaughter of Jost Heydt, the German baron who settled so early in the valley. The couple produced the second Shenandoah John, who married Elizabeth Walters, an English land-heiress of Alexandria, Virginia. They developed a plantation just south of Overall Run, where the Blue Ridge crowds the Shenandoah River. In addition to raising diverse crops with the help of slaves, they had a busy up-and-down sawmill and a gristmill that produced flour for shipment downriver in flatboats, along with the lumber, tanbark, tobacco, and other products.

About the time of the Declaration of Independence, John and Elizabeth had a son Isaac, who would grow up and multiply the already extensive landholdings. When Isaac was about 20, and alternating snatches of higher education at a distance with energetic work for his

Isaac Overall plantation house in decline at age one hundred and more. Located on a ridge above Overall Run, it was headquarters for 28,000 acres of the park-land, along with several thousand acres of valley land, for more than a century. The old structure on the lower left is believed to have housed slaves. (*Overall Papers*)

father at home, they built a new plantation house. It remained for almost a century the central landmark of the village that was first called Centre Mills, then Mill-ford (Milford), then Overall. When stagecoaches began running along the high bank of the Shenandoah, the big porch was extended so passengers could step directly under the roof and out of the rain. The location was about a hundred yards east of the present U.S. 340.

Ambitious Isaac married Mary Carson, who was Irish and a sister of Col. William Carson and two other prominent landholders a few miles northward. Early in the 1800s, perhaps when the children were coming, he built his own mansion house on a rise upstream and across the creek from his father's. In time that involved him in two different counties, Warren County north of Overall Run, Page County to the south. Isaac's house was of mountain logs and valley limestone. I saw it in the 1930s from the outside and don't remember it as especially big, but stories of houseguests and lavish entertainments suggest it had quite a few rooms. The logs were smoothly covered with white plaster. A large chimney of stone towered from the center.

Isaac served in the War of 1812 and from then on was called Colonel. In September 1826, at age 47, Mary Carson Overall died, leaving Isaac, five daughters, and two sons. Isaac's father John died two years later, and most members of Isaac's generation were leaving for large cities or new homes in the West. Though saddened by deaths and farewells, Colonel Isaac and his family thrived. Carson land inherited through Mary and more of the Overall land came into Isaac's responsibility. All the children had opportunities for advanced education, and some of them chose the chief cities of the East. The oldest son made his home in New York, but the youngest was much interested in managing the plantation. Isaac had friends from Boston to South Carolina, and visits and visitors were frequent. The work at home went on through it all.

Something kept gnawing at Isaac, though. His grandfather John had come to the Shenandoah Valley hoping to find precious metals. The Swiss explorer Michel had found an Indian silver mine in the Shenandoah mountains—but lost it. Isaac's grandfather looked but couldn't find silver; his father looked, too, and gave up. Isaac was more interested in the mountains than the lowlands. Immensely fond of horses, he rode the logging trails, often alone. He began to find colorful bits of copper ore and concluded that there must be silver, somewhere—perhaps in that rocky outcrop up whatever trail he was riding.

In 1833 Isaac bought 28,000 acres of the Blue Ridge adjacent to his lowlands. The great tract stretched from Dades Gap (in the vicinity of Mount Marshall) ten straight-line miles southwest to Beahms Gap east of the Redwell-Isabella iron furnace and averaged four miles wide, extending from the Blue Ridge crest down to the valley edge. The boundary had been set by James Barbour in his smaller Big Survey, dated June 22, 1795. Much of the southwestern timberland had been denuded to make charcoal for smelting iron. Iron, too, had come from ore banks inside the big tract. Signs of mineralization kept appearing; when Isaac found the rich mine he felt was there, he'd own it!

I recently visited the site of Isaac's house again, guided by a man who'd grown up nearby. We stood under black walnut trees that had taken over, and from his memories and my research and talks with Overall descendants *we evoked a summer day of 1836. Colonel Isaac was in late middle age but still vigorous. He'd been helping to organize Warren County and had agreed to be sheriff to help get things started right. As the largest landowner, he had a duty. But his main interest was in Page County just now, with rumors that his big buyer of charcoal, Isabella Furnace, might be going broke. He was worrying, too, about his oldest son. Why didn't Isaac H. write to him?*

As Isaac finished breakfast with the girls, daughter Jane said she wouldn't be going on the ride today. She was almost 30 and not yet married. She felt awkward riding in the mountains and wasn't sure she liked horses anymore, especially when a young man like their house guest T.H.L. [we know him only by his initials] from Philadelphia would be watching. She had a reputation for pickling tomatoes, as no one else could, and today the tomatoes were just right. Oldest daughter Maria Louisa was prospering with husband Andrew Pitman on the far side of the Massanutten. Daughter Mary Ann had also married and was living in Front Royal with her husband, Gibson N. Roy.

Son William C., the most faithful worker in the family, was out running the sawmill, assisted by two slaves. He had already set others to work in the tobacco, which, just now, was bringing in the largest income—more than lumber, livestock, tanbark, brandy, or grain, milled or unmilled.

Isaac went out to the stables. Daughter Ann P., the most religious one, and daughter Julia, the youngest, age 23 and beautiful, were already there. So was T.H.L., who'd been a beau to all the girls at one time or another but now seemed set on Julia. The young people raced on ahead. It would be a long ride to Jeremys Run. They were off to see if the contracting collier was at work and be sure he was careful not to let his fire escape into the forest. Isaac knew Ann would be scolding the collier for destroying the forest and leaving a mess. She loved nature as well as God, and she'd be glad if Isabella was failing. An appetite for 36 tons of "coal" every 24 hours took a scary toll on the trees.

Isaac rode steadily, watching along the way for signs of how the acorn crop would be; many would be needed to fatten the plantation's hogs in the fall. He watched also for mineral colors in the rocks. Quite far back but in sight when Isaac turned was his personal slave Charles, riding along to carry and serve the picnic. The ride would take all day—and never leave Overall land.

Isaac touched his heels to his horse and went a little faster. Ahead he saw Julia resisting T.H.L.'s efforts to speed her pace. She stopped her horse, even trotted back along the trail a bit. T.H.L. went on ahead as if she'd scolded him. When Isaac came up with her, she smiled brightly and laughed. Before he could say anything, she coaxed that today he must show them his silver mine—why did he always evade? He'd forgotten what it was he'd let slip about a mine; most likely that he'd seen a promising vein. But the assay had shown no silver, and less than 10 percent copper. In the past he'd never told details of failures, or even admitted them, and he wasn't about to do so now. He'd been sounding out geologists and mineralogists in a general way when on his trips, thinking of asking them to come and inspect the "copper land" but not asking them. He wanted to make a solid discovery himself.

Descendants here don't know exactly when Isaac died, or from what cause, but county records of 1843 show the distribution of his estate. There doesn't seem to have been a will. He probably never thought his

Isaac Overall letter dated June 22, 1835, when he was speeding southward through Virginia into North Carolina, traveling 55 or 60 miles a day, "never less than 20 or 25 miles before breakfast," in a barouche. The letter is addressed to his son-in-law. The fast trip was to find "Negroes." Nothing else is known now about the situation. Maybe the Colonel was representing Warren County, which was in process of organization; as soon as the county became official he was the first "high sheriff." (Overall papers) time might be close. An inventory of his personal property listed 17 horses, a quantity of lumber, equipment at the sawmill, equipment at the still house, tools and other contents of the blacksmith shop, substantial amounts of grains and flour in the upper story of the gristmill, two Negro men called Charles and Bill, a pair of card tables, an eight-day clock, a pianoforte, many books, two globes and a large map of the United States, personal furniture, a backgammon box, a looking glass, and a military sword.

Isaac was buried in a little cemetery on a hill in Overall, near the grave of his father, John. The lowland real estate apparently remained intact for the present, perhaps with the field and forest workers already the property of William. Isaac H. came from New York. He had power of attorney but let William go on managing the estate. A seven-way distribution of money was wanted—at least by Isaac H., who prevailed. On December 7, 1843, the names of all seven children appeared on a document (recorded in Warren County) selling to John Baker the 28,000 acres lying in the counties of Warren, Page, and Rappahannock on the Blue Ridge Mountains.

Baker must have defaulted, for on July 26, 1847, the "heirs of law of the late Col. Isaac Overall" sold the same domain to Knowles Taylor of New York City. The property was to be developed by a "Shenandoah Copper Mining Co." A months-long investigation was made on the ground by Richard C. Taylor of Philadelphia, said to be a professor of geology recently arrived from Britain. I find no answer to the natural question—whether he was related to Knowles. Professor Taylor condensed his findings into 37 handwritten pages. He had followed 14 different mineral veins both north and south of Overall Run, some of them miles long, and spoke with confidence of "the large quantity of copper ore." The values were mostly in "grey Sulphuret" but also in "green and blue carbonates . . . yellow Copper pyrites, the red oxide, the purple or variegated copper, and masses of the native metal and silicate of copper." Some veins, he wrote, were "40 feet in breadth . . . already proven to prevail eight miles in length." The concentration, however, was not rich, and large quantities of ore would have to be processed to bring success.

Knowles Taylor must have been enthusiastic, but he died soon afterward. His heirs couldn't pay for the property. There was a long lawsuit, and in 1858 the courts gave the 28,000 acres back to the Overall heirs. The Taylor report would be copied many times in long-continuing efforts to get the "copper land" into production. Though there were bits of silver in the ore, Isaac's dream of a rich silver mine faded out. The Overall heirs sold quite a few tracts of fifty to several hundred acres each to buyers interested in timber or farming or home building, but they

Maria Louisa Overall Pitman, Isaac and
Mary Overall's oldest child, married
Andrew Pitman, a German plantation
owner. She tried most of her life to realize
her father's dream of mining silver and
copper from the extensive Blue Ridge
estate. (From old glass photo plate,
Overall papers)

always retained the mineral rights as they knew Colonel Isaac would have
done.

Most of the mountain land was still being managed by William, who
didn't seem as much interested in minerals as in timber, crops, livestock,
orchards, distillery, and both sawmill and gristmill. Maria Louisa Overall
Pitman and her husband Andrew Pitman tried most persistently to get
mining started or to sell the land at a price that recognized the value of
the copper. The heirs finally decided the 40-square-mile tract was too big
for one likely buyer or for the heirs to manage in one unit. In 1871 it was
surveyed for division among Isaac's seven children. A mere 931 acres
were sold to defray expenses of the survey and other costs.

The map of the division in land records of the counties and the park
lacks geographic detail, so I'll have to guess a little in telling where each
subdomain was situated. Isaac H. received 3,922 acres, including
Neighbor Mountain. He bought the northernmost 3,238 acres that were
sister Jane's share. Jane was now married to A. T. Beecher, considered
in family tradition a relative of Harriet Beecher Stowe, author of *Uncle
Tom's Cabin*. Both Isaac H. and Jane lived in New York and, with the
Civil War still vivid in Virginia, they were considered next to deserters,
especially after Isaac H. sold his share and most of Jane's to strangers.

Jane Overall Beecher, Isaac and Mary Overall's daughter who lived in New York and may not have been always in love with the old South. (From tintype, Overall papers)

Mary Ann (Mrs. Gibson N. Roy), got 2,157 acres around Hogback Mountain. Apparently she let brother William manage her share for decades, but eventually she or her heirs disposed of a square mile or more. The Roys had lots of mountain land, having, through a marriage, fallen heir to Mathews family holdings. William also may have retrieved part of the land sold by Isaac H. But at park-land–buying time Neighbor Mountain was owned by Ellen Burrill, widow of James Burrill, a wealthy Englishman who came to America about 1890. And a 600-acre tract, once part of Mary Ann's share, was owned by "J. R. Millar (New York Life Ins. Co.)"—but when checks were made out they went to H. R. Millar and S. R. Millar. (See Appendix 3 and Appendix 4 for land payment facts.)

Maria Louisa, firstborn of the family, got 2,739 acres, apparently including Elkwallow and most of the Compton Run area. She and her family moved to a home called Spurmont, near the north end of Massanutten Mountain. From Spurmont they could at least see their Blue Ridge land. She and her husband, Andrew Pitman, profited from the Blue Ridge a little, as had Colonel Isaac, making deals for timber or tanbark.

Pitmans brought to the Overalls the traditions of German farmers who cherished the soil and were the main white influence in several park-land counties. Though Andrew, like nearly every Overall, was loyal to the South, many of his close relatives admired the Union. One of these, Levi Pitman, kept a diary from the 1840s to the 1890s that evokes the valley-and-mountain life and the German character that was important here. I'll select a few excerpts:

June 12, 1845. At 7 O'Clock this Thursday morning I was married to Miss Rachel Windle. Our courtship was a brief one. I visited her first on Whitsuntide. In two weeks after, I visited her the second time when we made the marriage contract. In two days after, I went there to ask her father's consent which was cheerfully granted. The first Saturday in June I visited again which was the last time before the wedding.

April 11, 1846. My wife was delivered of a fine son in the presence of my mother, Mrs. Sibert, Mrs. Sonnenstein (midwife) and myself.

Oct. 19, 1847. This day our new Church was dedicated. . . . The House was crowded and did not contain half that were there. The first sermon was in German by Rev. Burtner and then one in English by Rev. Markwood.

Sept. 29-30. Brother Eberhard . . . preached a good sermon in German Sunday. Many people got the blessing and were happy with the Lord. I was concerned for my salvation, took my Bible . . . and went into the woods to pray.

Oct. 14, 1849. 11 persons were baptized in the river by Rev. Gregg.

Peregrine Falcons with chestnut burrs. A bundle of slightly smudged pencil drawings created about 1841 by park-land owner Ann P. Overall Jolliffe, daughter of Col. Isaac Overall, was saved with other family papers. (Courtesy of Frances Heiskell and Thelma Fristoe)

Nov. 13. A colored man was condemned after his trial to be hung in Woodstock later part of this December for having abused a Miss Walker.

April 13, 1850. Father ate some dinner about 12 o'clock but toward evening he became very sick, his breath laborous until about ten min. past six in the evening he calmly expired in the advanced age of 78. . . . His posterity numbers 99. . . . It was truly a solemn scene to see a fellow creature pass away from among men. W. Sibert and H. Peer dressed and laid out the body. A lot of young people came in to wake alnight.

April 28, 1853. We planted potatoes—a pleasant warm day.

May 10. I commenced planting my corn. I put guano in each hill, covered it with a little dirt, and then put in the corn and covered it.

May 31. Over to Jacob Rosenbergers where I helped raise his barn. There were upwards of 30 hands present.

April 18, 1857. An interesting session of the U.B. Church conference. Joseph Funkhouser . . . bought and sold a colored boy to a slave trader. It was decided that he be admonished. Rev. Winto was chosen to do it.

Nov. 6, 1860. I voted in the Court House. The Republican ticket—for President Mr. Abraham Lincoln of Ill. . . . I was an elector for the party.

Feb. 6, 1861. I stopped at Tobias Eshelman's where I had a short conversation with him on the subject of politics. I was defending the Republican Party . . . when his wife ordered me out of the house.

Apr. 20. I went to Abr. Barb's and went with him to Strasburg before Obed Funk Esq. to make oath that I will be a loyal and law-abiding citizen of the Commonwealth and will never agitate directly or indirectly the subject of abolition. Civil War was inaugurated today at Fort Sumter.

In 1845 Levi Pitman had reported making "swadling cradles . . . also several cradles for harvesting grain." But in 1880 he recorded technological advances taking place in the valley (while technology in the mountains generally did not advance): "We made arrangements to have our wheat threshed out . . . with Dan Spiker's steam Power." And, "I ordered a 'Washing Machine' from New York by postal order $3.00." He even wrote of a photographer briefly renting a room in his house, hoping people would come to have their "likenesses made."

All through Levi's diary are references to deaths—from scarlet fever, typhoid, smallpox, tuberculosis, trees being felled—and to friends and relatives migrating westward, to Ohio, Indiana, a few even to Nebraska. A common scene throughout the half century was cattle being driven to the market from both valley and mountains, needing overnight pasture along the way; as many as 750 head stopped in one herd at his farm. Each year, he wrote of going to the mountain to pick whortleberries; later in the diary they're called huckleberries. There were references also to both valley and mountain residents gathering chestnuts, black walnuts, and other wild foods—as the Indians had years before.

Despite his preference for the Union, Levi stayed on good terms with Andrew and Maria, even during the war itself. He often visited them, though realizing they strongly favored the Confederacy. Once, when he was tuning Maria's piano, he simply couldn't get the tone right. So he stayed overnight—though he was expected at home and couldn't let his family know—and put in another day to perfect the job.

Maria died in 1893 at age 87; her husband Andrew Pitman had died at age 82 and diarist Levi Pitman, at age 85. Maria's executrix, daughter Mary Catherine Pitman, struck trouble. Squatters were living on the Rappahannock part of the inheritance. She evicted some, but one got a temporary injunction and sued to make it permanent. The case of *John A. Keyser* v. *Maria L. Pitman's Executrix*—sometimes v. *Mary C. Pitman et als.*—was pondered from 1898 to 1902. At last the judge put the puzzle before a jury (Rappahannock citizens, of course, in Rappahannock court), and the jury gave the land to Keyser. The judge, thus bolstered, declared he would favor all longtime squatters on Overall land in the county, explaining that this land was lost to the owners on account of their living far away in Page and Warren counties and not supervising this end of their properties.

Ann P. Overall Jolliffe got 3,412 acres in the 1871 division, including Jeremys Run, and she held on firmly until death. *I imagine her along Jeremys Run Trail again, not riding now but walking, maybe stopping to make her pencil drawings of flowers and birds. She was often lonely. Perhaps more than anyone else in the family she loved nature. I feel she would be pleased to see the restoration of forests and wildlife in the park.*

Ann's marriage to James S. Jolliffe had taken her to Pennsylvania. At a time now unknown, they were divorced, but she went on living there, letting William manage her Virginia land with only brief inspection visits and comments. She wrote thoughtful pamphlets applying Christianity to life. Her eloquent words showed she felt trouble was a gift from God for building strength and character. Two of the pamphlets, saved here, had been published in 1867 by James S. Claxton, Philadelphia. One was entitled *The Mission of Suffering* and was addressed "To a Pastor in

Trying Circumstances." She gave the impression of having lived through the gamut of trials and having found in Christ "the strength to suffer joyfully."

Ann's last will and testament, recorded at the Warren County Court House in 1886, left her share of the "copper land" to her brother William and his children (except a one-seventh share to a friend in Charleston, South Carolina). Her "farm at Milford" (Overall) she wanted sold to pay debts. Her personal property, including many books, was left to her sister Julia A. Overall. Only a 13-acre pasture on her Blue Ridge domain was open land. All the rest was forested, though mostly with trees too small to have commercial value since the market for charcoal in large quantities was gone.

Julia stayed closer to the 3,186 acres allotted to her, extending from near Rileyville in Page County and up over the crest into Thornton Hollow, Rappahannock County. She lived for a long time with William and his family at the old Colonel Isaac house, then moved to Front Royal—where William also maintained a house for many years. Having Isaac's love of horses, as well as of landholding, Julia must have ridden

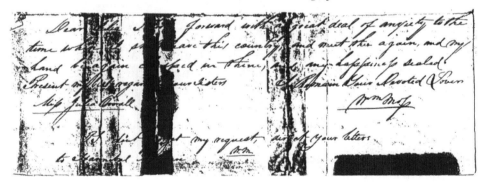

Susan J. Pitman Heiskell, daughter of
Maria Overall and Andrew Pitman, was
considered to resemble her Aunt Julia, a
most attractive belle. Sue was born in 1845
and was very much alive beside the park to
receive her share of the state's payment for
park-land. She died at age 97 during
World War II. (Overall papers)

the Blue Ridge trails frequently. Perhaps there were pleasure parties that included suitors; perhaps she sometimes rode with William, checking on work in progress or planning new projects.

Her niece, Susan Pitman Heiskell, the daughter of Maria and Andrew Pitman and a great hoarder of family documents, knew her especially well, being a somewhat similar person herself, though one-third of a century younger. Sue wrote in 1931: "Julia Overall was a celebrated beauty, said to be the handsomest woman in the Shenandoah Valley. . . .She never married, was a great belle. Two gentlemen committed suicide because she refused them." Like many of the Overalls, Julia exchanged letters and sometimes long visits in person with people of eastern cities.

Some of the letters she received in colorful envelopes were saved. One, dated December 7, 1839, said, "There is nothing on earth I should prize so highly as one line from you, a single sentence if in that you said you still loved me. . . . Dear Julia, I look forward with a great deal of anxiety to the time when I shall . . . meet thee again and my hand be again clasped in thine, and my happiness sealed. . . . I Remain Your Devoted Lover, Wm. Moss." Another, headed "Philadelphia, February 26th, 1843," includes words of love and longing as well as vivid insights into life at Overall:

Are the *Angels* all single yet, or alive? for indeed Julia I have not heard anything of your family for about two years. . . . Perhaps this may

"Aunt" Betty Gaskin, the "mammy" at the Maria Overall-Andrew Pitman plantation. She was a member of the Methodist Church in Edinburg when she died. She "raised" Sue Pitman Heiskell, and Sue expressed lasting love for her even when more than 90 years old. (Overall papers)

(unconsciously) be addressed to a *Married Lady.* If so, I hope the husband of Julia will appreciate her as she deserves and add to his numbers of friends the devoted friend of *Miss Overall*—"Remember me not as a lover whose hopes have been crossed, whose bosom can never recover the light it has lost." No, no—to continue the quotation, "As a sister remembers a brother" I would have you remember me. . . .

I have often wondered whether sister Jane does the pickling of your Tomatoes as usual—and whether she is quizzical as formerly—and whether she ever falls from Stupid Horses when accompanied by Stupid Cavaliers—and whether—she is married. I have almost a mind not to mention Ann at all, she did not answer some letters I wrote her—but I'll be more charitable—and will beg of you to give my kindest remembrances to her—and if she has no beaux, which is hardly possible, will send her a "nice young man this summer."

The letter is signed "T.H.L.," after which there's a P.S.: "Please give my respects to your Father and William." I fear Colonel Isaac was dying or dead when the letter was written.

Julia lived to the age of 84, and, when she was buried in 1897 at Front Royal, the paper said she was the last survivor of Col. Isaac Overall. It credited her with an important part in making the home at Overall Run "proverbial for genuine hospitality" and said she had retained all her long life her characteristic "goodness of heart . . . beauty of person . . . brightness of mind."

The 1871 division gave directly to William Carson Overall only 2,226 acres of the mountain empire in two pieces, most likely the vicinity of Mathews Arm Campground and that portion of park-land nearest the old home (the immediately surrounding cropland having come to him otherwise). William had lived in the old house ever since birth, married Selina Jolliffe (sister of James S. who married Ann?), and had six daughters. The family apparently had a home in Front Royal, while also using the Colonel Isaac house on Overall Run. The only time William left home territory for more than a few days was when he served in the Confederate Army and earned the title of Captain. For more than four decades he was widely considered the monarch of an only slightly dwindled 40 square miles now within the park. It was mostly after his death in 1885 that serious fragmentation began.

Captain William's dedication prompted him to do what he thought his father would have done. Suitable lower areas were farmed or grazed. There were probably a dozen slaves until the war and about the same number of workers for decades afterward. There must have been many horses for plowing and hauling and riding. Friends still came from the cities for enjoyment, including excursions into the mountains and fishing on the river.

The gristmill and sawmill, apple mill and distillery, blacksmith shop and other facilities continued in operation. There was no longer an iron furnace to supply with "coal." Still, the higher and steeper vastnesses were managed mostly on the old pattern, forests being "cut over" for lumber and tanbark every 30 years or so. Rights to harvest specified sections of forest were often granted to jobbers, who would pay a percentage of sale income to the owner. From time to time there were also

Heirs of Isaac and Isaac's children tried hard to hold the immense tracts of mountain land, but lost hundreds of acres to squatters, mostly in Rappahannock County. This poster was part of the effort; so was action in the courts. (Overall papers)

NOTICE.

All trespassers are hereby notified to keep off of the Barbour Survey and the lands known as the Nail and Clark fields, the lots Nos. 3 and 4, assigned to Maria L. Pitman, &c., in the division of the lands of Isaac Overall. Any persons trespassing on this land will be prosecuted to the full extent of the law. There is being a strict watch kept for trespassers.

(Signed)
    MARY C. PITMAN, Ex'or.
March 14, 1898.

agreements for developing mines, but few led to production. Overall mountain lands had few "tenants" in residence. An 1866 map shows a "mountain settlement" and a "Richard" or "Rickert" family above Rileyville on Mine Run that may or may not have been inside the Overall boundary. Perhaps William forgot the far "back end" of the empire in Rappahannock or, as he aged, simply lacked energy to look after it.

The railroad came in the 1880s, soon reducing the amount of freight shipped downriver on flatboats. For a while there was almost a town, including a store, a doctor (Zachariah Compton), and the Borden Stave Mill; it employed up to 50 men, most likely drawing on Overall trees. Dr. Compton bought the old John Overall house and brought howls from an Overall grandson visiting after a long absence: "I looked in vain for the house in which I was born. Dr. Compton had torn down that Colonial landmark to make room for a new house. It looked like vandalism, Cousin!" The letter, dated 1884, was to Maria.

After Captain William died, one of his daughters, Harriet Tyson Overall, known as "Miss Hattie," lived on at the Colonel Isaac house. The barn was still there—and horses, though it's unlikely Miss Hattie herself could ever ride them. She was born somewhat crippled and never married but was said to be strong of mind. She traveled on the train sometimes, and always the conductor helped her up the metal steps into the passenger car. She moved about the neighborhood with horse and buggy. A black man named Arthur Brook worked for her, taking care of the yard, pasture, barn, and livestock, perhaps living on the Heiskell place at Compton not far away. A black woman helped her in the house sometimes.

The man who envisioned with me a summer day in Colonel Isaac's reign remembered an anecdote about Miss Hattie. She was in the kitchen alone, straining to reach into a flour barrel where the supply was low. She fell into it head down. The flour could have smothered her, but someone—possibly Arthur Brook working outside within earshot—rescued her in time. Miss Hattie moved to Washington, D.C., before the park was established. She was paid for quite a few remnants of Colonel Isaac's and Captain William's domain, including, after all, sizable holdings in Rappahannock County as well as on the western slopes. (In the list of landowners, Appendix 3, she was among the Wm. C. Overall heirs.)

Miss Hattie was the last person named Overall to live in the Colonel Isaac house, which stood there until about 1940, but she wasn't the last of Isaac's and Mary's descendants to live where the mountains of Overall-land cast their morning shadows. There was another granddaughter, Susan J. Pitman, born to Maria and Andrew in 1845, who married Francis Lovett Heiskell in 1874. They were still living at Compton in

John William Overall, a nephew of
Colonel Isaac, was editor of the *New York
Mercury*. Born and raised at Overall, he
fondly remembered the Blue Ridge and the
Overall homes. Nostalgic letters he wrote
to his cousins here, mostly in the 1890s,
give a living picture of those Overalls who
owned and used one-seventh of the land
that became Shenandoah National Park.
(Overall papers)

1931, after 57 years of marriage. Francis was 81 and Sue, 86. Around that
time Francis helped an engineer in surveys for park-land. Sue was a poet
and a preserver of family papers and traditions. She survived until World
War II, coming within two years and a small fraction of age 100.

The records and mementoes were passed on to her granddaughter,
Frances Heiskell of Compton, who died in 1987 after helping me
mightily in gathering and interpreting information, not only about the
Overalls but about other people and situations of the park region's past
as well. Frances and her sister Thelma Fristoe and Robert Keys of Front
Royal, Elza Hutton and Norma Smith of Luray (descendants of the
original Shenandoah Overalls via Mamie R. McKay, another poet and
genealogist) are thus both sources and parts of this story of the
generations of Overalls that spanned and wove themselves into the whole
white people's history of Shenandoah National Park.

CHAPTER XI

Farmer-Grazers and Tenants

After a century of powdered-wig ownership and plantation dominance of around nine-tenths of the park-land, the plantation system here began coming apart at the seams. Much of the land had been "worn out" through cycles of clearing, cropping, and grazing, followed by too-short returns to forest. The economy was slipping. Prices paid by major markets often failed to keep up with costs. Younger planters were migrating southwestward in large numbers. Hard-pressed elders were pessimistically neglecting fields tangled with broom sedge, briers, and saplings of scrub pine and thorny locust, whether in lowland or mountain. Or they were selling many acres in efforts to make financial ends meet.

Buyers of hundreds or thousands of acres in the Blue Ridge might be valley-piedmont investors looking toward future timber production, or Yankees—especially Pennsylvanians and New Yorkers—teased by mineral prospects. But increasingly after 1830 the buyers of the most fertile park-land, especially along or near the Blue Ridge crest where the base rock was the old lava or granite, were lowland farmer-grazers seeking mountain pastures to double or triple their beef-cattle production. Collapse of the 48,000-acre plantation between Milam and Thornton gaps, after the death of Thomas Shirley in the mid-1800s, speeded the process. The Civil War clinched it. Lowland farmers, mostly of German descent, had taken over conclusively from descendants of Anglican gentry, while mountain residents clinging to small bits of the land had weathered the transformation almost without noticing.

When the park-land was being bought in the 1930s, at least 50 square miles of it were grasslands used for summer grazing. In addition to the vast pastures, the farmers of nearby lowlands owned thousands of acres of adjacent rocky ridges that were producing shingles, fence posts and

Cattle grazed immense areas of the Blue Ridge before the park was established. This picture was taken near Milam Gap south of Big Meadows in the early 1930s. (From Edward Steere, "The Shenandoah National Park," 1935)

rails, firewood for heating both mountain and lowland houses, and sometimes significant quantities of tanbark and lumber. For nearly a century this lowland-highland combination had been the dominating lifeway of the park-land. I'll explore its complexities and character.

One of the 40 or so control centers was the old Varner farm on East Hawksbill Creek below Stony Man Mountain. The dark side of the Blue Ridge looks like a wall of mystery from this farm at sunrise, filling half the view. Only later do the side ridges and hollows show. Louise Long and Dorothy Musselman, sisters, live there now. They were born Varners, descendants of a German family that settled in the mid-1700s, one of the four families welcomed by the lone Indian medicine man whose fellow villagers had disappeared. German-Swiss-Americans had raised crops and livestock there for ten generations.

Louise married Arthur R. Long, Jr., whose family farmed along the main Hawksbill Creek and summered cattle at two Ridge locations. She thus has intimate associations with three great mountain pastures, one each in Page, Madison, and Rappahannock counties. She remembers going with her grandfather in a buckboard when she was a little girl to see how the cattle were doing. They jolted past the "Brick Church" and on up Rocky Branch. There'd been floods, and the road was gone, so they drove in the creek. They spent the night at friend Ed Hershberger's summer-grazing ranch near Beahms Gap, then jolted on down to Spiencop (also spelled Spion Copse) on the North Fork of the Thornton River below Elkwallow.

They were greeted by Jake and Jeff Dwyer, tenants on the grazing property, and their families. The Dwyer children gave Louise hazelnuts they'd gathered. Louise "loved to go" to Spiencop, but worried about howling wildcats and venomous snakes. One of the Mrs. Dwyers had

The Varner family farmhouse on East Hawksbill Creek below Stony Man Mountain. The house, though built in the 18th century, is still standing in good condition. It was the home of Jesse Varner in the 20th century. People living in such places beside the Blue Ridge owned and industriously managed the richest resources of the park-land, a vast doman of bluegrass sod flanked by forest. (Courtesy of Louise Varner Long and Dorothy Varner Musselman)

been bitten by a snake in the garden and had died. Three Varner brothers, "Grandpa, Uncle Jake and Uncle Martin," put cattle on this rich pasture. Earlier, the pastureland had belonged to great-grandfather Hamilton Varner. Sometime before park establishment a fourth partner, Charles (Isaac?) Spitler, joined the ownership.

In a log barn there each of the four had places for their horses. They also had a bedroom each. The different owners would sometimes stay for weeks, enjoying the cool mountains and gathering chestnuts while they looked after the cattle. Spiencop also had the Hudson-Weaver apple orchards and two Hudson summer homes. Charles Spitler, Jr., says he and his father sometimes went up in a wagon and brought back a load of apples. He still has an old "slide" to put one wagon wheel in—it serves as a brake on steep slopes by keeping that wheel from going around— and a Buena Vista saddle, his father's, and old saddle pockets, his grandfather's. Some Blue Ridge cattlemen used western saddles, which have horns for holding a lasso rope, while others preferred eastern saddles that lack horns.

After Louise was married there were three different brothers—her husband Arthur and two other Longs. Before the park, Arthur had a fine grazing place on Thorofare Mountain between Skyland and Nicholson Hollow. The tenant was Charlie "Buck" Corbin. I visited several times with Buck at his later-years home outside the park, then interviewed him for two hours on his life in the park. He mourned the loss of the "great pasturelands"—which belonged to Arthur W. Long, succeeded by the

Tenants at the grazing place of the Varners—at Spiencop, North Fork, of Thornton River, Rappahannock County—now in the park. The man on the right with a small boy is believed to be Jake Dwyer; his wife had died of snakebite. In the center are Mr. and Mrs. Jeff Dwyer. The young ladies are Dwyers, too. Though a helpful tenant here, Jake Dwyer and quite a few other Dwyers had some land of their own not far away. (Courtesy of Louise Varner Long and Dorothy Varner Musselman)

younger Arthur—as well as of his own homeplace. About 50 of Arthur's cattle grazed there, and Buck kept a watchful eye on them. The other Long place was between upper Tanners Ridge and upper Long Ridge. Though typical of grazing properties taken for the park, it escaped that fate in a fund crunch, and so it continued as before and furnished more recent memories.

The Long brothers assembled their cattle in April at the old Long farm. The herd of about three hundred would be moved out early along the road to Tanners Ridge. Several men on horses worked alongside to keep cattle out of bordering properties. There would be a flagman in front and another behind to warn approaching traffic. Arthur Sr., not so young

The Varners' mountain house at Spiencop with some of the men who worked with cattle there. The Varner families sometimes vacationed at Spiencop for days or weeks when the valley was hot and the mountains cool. (Courtesy of Louise Varner Long and Dorothy Varner Musselman)

any more, would usually drive a truck. If any calves got tired, they'd be given a ride. Some of the cattle had been to The Ridge before and led the herd eagerly. Though the distance was close to ten miles, they'd reach the mountain pasture by noon.

The tenants up there were Carrie and Joe Thomas. The Longs reserved one room only in their big old mountain house; the tenants used the rest. One or more Long brothers would ride up about once a week to be sure the cattle, mostly brown-red shorthorns, were thriving. Louise and her husband rode up together many times and spent the night. Though the house wasn't fancy—the wallpaper was old newspapers— Carrie kept it spotlessly clean. Her cooking tasted extradelicious. She'd have hoecake with every meal. She'd fry pork, then cut up and fry potatoes in the pork grease. She did all the cooking on a big cast-iron wood-burning stove. The Thomases had married children who still lived in the new park but would settle elsewhere soon. "They'd come at night and sing. We had a great time!"

In the spring after getting the cattle up there, everybody might go "merkel hunting" (morels, spring mushrooms) in the moist woods, often

Three Varner partners and several associates at a long-ago log home converted to storage shed, holding tools, salt, and other supplies. The picture was probably taken about 1900. In the foreground, left to right, are Jake, James, and Martin Varner. At the peak of the roof is young Jesse, who in maturity would take over management from his father, James. (Courtesy of Louise Varner Long and Dorothy Varner Musselman)

finding large amounts, enough to give some to friends or kin in the valley. Later they'd pick berries. These Blue Ridge places were resources for recreation as well as production.

Livestock had come to Virginia with the first settlers in 1607. Four years later Lord Delaware reported, "The kine all this last Winter, though the ground was covered most with snow, and the season sharpe, lived without other feeding than the grasse they found, with which they prospered well, and many of them ready to fall with Calve." It soon appeared wise, though, to give the stock—cattle, horses, goats, sheep, chickens—a little shelter and emergency feed and to protect them from Indians and unauthorized whites.

"Herding" advanced into the wilderness ahead of settlement. Despite wolves and other predators, cattle, horses, and hogs thrived, though sheep needed special guarding. In the lowlands on both sides of the Blue Ridge natural meadow furnished grass, wild pea vines, and other forage. Soon there were two categories of introduced stock—gone-wild and owned.

Laws were passed to help distinguish them and to regulate hunting or managing. Owned animals were earmarked and recovered in annual roundups. For a long time Virginia was open range; livestock fed legally anywhere they could go; farmers had to fence them out or risk total loss. Owned herds were guarded and moved to fresh feed by *cowboys*—this term used here long before the Revolution.

Cowpens and cabins were built at places where cattle needed to be rounded up. Some of these were outlying quarters of plantations; others were contrarily independent. Some became lasting homes of hunter-herder-gardeners—squatters at first, most likely, and later owners or, more likely, "tenants" on vast pastures as legal owners became more assertive. Generally speaking, the powdered-wig owners didn't inspect or regulate their back-country lands and remote bases or quarters anywhere near as closely as did the later, German owners.

During most of the white history of this region, great herds of cattle were driven from the mountains long distances to major markets. Virginia raised more cattle than any other colony or state until Texas took the lead about 1845. Appalachian production continued high, and even in 1927 a pamphlet issued by the U.S. Department of Agriculture recognized these mountains as "one of the most important beef-producing sections of the United States." It said Blue Ridge bluegrass added more weight to cattle during the summer than the richest lowland pastures.

Lila Meadows (born Offenbacker, German name wedding English name), age 90 when I interviewed her in 1986, and her husband, Robert, had been tenants on grazing lands of Frank and Grover Koontz near the park's Bearfence Mountain. Robert apparently grew up here, but before marriage he'd worked in Washington, D.C. Lila was raised on Tanners Ridge. Her mother was born a Cave (English) and sometimes told of wolves coming to get ripening corn in Dark Hollow. Wolves would tear people all to pieces to get corn, Lila's mother said, so everybody ran to the cabin when wolves howled.

There wasn't any formal agreement of tenancy; everyone seemed to understand the relationship already. The tenants would "salt the cattle"— that is, they'd notice if the salt the owners had put out was gone and they'd put a new supply on rocks where cattle could lick it up. The salt was fine then, like table salt, not big cubes of rock salt. If the fence was down anywhere, they'd make emergency repairs.

A tenant and family lived in the cabin and took care of it. They grew vegetables, often with separate patches for potatoes and corn, and orchard fruit. It was customary, though not required, for the tenant family to make small gifts of wild nuts or berries, or maybe a few heads of the

Blue Ridge livestock men raised and harvested hay on their farms in the lowlands and fed it to wintering livestock there. (Courtesy of Dr. and Mrs. Eric Rhodes)

superior cabbage that grew in mountain gardens, to the owner family when they came, perhaps also to feed and lodge them occasionally unless the owners had a summer house for their own use, as many did. The owners, too, would bring small gifts, maybe toys, maybe coffee or sugar. Lila remembered the Koontzes often brought big fish from the Shenandoah River. If there were days of work to be done, such as mowing briers with scythes, the owner might hire the tenant and strong sons and pay wages.

The tenant paid no rent, either in cash or a set share of production. The owner paid nothing for the regular watching and emergency coping. Janie Bailey Mauck Spitler, long a civic leader in Page County, whose second husband had had Blue Ridge grazing lands and who now looks after the valley farm, aided by a tenant, tried in a 1986 interview to explain the puzzling arrangement: Each family that had cattle on The Ridge had a family or two of mountain people keeping an eye on the place and the livestock. Such tenants were a real asset to the owner. Though some helped a lot and others not so much, they were loyal to the owner and he to them. Both tenant family and owner family might have been parts of the scene from generations back. The more recent owners must have "inherited" many tenants from previous owners, English gentry. "There was no contract," Janie Spitler said. "It was *noblesse oblige*." If the place was sold, the new owner customarily acquired the tenants along with the land and felt responsible for them.

Tenants didn't own the land, but many felt they belonged to it—and it, in a deeper than legal way, to them.

What situation in the lowlands completed this prevalent combination, which embraced at least half the park-land's mountain people along with many families of owners and farm workers in valley or piedmont? The lowland farms mostly had two to four hundred acres of fertile soil, a solid old house, immense barns, and quite a few other outbuildings, as well as orchards and fields of corn, wheat, hay and other crops. The landowners, though seldom highly educated in an academic way, were capable citizens likely to be near the forefront of agricultural advancement. They treasured the soil and used superior seed and livestock breeds after their merits had been proved. Quite a few of these owners at park-purchase time in the 1930s had assets of several hundred thousand dollars; a number were said to be almost millionaires, being owners of businesses in the towns as well as of farms and mountain pastures. Though most of them had a lot, they risked a lot, including drought and storm and the Great Depression, which their assets might, or might not, survive.

Aided by old accounts kept by Reuben Long, great-grandfather of Arthur R. Long, Jr., we can get glimpses of the long operation centering beside Hawksbill Creek a few miles south of Luray as far back as September 1831. William Marchel was paid that month for work in the farm's blacksmith shop; he had reconditioned iron tools and shoed horses. What Marchel had drawn from the farm's commissary balanced what he'd earned. One transaction was "credit to 3½ days work in shop at one bushel of wheat per day, $3.50." There were about a dozen farmhands, but most of them worked there only 6 to 15 days in a typical month. Louise Long believes they had small farms of their own nearby but needed to earn more.

Cattle were already being put "on The Ridge" each April and brought down each October. Church Tomas was the earliest tenant on Tanners Ridge mentioned in this account book, but there were probably earlier account books not saved. Phillip Long was handling mountain affairs. He picked up supplies for Tomas, mostly food incidentals, not staples. He also drew a little money to take to Tomas, to pay Henry Buck and Enuc Jinkins "for working on the Ridge." In 1870 the name of John Tomas begins to appear in place of Church Tomas. John was drawing supplies and earning credit for several full days of work, cutting brush and building fence, also for "makein 2,500 shingles."

Once the Long youngsters must have got hold of the account book. Where Reuben Long had written his name there were childlike challenges: "John F. Long's Book," then "Jos. M. Long's Book March 12th 1869." Moralistic sentences were repeated as if for penmanship practice: "A man today in rich array tomorrow may be laid away. A Man today in rich array tomorrow may be clothed in Clay. . . . A cow does not know the value of her tail till she loses it."

The farm had a legal distillery, with a John Blar paid by the day for stilling from 1852 to 1860. During one period he made 290 gallons of liquor for valley people, and two gallons out of each five were kept as toll. It's noted down that Reuben Long paid $536.40 in liquor tax in 1864; that's either a mistake or they were doing vastly more liquor business than I'd expect. Much of the product was apple brandy. People would bring loads of apples. One load usually made about two tubs of cider. Henry Huffman must have brought unusually large loads in the fall of 1854; two of them made eight tubs of cider, then from that cider, 41 gallons of brandy.

We can get similar glimpses of Hamilton Varner, Louise's great-grandfather, beginning just after the Civil War. In 1866, from February through November, Ian Moier drew 525 pounds of hemp from the Varner stock at 10¢ a pound. Benjamin Foster coopered flour barrels for

Matilda Varner, wife of Hamilton Varner, parents of Jake, Martin, and James. Mr. and Mrs. Hamilton Varner were responsible for the extensive mountain-and-valley operation, involving dozens of workers, from Civil War time until the 1880s, when James began taking over. (Courtesy of Louise Varner Long and Dorothy Varner Musselman)

the Varners and was credited with 30¢ a barrel. Several men were involved with cattle on The Ridge—Edwin Varner, Poe Aleshire, Joseph Richard. Aleshire made 4,000 shingles up there in 1869 and was credited $14 for them. Andrew J. Cave, probably a mountain resident, did old-time work for the Varners up there in the 1870s and 1880s—cutting 53 loads of wood at 16¢ a load, for instance, and splitting 775 rails for $5. Hamilton's son James was taking over the management in the 1880s and seemed to have about 150 cattle on The Ridge, but he liked horses best and recorded dates of births and names of the colts in the account book. There's mention of 62 calves born in 1890 but no mention of the mother cows and no calves named.

The German-origin Longs and Varners and their English-origin tenants illustrate the pattern that produced great herds of cattle from Hogback on the north to Bearfence or beyond above Elkton. The north end of the park-land for many years had some English-origin owner-grazers and the south end some Scotch-Irish with substantial produc-tion—quite a few families with a hundred or more cattle each on mountain pastureland.

The lives of the farmer-grazers, financially comfortable as they seemed to be much of the time, were likely as adventurous as the lives of western ranchers and cowboys. There were wolves, bears, and cougars

Lizzie Lineberger Varner and husband
James A. Varner were responsible for the
Page-Rappahannock livestock
combination from the 1880s until about
1908, when their son Jesse L. Varner was
taking over much of the load. (Courtesy of
Louise Varner Long and Dorothy Varner
Musselman)

(usually called *painters* in the Blue Ridge) when Reuben Long and
Hamilton Varner and dozens of other lowland farmers had their cattle
grazing the mountain pastures. This region wasn't notorious for cattle
rustling, but there were hazards enough.

In the drought of 1930 all the grass parched. The cattle ate bark and
twig wood. Forest fires swept The Ridge, sometimes roaring at high
speed across the pasturelands in great arcs as if Indians were fire-hunting.
Herds stampeded. Owners aware of the danger were up there to do what
they could. On the Spitler Ranch near Franklin Cliffs a frantic herd was
caught between a swiftly snaking line of fire and a wire fence. The
cowboys tried chasing them back through the line where the flames were
weakest, into the already burned area. They couldn't do it, but they
bought enough time for the quick-thinking owner to use his wire cutter.
He opened the barbwire fence just before the stampede came down on
him. Though scattered far, all the cattle were ultimately found safe. On
another grazing property atop The Ridge, a Joseph Spitler suffered a
heart attack on horseback while trying to control his cattle, and he died
up there far from medical help.

There were half a dozen or more big pastures owned by distantly
related Spitlers at various places on The Ridge. Jim Woodward was tenant
on Samuel and Bernard Spitler's place. The Woodwards moved from the
old tenant house to the owners' newer and warmer house for the winter,
then back to the tenant house in April. There was often that kind of
sympathy. Owners and tenants were concerned about each other.

The Bernard Spitler ranch house overlooked the route of Skyline Drive a mile and a half north of Franklin Cliffs. Spitler Knoll and Spitler Hill were named for Bernard's father, Samuel. These Spitlers—of Swiss origin—ran their Blue Ridge cattle "spread" in wild western style. Bernard went to Wyoming and got western cattle and equipment including chaps, western saddle with horn to hold the lasso, western hats and quirts, branding irons, and Colt revolver. They took pride in their well-built mountain house, used it heavily in spring, summer, and fall, but they let their tenant family live in it during the winter because it would keep them warm and comfortable. (Courtesy of Bernard H. Spitler, Jr.)

The Spitlers had a sawmill up there and sold lumber to the railroad. Once the railroad wanted trestle timbers at least 40 feet long. The Spitlers and Woodward, with some help from the valley farm, produced them. These Spitlers also sold tanbark and never wasted the trees after peeling them. They sawed and sold them.

One day three Spitler cattle got through a fence and disappeared. Bernard Sr. tracked them into Nicholson Hollow, a place reputed to be so lawless even the sheriff had to get permission from "the King" before entering. Bernard risked it. Carrying his rifle, he went down and found his cattle. He also found tall, lean men with old rifles, eyeing him. He tried to hire them to help drive his cattle back up, but they put him off. They took him to see Aaron Nicholson, "the King of Free-State Hollow." The King offered him a drink. He declined. Then, seeing the expression on the King's face, he reconsidered. The brandy was powerful but good. When they'd finished drinking together, the King guaranteed the men would bring the lost cattle up to the ranch, when the day got cool, if he would pay them now. And they did, friendly as could be.

Another time, though, with a different "mountaineer," Bernard Sr. had to threaten shooting to persuade the fellow he couldn't get away with leaving the Spitler gate open whenever he didn't happen to feel like closing it. Bernard Sr. lived ranching. He went out west in 1915 and came back with a Wyoming saddle, western chaps, western hats, and a big Colt revolver.

There was never a shortage of danger. Thunderstorms could be extraordinarily fierce on the mountain. Once the Longs lost 11 cattle when lightning struck a forest tree where they'd clustered. Yet most of the farmer-grazers' mountain memories were of pleasant times—except the unforgettable, final event when the state took their mountain to make the national park.

CHAPTER XII

Millers, Townsmen, and Railroaders

Most whites were unprepared to survive on wild plants and wild meat. They needed meal from Indian corn in larger, more regular amounts than had the Woodland Indians. Corn could be ground by hand, with mortar and pestle, slowly and laboriously, but settlers were unwilling to do this. Thus gristmills were necessities in the early centuries of settlement. Meal and flour must be fresh, so trips to the mill were frequent.

For people not part of a plantation, gristmills were also the nearest thing to community centers around the Blue Ridge until the towns grew. Though the early mills were built and operated as plantation facilities, nearly all of them served everyone else in their vicinities who ate bread, whether of corn or another grain. A commissary or store usually went along with the mill, so all supplies could be obtained there. The millers and their helpers put in long hours every day, except possibly Sunday. Still, you couldn't make a "quick trip" to the mill, the grain was put to grind while you waited and visited. People met neighbors there, and learned and interpreted news there.

A gristmill just below what's now Sperryville must have been built in the 1730s if not before, near the junction of the north and south forks of Thornton River. The early settlers west of the Blue Ridge, even west of the Massanutten, knew about it. In 1740 they petitioned for a road to improve their access to it, and they called it Thornton's Mill.

Within a few decades there were a hundred or more gristmills around the foot of the Blue Ridge, where mountain people as well as lowland people brought their corn to be ground on shares. Very few mills were inside what's become the park boundary. The best locations were where the streams had dependability and strength of flow and where the farming population and production would assure enough grain to make the

Lam's Mill, inside the park near U.S. 33 east of Swift Run Gap, was still capable of grinding corn into meal when the park was established. It was saved for years as a potential historical exhibit, but no funds to maintain such exhibits were appropriated. Time took its toll. The waterwheel and log-and-weatherboard building decayed. (NPS)

operation worthwhile. Mills higher up probably didn't last long, unless they were located on a main highway. Along U.S. 211, inside the park line above Sperryville, there was an old Triplett Mill, later belonging to Addison W. Clark and having an up-and-down sawmill operating from the same waterpower and producing rough lumber. Buildings and at least some of the equipment were there when the land was bought for the park, though I seem to remember the mill being called Atkins Mill then.

Even after the park was established, picturesque old Lam's Mill, with a big waterwheel and mill equipment inside, was popular with photographers near U.S. 33 east of Swift Run Gap. This mill was said to have been running just before the land was bought for the park. Civil War maps called it Dunn's Mill, and other sources say it was operated for a time by John Dunn but was originally built in 1836 by George W. Dean. Perhaps Dean's plantation was a successor to the Kirtley family's Swift Run Gap plantation of the 1700s.

In 1869 the Showacre family acquired this mill, along with a tannery just across the road. Most of our facts come from this connection, through a 1938 letter from Charles Showacre of Cumberland, Maryland, to George Shifflett, who was then caretaker at the mill. Charles said he was born across the road from the old mill in 1870. His father operated the tannery, and his brother John, ten years his senior, was soon operating the mill. The state bought the site from the W. J. Lam estate, hence the name applied to the mill in the 1930s. There'd been other owners between the Showacres and Lams—Suel McDaniel, James Offield, Joe Shiflett.

A mill site on the Hazel River in the park is still findable, reportedly with a heavy old burrstone. But I haven't found any history of this mill and guess it was relatively short-lived. Another one in the park seems to have existed for some 60 years. The site of that Silas Utz gristmill (and up-and-down sawmill) is along the Rapidan River, about four miles below Camp Hoover, at an elevation of approximately 1,200 feet. The mill installation was part of a thousand-acre plantation. The gristmill is said to have existed from 1830 until the river washed it away in 1893. Burrstones were reported in 1936 to be visible in the river about a hundred yards below the mill site. I don't know if they're still there. County records show Utzes owned the plantation for at least three generations, but in 1919 they sold 380 acres of it, including the plantation house Rockland, a large orchard, and the mill site to Dave L. Breeden, who owned that land until the park came.

The gristmill that served the largest concentration of park-land residents—Hazel Mountain-Hughes River-Old Rag vicinity—was situated at what came to be called Nethers outside the park on the Hughes River. It may have been started as early as 1794 after an enthusiastic developer named Benjamin Lillard convinced Rowland Yowell that a mill would do a good business there. It was built on a 90-acre tract that Yowell bought from James Ward for $1,000. I find "Yowel's Mill" at the site on a map issued in 1821. There's some evidence of construction in 1824, but that must have been a rebuilding or an addition.

A great deal of knowledge and effort goes into a gristmill, even one of the old "simple" ones designed mostly to turn out cornmeal. For dependable power there's nearly always a dam in the stream, and a diversion of water into a millrace to come at the big waterwheel at the right level (some are undershot, others overshot). The homemade overshot waterwheel first installed by Yowell was replaced about 1869 by a turbine that served until the 1890s. Then a new overshot wheel was installed to get more power from less water, as the flow seemed to have been declining for years.

The older mills have carved wooden gears and pulleys and belts to help deliver the power where it's needed. A sizable building several floors high is necessary. Heavy stones—great thick circles—do the grinding. Usually they come from expert stonemen at a distance, and the hauling could be quite a problem. It's said that the original burrstones at Nethers came from France and were replaced in 1902 with stones from Massanut-

W. A. Brown was postmaster at Oldrag, one of a very few concentrations of families in the park-land large enough to afford a post office. This post office was abolished following park establishment and the decision that the mountain residents would have to move out. (Photo by Arthur Rothstein, 1935, from Farm Security Administration collection, Virginia State Library)

ten Mountain. Other mills beside the park seem to have brought stones from Pennsylvania and other medium-far places.

The bottom stone is anchored down. The upper one can be raised and lowered, and it turns to do the grinding. Grooves are chiseled into the stones, and these grooves have to be sharpened with hammer and chisel at intervals in order to keep the stones grinding well. The meal works along the grooves and into a bin as the top stone turns.

Nethers Mill with its store was so much a community center that the voters came to cast their ballots at a polling place in the lower room. Among the customers from the park-land were Nicholsons, Corbins, Jenkinses, Weakleys, and Dodsons. The millers kept one-eighth of the cornmeal as toll, which they sold to other customers or hauled by oxen and sled, or later oxen or horses and a Fishback wagon made nearby, to Gordonsville for shipment to far markets via railroad.

Nethers Mill was the first in this section to install equipment for grinding buckwheat. Rye and wheat were also ground; the coarse, whole-

Nethers, Virginia, outside the park along Hughes River near Old Rag Mountain, had a gristmill that pulled business from both mountains and lowland. A store and a post office and a polling place—a community center—grew at the mill. It was Yowell's Mill at first, about 1794, and Nethers Mill much later. The post office was established in 1885. Both post office and mill closed down in the mid-1940s. (Photo by Arthur Rothstein, from the Farm Security Administration collection, Virginia State Library)

grain flour was used for making brownish bread. Some housewives sifted this rough "mountain flour" to remove the bran and other hard or dark parts, which were fed to livestock. The flour that was left was almost white. The mill wasn't equipped to produce bleached, branless white flour, but Tip Nethers had a stock of such flour bought from the old Thornton Mill (which was now called Fletcher's Mill) in case any customer insisted on this extrarefined product.

George Corbin, who lived nearly five miles up the main Hughes River, brought some of just about every kind of grain raised in that vicinity—corn, wheat, rye, and buckwheat. The buckwheat was for pancakes, which George and his family and associates greatly liked with sorghum molasses made from "cane" that they grew. All the grain would be well cleaned, weed seeds and other trash removed from it, before they took it to the mill. It should be completely ready to grind, and you could then get it done while you visited and go back home with it. George's father, Madison Corbin, back around the turn of the century, had a wagon and two horses. They hauled tanbark in it and drove the wagon to the mill and the store when grain was to be ground or supplies picked up—such as sacks of sugar to be used with ground corn in fermenting mash for making moonshine.

Tip Nethers and his mill weren't speedy, but they were ready to get grinding at any reasonable time. Tip would explain that cornmeal is best flavored if ground slowly so as not to get "cooked by the heat of grinding." He might explain, too, that "there ain't much water in Hughes River these days"—which meant the waterwheel didn't turn very fast. This mill lasted for 151 years before Tip closed it forever in 1945. Tip Nethers might not haunt the park itself very much, but he haunts near enough to count.

Mountain residents and rural lowlanders liked the old mills. They liked the stores that often went with them and the horseshoe-pitching ground alongside and the post office service by the miller or storekeeper or wife. But the time would come when the economic trend the mills inaugurated would reach giant size and swallow the rural services, making "independent living" close to impossible.

Browntown, situated below Mount Marshall with national park on three sides of it, can serve as an example. It grew from gristmills that located along Gooney Run in this manor of Lord Fairfax that now forms much of the park's north end. Among builders and operators of Gooney Run mills were the Boyds, Humes, and Rudacilles in the late 1700s. The Browns built mills at several different sites on the stream, and Abraham Brown's site somehow proved especially attractive to business and industry.

The growing hamlet was informally called Brown's Mill, but when it got a post office with John Hambaugh as postmaster in 1812 it was officially Hambaugh for a while, though Browntown got to be both popular and official in the long run.

The business-industrial movement took over from the plantation system after the Civil War and began pushing destiny. Browntown gobbled park region resources, pulling both mountain and lowland people into its orbit. A large tannery (detail in Chapter 13) employed 150 or more people and drained the forests of chestnut oak for its tanbark. Other factories followed, using mountain resources. Busily employed in factory jobs or in extracting raw materials for the factories, people had little time for the complex old homecrafts. Spinning wheels and looms got pushed out into storage sheds or up into attics, along with tanning vats and cobblers' benches and lasts. Browntown stores offered fabrics, clothing, shoes—whatever anyone might need or want. There were distilleries and

A wooden flume carried water from the South Fork of Thornton River and released it atop the wooden "overshot" waterwheel to turn the machinery in this mill long situated beside the Lee Highway (U.S. 2ll) on park-land above Sperryville. In the 1700s and 1800s there were dozens of gristmills on substantial streams along both eastern and western edges of the park-land but few inside the boundary. (NPS)

taverns, churches, schools, and transportation facilities to and from far cities. Browntown's volume of commerce and industry was high for decades, but a new phase of economic and technological "progress" was in the making and even the Gooney Run gristmills would die.

Front Royal, the only sizable town touching the park, began as a junction of trails crossing Chester and Manassas gaps and reaching Chester Ferry across the Shenandoah River. Soon, of course, it had a gristmill and a store. It also had wild Saturday nights that earned it the name Hell Town. In 1788 it got the name Front Royal, maybe from a drill sergeant who kept ordering his militiamen to "front the royal oak," perhaps soon shortening the order to "Front Royal!"

In 1805 Front Royal had 60 houses, a Methodist chapel, an academy, a mill, and several stores. In 1836 it became county seat of new Warren County. People there were manufacturing excellent wagons that sold widely, and in 1854 a railroad came through Manassas Gap with "the cars" stopping in Front Royal to load and unload freight and passengers. The population at the start of the Civil War was around five hundred. The war left the town in ruins, railroad and bridges wiped out, buildings damaged, the economy paralyzed. It recovered fast, however, and went on growing.

We could go on like this all around the park, though few other towns are as close to the boundary as these two in Warren County, but the pattern and the meaning to the people would be similar. The home and close-to-home life-support system was being sucked away. The staff of life was ceasing to be corn or even mountain flour; it was becoming white flour, and bigger mills farther away were making white flour more efficiently than little mills could.

The trend pervaded almost every aspect of living, but the cost was high. More and more cabins became vacant. People followed jobs and services of commerce and industry. Remote populations thinned. Small towns got smaller; bigger towns got a little bigger; cities much farther away grabbed most of the growth and prosperity. People of the park-land were too few to enter into this competition, though they were fundamentally affected. Some commercial operations had come in along highways crossing Thornton and Swift Run gaps, but no concentrations ever approached town size. There were several post offices representing small populations—Hawsberry, on the old turnpike east of Panorama at about 1,400-feet elevation; Oldrag, established in 1919 on the divide between Weakley and Berry hollows at about 2,000-feet elevation; Beahm, about a mile west of Panorama on U.S. 211, Page County; Skyland, on Stony Man at about 3,500-feet elevation; and Simmons Gap, at the old mission and school, about 2,250-feet elevation. There was mail service to Black Rock Springs, but I'm not sure there was an official post office.

This country store is believed to have been in Page County within walking-shopping distance of mountain homes. Even such small stores as this were rare inside the park-land. (Photo by Wallace Rhodes, courtesy of Dr. and Mrs. Eric Rhodes)

None of these small clusters of people could slow the cityward shift of the economy. Because they were so scattered, mountain people never built economic or political influence. There were no local governments in the park-land, rarely any lasting interest by residents in political matters—except, for a few years, the political questions of the Civil War. The people mostly accepted fate—"What is to be will be."

The most potent development, in its long-range effect on owners and residents of park-land and neighboring territory, was the steam-powered railroad. Hauling freight in cumbersome wagons or on risky flatboats or slow barges might be all right, but railroads would be better—so said eminent engineer Claude Crozet and other farsighted thinkers in 1830. The Virginia Board of Public Works, however, did not agree.

In the next 15 years some railroad mileage was built—for instance, from Richmond up the piedmont to Louisa. This Louisa Railroad was extended in 1840 to Gordonsville and in the 1850s was named Virginia Central. Promoters of Staunton and the rest of Augusta were urging its extension across the Blue Ridge into the valley. The promotional pressure increased and aimed for a tunnel under Rockfish Gap. Rails were laid on both east and west slopes of the Blue Ridge. Experiments tried using extra locomotives to take trains across the steep grade of Rockfish summit. Augusta historian Joseph A. Waddell reported there was rail service to Staunton from the piedmont from 1854 on. But the extra locomotives were no adequate substitute for the tunnel that was already under construction.

Claude Crozet had served two separate terms as principal engineer of the Virginia Board of Public Works, building turnpikes and canals, but he had lost support each term through being ahead of the times. Now chief engineer of the Blue Ridge Railroad, a private firm, he was determined to prove that railroads were not just a curiosity but a faster and less expensive system of large-volume transportation. The Blue Ridge Tunnel, the first great structure of this type in the country, was going through the mountain rock about five hundred feet below the level of Rockfish summit. Crozet had estimated the cost at $200,000, and construction had started in 1850.

The next year a carriage traveler on the turnpike took note of the stupendous project. "We passed under an arch composed of mason work over which the railroad is carried," Mary Jane Boggs wrote, regretting there was no time to go down to the tunnel mouth. The tunnel "will require a great amount of labor to complete," she said, noticing the men were there in large numbers. Nearly all were recently arrived Irishmen, who worked hard for modest pay. After all, they'd been starving in the potato famine before they came to America, but they sometimes got out of control.

Waddell described an "Irish Rebellion" of February 11, 1850. Two varieties of fighting Irish tangled. "Corkonians" of the Blue Ridge Tunnel attacked "Fardowners" who worked on grading nearer Waynesboro and lived in a big frame house there. A crowd of Corks estimated at 235 beat up the Fardowners (numbers not given), broke into their boxes of belongings, tore up their clothes, burned the big house, and then went on back to the mountain and their rock blasting and shoveling.

The event was startling and got magnified in the telling and retelling. There was talk of human heads rolling about like pumpkins. The Augusta civil authorities called in the military, and a detachment marched to Waynesboro and rested, waiting for cover of darkness to make their attack on the deadly Corks of the Blue Ridge. But when the military got up there, the Corks proved not to be in a fighting mood. A few supposed leaders were arrested. More men were arrested along the road back down, almost every man whose accent sounded the least bit Irish. Fifty prisoners were taken to Staunton. By then the event was being seen in truer perspective. Nobody was missing. No human heads or corpses could be

Claude Crozet, the eminent engineer who planned the railroad tunnel under Rockfish Gap and supervised the construction. (From Howard Newlon, Jr., and Nathaniel Mason Pawlett, *Backsights*, 1985)

found. The citizenry was beginning to feel amusement instead of horror. Only two or three of the 50 arrested could be convicted of anything, and these of minor offenses only. Irishmen were understood to be fighters and they'd fought. So what?

The tunneling went on from 1850 until 1858. The cost rose to $488,000, more than double Crozet's estimate. But the result was magnificent. The completed railroad was an important and lasting success—for business and industry, that is, but not for people depending on gristmills and other old-style services near their remote homes.

Meanwhile, the northern end of the Blue Ridge stretch that's now the national park was involved in "progress," too. A railroad connecting with ports near Washington, D.C., was planned to cross Manassas Gap—a low pass, needing grading but not a tunnel—into Front Royal and on to Strasburg. This project also relied on Irish labor. By 1852 the line had reached the eastern foothills of the Blue Ridge, but no funds were available to bring it over the pass. Front Royal and Warren County developers raised $45,000, and the first train smoked, puffed, and steamed into Front Royal on October 10, 1854.

The park-land was enclosed in parentheses, south and north, but it would be the railroad all along the western foot of the Blue Ridge that would change life in mountains and valley most fundamentally. Its coming was slow, a few miles now, maybe more later. During the Civil War there was a Baltimore and Ohio Railroad main line track from Harpers Ferry to Martinsburg, with a connection by a different company to Winchester, but no railroad along the valley in the park region.

A Stonewall Jackson legend fits in here. He's credited with capturing Federal locomotives and railroad cars near Harpers Ferry in 1861 and

The Shenandoah Valley Railroad, completed along the west side of the park-land in 1882, changed life forever here. Larger mills at a distance soon replaced the local mills that rural and mountain people depended on, and it was the same with other facilities and services. The park's Knob and Neighbor mountains loom in the background. (Courtesy of Dr. and Mrs. Eric Rhodes)

pulling them many railless miles to augment the railroad equipment of the Confederacy. One version has him hauling four small locomotives over the Valley Pike (U.S. 11) from Winchester to Strasburg, where he put them on the Manassas Gap Railroad. Later that year he is said to have hauled 14 much larger locomotives, needing 40 horses to pull one, all the way to Staunton to put them on the rails to cross Rockfish. Another version, likely more accurate, involves 56 locomotives and 300 cars. About 35 of the locomotives were badly damaged, but the rest were pulled on the wagon roads to Strasburg. At least 80 railroad cars were similarly moved to Confederate rails. Capt. Thomas R. Sharp was in charge of this work for Stonewall from the spring of 1861 on to October. The booty included also nine miles of rails, $40,000 worth of machinists' tools, and a lot of telegraph wire.

Valley towns were trying hard after the war to fill gaps in the line between Hagerstown and Roanoke. In 1870 Augusta County voters defeated a proposition to subscribe $300,000 worth of stock in the Valley Railroad Company. The issue came up again the next year, this time phrased as $200,000 in "Valley Railroad" and $100,000 in "Shenandoah Valley Railroad," two different companies, two different routes, but again it lost.

Nevertheless, by 1879 the railroad was completed from Shepherds-town, West Virginia, to Riverton, near Front Royal, and closing in on our area from around Roanoke, too. Soon it was connected from Shepherdstown to Hagerstown, where main lines joined with chief port cities on the Atlantic. Some of the very last construction was in Page County during 1880 and 1881. Building long, high trestles in the Rileyville-Compton-Overall section, beside the park, was expensive and time consuming. Soon there was a connection on the south at Waynes-boro Junction. The first passenger train inaugurated the full Shenandoah Valley Railroad (later Norfolk and Western, then Norfolk Southern) on June 18, 1882, taking about ten hours from Hagerstown to Roanoke. This train traveled at 30 miles per hour, except that where the track construction was very recent, so not settled solidly, the speed was held down to 15 or 20.

Almost everyone enjoyed having the railroad. Even the people of the mountain hollows liked the music of the steam whistle and the dreams of far, romantic places that it stirred. The rails brought the world to all the towns along it, but they'd soon make the old ways of living more difficult.

CHAPTER XIII

Lumbermen and Barkers

The forest grows so fast from naked ground on these mountains in this climate that we tend to suppose it was always here. Yet people came before this forest came; the mountains in that frigid time had only low-growing plants with an occasional spot or line of spruces. Even since the white people came, the park-land forest of hardwoods with a few evergreens has been cut or burned repeatedly, though never all at one time.

The Indians used the forest for firewood, wigwams, and other structures, spear handles and throwers, tool handles, bows and arrows, digging sticks for agriculture, and other useful or decorative things. They hunted and gathered food in the forest, and also found fibers and medicines there. They deadened many trees by girdling, and they burned parts of the forest, sometimes to encircle herds of prey, sometimes to create garden space, sometimes to maintain or enlarge vast meadows where bison and elk would thrive.

Early whites imitated the Indians in using the forest, though bringing in their different patterns. Soon big operators arrived, who didn't just use but used up. The ax was standard equipment for a pioneer. Under ax-deadened trees he planted his first crops and fruit trees; they'd grow best where no forest leaves would shut off the sun. When he had more time, in winter maybe, he might remove the dead trees and use the wood to feed heating fires or to make crude chairs and tables and beds. Or the trees might stand while fungi and rot ate them.

The soil was considered exhausted after a few years, and new ground would be planted. The homeplace sometimes showed three successive deadenings—abandoned, currently cultivated, and new—with stark trees standing on all three. Well-financed planter-pioneers might use the deadening method at first, but soon they'd be harvesting and using all the trees. After a few years they'd have plenty of axes and saws, imported from Europe or made by skilled craftsmen in Virginia, and they'd have plenty of labor.

Fallen American chestnut, found in 1918 along Rapidan River in the Blue Ridge. The oriental blight that would kill all the wild chestnut trees (though not the roots) was just reaching this region. This giant, 21 feet in trunk circumference, didn't succumb to blight or to humans but to powerful wind or old age. During preceding millenniums chestnuts had been the most numerous trees in much of the park-land. (Miller E. Roudabush)

This up-and-down sawmill was in the park beside U.S. 211 between Sperryville and Thornton Gap when the park was established. Such mills, powered from waterwheels, were generally used here until after the Civil War to turn logs into lumber. Boards found in most log houses in the park region carried the straight marks of such saws, though a few boards in the very oldest cabins might have straight marks of a still older system—two men working the long saw, one above the log, the other in a sawdusty pit beneath. (SNP archives)

By the time of water-powered up-and-down sawmills, the pioneers would have two-man crosscut saws. The ax would cut a notch into the trunk on the side toward which the tree should fall, then the crosscut saw would cut from the opposite side toward the notch. This standard method helped place the falling tree in the most convenient place for trimming and sectioning and reduce danger to loggers and damage to other trees.

Many trees were made into houses, barns, mills, and other buildings, shingles for roofs or siding, rails for fences, firewood for heating, charcoal for ironworking, tanbark for making leather. Another primary incentive for cutting trees was desire for more sunlit land to grow more tobacco (and, of course, other crops) and to grow more cattle, all for the owners' use in some degree, yet mostly in the larger operations to make money. Still another incentive felt urgently by planters was the need to keep their slaves busy in winter when work with crops was at a standstill.

Products of the up-and-down sawmills soon were finding markets downstream. Plantations in use for decades might already be running out of timber; some were mostly meadow or brushland when they were founded. Firewood was moving down country in substantial amounts almost from the beginning. As far back as the 1760s the West Indies were buying barrel staves and other wood products from Virginia. Britain was buying staves, too, along with clapboards and shingles. As soon as there were wagon roads crossing the Blue Ridge and flatboats on the Shenandoah and James rivers, wood products were part of the freight. Most of the barns, mills, and other large buildings in the valley were burned during the last year of the Civil War. Rebuilding took a great flow of lumber. Railroads wanted loads of ties to anchor the rails and big beams for trestles and unending supplies of lumber to haul cityward.

Mountain residents saw what was going on and wanted their shares, but few of them owned enough acreage to participate beyond bartering a few logs, snaked to the mill, for a share of the lumber. Log cabins did sometimes get covered with weatherboards thus earned, and the people could get wood of the different kinds they needed for their buildings or furniture or fences or white-oak–splint baskets. Some mountain families made furniture, fence rails, shingles, or tool handles, which they sold in small quantities. There was no naval stores industry in this kind of forest, but timber operations employed a few mountain men. After the Civil War, many mountain families peeled tanbark and had small quantities in piles, like money in the bank, ready to haul and sell to pay for something they might urgently want. But nearly all the large timber tracts were owned by people who lived outside the park-land, though most of them within a mile or two, like the farmer-grazers. Neighbors outside the mountains were also the jobbers in cutting timber and sawing lumber.

The impact of mountain residents on the park-land forest resembled that once made by Indians—hardly noticeable—but the impact of the nonresidents was beginning to show, even from a distance.

Small tanneries, sometimes called tanyards, had functioned at most plantations in the early years. Some of these expanded moderately, serving customers of a wide neighborhood. Tom Carr, for instance, had an old-fashioned leather operation going in Sugar Hollow, along Moormans River, in the park's south district, recently enough for his daughter Mrs. Arlene Carr Abel to describe it from her own memory to interviewer Dorothy Noble Smith in 1979. Tom's father had operated the tannery earlier; quite likely it had started generations back.

As customary, Tom Carr used chestnut-oak bark as the source of tannin. The trees were felled and peeled when sap was flowing heavily in spring, and the bark was stacked to dry. There was a big iron device operated by a horse going around and around to turn this mill, thus grinding the bark. There were big vats to put the bark in and clear water vats and lime vats to put the hides in after they'd been scraped. You straighten the hide out and flatten it down and put ground-up bark over it. Then another hide, and more bark, until that vat is full. Add water and let it sit, sometimes probing in and looking at samples to see how the process is doing. At the right point, you take the leather out and put linseed oil on it and manipulate it until it's nice and soft. If you wanted to make it black, you put it in an iron pot and added other iron things and water. Tom Carr made harness and shoes and other things from leather he tanned.

Dozens of neighborhood tanneries were drawing chestnut-oak bark from the park-land in the 1700s and 1800s. They used local hides and served local customers. There was also a market in coastal areas and even in Europe for tanning materials from the Blue Ridge, including chestnut-oak bark and sumac, which was also used as a dye. Tanbark was frequent cargo on wagons moving across mountain passes and in gundolas moving down the Shenandoah River. In 1890, according to the Page County newspaper, more than 20,000 tons of tanbark annually was being shipped on the Shenandoah Valley Railroad from Stanley alone. About that same time, according to the Warren County paper, one week's railroad freight leaving Front Royal included 40,000 pounds of quercitron (black-oak inner bark used in tanning and as a yellow dye), 67,000 pounds of sumac, and 260,000 of tanbark.

Industrial tanneries, employing one to four hundred people each, began coming into existence along this part of the Blue Ridge after the Civil War. They consumed endless amounts of chestnut-oak bark, and

Steam-powered circular saws produced most of the lumber in the park-land during the active period of timber cutting between the Civil War and the end of World War I. The circular saw (just to the right of center, by the man's elbow) cuts lengthwise through the log as it's moved past, also by steam power. The steam engine, puffing wood smoke (below) transmits the power by way of the wide belt. (NPS)

they hired local people, some from the mountains, but they seldom used local hides or catered to local needs. The biggest of all, Virginia Oak Tannery at Luray, was started by the Deford Company in 1882. For many years it used only Blue Ridge oak bark. It specialized in shoe-sole leather, and the number of cattle hides processed, nearly all from Midwestern packinghouses, climbed as high as 1,500 a day.

Deford owned big acreages of mountain land. An item in a Luray paper in 1886 said a George W. Stanley was "barking" for the oak tannery and had "erected another large bark shed . . . and put up a new Fairbanks scale." Lewis Willis, an elderly resident near Marys Rock, was a tanbark jobber in the early 1900s, dealing mostly with the Luray tannery. He bought barking rights from owners of mountain forest, contracted with the tannery, and pulled together the men and equipment to fulfill the contracts. A 1,270-acre Deford tract in Albemarle County, surprisingly far away from the tannery, was bought for the park in 1933. It had been cut over about 1910-11 and was in line to be barked again, but there'd been bad fires and the harvest might have been scant.

Barking used up chestnut oaks but not the whole diversified forest. Sometimes the peeled logs were just left to rot. Other times, though, a jobber would do well by selling the chestnut-oak logs to a sawmill while selling the bark to a tannery. Much park-land forest did get quite completely consumed. Some full-time lumber producers, though living in small towns not far from the mountains, worked on a medium-large scale. In the early 1900s, for instance, James O. Bailey of Luray had quite a few sawmills, more or less portable. He'd buy the timber in big tracts of Blue Ridge land—hundreds, sometimes thousands of acres. Each sawmill had its own crew to do all the tasks of timbering. They'd put up large frame shacks in the forest with bunks and a kitchen with a cook, and they'd stay there and work, clear-cutting the whole forest and making it into lumber. Big lumber piles accumulated by the railroad ready to be shipped to cities.

An operation on the Staunton River, now in the park, had a busy logging railroad right out in the forest in the 1920s. Big crews with powerful equipment took out lots of timber. But they didn't disturb the upper canyon of the Staunton, where about 1,100 acres of old forest, nearly all that was actually left "virgin" in the entire park area, survived below The Sag until park-purchase time.

A deeply connected representative of timbering and tanbarking on the park-land, about whom I've learned meaningful details, was John J. Miller. He had a plantation-sized place called Mountain Green near Washington, Virginia. Maybe as far back as the Civil War he owned, in addition to lower land, 3,500 acres of forested park-land in Rappahannock County.

Because such holdings as Miller's could supply seemingly endless tanbark, three Marylanders set up the Cover Brothers Tannery at Browntown in 1874. About 100 men were employed full-time and as many as 150 extra each spring for bark peeling and hauling. The Covers had many big mules for use in barking. When they got more tanbark than their tannery required, they'd ship it to distant markets.

In 1883 Miller and the Covers signed a contract. Miller committed himself to furnish a minimum of a thousand cords of tanbark a year for 25 years. They would pay him $7 a cord (said to weigh 2,240 pounds) for all the good bark he could deliver to their plant. He set his wagons, teams, and hands to making roads on all the chestnut-oak ridges of his vast forest. His production of bark fluctuated. Perhaps he had other work demanding his crews and equipment. If the Covers came, as sometimes they did, with their own men and equipment to get the bark from the undisturbed forest, they paid Miller only $1.25 a cord for what they took. They seemed always eager for bark. They'd pay small suppliers, sometimes mountain men helped by their sons, $6 a cord for good bark delivered in May and June, later in the year only $4.50.

In two decades just about all the chestnut oaks within reach must have been used up. In 1904 Miller bought 3,131 acres in adjoining Warren County from John Hodder, a Browntown manufacturer of products using hardwood trees—tool handles, wagonwheel spokes, many things widely used in preplastic years. Hodder had bought the same big tract from George C. Jenkins and wife. It was nearly all of the northernmost division of Col. Isaac Overall's mountain empire, which had been daughter Jane's share and must have come by way of Isaac H., the son who lacked the typically strong Overall landholding instinct. The land included the west slope of Mount Marshall and the northwest slope of Hogback, with Gravel Springs Gap near the middle.

These chestnut shingles served their time—about 50 years. They have long since shown ridges and valleys because the soft part between the hard grain (annual ring when you have a complete cross-section of log) has worn down. Mountain men often earned a little money by splitting out shingles.

Bark cover repels cold weather. Indian wigwams and mountain cabins were sometimes covered with bark peeled from trees. Far greater numbers of trees, especially chestnut oak, were peeled to get tanbark. Notice woman chopping wood. (NPS)

Miller thus owned 6,666 acres, as he figured it, inside the present park boundary. He should have been ready to supply the Covers for the rest of his contract term—and a decade, at least, beyond that. But either he and the Covers quarreled or careful exploration of the new land revealed a shortage of chestnut oak. The Covers, saying the bark supply handy to Browntown was exhausted, closed that tannery and went into a similar operation at Elkton, buying much bark for many years from the Rockingham part of the Blue Ridge and from over the crest in Greene County, some hauled across Powell Gap.

The John J. Miller Manufacturing Company was organized, with C. T. Edmonds as Miller's partner and general manager, to produce staves and heading of American chestnut, which still existed in large amounts on the Miller land. After getting this business going, they succumbed to an attractive-sounding offer and sold out to a Philadelphia concern, which would operate as the Rappahannock Lumber Company. This company produced heavily for several years, but in 1907 it failed to make payment in accord with the contract.

Miller repossessed, and Edmonds resumed management of the business, which was large and widespread. There were log drags and logging roads all around, sawmills operating, shacks erected to lodge workmen and kitchens to feed them. I'm told there was a logging flume somewhere on Mount Marshall's slopes. The business had a shop where a George Cooper coopered barrels.

Mountain people made fine baskets of split white oak. They selected young trees with great care. The splints were wonderfully flexible yet stiffened with time. The basket maker here is Eddie Nicholson (right). His friend is Charlie "Buck" Corbin. Both lived in the Old Rag—Skyland area of the park when younger.

Miller helped or, to some extent, bossed Edmonds. On his own, he dealt independently with timber other than the American chestnut. American chestnut trees were soon dying because of the oriental blight, but the wood was still usable. In 1922 Miller sold timber rights on all his mountain land to William H. Grannis of Baltimore for $10 an acre. The sum of $10,000 was paid on the signing, and there were to be substantial annual payments for a decade, while the timber was being cut, to make the total $66,660.

It seems Miller had high expectation of mineral values, too, as Col. Isaac Overall had had much earlier. The "Indian Copper Mine" above Big Devil Stairs was on Miller's land. He contracted with Alfred B. Isles to

Timber cutting wiped out large areas of Blue Ridge forest. Where the soil was fertile (usually from granites or basaltic greenstone in the park) and not too steep, the cleared areas might become livestock pasture—as here southeast of Stony Man Mountain (on horizon left of center). If not prevented by regular grazing or brush cutting, young forest would start surprisingly fast, beginning another cycle of timber growth. (NPS)

mine any and all mineral on the 6,666 acres, paying 10 percent royalty on all sales of ore. I don't think Isles made any down payment, but one way or another Miller was doing well with his ten square miles of parkland.

One day in 1925, though, his personal part came to an abrupt end. He was bringing out heavy logs on a heavy wagon. While he was driving down a steep slope, all braking arrangements suddenly failed, and the wagon went out of control. Miller was killed.

The 19th-century belief that the American forest was inexhaustible was Miller's belief in relation to his own forest. Despite incredible amounts of diverse production of wood products, this forest continued to look very green and to possess innumerable trees. Miller had apparently told his heirs it was still "virgin." When Virginia was investigating the land for the national park, the heirs, some living far away, asked $15 an acre or $100,000 for the 6,666 acres and told the man from the Virginia State Commission on Conservation and Development that this was "the only tract of virgin timber in this mountain." The state man couldn't see this spindly forest that way at all, so the question went to an appraisal board.

State witnesses said there was virtually no timber of value on the entire tract. They pointed to the exhaustion of chestnut oak from tanbarking.

A very few red oaks survive from Indian times. This one, on a unique-in-the-park 1,100-acre tract in upper Staunton River, where live timber was never cut, is six feet through the trunk at breast height. Persons included to indicate size of tree are the author and Ruth Smith, a botanist now focusing on Indian use of plant materials. (Ed Smith)

They said Grannis had installed a high-speed, multiple-band-saw operation to cope swiftly with large volumes of remaining species but could feed the mill from the whole 6,666 acres for only a short time. Grannis had then defaulted and let the contract slip.

The heirs couldn't believe the beautiful forest of seemingly endless extent was really, in effect, gone. Miller's old partner, Edmonds, was put under oath and required to tell what he knew—from earlier years plus a recent special reconnaissance. He gave the history since 1903, confirming the chestnut oak was used up in serving the Cover tannery. Further, he said the Virginia Hardwood Manufacturing Company of Browntown had removed all the accessible ash, hickory, and oak, down to small size— maybe five-inch diameter—for making tool handles. This company had operated several mills on the tract. The Miller company itself had "removed practically all of the available chestnut and softwood timber and hardwoods suitable for the manufacture of staves and heading." Except for locust, all the accessible timber had been used up before the national park was ever suggested, and the locust was then sold locally.

Records show payment for the big tract was made up of compromises—but none anywhere near the asking price of $15 an acre. It mostly went for around $4 for "cove" land, $2 for "slope," and 75¢ for "ridge." The Miller estate received $28,441 for the tract in the two counties; it turned out on official survey to have 6,003 acres. This tract was typical of almost all parts of the park-land supposed to be forested; additional examples might be identified in Appendix 3.

The forests of the Southern Appalachian Mountains were following the lowland forests into oblivion, and a few people around 1900 began to recognize the loss. The science of forestry accumulated evidence of "wasteful lumbering and ravages of uncontrolled fires." In all the long past there had been no organized effort to prevent or fight forest fires. On top of that, the forests had suffered intentional burning by both Indians and whites.

In 1902 President Theodore Roosevelt issued a report showing what was wrong and pointing out "the necessity of protecting through wise use a mountain region whose influence flows far beyond its borders with the waters of the rivers to which it gives rise." In some sections the report specifically referred to the Shenandoah-Blue Ridge, but mostly it discussed the whole vast region. Photos showed examples of drastic erosion in the mountains after logging and heavy flood damage in the lowlands nearby. Some mountains were shown stripped of both forest and soil. Water-supply systems and river navigation were shown to be suffering, as well as mills whose waterwheels needed regular stream flow. I think of the Nethers Mill beside the park and Tip Nether's conviction the Hughes River flow was dwindling; Elkton people, too, complained that the mountain streams flowed "muddy."

Roosevelt pointed out that "a clean lumber job is seldom seen. There is great waste of good timber. . . . Care is seldom taken to throw trees where they will do the least harm to themselves and to others." The revelation of damage so far along produced a decades-long effort to set aside "forest reserves" throughout the Appalachians.

Advocates of a national park in the Blue Ridge between Front Royal and Waynesboro would claim in 1924 that the mountain forests were "virgin" or "primeval." They apparently had the same cast of mind as had John J. Miller about his 6,666 acres. A professional report of 1914, detailing the true situation, somehow hadn't reached these advocates. Clifford Hall of the U.S. Forest Service, looking for lands suitable for the national forest reserves between Simmons and Manassas gaps—about two-thirds of this park—found little to encourage him.

Cut-over land become pasture gave open panoramic views in the park's north district when Skyline Drive was being graded. Sizable orchards are at left center; large quantities of apples were produced from park-land. (NPS)

Lumbering, Hall reported, was "an important industry" here, though carried on in "small-scale operations," mostly with portable sawmills. The chief products were lumber, tanbark, and crossties for railroads. Nearly all the worthwhile timber was gone from the west slopes of the Blue Ridge. One hundred eighty years of cutting, plus "the common practice of burning the woods," had caused erosion and extreme ups and downs in the flow of streams. "Scrubby growth of worthless brush" passed for forest on much of the west slope.

The east slopes had resisted fire to a greater extent, being more moist, and might have enough timber "to maintain the industry for some years." Hall found 9,700 acres that could still be called "virgin forest" in 1914, but it was rapidly dwindling. He estimated that about 20 percent of the mountain area was actually cleared—15 percent in grass and 5 percent cultivated. Other estimates have seen the park-land as 30 percent cleared. There was quite a lot of mountain grazing outside Hall's study area, south of Simmons Gap, mostly east of the crest.

Hall didn't see mountain residents as significant in his study of suitability for national forest reserves, but he did not recommend the Simmons-Manassas area. He said it "is so cut up by rather high-priced grazing lands as to make the desirability . . . at least questionable." If advocates of the park had known what Hall knew they might not have recommended establishing a national park here. Still, though mostly depleted of "timber," the forest glowed with scenic beauty and possessed a resilience that would amaze experts as well as residents and sightseers.

CHAPTER XIV

The Mountain Folk Image

Only after people from Europe and Africa had lived in these mountains for a century and a half (roughly 1700–1850), coming and going or staying a decade or several generations, did anyone consider mountain people here lastingly different from lowland people. Horace Kephart, author of *Our Southern Highlanders* (1913) found his earliest reference to mountaineers in an 1845 story by Edgar Allan Poe. It said "fierce and uncouth races" occupied wild mountains of western Virginia. Before that, elevation or topography of home didn't add up to identity. You might be gentry, tenant, servant, soldier, hunter-trapper, bandit, Irish, Welsh, German, herder, farmer, but you didn't recognize yourself as mountaineer.

The earliest reference to mountaineers I've found for the Shenandoah–Blue Ridge was in the diary of Lucy Rebecca Buck, Bel Air plantation, Front Royal, on June 23, 1863. Lucy was telling about her cousin Walter Buck of Belmont plantation on Dickey Ridge being brought home from the war for burial. She wrote that he was "regarded by the mountain people as a kind of Sir William Wallace" (a famous Scot of long ago, a patriot and military leader). Also during the Civil War, Lucy's family hired a "mountain girl" to do work the runaway slaves had abandoned.

By 1880 or so, southern mountaineers had become a character type in American fiction, set mostly in eastern Tennessee, Kentucky, West Virginia, southwestern Virginia, and western North Carolina. The stereotype probably didn't fit reality anywhere with complete accuracy, but it was farther off the mark here than in most of the Appalachians. Still, outsiders found people living in log cabins in hollows here, sometimes carrying old rifles and otherwise looking the part. Romanticists considered them noble primitives or dangerous barbarians. Missionary-educators thought they were "lost sheep." Sociologists and social workers were sure they needed "help."

Who were mountain folk? The Buck family was not, though they went on living in the Blue Ridge. The Foxes were neighbors of the Bucks,

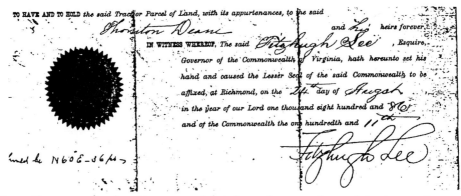

TO HAVE AND TO HOLD *the said Tract or Parcel of Land, with its appurtenances, to the said*

Thornton Dean *and his heirs forever.*

IN WITNESS WHEREOF, *The said* *Fitzhugh Lee* , *Esquire,*

Governor of the Commonwealth of Virginia, hath hereunto set his

hand and caused the Lesser Seal of the said Commonwealth to be

affixed, at Richmond, on the 24 day of August

in the year of our Lord one thousand eight hundred and 86

and of the Commonwealth the one hundredth and 11th

About 42 percent of park residents owned their homeplaces or other park-land, according to the census of 1934. This deed was one of the last granted by the governor of Virginia. It was long assumed that all state land had gone into private ownership, but even when park-land was being bought in the 1930s the surveyors discovered two sizable tracts that were "vacant"—had no owners. (Courtesy of John W. "Bill" Wilson)

and they weren't mountain folk then either. Thomas Fox bought his 450-acre plantation on Dickey Ridge from Marcus Buck in 1856 for $5,000, built a home and farmed with the help of slaves. These Foxes were gentry, most likely kin of Col. David Fox, who moved from tidewater to the upper reaches of the Rappahannock, and if you're gentry you're not mountain folk, or so it has been supposed.

When slavery was abolished Thomas Fox and family did the work of raising crops and livestock themselves. Samuel George "Buddy" Fox, grandson of Thomas, son of Lemuel, was born in 1892, not far from where the Skyline Drive would be built. In a 1977 interview by Patricia Brinklow, Buddy remembered that Thomas and Lemuel talked about their former slaves and about a slave burial ground on Dickey Ridge. Thomas had been educated. Lemuel had not, but his wife Lucy, raised in Browntown, had learned to "read real well." Buddy walked three and one-half miles to Arco school in Harmony Hollow, but often the snow got too deep, and it might be a month or more before he could go back.

Buddy and the other children had to take care of livestock, at least a hundred cattle, also sheep, hogs, and horses. "We had to do a lot before we went to school . . . and when we got back . . . by the time we got done working, it was time to go to bed. We worked a lot by the light of kerosene lanterns." In summer there'd be corn and other crops demanding even more work.

They cut trees and peeled tanbark and hauled many loads to the Cover tannery at Browntown, starting with six horses at 4 A.M. and getting back at 9 P.M., making as much as $8 a day each—"big money them days." Of course, with ten children, there were many hands for the work—but no

Mrs. Dodson and child, presumably of the Hazel-Nicholson Hollow area inside the park, where many Dodsons lived and where the photographer, Arthur Rothstein of the Farm Security Administration, took quite a few pictures. (From Virginia State Library)

John Russ Nicholson using apple peeler. Russ lived in Nicholson ("Free-State") Hollow. His son wrote a long poem urging that elderly persons be allowed to remain in the park. Russ was put on the secretary of the interior's lifetime list to continue in his old home as long as he lived, but he died before the day of exodus arrived. (Photo by Arthur Rothstein, from the Farm Security Administration collection, Virginia State Library)

servants or employees in that generation. The women made quilts and mattresses and pillows filled with feathers. Though sheep were sheared, all the wool was sold; no spinning or weaving was done at home anymore. Store-bought goods were available in Browntown and Front Royal.

When someone died "up there," two Updikes would come to the house, "do the embalming in the living room—no funeral homes then." There was the "old Bowman mill . . . old-time water mill" not far down-hollow. Bowman used to grind all kinds of stuff, corn, flour, wheat, mush for hogs. ". . . He would take out a toll for the work." They had great fun at Christmas. "My mother and sisters always put up the tree on Christmas Eve." There were presents in stockings and "all kinds of candy and fireworks." Noisy fireworks at Christmas were customary in much of the park region.

Buddy remembered moonshine—which, of course, is part of the mountain folk image, though common in the lowlands, too. "Lem . . . used to set his still below the old house at the spring. Had an old 60-gallon

Mountain cultivation patterns. Most of the park-land people didn't think of themselves as farmers, but the typical family had a garden, a corn patch, a potato patch, fruit trees, a hog or two, and a milk cow. A census in 1934 showed, however, that 148 out of 465 families raised no corn, 116 families raised no potatoes, and 44 families cultivated no ground at all. (Courtesy of Dr. and Mrs. Eric Rhodes)

still. My God, yeah. He use to make moonshine all the time." It was for him and his friends, not for sale. But neighbors—"old Mrs. Lockhart . . . and the Pomeroys . . . use to sell it." Sometimes the officers caught them—"made 'em pay a fine, maybe lock 'em up fer a day. Turn 'em out, they'd go back, clean up, set up again."

Buddy denied believing in superstitions, but he knew that a bird getting into a house meant someone was going to die. And when you hear the first call of the whippoorwill you're supposed to turn a somersault, and that means your back's not going to ache any more that year. And when you hear "the old big owl in the mountains holler, hear it late in the evening, you just might as well prepare for snow. I believe in that."

The Foxes were gentry in 1856. Half a century later they were giving a pretty fair reflection of the mountain folk image—except they weren't Scotch-Irish and they weren't feuding with anybody.

What made mountain folk in the Shenandoah–Blue Ridge from Civil War time to park establishment, I gather, wasn't social class or origin exactly, or education or lack thereof, but mainly a persistent fondness for living in mountains or a habit of doing so. I must be careful about generalizing; the more we sample, the more we find diversity here. Most

Simmons Gap mission, on top of the Blue Ridge in the park's south district, was one of a dozen or more missions with schools working to save the "lost sheep". These missions and schools resulted from the life-dedication of Archdeacon Frederick William Neve, a clergyman from England who had ridden a small horse named Old Harry into the mountains to make himself "a thousandfold more useful." (NPS)

mountain families on this park-land were English, but some were German, Scottish, Irish, Welsh, or French. Some owned land; more than half did not. Some went to college; some couldn't read or even write their names. Most families cultivated one to eight acres, but a few, ten times that much.

Sola K. Sours (family of German origin) used most of his 292 acres on Beecher Ridge—surface, that is, as mining rights had been reserved by the Overalls—to feed his livestock. He went farther than that; he became notorious for using many miles of the Blue Ridge for his hogs. In Page, Rappahannock, and Warren counties people feared "Soly" Sours's "ole big hogs." After 1900 a law prohibited hogs from running wild, but in 1934 the Page County newspaper reported that about a hundred of Sours's far-ranging hogs had been shot by unknown persons. Sours was said to be gathering his mobile property, but in January 1936, inside the just barely established national park, another resident, Henry Jewell, was suddenly charged by a 750-pound wild hog that killed all five of his hounds in one furious flurry. Jewell later shot the beast.

Lonnie Lee Conley sometimes had a garden and a cow, but mostly he was a carpenter specializing in making handles for tools. Conleys were both mountain people and lowland people. According to Bill Lumpkin, Jr., of Greene County, Lonnie was born in Rockbridge County. When he was 12, his father George Washington Conley bought park-land on Hightop Mountain and moved the family there. In his late teens Lonnie worked with the federal Civilian Conservation Corps building stone walls along the Skyline Drive. After the exodus of park residents, he adventured in various cities before returning to the mountains and his handles and at long last a grave near his boyhood home by the old Hightop Pentacostal Church.

The Via family also included both mountain and lowland residents. William Via, Sr., French Huguenot, moved up the piedmont to Albemarle about 1730. He and his descendants raised tobacco, grains, livestock, and apples. They advanced up a branch of the Doyle River, then spread over what's called Via Gap on today's maps into a fertile, secluded Shangri-La called Sugar Hollow. In some generations they made lots of *legal* brandy and whiskey. A Via of Sugar Hollow would ultimately fight through the U.S. Supreme Court, trying to prevent the taking of private land to become national park.

A notable park-land woman was Mary Catherine Cave Thomas who, according to a descendant, lived to the age of 103. Her home was west of Tanners Ridge Overlook on the Skyline Drive near the edge of Big Meadows. She had visions, before the park had ever been mentioned, of big machines digging up the mountain pastures, of "droves of people going by," of bright lights shining in her window. She'd say to great-grandchildren, "Hang something over this window so the lights don't hurt my eyes." It was thought she was losing her mind, but later, when the Skyline Drive was built, people realized she had accurately envisioned the future.

In the 1930s, just outside the park's north entrance, Richard E. Beaty had a roadside stand where he sold my first Shenandoah guidebook and two books of his own. Beaty had left Harmony Hollow as a young man and lived 20-some years in Washington State, often longing for his boyhood home. He wrote a small novel, *The Mountain Angels*, out of homesickness. Though fictional, it's filled with an authentic reliving of the freedom in these mountains, of finding wild strawberries, huckleberries, wild grapes, chestnuts, hazelnuts, hickory nuts, honey in bee trees, and the sweetest persimmons.

It also deals with people of different origins, white and black. In his frank preface, Beaty hints sympathy with black people and a tendency— not uncommon among park-land residents—to prefer the Union over the Confederacy. He's critical of "deserters from the Southern army" who formed "bands of thieves and cutthroats that took advantage of a war torn country." One of his characters before the Civil War is a free black woman, descended from slaves released in large numbers by an early Virginia planter. Beaty must have been acquainted with such people in real life. Though blacks, other than as slaves, were quite rare in the park-

Mountain people were experts at "trouting." This barefoot lad was fishing along
Jeremys Run when a park-promotion photographer, Harry Staley, came along in the
mid-1920s. (Harry Staley)

land's past, this Beaty glimpse belatedly intrigues me, as do black
cemeteries in the park and ownership of an 812-acre park-land tract in
Augusta mountains by "John West estate (colored)." There should be
further research for black participation in the park's past.

Blue Ridge people, like many other early Americans, felt the
supernatural in almost everything. Clyde Knight, in his *Pathways to
Remember*, a deeply genuine recent book, said witchcraft upset his
community—Bacon Hollow, below the park's Powell Gap—and other
people both in the piedmont and the mountain in this present century.
When he was a boy, witches with evil powers were believed actively in
league with the devil. They could change themselves into nonhuman
forms. Cows might suddenly stop giving milk because of witchery.
People quickly destroyed fingernail trimmings or cut-off hair, because
witches might lay a curse on you through them. Many people in remote
areas, mountain or not, believed in ha'nts returning from the dead to scare
or torture—sometimes maybe to cheer—the living.

Evil was usually more than canceled out by good. Where no churches
were handy, a mountain man, educated or not, might "get the call" and
become a preacher. George Buracker who lived east of Big Meadows had
public prayer services in his home, then preached at Sunday services in
the new school that President and Mrs. Hoover created near their camp
on the Rapidan. Warren Corbin got the call and created a church in
Nicholson Hollow. Gordon A. "Gurd" Cave, of the Caves mentioned
at the end of Chapter 4, preached in Dark Hollow and built a church
alongside the Gordonsville–New Market Turnpike. He also traveled to
preach in the Shenandoah Valley.

In October 1933, Gurd Cave wrote to the Virginia conservation
commission: "I have lived hear all my life and have had my father's

Moonshine still found in Hazel "country," now part of the national park. Not all residents of the mountain made and sold illegal liquor; some had made legal (government-licensed) commercial liquor for decades, and some made a little whiskey or brandy for their own use but not to sell. The "census" of 1934 found that only 17 of the 465 resident families had cash income from moonshine, while 49 sold farm crops for money, and 331 got cash by working at the Skyland resort or at farms in lowlands. (NPS)

Old copper "worm" from a good-sized still was found near a spring about a mile below (west) of Jewell Hollow Overlook on the Skyline Drive.

possession which he left me. . . . i have never rented of no body . . . but have lived as a squatter and i claim my rights." Though Charles Koontz of Stanley had the deed to the large tract on which Cave had settled without permission, the state honored the time-and-use–established rights and paid separately for the long-used home and land and for the church. After leaving the park, Cave built another church and continued his evangelism. He and his wife also operated a store. They celebrated their 60th wedding anniversary in 1966.

Park-land residents fitted the mountain folk image in some ways but not in others. Most of them were inclined toward religion and toward independent living in isolation from, and indifference to, the "civilizing" influences of the world. Some of them played fiddles, sang unwritten songs, told unwritten tales, made and drank moonshine. Sometimes the men fought, usually when drinking heavily. Here and there, at times, as elsewhere, a murder happened. But these people differed in ancestry and major aspects of behavior from the popular image of mountain folk. Few of them were Scotch-Irish, and they were not noted for opposing clans carrying on deadly feuds from one generation to another.

Efforts to define Shenandoah park region people are bound to be either endless or partly wrong. Approximately five hundred families were here before a national park effort began, less than two per square mile. They were an unorganized, nonhomogeneous, tiny minority in each of the eight counties, in contrast to more typical mountaineers, who were homogeneous populations that formed strong majorities in nearly two hundred counties elsewhere in the Appalachians. Being so few and so far scattered here, they had no opportunity for, hence little interest in, local political influence. Sometimes, though, quite a few of them voted for favorites among candidates for national positions.

An unidentified mountain man plowing a rocky slope, behind a reluctantly pulling mule. Corn was to be planted here. Despite steepness and boulders, much of the Blue Ridge had fertile soil. In places, however, there were grievous losses from erosion. (NPS)

Early in the 1880s, Episcopalians (Anglicans) of Augusta and Rockingham counties started what they called "the work among the mountain folk" who were "for the most part destitute." By 1887 the Grace Memorial Church had been completed on the battlefield of Port Republic, and the bishop had consecrated it to "the gospel of peace" and declared "the hills around it echo to the hymns of redemption." A missionary to the mountain people here was Eleanor Wheat, a great-great-granddaughter of Thomas Lewis, who had lived nearby. A 1912 report by Rev. J. R. Ellis tells of a mission at "historic Brown's Gap" and of four schools along the Blue Ridge being attended by approximately two hundred children. Though Virginia had public schools serving places where families weren't exactly few, the financing wasn't adequate to serve remote places with scant and scattered populations.

The Church of the Brethren, launched in this region by early German farmers, did missionary and educational work on both sides of the Blue Ridge. Clyde Knight tells about Rev. Mr. S. A. Sanger, for instance, who spent 35 years, starting about 1886, helping to educate people in the mountains of Greene County. Knight also credits Miss Nelie Wampler of this church and its Bridgewater College for valuable educational effort in the Blue Ridge, starting at the one-room Bacon Hollow school in 1909. Other churches and different institutions and individuals, sometimes mountain residents themselves, started schools or helped keep them going.

The vastest mission and school operation on the park-land was set in motion by an Episcopal clergyman named Frederick William Neve, the kind of person around whom legends grow. Born in Kent in 1855, graduated from Oxford in 1879 with further degrees to follow, ordained priest in 1881, Neve served parishes in England for seven years. He reached Virginia on May 6, 1888, and began serving in Albemarle County. He tells:

> A mountaineer who used to come to Church . . . would always bring me an Albemarle Pippin and hand it to me . . . without saying a word. One Sunday, however, he broke the silence and said, "I want to jine the Church." So I rode up to his little cabin on top of the mountain. . . . He dragged a box out from under the bed and produced an old fiddle, gazing anxiously at me to see whether I disapproved. I asked him to play something and from the quavering notes I made out the tune of, "Jesus, Lover of My Soul."

Neve rode in the mountains often, asking himself what he could do for "the poor people . . . shut off from civilization for generations." His eyes were crossed, and the Blue Ridge people were soon telling each other, "One of his eyes is on the mountains and the other is on us." He

Prudent families put up hay to help feed cows or other domestic "critturs" when winter got rough, though it was possible for such animals to survive until spring by browsing the forest.

rode a small horse called Old Harry, and his legs almost touched the ground, especially on steep slopes, but he got where he wanted to go when he wanted to get there, regardless of weather or other difficulties. Often he slept in cabin lofts between feather mattresses, with bacon slabs hanging from the rafters and pumpkins in a corner, snow maybe sifting lightly into the loft and covering everything with white dust. He felt the people were deprived spiritually, medically, and educationally. He envisioned missions and schools at ten-mile intervals along the top of the Blue Ridge to serve and save them all.

Neve's stories brought response from people at a distance. He proved capable of raising funds, perhaps partly because he mixed dire reports with humor aimed at himself. One anecdote was about the seat splitting out of borrowed pants as he leaned over to baptize some people in a creek; he had to sneak out of there through the bushes. Another had him insisting he would walk from a funeral to the cemetery, while all the people insisted he must ride. The people won, and he had to ride in the undertaker's lap on top of the horse-drawn hearse.

In 1900, encouraged by donations from church women in Richmond, Neve hired a young lady teacher and took her up to Simmons Gap. "We had no equipment and scarcely any money," he wrote later, "but I felt that the people were the lost sheep of the Good Shepherd and that if we would try to find them for Him He would undoubtedly bless our efforts." Four years later the bishop of Virginia appointed Neve the archdeacon of the Blue Ridge. The work launched by the valley Episcopalians was added to his system.

The first teacher was Angeline Fitzhugh. The Simmons Gap school building was a small frame structure, never painted. Shenandoah park

Stone sledge or stone boat may be the proper identity of the framework of thick boards—and broken metal runner—in the foreground, its front right corner almost touching the dog. With heavy planks on top and horses or oxen to pull, it helped clear big boulders off cropland, maybe to be built into massive stone fences. This was probably the home of Anna Eliza Dean, lifetime resident, Hensley Hollow, 1935. Boulders are still in evidence at that site, arranged in fences or supporting terraces with patches or fields. (NPS)

ranger Roy Sullivan, widely known for being struck repeatedly by lightning, yet finally dying from another cause, attended school there through the seventh grade. He remembered about 35 students in that one-teacher school. They came from approximately 15 families living within a four-mile circle; most of them, like his own family, were just outside present park-land, which is narrow here. Quite a few of the families were turnpike-and-railroad-constructing Irish, and large, Sullivan told me, but well supplied with food and other necessities.

Roy's parents had a farm with many cattle, sheep, hogs, and chickens. They hauled tanbark to Elkton and got a good price for it. They also sold chestnut rails, locust posts, hickory handles, chairs with white-oak–splint bottoms, and, when chestnuts were ripe, several hundred pounds of them a day at 4–5¢ a pound. Some neighbors hunted and trapped fox and bobcat for furs. Roy's grandfather, Ira Sullivan, had hunted bears and sold skin and meat for $5. Roy hunted rabbits and sold them for 25¢ each to the George Herring store down northwest on the road toward Elkton.

Archdeacon Neve kept riding up on Old Harry. In 1902 he started another school and mission on Frazier Mountain (now Loft). The Fraziers who lived there were Scotch-Irish, an ancestry rare on park-land. Some Fraziers were landowners; others, tenants. Miley Frazier was a tenant on the vast cattle range of Scotch-Irish Pattersons.

Neve kept praying to become "a thousandfold more useful," and he kept expanding the work. A stone chapel was built at Simmons Gap in

1908. There were more and more women workers, mostly volunteers. Some received small salaries when, occasionally, funds were ample, but many women remained volunteers in the mountains decade after decade, teaching school, tending the sick, holding church services. Soon there were missions and schools inside and outside the present park boundary all the way from the south end north to Big Meadows. Sooner or later a stone church would be built at the different sites. Among those not already named were Mission Home, with a church, hospital, and school, in the foothills east of Simmons Gap and Loft Mountain; Bacon Hollow school; Pocosan (Pocosin) Mission, including both the upper mission and school inside the park, north of Dean Mountain, and lower mission in flatter lands to the east; Tanners Ridge school and chapel at the park boundary near Big Meadows; and Pine Grove mission church in the hollow down below and westward.

Scientifically oriented work among the mountain folk started ten miles north of the northernmost of Neve's institutions. Business and professional people had been summering at the Skyland resort for two decades. Being in a different cultural compartment, as were the clergymen, they, too, saw the mountain residents as destitute or deprived, though also as intriguing characters. To the mountain folk, the city folk were, in turn, characters. These groups of so-different cultures entertained each other, with the Blue Ridge folk often most aware of this role. They were amused by city folks' unsophisticated reactions to them and to wild nature, and they were pulled toward taking advantage.

The mountain families didn't consider themselves destitute, but some "read" the affluent visitors' minds and played up to them, partly because it was fun and partly for the gifts. They'd put on their worst clothes instead of their best when likely to meet the city people. They'd go barefooted when they might not otherwise. The men would make a point of carrying old guns. Some would intentionally overuse words and phrases that caused puzzlement or amusement. Yet their acting was seldom so very far from their reality. In regular life their clothes were sometimes old and brier torn; they had things to do that dress-up clothes weren't suited for. Many of them honestly liked to go barefoot, especially the young ones. Their regular language did include old-English oddities. A sack was a *poke*, and they usually *toted* it instead of carried it. Birds might make *nest-es* (two syllables), and the things holding up fences might be *post-es*. Brush was most often *bresh*. Poison was *pizen*. A snake *querled* up, not coiled up.

In the 1920s Dr. Roy Lyman Sexton—as a Skyland guest and a leader in the Potomac Appalachian Trail Club, Washington, D.C.—began

Picket fences were a common feature of mountain yards and gardens. Records indicate this was the Seldon Dodson home in the Madison County part of the park in the mid-1930s. (NPS)

worrying that the mountain diet didn't give adequate nutrition and that marriages between relatives were doing genetic damage. He and helpers he recruited immunized some of the people against likely diseases. George Corbin of Nicholson Hollow, the quintessential home of park-land folk, remembered Dr. Sexton as the man who carried a movie camera and "took the folks' tonsils out."

Dr. Sexton reported "astounding conditions," but after becoming better acquainted he found most mountain folk thrifty and healthy. He credited cabbage "which they bury in the ground and thus have a continuous supply the year around." However, he called the folk "the forgotten people of the Shenandoah" and, like Archdeacon Neve, thought they needed to be saved.

Articles were published about the direst living conditions. Social workers and theorists came to look. One result was a 1933 book called *Hollow Folk*, which the authors Mandel Sherman and Thomas R. Henry claimed contained "a wealth of material for scientists" about "the growth and decline of human culture." The descriptions of life in the Skyland–Old Rag area weren't intended to be complete; details were selected to support a theoretical framework. Unfortunately, the theory insulted the people, and the book has been widely hated.

The foundation idea seems to have been that the lifeway of restlessly striving city folk was best, representing civilization as it ought to be, and that lifeways and people got worse as they differed from this city style. Rural lowland thoroughly interconnected with cities might rate a B. As city connections and imitation dwindled, ratings dropped. Nicholson Hollow was presented around D level; Corbin Hollow got an F.

There was a wide gulf between cultures. Looking from a distance into something foreign to their understanding, the authors complained that these strange people had few neuroses and were "without the sense of insecurity so common among people in other situations"; most of them seemed "to have no wish to escape from reality." So, you see, it's most civilized to have drastic conflicts, to become neurotic, to feel insecure, and to wish to escape reality.

I'll put aside the *Hollow Folk* book and try to fathom the cultural contrast. From within each side that side looks right. Yet something seems to have turned a bit that shouldn't have. A large part of the original American dream, whether dreamed by a Jost Heydt with chests of gold or by an Amos Corbin, who reached Corbin Hollow without funds to buy land but made a home anyway, was to live uncrowded in peace and freedom surrounded by beauty and abundance. This dream came true for a large proportion of the park-land people. Few of them ever had much money, but far from being deprived, they could and usually did draw on a greater diversity of abundance than the average lowlander could afford.

Sparkling pure water came from the depths. The soil produced richly not far from the kitchen door. Apple trees were handy. Wild berries and nuts grew nearby, the tasty black walnuts right in the yard. Hogs fattened on natural foods. Cows thrived on mountain grass and shrubs. Even after the larger wild animals were gone, there were rabbits, squirrels, groundhogs, opossums, raccoons. Many kinds of foods could be, and were, kept for winter "canned" or smoked or stored in a root cellar. Fish were easy to catch when you knew their habits. Firewood was all around. If lumber was needed to repair the house or add another outbuilding, trees could be cut, and a nearby mill would saw them on shares, no cash needed. Furniture, baskets, and other useful things could also be made.

Most mountain men worked hard at times, but they probably enjoyed more leisure than the average man of the dominant culture. Mountain women worked more hours than most of the men but seldom under pressure equaling that imposed by urban and suburban conditions. Spinning and weaving at home had generally ceased after the Civil War, but cloth and other things were buyable with eggs or berries or chestnuts or shelled-out walnuts.

A balanced view of park-land residents, gleaned from acquaintance with every family at the time of park establishment, was written by "the Homestead Lady," Mozelle R. Cowden (later Brown). Though no

A graceful home with apple tree and picket-fenced garden plot. Mountain homes in the drought-and-depression–plagued 1930s varied from tumbledown to stubbornly neat to ruggedly beautiful. (NPS)

family was actually typical, the "statistically" typical family had five members, the parents educated one to four years, the children mostly not in school. The log house was reasonably clean and had flowers around the door. Vegetables, dried apples and beans, kraut, potatoes, pumpkins, and cabbage were stored for winter. The family had a hog, some chickens, and a cow. Money income was $100–$150 a year. Health was good, except for teeth. The Homestead Lady didn't observe many drunkards or violent people. She found mountain residents kind and helpful, frugal, accurate in what they said, possessing a keen sense of justice. She liked them but thought it was fortunate they would soon be moving closer to doctors, dentists, and schools.

Life in the mountains was getting more difficult because the local support industries such as mills were dying out, soil fertility was weakening, chestnut trees had died, and the lifeway outside the mountains was diverging from that inside. Yet the mountain people felt they were living a good life, more enjoyable in many ways than that of most city people, and I agree. This book celebrates the people who lived in, or otherwise used and loved, the park's mountains.

CHAPTER XV

National Park Dreamers

A teenage boy named George Freeman Pollock traveled by train to Luray in 1886 and persuaded a farmer to guide him up Stony Man Mountain. He'd come to examine a copper mine in which his father owned much stock, but the autumn-colored, hazily magic, mountain-and-valley scenery took possession of him. "Then and there," he would write years later, "I made up my mind to consecrate my life to the development of this, my father's land." His purpose was human enjoyment, not minerals or timber. He would "tell the world" and show the world how wonderful Stony Man was.

Born in Brooklyn in 1869, Pollock was raised in Washington, D.C., and Massachusetts. His father and mother wanted him to become a teacher, but he longed to be a naturalist adventuring in wilderness. He persuaded Smithsonian Institution to accept wild specimens he collected, and he had hoped to catch some on his first trip to the Blue Ridge. But he forgot to try for specimens, just as he forgot to look at the mine, in his amazement over the scenery. Pollock was like that, a dreamer, a reacher for the far out or the impossible. Always a small person physically, he would become one of the giants in the genesis of Shenandoah National Park.

Young Pollock hurried home and persuaded his father and several friends to come and see Stony Man. He brought other parties out to camp on a high, almost-level site below the peak. In 1889, while he was still a minor, a Blue Ridge Park Association was formed in Washington, with his father as a director. A promotional pamphlet said the members were "gentlemen, business men, men of affairs, artists and professionals, men of letters and students, from Washington, Boston and New York." Similar people were invited to join—"to maintain here . . . a health resort, where the weary men may flee and find abundant rest and freedom."

Though our teenager had inspired that organization, he soon got impatient and tried a different move to turn his dream of a superbly scenic resort into reality. He initiated a partnership—"Kearney, English &

Pollock, Mill Owners, Builders and Contractors, also Proprietors of the Blue Ridge Park Livery Stables, Stony Man, Page Co., Virginia." The company would produce lumber on the site and erect any structures ordered. But orders were slow. To raise desperately needed funds, the determined youth executed a handwritten contract, selling all the chestnut-oak bark lying on a ridgetop tract to which his father's title was at least somewhat clear. Revenue from this deal helped keep the still-nebulous dream alive.

Then the elder Pollock died. Business partners and greedy officers of the association tried to squeeze young Pollock out. He fought back, held on, and finally got a beginning of his dream into solid form—several cabins on the Stony Man shelf. In his 20s, seriously short of operating capital, he attracted a socially prominent couple who would, if pleased, influence many prosperous friends to join his Stony Man Camp clientele. Carrying their luggage, he conducted them to their cabin. When he opened the door, he was shocked to see a rattlesnake coiled in the center of the room. Turning, he said quietly, "'The cabin isn't quite ready," and closed the door behind him. Quickly he opened the back window. He grabbed the venomous snake bare-handed and threw it out. Then he welcomed the guests in.

Pollock wanted everything for his guests and often spent more than he took in. He had a keen sense of drama and entertained with varied spectacles, usually with himself at center stage—demonstrating good judgment, as he really was a great showman. He became notorious for tremendous bonfires at Skyland, easily visible from the valley below. He must have felt Indians haunting old Stony Man, and he began a line of dreaming that would lead to costumed pageants featuring Indian characters and romantic events, such as "The Wedding of Wetona."

Mountain residents worked for him. They also peddled moonshine and wildflowers, nuts, and berries, sometimes white-oak–splint baskets, a handcrafted product they'd continued to make. Sometimes, drinking too much of their own whiskey or brandy, they became troublesome. But Pollock coped well and turned the "mountaineers" into a continuing pageant helping to entertain his guests. A villainous-acting mountain resident named Fletcher threatened him with a large pistol, apparently trying to scare him off the mountain. But Pollock didn't scare well at all. He began carrying a pistol, too, practicing till he was an expert, and he brought a monstrous dog from Washington, D.C. Fletcher was the one who left the area. Another brush was with Aaron Nicholson, the imposing "King of Free-State Hollow," who claimed to own a great sweep of the mountain including much of Pollock's land. But Aaron, too, failed to gain dominance over "the Little Chief of Stony Man Camp."

Black Rock Springs Hotel, in what has become the park's south district, preceded Stony Man Camp or Skyland by more than half a century. Even earlier, Thomas Jefferson and a few others were enjoying the scenic beauty and recreational opportunities of the Blue Ridge. (From an old, old glass-plate photograph, courtesy of Arnold L. Via)

Nicholson and Pollock, two strong men, came to respect each other. Not because of Pollock, the quintessential "mountaineer" moved out of the park-land early in the 1900s and lived his concluding years on lower land.

Pollock may not have known that Thomas Jefferson, riding horseback, was more than a century ahead of him in discovering and praising Blue Ridge scenery. If he had, he might have dramatized himself as Jefferson. But Teddy Roosevelt fitted his nature better, and he began dressing like that rough-rider in fringed buckskin. Pollock blew a bugle to awaken guests and to mobilize horseback excursions to The Limberlost and White Oak Falls or Crescent Rock or Stony Man peak. He yodeled. He performed by handling large, live rattlesnakes and by telling dramatic stories, many of them about his adventures with the mountaineers.

It's unlikely Pollock knew in the early years that he had a long-established competitor—the Black Rock Springs Hotel, high on the Blue Ridge, 45 miles south. It was a summering place for socialites, mostly from tidewater Virginia and from Baltimore and Philadelphia. Annual stays at high-elevation resorts were considered a must for children of successful planters and businessmen, to avoid malaria, according to Shenandoah Valley historian John Wayland. Stories were told of long-ago brides and grooms who first met at Black Rock Springs, which was promoted as "superior to all the spas of Europe" and may have been operating as early as 1830 inside the present park boundary.

The Black Rock Springs Hotel burned three times. Pollock must have sympathized when the big fire of 1909 came over the mountains and destroyed this competitor just as his own similar business was growing rapidly. The hotel building had accommodated three dozen people at a time. There were also 30 private cottages, all wiped out along with bridges on the road up to the resort. The news would have given Pollock an uneasy feeling but maybe also a boost. Summer residents of Black Rock might become summer residents of Skyland; he was always reaching out, personally and through impressive booklets and newsletters. But, proud as he was of Furnace Spring at his Stony Man Camp, he didn't decide to feature "the waters." He did construct a swimming pool, however, and have a wild pool ready for guests near a White Oak waterfall, and his guests did enjoy mountain spring water. And he did have a ballroom, perhaps equal to the one that had burned at Black Rock, and as that hotel resort had done he hired musicians, many of them black, to play for the dancing and other festivities.

By 1910 there were many bark-covered cabins and an ornately rustic dining hall on the high shelf of Stony Man. Horseback trails led to scenic attractions that are still among the most popular in the park. When forest fires or human depredation threatened, Pollock fought to protect the scenery, regretting now that he'd been forced to sell so many chestnut oaks. Stony Man Camp became Skyland, a "dude ranch and resort" so large it had its own post office.

About the time Pollock was getting up his courage to propose to a "Spanish-type" beauty named Addie Nairn, who had inherited a "handsome fortune"—the quoted words are his—she was building stone-buttressed Massanutten Cottage at Skyland. This cottage, soon the Pollocks' home when they were on the mountain, is saved now as a historic structure. Pollock's financial dependability increased after the marriage. His wife might help when he was in the worst predicaments, but still he ran up bills he couldn't pay. She was a strong woman and wisely refrained from rescuing him consistently. An especially note-worthy sharing of costs happened in 1920 when Mr. and Mrs. Pollock paid $1,000 to a timber cutter named Grim to save a hundred of the choicest "virgin" hemlocks in The Limberlost, which was near Skyland but not on Pollock property.

Guests came not only from far cities but sometimes also from nearby lowlands. Miller E. Roudabush, a leading flour miller of Page County and a pioneer in generating electricity from Shenandoah River waterpower, often brought his family up the "carriage road." The Roudabushes usually stayed at Fell Cottage. Roudabush often rode far by himself, exploring the Blue Ridge. He enjoyed visiting mountain people. He arranged for a Thomas girl to be raised by his mother in the valley. She prospered there but chose to return to the Blue Ridge—demonstrating

Miller E. Roudabush, gristmill owner and leading businessman of Page County, along with friends, used the park-land recreationally and quite regularly, beginning a decade before the park was proposed. Roudabush camped and fished along Rapidan River every year beginning in 1914. Jeremys Run became a favorite stream in the 1920s. He knew and enjoyed people living full-time in the mountains. The vehicles here on high grassland are loaded with recreational supplies and equipment. (Photo by Miller E. Roudabush, lent by his daughter, Jessie Ann Price).

Young George Freeman Pollock at a playful time when the elaborate, bark-covered dining hall at Skyland was new. (Anonymous)

Well-dressed ladies enjoyed the great cliffs of Stony Man many years before there was a national park here. Skyland was described then as a "dude ranch and resort." (Zerkel collection, SNP archives)

that some people just naturally love mountain life. She married in the mountains and was the mother of Ray Buracker, the boy who would give President Hoover an opossum and thus bring an excellent small school to the Blue Ridge.

A prominent lumberman of the valley, James O. Bailey, and his family often stayed at Skyland. Bailey sometimes lent money to Pollock. Janie Bailey (now Janie Spitler) remembers Skyland when the light was from coal oil lamps and the heat only from fireplaces, mountain men keeping wood supplies on the porches of all cottages. Later, Janie was a summer telephone girl at Skyland. The possibility of a national park had been mentioned, and many VIPs were calling. She got to know Mrs. Pollock best. Addie Nairn Pollock wasn't as gregarious as George, Janie remembers. The summers were long for her, but she was a delightful person. She read a great deal. One summer she invited Janie up alone— she had "Massanutten Cottage looking so beautiful!" She gave her guest a splendid amethyst (Janie's birthstone).

The Skyland environment and program had resemblances to those of western national parks in that era, but Pollock didn't originate the idea of a national park here. Ever since the 1880s there'd been a dream of an immense Southern Appalachian park, but the movement didn't spring directly from that southern dream. The first mention here was by a secretary of the Front Royal-Riverton Board of Trade, Hugh E. Naylor. As long ago as World War I, Naylor was urging his organization to campaign for a national park near Front Royal—to help build travel business—but this idea didn't lead to action either.

The spark with a direct connection came from Stephen T. Mather, the forceful first director of the National Park Service. Mather had been dreaming since 1919 of a large national park in the Appalachians, a park that would be an eastern equivalent of Yosemite or Rocky Mountain. He was interested, of course, in conservation of the East's forest and wildlife, but he had a political motive, too. He worried that a park system with "crown jewels" only in the West might fail to hold majority support in Congress when funds were scarce. He needed citizen support where most of the people lived.

Mather finally put his dream into his annual report of 1923, published early in 1924. His boss, Dr. Hubert Work, the secretary of the interior, transformed the spark into a torch. Mather and Work chose five men with nationwide reputations in national park-type recreation to become an advisory committee and discover a top-quality site containing 500,000 or more acres (for a list of committee members for this and other groups formed to work toward park establishment, see Appendix 2). The

Massanutten Lodge, now historic as the Skyland home of the Pollocks, was built in 1918 on the initiative and at the expense of Mrs. Pollock, recently Addie Nairn. The stonework was done by notorious mountain man Charlie (C. D.) Sisk.

Horses were part of the Skyland personality and helped create strong supporters of the national park proposal. Mrs. Pollock (on a white horse) and Mr. Pollock are prominent side by side at front center. (Photo by Harry Staley from the Zerkel collection, SNP archives)

chairman was Dr. Henry W. Temple, a congressman from Pennsylvania, formerly a professor of history with special interest in bison-Indian trails.

When the Southern Appalachian National Park Committee first met in March 1924, more than 20 sites had already been suggested. Shenandoah Valley businessmen, including Naylor, had their idea in—create a national park by transferring lands from the national forest in the valley region. No one had suggested Skyland and vicinity. The committee was overworked with inspections, none near the Shenandoah. Rumor said Great Smoky Mountains would easily win.

Harold Allen, a government attorney well acquainted with Pollock and Skyland, couldn't keep sitting idly by. He'd clipped the news story when the committee was formed months before and sent it to Pollock with a note asking, "Why not Skyland?" Allen had waited and worried. Now he went to see park committeeman Col. Glenn S. Smith, an engineer with the U.S. Geological Survey, and was told no committee member was ready to believe a suitable site could exist within a hundred miles of the nation's capital. Allen told Smith they'd better open their minds, and Smith gave him a questionnaire to answer.

Pollock always remembered when Mr. and Mrs. Allen arrived at Skyland with the questionnaire. He'd been busy when he received Harold's note, but the main trouble was he just hadn't been able to make up his mind. Now he felt challenged. He'd dedicated himself to telling the world about Stony Man, hadn't he?

Allen, Pollock, and George H. Judd, a partner in the Washington plant that printed the *National Geographic*, sat down together in Judd's

An early bumper sticker and a persuasive pamphlet helped multiply advocates of the national park. (SNP archives)

cottage, out on the ridge point that seemed to soar over the deep valley. They talked and got up at intervals to pace among the furniture. Soon they were dictating a rough draft of questionnaire answers to Pollock's stenographer. Pollock claimed familiarity with 50,000 acres and general knowledge farther along the range. He proposed to explore at his own expense and report further. "We all got excited with the task as it progressed," he later wrote. "And no wonder! Just to recount the natural features . . . convinced us that we had a real national park site to present, and were perhaps making history."

Those first answers dealt with the area between Thornton and Fishers gaps. Enthusiasm soared beyond the truth here and there: "Numerous mountain peaks over 4,000 feet high," for instance, when there were but two; "large portions of this area . . . never touched with the axe," the whole area "absolutely free" of "improvements," and "no devastation by fire throughout the entire region." But a lot was true—magnificent panoramic views, beautiful streams with waterfalls and pools, fine hemlock, oak, ash, tulip poplar, chestnut, and an opportunity for a permanent bird and mammal refuge. The lyric climax was reached with these words: "In autumn, with the profusion of fall flowers and berries everywhere and the varied and brilliant coloring of the giant trees, mass

Pollock (pointing here) took advantage of every opportunity to show and praise the scenic beauty of the Blue Ridge. His friends and guests were mostly people of influence in major American cities—Boston, New York, Philadelphia, Baltimore, Washington, D.C., and on south. (Zerkel collection, SNP archives)

color effects greet the eye in every direction, indescribable in beauty and grandeur."

Pollock quickly got testimonial letters from influential people who had been guests at Skyland. With a Washington friend who knew the government from the inside, he called on Colonel Smith and, so he reported, "talked loud and long." Smith failed to resist him. Smith and fellow committeeman William A. Welch, the manager of Palisades Interstate Park in New York and New Jersey, reached Luray on September 12 and were met by "two delegations," one favoring Massanutten Mountain, the other the Blue Ridge. Luray real estate broker L. Ferdinand Zerkel, a director of the new regional chamber of commerce, Shenandoah Valley, Inc., had organized the greeting, complete with a brass band. Zerkel scored a big diplomatic success that day, turning Naylor and his whole promotional institution into backers of Skyland-Blue Ridge. Pollock took care of impressing Smith and Welch, and they said they'd come back when they had more time and they'd try to bring the whole advisory committee.

Zerkel would qualify as one of a half-dozen crucial workers for this national park. Though not immediately overwhelming, he had endless staying power and could interrelate the most complex affairs. If a national park were created here, his real estate business would increase, of course, yet he was but mildly selfish. He simply loved to get people together, especially "enemies" who hadn't yet realized they'd gain more from cooperating than from competing. Mr. and Mrs. Zerkel were collectors of relics from the long past, including Indians, and hoped to open a museum in Luray, though they guessed it wouldn't pay for itself (which later proved true).

"Everybody" had to see White Oak Canyon. Here's an influential group at the top of one of the many waterfalls there. Pollock is at right against the bedrock, his mobilizing bugle in his lap. (Zerkel collection, SNP archives)

Pollock and Zerkel became president and board chairman of the Northern Virginia Park Association, which was formed to win over the park selection committee. Pollock, who was intimately familiar with the pattern of land ownership and use, and Zerkel, a real estate professional, must have seen the near-impossibility of acquiring all the private land here for a great national park, and they must have known that such a thing had never been done before—anywhere. But they were too deeply involved to hesitate now. Zerkel organized and indoctrinated Shenandoah Valley business leaders along with other leaders around Virginia and in Washington.

Pollock's life flowered that fall, as if all his friendships and all his experiences had been preparation for convincing people that this part of the Blue Ridge was created to become a national park. Everyone he could reach got the treatment. Promotional material included the association's 16-page pamphlet, "A National Park near the Nation's Capital," and a flood of personally dictated letters. Pollock invited influential people to Skyland as his personal guests. He invited photographers and guided them to scenic places when illumination and recreational action were right. He (and Addie Nairn Pollock?) paid out thousands of dollars for new trails and for viewing towers above treetop level on mountaintops. He furnished horses and accompanied dignitaries to interpret the mountain forest that he considered "primeval"—though it was far from meeting conservationists' definition of the word.

Secretary Work's committeemen came—all but one—and spent a week or more inspecting the area, acting pleased. Perhaps even more meaningful for the long pull was the arrival, to join one expedition's finale, of the Virginia governor, E. Lee Trinkle. The governor was seeing Virginia in a contest with other states. At stake was urgently needed economic advancement; Virginia had lagged behind its potential ever since the Civil War. But Governor Trinkle was seeing even more, a possible return of the Virginia Commonwealth to its early eminence and glory. The park challenge was becoming to him an affair of honor, of reawakening the great Virginia spirit.

Pollock worried about the one committeeman who hadn't so much as acknowledged the many invitations he'd received—Harlan P. Kelsey, a landscape architect and botanist of Salem, Massachusetts, a former president of the Appalachian Mountain Club, and a firm advocate of Great Smoky. Pollock tried all the pressures. Finally, through Zerkel's friends of Shenandoah Valley, Inc., including Naylor, the reluctant Kelsey was brought to Front Royal. He was wined and dined there, and Col. H. J. Benchoff, a star orator, opened a way for him to reconcile his fondness for Smoky with a national park here:

Left: Harry Staley, master photographer, on Black Rock in the south district. His heavy and cumbersome camera went with him everywhere and powerfully advanced selection of the Blue Ridge as an appropriate location for the East's first vast national park. (Zerkel collection, SNP archives) *Right*: The Pollocks and Shenandoah Valley, Inc., spent $15,000 for viewing towers that put observers, including park-selection examiners, above the tree canopy for 360-degree panoramas. (Zerkel collection, SNP archives)

> Standing where I am tonight, a radius of four hundred miles includes . . . a population amounting to almost one-third of that of the whole country. . . . And as this is to be a park to meet the needs of the greatest number who will be attracted, it is not necessary to establish it so far from our Nation's Capital. Let us establish it here, and let us establish another later, farther down the line.

Next morning early, the valley leaders delivered Kelsey to Pollock. Naylor—who'd once favored Massanutten over the Blue Ridge, had had north district viewing towers built and horses hired with valley funds. The Kelsey inspection became one of Pollock's dramatic stories.

The party of 15 rode "over old logging roads and trails through a primeval forest" on the east slope of Mount Marshall. They inspected The Peak, then crossed over to the valley slope, riding the last ten miles in darkness. Pollock, who rode every day, got sore from so many hours on horseback, but Kelsey now wanted more equally strenuous days. Though the weather was bad next day, Pollock guided his once-reluctant guest from Luray to Big Meadows, then down to Bob Graves's bungalow near Doubletop. Kelsey rode up lofty Fork Mountain without Pollock and came back "inspired" by seeing the center of the proposed park from the tower Pollock's men had built, carrying the lumber "five miles" by hand.

Pollock then led Kelsey, in wind and cold, via Weakley's Ranch, Umbrella Rocks, Franklin Cliffs, Cowboy Fields, Spitler's Ranch, "the grand old peak of Hawksbill, and thence up the Devil's Stairway to Crescent Rock and through the Limberlost Swamp to Skyland." Strongly hungry by now and near exhaustion, they smelled the "heavenly aroma" of roasting duck. But there was a moon, and the air was clear except for mist around the peaks. It was "now or never" for Kelsey to see the view from Stony Man peak. Alone, the two urged their horses up the trail and tied them at the base of the tower. Pollock wrote:

> The tower rocked in a wind so strong that the skirt of my poncho was flapped up over my head as we climbed the narrow ladder. . . . I pointed out Old Rag Mountain to the east, clearly defined in the moonlight, and Mount Marshall, thirty miles away to the north. Completing the magic circle were the Piedmont Valley in mysterious mist to the east, the Shenandoah Valley with its faintly twinkling diamond and ruby lights to the west. . . . For accompaniment to this glorious outlook we could clearly hear the booming of waterfalls . . . below us to the west. And as we gazed entranced, our fragile tower was swaying, swaying, giving us the effect of a ship at sea. It was all almost unearthly, but it was very grand.

On December 12, 1924, Kelsey and the rest of the committee adopted what Colonel Benchoff had urged—"creation of the first national park in the Southern Appalachians" in the Virginia Blue Ridge between Front Royal and Waynesboro, with the hope "that its success will encourage the Congress to create a second park in the Great Smoky Mountains."

The committee's report made news all around the nation. Most of the articles spoke of seven hundred square miles of "primeval wilderness" that had somehow survived the forces of exploitation. Trinkle, Virginia's head booster, led a "battalion of 300" to Washington to push legislation through Congress quickly. When the time came for hearings, the main Shenandoah fear was the accusation of North Carolina newspapers that the Skyland–Blue Ridge area was so far from primeval that making it a park would throw 15,000 people out of their homes. Zerkel and Pollock prepared to refute that damaging contention.

Though they must have realized the accusation represented one valid way of seeing the facts, I'm quite sure they felt the mountains were as wild as anybody would want them to be—and no one would be thrown out. Surely the "mountaineers" would be kept as part of the natural environment. Surely the cattle would still graze on the vast pasturelands, keeping them open for the panoramic views. Surely Pollock himself would continue to operate Skyland as he had for decades. Some kind of leasing policy would take care of such things.

It didn't matter at the moment, anyhow. The accusation never came up in the congressional hearings. What was getting the attention was the

National park experts and energizers line up by the Skyland dining hall during the
National Conference on State Parks in 1925. Second from left is Pollock, then come four
not identified, then Glenn S. Smith, secretary of Southern Appalachian National Park
Committee; Stephen T. Mather, National Park Service director; governor of Virginia, E.
Lee Trinkle; U.S. secretary of the interior, Hubert Work; A. C. Carson, Front Royal
attorney and judge; Congressman Henry W. Temple, chairman of the SANP committee;
Gilbert Grosvenor, editor and head of *National Geographic*; and George H. Judd of Judd
and Detweiler, Printers, Washington, D.C., who owned a splendid cottage at Skyland.
(Zerkel collection, SNP archives)

insistence of the Smoky people that their park be on a par with Shenandoah and then the insistence of Kentuckians that a Mammoth Cave park
be in the bill, too. Secretary Work and key congressmen agreed on
Smoky; so did Trinkle and other Virginians. But almost nobody was
ready for Mammoth Cave—yet. As it turned out, that didn't matter very
much either. The final bill wouldn't establish any parks. It would just give
a bit of official status to the Temple committee, changing it to commission, and give it a few thousand dollars to hire a clerk and for members
to scout where boundaries might be if any park were to be established and
if anybody might donate any suitable land or money to buy some.
Congress had never appropriated money to buy national parks and wasn't
about to start doing so.

The three-park bill did pass in February 1925, and it was a door open
a crack where it had been locked before, open enough for Shenandoah
enthusiasts to push farther. That seemed to mean: Raise land-purchase
money. Secretary Work interpreted the bill to mean that, between
Shenandoah and Smoky, the park that raised the most the fastest was most
likely to win the favor of the Interior Department and of Congress.

Park supporters, including the Temple commission, seemed puzzled for several months. How does anyone proceed to make hundreds of thousands of acres of private land, populated and used by unknown numbers of people for two centuries, into a national park? There was no precedent. Not knowing what else to do, Pollock invited the fifth annual National Conference on State Parks to Skyland for the last week in May 1925. He outdid himself telling and showing the attractions of the Blue Ridge. Delegates from all over the country had a great time.

The most significant thing that happened, though, was that Dan Wine, secretary of Shenandoah Valley, Inc., and of the Northern Virginia Park Association, had an idea. In conversation between formal sessions, when the problem of establishing Shenandoah was being casually tossed around, he said something like "Buy an Acre at $6." That was it! If thousands of people would just buy one acre . . . The recently retired board chairman of an automobile company, quick on the draw, handed Dan Wine the money for ten acres. Others caught the fever and "bought"— or pledged.

Diplomat and workhorse Ferdinand Zerkel soon found himself saddled with a full-time job as executive secretary of the nonprofit Shenandoah National Park Association, campaigning statewide for $2.5 million. He was to receive $3,000 a year plus expenses "to be paid as funds are available." Academy headmaster and orator Colonel Benchoff was elected president; Wine, secretary. Pollock, not as much given to raising money as to spending it, avoided involvement. But he couldn't resist making a showy pledge of one thousand acres of park-land, not the money for it but the land deed itself.

Zerkel and Benchoff—and helpers including Governor Trinkle and soon-to-be governor, Harry Flood Byrd, who had a cottage at Skyland— organized Virginia, perhaps more completely than it had been organized for any project since the Civil War. The newly organized State Chamber of Commerce cooperated. Trinkle, a large and heavy man, traveled widely and energetically, boosting state patriotism, not just the park but anything that would bring business to Virginia. He soon said he'd lost 40 pounds in the effort. Byrd called the park "the greatest opportunity for economic advancement" and headed a front of well-known names representing all of Virginia.

Fund-raising professionals from New York were engaged. Pathé News made a movie of park region scenery and recreational action. Zerkel, Trinkle, and others wrote articles for national magazines. The new association's official pamphlet quoted Dr. W. J. Showalter of *National Geographic* as saying this park would bring into Virginia "at least one hundred million dollars annually." Volunteer coordinators throughout

Shenandoah
National Park
In Virginia

VIRGINIA
FIRST IN THE HEART OF THE NATION.

VIRGINIA STATE CHAMBER OF COMMERCE
GRACE-AMERICAN BUILDING
RICHMOND
1925

Virginia State Chamber of Commerce, newly organized to help Virginia rise again in the business world, put its weight behind the park proposal with an informative pamphlet featuring photographs in color (rare then in print), tastefully but not garishly tinted by hand. (NPS) the state recruited volunteer contact persons. Over and over, in many different words, it was said that the park was for the prosperity and the honor of Virginia.

There were rushes and stalls, of course. During the stalls Virginians were challenged by alleged park-fund achievements for Smoky or Mammoth Cave. Other states could not be allowed to win. Pollock helped through one stall by distributing a scary appeal to clients of Skyland. He said park protection had to be achieved quickly. Otherwise, "these mountains . . . will be covered with dead chestnut trees." Only the National Park Service could cope with the menace caused by an oriental fungus. The dry, flammable trees had to be removed before they could catch fire and spread it until all the beautiful scenery is gone "never to be replaced."

In another stall, a pep meeting was held at Richmond, Governor Trinkle and Governor-Elect Byrd presiding together. The president of the University of Virginia said, "It would be a tragic misfortune if Virginia should pass up this opportunity to obtain a national park." Very little was said about conservation during the furor of effort. When Byrd took office, he accepted chairmanship of a Statewide Fund-Getters Committee, saying the park would bring "enormous increases of the amount of cash going into the various normal channels of trade." The *Richmond Times-Dispatch* ran articles about western national parks, with frequent Blue Ridge pictures, equally scenic, to prove that Virginia deserved a place in the same world-renowned category.

The Shenandoah National Park Association, Inc., went to great lengths—or heights—to promote the park and raise money from Virginia citizens to buy the park-land from its private owners. (Zerkel collection, SNP archives)

Schoolchildren, it was said, were contributing nickels and dimes. The records credit railroads and a few other major travel businesses with $10,000 each. By far the largest amounts were pledged by business and professional men. On April 1, 1926, the deadline set by the Temple commission, the Virginia total was given by Zerkel, Benchoff, and Hollis Rinehart of Charlottesville, the association's treasurer, as $1,249,154 in pledges and cash. Though far short of the goal, the achievement was considered to prove a significant revival of the Virginia spirit. Meaningful amounts came from all over the state. The park campaign, Zerkel said, had broken down "the age-old jealousies . . . between the Old Dominion's 'Five Grand Divisions': The Valley, Piedmont, Southside, Tidewater, and Southwest."

The Temple commission and Secretary Work urged Congress to pass legislation that would actually authorize the establishment of both Shenandoah and Great Smoky as national parks when minimum acreages "have been transferred in fee simple to the United States." The minimum for Shenandoah was 385,500 acres. Congress responded quickly, and President Calvin Coolidge signed the Shenandoah-Smoky bill on May 22, 1926.

CHAPTER XVI

Conservation-Developers

When Harry Flood Byrd became governor early in 1926, he was determined to lift Virginia toward the prosperity and prestige it had enjoyed before the Civil War. He and the legislature quickly created the Virginia State Commission on Conservation and Development. Byrd persuaded his friend and campaign manager Will Carson to become chairman, partly because Carson had this paradoxical idea that Virginia could increase its development, with dignity instead of crass boosterism, by conserving its natural resources and historic traditions. For eight and one-half years Carson would risk his high political and industrial promise, sometimes his life, in acquiring the Shenandoah park-land from reluctant owners.

Carson "was a big, handsome, popular businessman and civic leader whom I have always regarded as the founder of Shenandoah National Park," wrote 96-year-old Horace M. Albright on Shenandoah's 50th anniversary. Albright was remembering when he was Park Service director following Mather, and Carson was working personally in the Blue Ridge with President Hoover, then with President Roosevelt.

People coming within range of Will Carson's personality might guess he was Irish, and he was. Born at Enniskillen in 1870, William Edward Carson attended school in Ireland, then at age 15 came to Riverton, near Front Royal, at the north end of what would be the park. His father had bought extensive limestone lands here and manufactured and sold burned lime and later hydrated lime. Will was soon working at the lime plant, and he became manager in 1895. After his father died in 1910, he introduced "Flamingo" for masonry mortar and gained a large volume of business. The National Lime Manufacturers' Association elected him president, and he became a leader in creating the U.S. Bureau of Mines and the Federal Reserve System. During World War I he was with the U.S. War Industry Board. All he'd learned in such experience—and more—would be needed to establish "the impossible park," the term many knowledgeable people applied to the Shenandoah proposal.

Virginia's new State Commission on Conservation and Development gathers with
Governor Harry F. Byrd and Chairman William E. Carson on the cliffs of Stony Man.
Also present were George Pollock, Arno B. Cammerer of NPS, L. Ferdinand Zerkel of
the Shenandoah National Park Association, and Glenn S. Smith of the Southern
Appalachian National Park Committee and the U.S. Geological Survey. (Photo by
Harry Staley, Zerkel collection, SNP archives)

Governor Byrd (right) and Chairman Carson in "Byrd Bath"—otherwise a mighty chilly White Oak Canyon pool. (Zerkel collection, SNP archives)

Carson and his six fellow commissioners and Byrd during his four years as governor were a team. As the conservation-development leader willing to give the most time (for $1 a year), Carson generated ideas, discussed them with the others, and then meshed them with reality, aided by the commission's staff. He soon saw that achieving the 385,500-acre minimum size for the park literally was impossible. That much suitable park-land simply didn't exist between Front Royal and Waynesboro. This "primeval wilderness" was populated by at least 30,000 people. The Shenandoah law must be amended.

Exploring diplomatically toward common ground, Carson wrote to Secretary of the Interior Work. Then he turned to another park puzzle, Zerkel's and Benchoff's hard-won land fund. There were 22,500 pledges, and he had the commission office mail collection notices for all of them. Two months later the payments totaled $409,368. Nearly four hundred notices came back from the post office unclaimed. It would be a miracle if anywhere near the $1.25 million pledged was ever collected, and even the full amount would hardly begin to buy the minimum acreage.

The Temple commission demanded that Virginia start buying land. The governor, Senator Claude A. Swanson, Colonel Benchoff, and several other influential men went to Washington with Carson. They said they had to see their way to actual park establishment before they could legally or morally spend pledged funds, and they simply couldn't see the wilderness park of 385,500 acres as realistic. A smaller park might be possible, and they asked for cooperation toward reducing the minimum. Work showed anger. He accused them of trying to capture an "invaluable asset," which a national park would be, "and have the national government pay for it." He dismissed the delegation. "I cannot, con-

Dinner was served to the state commission and associates at Bob Graves's Honeymoon Cottage, Doubletop Mountain area. Shown here (left to right, top photo) are Smith, Pollock, Carson, Byrd, host Robert Graves of Madison County, and Cammerer. (Photo by Harry Staley, Zerkel collection, SNP archives) Also at dinner ((left to right, bottom photo); L. Ferdinand Zerkel, executive secretary of the Shenandoah National Park Association; two members of state commission not identified (Coleman Wortham, Junius P. Fishburn, E. Griffith Dodson, or Rufus Roberts?); commission members Lee Long, mountain-and-valley landowner and cattleman, and Thomas L. Farrar of Charlottesville. (Photo by Harry Staley, Zerkel collection, SNP archives)

scientiously, with the information I have in hand," he insisted, "allow a reduction in the acreage."

Carson flared up, too, but he cooled off and realized the way forward was to get the facts in solid detail. Civil engineer Fred T. Amiss of Luray was sent out to investigate land ownership. Amiss (pronounced *Amos*) and helpers talked with mountain residents and studied county deed books. Most residents didn't own the land they lived on. Most tracts had changed ownership a dozen or more times since the early 1700s, only a few staying in one family line. Almost no present owners wanted to sell. Few residents would move out voluntarily. Some said they'd defend their homes with their guns.

The minimum acreage then required would contain about six thousand tracts, 20 or so with more than a thousand acres each, others less, all the way down to building lot size. There wasn't any way of shaping the acreage contiguously without including more than three thousand homes with families (tenants or owners or squatters) living in them year around. An effort to take so much would surely stir rebellion. The current commercial value of the minimum acreage was "somewhere between eight and ten million dollars," Amiss said.

Secretary Work agreed to a "resurvey," not to reduce the total, he insisted, but to find the right 385,500 acres. The task was assigned to Arno B. Cammerer, one of Director Mather's most able executives; he was later NPS director himself and considered one of those crucially responsible for this park's establishment. Cammerer put in a full month, traveling where he could by car but often on horseback or afoot. As Carson had predicted, he couldn't find enough suitable acres. He drew a line—called the Cammerer Line ever since—around 327,000 acres and said that would make a good park. In the course of his work Cammerer noticed the "comparatively level places" and the flowing springs on top of the Blue Ridge and made the first suggestion that visitor facilities be located up there. Shenandoah, with facilities in the center on the range crest rather than near the fringes, would, he said, thus "differ from all other parks" in its development.

Congress cut the minimum to the Cammerer Line. Carson still wouldn't buy a square inch of land, but he'd try hard to pull Cammerer's plan inside the limits of the possible. He liked Cammerer and felt they could work together.

The incredible complexities and the years needed to sort them out gave time for diverse feeling, thinking, and doing throughout Virginia and beyond. Influential conservationists, learning that the forest wasn't literally primeval but had been cut over every 30 or so years for two

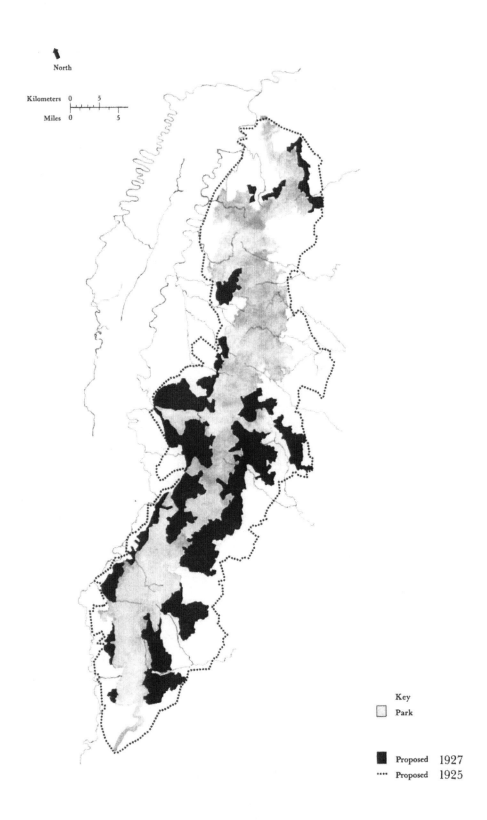

North

Kilometers 0   5
Miles   0   5

Key
☐ Park

■ Proposed 1927
•••• Proposed 1925

centuries, began doubting the appropriateness of full national park status. A Virginia citizen issued pamphlets arguing against the national connection, favoring a state park. Carson's confidence sometimes slipped. Though he never considered giving up national status, he once found himself tracing all the changes wrought here by humanity, and looking at people now living in the proposed area, and wondering if a national historical park might be most appropriate. In the early years, he apparently never supposed residents would have to be moved out entirely, but a tentative idea of his that maybe one section of the park should be set aside for them, with other sections to be vacated, did get on the record.

There were diverse surges favorable to the park. Dr. Frank Bohn of the *New York Times*, while attending a reunion of long-ago passengers on Shenandoah Valley trains, learned of the park's plight. He made an impassioned speech, from which newspapers quoted:

> Build industrialism in this Valley as the Saints of old built the Church. . . . Say to the million people who are to come into Virginia to make their homes here, that you invite all of them to live life more abundantly. . . . The mountains and fresh air will make abundant life possible even with industrialism—abundant life no longer possible in crowded cities. . . . Save the mountains as a spot where the masses can get a breath of sweet fresh air. . . . The price of the Blue Ridge must not kill the park.

The influential *Times* published many articles promoting park establishment.

The Appalachian Trail movement, another important force pushing for this park, flowed from the same overcrowded industrialism. It grew from a proposal by Benton MacKaye for a two-thousand-mile hiking trail along the Appalachian range from Maine to Georgia, first publicized nationally in October 1921. MacKaye stirred keen interest in Washington, D.C., and elsewhere, and it became obvious that the trail should traverse the Shenandoah park region. Medical doctor Halstead Shipman Hedges of Charlottesville was probably the first to scout the Shenandoah–Blue Ridge for an Appalachian Trail route. Beginning in 1922 with a hiking-camping trip from Swift Run Gap to Waynesboro, Dr. Hedges's efforts came ahead of the park's conception but continued through the incubation period.

The Potomac Appalachian Trail Club (PATC), organized in Washington, D.C., held its first meeting in November 1927. Its basic charter set forth two purposes: to create and maintain a trail along this part of the Blue Ridge, and to foster establishment of a Shenandoah national park. In the next year, when the Cammerer Line was drawn, hiker-trail builders were busy in groups here and busy, too, fostering the park in Washington, D.C., where many of them were influential.

Fred T. Amiss, civil engineer of Luray, was sent by the state's Carson commission into the mountains and the court houses to find out exactly what land was owned by what people and how much it was worth. Amiss became the most knowledgeable person of all, most likely, about the resident families, about the landowners, and about the tracts. (Courtesy of Mrs. F. Thomas Amiss)

Myron H. Avery, a lawyer with the government, was the first president of PATC and for many years chairman of the whole Appalachian Trail organization. He measured many park-land trails with a bicycle wheel and launched a program of volunteer work in the park region that has continued to this day and could never have been afforded if wages were involved. Pollock was an early trail club member. So were Zerkel, Harold Allen, and Roy Lyman Sexton, the doctor who got interested in the "mountaineers'" health. Dr. Sexton donated "the first permanent shelter on the Appalachian Trail south of New England." It was built near The Pinnacle in 1930 by mountain masons and carpenters.

Along about this time, Zerkel and his wife joined with Sexton to save a child of Corbin Hollow who seemed declining toward death. Zerkel never talked about it to me, but I understand the child was diagnosed and treated by the doctor and cared for at the Page Hospital in Luray. There was said to be recovery to health, weight, strength, and intelligence normal to American children.

Different agencies of federal and state government helped toward park establishment. A large majority of Virginians and of Americans generally, I think, would always have answered yes if asked whether they favored establishing this park. Only a small minority would have answered no, but a few of these might have added some profanity.

When the Carson commission needed a detailed topographic map for determining and recording exact relationships of the poorly marked land tracts, each of which had been described in deeds independently (no common anchor point or meridian), the U.S. Geological Survey was eager to oblige—as soon as Congress would supply funds. Carson speeded the start by advancing $10,000 of his personal money. The large-scale topographic sections enclosed by the Cammerer Line cost $80,000. They showed accurately even the locations of mountain homes.

The Virginia General Assembly became more and more willing to bolster the honor of Virginia through helping establish the national park. Though collection of the Zerkel-Benchoff pledges had been thorough, at least by comparison with collection of similar pledges for Great Smoky, the total didn't reach $1 million, only $908,069.60. The legislature realized that an earlier law, expected to put $200,000 into the fund, had proved a dud. Early in 1928, it responded to a Byrd-Carson request and appropriated $1 million to help buy park-land. It also passed legislation to speed legal procedures. The Public Park Condemnation Act, drafted with the aid of Will Carson's lawyer-brother A. C. Carson, allowed all park tracts in one county to be grouped in one court case, reducing the total cases from thousands to just eight. Even "donated land," not very significant in total amount, would be put through the condemnation process, because total rights, erasing all possible confusions of title, were thus secured; the donation would be taken in dollar value.

But before condemnation started, the Carson commission had to be sure of enough money to pay whatever prices the process approved. The only way to come close was to complete its own surveys and appraisals of everything inside the Cammerer Line. There was almost $2 million now for land purchase, and the Temple commission had promised a national campaign to match Virginia funds (and funds North Carolina and Tennessee had raised for Smoky). The theoretical $4 million just might buy the 327,000 acres. But then events shattered hope. Smoky received $5 million from John D. Rockefeller, Jr., in March 1928, so was no longer interested in a joint national drive. Great Smoky Mountains National Park was assured and on its way to early establishment. The Temple commission fell apart and responded no more.

Carson felt betrayed. Cammerer, personally and unofficially, but with the consent of Secretary Work, volunteered spare time to help raise the missing $2 million from philanthropists and foundations. In 1928 the prospects looked excellent, but next year came the stock market crash, followed by the Great Depression. The Cammerer-Carson receipts would turn out to be a trifle more than one-tenth of $2 million—John D. Rockefeller, Jr., $163,631; Edsel Ford, $50,000; Ball Brothers of Indiana, $5,000; W. T. Grant, $1,000; and Thomas A. Edison Estate $250—not negligible but nowhere near enough to fill in the Cammerer boundary.

Reviewing the park's position, Carson realized that one abyss of oblivion after another had been narrowly avoided—but never really left behind! Now questions were being raised as to whether the new condemnation law was constitutional. A delay of uncertain duration would be necessary for a court test. Condemnation papers were filed in Warren County, and landowner Thomas Jackson Rudacille responded with a suit for an injunction against such taking of land. The Virginia court supported the new law in October 1929, but Rudacille then took his case to the state's Supreme Court of Appeals.

While waiting for the conclusive decision, Carson developed a money-stretching way of working with the jigsaw puzzle of mountain tracts. Coves and hollows with rich soil and homes might cost $20–$50 an acre. Cliffy ridges could be bought for about $1 an acre, and they made beautiful scenery. Drawing an irregular boundary that left out expensive land would get more acres in return for the too-small land fund. If the engineers and appraisers determined what lands and how many acres could be bought with the available fund, then he might get Congress to reduce the minimum to that number of acres. Realistically, though, the prospect looked dim.

"Town hall," Camp Hoover, represents arrival of powerful help in the effort to establish the national park. Will Carson, working directly and through others, persuaded the president to set up his multicottage "fishing camp" here. (SNP archives)

President Herbert Hoover fished for the native brook trout but also rode. On one Blue Ridge crest ride with the National Park Service director, he initiated construction of Skyline Drive as a drought-relief project. (SNP archives)

Carson had farseeingly acquired a powerful ally. After the election of 1928 he'd adopted an incredible strategy. President-elect Herbert Hoover was known to be tremendously fond of fishing for mountain trout, and now the grapevine said he was seeking a place near Washington, D.C., where he could escape both mosquitos and the "pneumatic hammer" of official life. The upper Rapidan River in the park-land was noted for native trout. Carson persuaded a fishing club that had secured Rapidan rights from the landowners to release them for use by the president.

As if by miracle—though resulting also from maneuvering of extraordinary skill and risk, such as Carson's personally guaranteeing $7,500 to help build a usable road into the Rapidan—the strategy functioned. Two months after his inauguration in March 1929 the president had slept "in one of five brown Army tents with wooden floors in place" where the Rapidan originates. Accompanying him was Ray Lyman Wilbur, successor to Dr. Work as secretary of the interior. The fishing camp grew with more solid structures, and before long Carson could write to Cammerer: "I spent six hours with the President, Mrs. Hoover and Secretary Wilbur . . . and the President has a very compre-

Lou Henry Hoover, First Lady, explored much of the park-land on horseback and studied its wildflowers on leisurely walks. (SNP archives)

hensive view of the park now, as has Secretary Wilbur. . . . I talked to both . . . about our problems . . and they are both with us."

Soon, while continuing to help the park toward establishment, the Hoovers worried about the mountain people and their adjustment to the coming situation. Partly as a result of a mysteriously promoted media event, in which a mountain lad named Ray Buracker gave the president a live opossum, the Hoovers became great friends of the mountain people. They built and operated an excellent elementary school, below Big Meadows, entirely at their personal expense. I have no clues connecting Will Carson to the "Possum Boy" or the school, but in those years Carson was responsible for so many near-miracles that I can't help suspecting he was somehow secretly involved.

Though the park seemed possible now, with Hoover's help and the unending national, even world, flow of news and features from "the president's" Blue Ridge, troubles persisted. Carson's park division staff head died, so the jigsaw of tracts for a feasible park took longer to put together. Rain failed, and forest fires that Pollock called "the worst in a lifetime" raged around Skyland, around Black Rock Springs, even near the president's camp. The people of the mountains, resenting the imminent park, weren't eager to help beyond fighting to save their own houses and outbuildings. Both opposition to the park and impatience to see it more quickly achieved were multiplying.

There had been wide expectation that Carson would follow Byrd as governor, but political complexities and Carson's dedication to the park intervened in 1930. If there had been any question who to blame, where the park "buck" stopped, there was none after Byrd's term expired. The buck stopped with Carson. Whatever might go wrong was his fault, and if he didn't achieve "the impossible park," nobody would.

NPS Director Albright, who knew Carson well, suspected at the time only part of the wide, wide range where his friend managed. In an interview many years after the event, Albright remembered a day at Camp Hoover when Carson wasn't there. Hoover led a party of horseback riders up along the range crest near Big Meadows:

> The President motioned me to come up alongside. . . . He told me that these mountains were just made for a highway. . . . And he said, I think everybody ought to have a chance to get the views from here. . . . The people should have this sensation that I have, this exhilaration, this experience that I have riding along here. He said, I want you to consider undertaking a survey right away . . . talk it over with Mr. Carson.

A skyline drive had been dreamed in 1924; the idea was originated perhaps by Pollock or Harold Allen or Zerkel, then seemed forgotten. But Carson was developing it. The fall before, he'd guided the president on horseback over a part of the route. The president had been surprised by the quality of scenery and had agreed to federal aid for a road if funds could be found. When drought dried up the mountains, Carson asked for drought relief funds to give mountain people jobs building the range-crest highway. The president was willing if Congress gave authority, so schemer Carson got a congressman to provide and push the needed bill.

Hoover not only gave the order for Skyline Drive; he also watched the advancing project on the ground. The *New York Times* reported the Carson commission was naming the road Hoover Highway, but somehow Skyline Drive prevailed. The naming may be the only part of the whole affair that slipped out of Carson's control. Though he couldn't get another dollar to add to the land-purchase fund, he got $1,570,479 for building Skyline Drive between Thornton and Swift Run gaps, with millions more to come. He staged a five-week Advance Opening—from Lee Highway (U.S. 211) via Skyland to Crescent Rock—in the bright autumn of 1932. The road and its panoramic views were so impressive,

Panoramic views the president called "the greatest in the world" justified Skyline Drive. The air was clearer then; the views mostly wider and free of foreground obstacles. Looking northward in 1934 from Buck Hollow Overlook, the view included Lee Highway and much cleared land now forested. On the high horizon were Hogback Mountain, two rounded peaks of Mount Marshall, and, at far right, The Peak. Looking westward, the most famous view included sharply defined farms in the valley, Massanutten Mountain, and far ranges of the Alleghenies in West Virginia. The boy in the rocks is Eric, son of the photographer Wallace Rhodes. (Courtesy of Dr. and Mrs. Eric Rhodes)

Left: Skyline Drive when new, seen past Little Stony Man Cliffs. (NPS) *Right*: Construction at Marys Rock Tunnel. The central section of the Skyline Drive was hurried so fast to employ men suffering hardships of drought and depression that contracts for roadwork south of Marys Rock were awarded before the tunnel was opened. Some contractors had to get to their projects up old wagon roads in the hollows. (NPS)

there was no way now that the American public could let park establishment fail.

While the Carson-Hoover-Albright scenic highway was winning high praise, Franklin D. Roosevelt defeated Hoover at the polls. Congress authorized Roosevelt's Civilian Conservation Corps among the first New Deal legislation, and on April 5, 1933, the president allotted $10 million by executive order to get this CCC started. The very next Sunday, April 9, Roosevelt, Secretary of the Interior Harold Ickes, Albright, and Carson were together in the Blue Ridge. Hoover had left his camp and Blue Ridge land to the park, for use by future presidents if they wished, otherwise for the public. Though FDR found the camp too rugged for him, he was much pleased by the mountains so close to Washington, D.C., and by the Skyline Drive. He wanted his first CCC camps here. Carson raced to get sites for the camps and the conservation projects.

James Ralph Lassiter, later to become Shenandoah's first superintendent, was quickly transferred from NPS's George Washington's Birthplace, where he'd been supervising roadwork. He set up an office in Luray, in Zerkel's building, and, with help from appropriate personnel of NPS Washington, began planning projects and hiring camp superintendents, foremen, and technicians trained in construction, forestry, landscape architecture, and other needed specialties. Since there was no national park, so no NPS funds, Lassiter and the whole staff would be paid by Emergency Conservation Work, the CCC-funded work-project auxiliary providing technically trained planners and supervising foremen who

President Roosevelt liked President Hoover's Skyline Drive so much that he wanted his first CCC camps here. The "boys" had to live in army tents at first but were in wooden barracks before winter got severe. This scene shows early Camp NP-3, a few miles north of Swift Run Gap. (NPS)

would keep the "boys" busy. FDR's wish was enough to make almost anything happen that spring.

Nonpark Shenandoah got the first two national park camps on May 15, 1933. Each camp had nearly two hundred boys in their late teens. The army was responsible for the camp facilities, clothes, food, and other necessities, while Lassiter's personnel supervised the work projects. More camps were added until the proposed park had more than a thousand men doing park-type work here.

Masses of CCC boys and the scattered mountain people, sometimes hiding, frightened each other at first. Most of the boys were from cities, and most of the mountain people had never seen a city. Yet common ground began to appear. One thing they shared quite obviously was a shortage of money made worse by the nationwide depression. A mountain lad told me, "When you get to know a CCC by hisself, he's like you, knocked around but keeping on going."

The area was intended by Congress and the administration to be a large national park exhibiting the primeval character of the Appalachians, so the emphasis was on a quick "return to nature," while also cleaning up the landscape and preparing to receive visitors in large numbers. Blight-killed chestnut trees were removed, as Pollock had earlier felt important. The boys manned fire towers and fought forest fires. Soon they'd be planting hundreds of trees a week—some bought, some raised in CCC nurseries here, some dug in the forest, even 15 feet tall, and replanted where the landscapers said trees were needed.

CCC crews transplanted many thousands of trees while "landscaping" the park, especially near the Skyline Drive. (NPS)

President FDR visited to see how the CCC was working. He liked what he saw. He remained personally interested in Shenandoah, kept funds coming to complete Skyline Drive, and did whatever he could to help Carson get the land so the park could become an official reality. Soon he and Mrs. Roosevelt, along with several policy-making executives, would be developing plans for resettling the mountain people in "homestead communities" outside the park itself.

Legality of the land condemnation was confirmed by Virginia's highest court. The depression convinced almost everyone that no additional park-purchase money could be raised, so Senator Swanson put a bill through Congress to lower the minimum acreage to 160,000, the amount Carson felt certain the funds in hand could pay for. Virginia political leaders continued to feel the state would gain greatly from the park. Most state and federal officials came around to a belief that both the park and the mountain people themselves would benefit if the people moved out, at least all but the elderly and their immediate households.

All relevant tracts were now accurately described and mapped. Appraisers had thoroughly studied the land, buildings, timber, orchards, even mineral prospects, and calculated the values. Blanket condemnation, county by county, was moving through the courts. Gov. John Garland Pollard, Byrd's successor, appointed circuit court judges to arbitration committees. The thousand-plus owners seemed resigned now—after many futile protests—to losing their land, but about one out of eight

Pocosin Cabin. The CCC built both lean-to shelters and snug cabins for hikers along the Maine-to-Georgia Appalachian Trail in the park. (NPS)

complained the payments were too small and requested arbitration. A few increases were approved.

After serving through the four-year terms of two governors and into the term of a third, Carson was able in August 1934 to deliver to the federal government all necessary deeds, signed by Gov. George C. Peery, to form Shenandoah National Park. He said in his official report that he'd often been "threatened with sudden death by infuriated landowners" but was sustained by "the zest of accomplishment, the joy of combat, the enthusiasm in doing what we were assured was impossible, and in the end the hope of high achievement" for the long-range "good of the people of the state."

There was an outburst of applause around Virginia, for the park especially but also for Carson's other outstanding services to the prosperity and dignity of Virginia. Citizens and newspaper editorials expressed disappointment that Will Carson hadn't become governor. Maybe he felt disappointed, too. But he settled back in his Warren County home—called Killahevlin in memory of his origin in Ireland—and gave no sign of political ambition. He discussed his park work calmly with the local Lions Club in Front Royal. The deeds waiting in Washington, D.C., for federal acceptance, he said, involved 1,088 tracts totaling 181,578 acres. A total of $2,258,910 had been spent in buying the land, $1,859,910 going to the landowners, the rest for overhead including costs of surveying, mapping, and appraising.

Carson had left his central position when he'd delivered the deeds to Washington. An unforeseen court case intervened (see Chapter 17), and

Big Meadows was famous for sail planes in early CCC years. Some of the motorless flights on Blue Ridge air currents lasted for hours, went as far as Pennsylvania, and threatened to break world records. (NPS)

he must have been on pins and needles in relative loneliness during the year of limbo. When word reached him the day after Christmas in 1935 that enough of the land had been accepted to make the park a reality at last, he started on impulse to see engineer-in-charge Lassiter at Luray, maybe for mutual congratulations. He hadn't thought to tell anyone where he was going. A blizzard caught him on the Skyline Drive, which he had so effectively promoted and his car got stuck in a snowdrift. He tried to dig out. There was no traffic, no help. He was totally alone.

His family checked 20 hospitals in the region. Virginia state police, private groups, and detachments from an army depot near Front Royal searched for him. Night came. Lassiter hadn't known he was coming, but before morning he might have guessed or even felt some telepathic impulse from this founder of the park, who must have been almost freezing. Lassiter mobilized three entire CCC camps, about six hundred men. Trucks moved in low gear along the Skyline Drive, with men clinging to the sides peering over the precipices until at last Carson was found, too cold now for congratulation or celebration but in urgent need of medical care. Many have wondered what he was thinking while alone all those hours in the blizzard in "his" great park.

Carson died in 1942 at the age of 71. Years later a previously unnamed 2,500-foot mountain, ten miles south of Front Royal, near the Skyline Drive, was named Carson Mountain in his honor. Perhaps he's there, in a way, but more likely everywhere in the park.

CHAPTER XVII

Embattled Owners

T he 1,300-plus families caught in the "blanket condemnation" represented just about the whole gamut of Virginia life. Some were park-land residents, but far more owners lived outside the park boundary in valley and piedmont. They were wealthy and poor, educated and illiterate, farmers, livestock men, industrialists, merchants, office workers, doctors, lawyers, laborers, moonshiners. A few welcomed the money for their land. Most resisted the taking, some with well-reasoned speeches or letters, some with threats to kill—which they never carried out because no one person ever seemed the villain—and some with court action.

The largest tract being taken showed on the owner's claim form as 24,100 acres. Mostly in Rockingham County, it extended into Albemarle, Augusta, and Greene counties as well. Mineral rights in an additional 1,500 acres were part of the holding. This empire covered the west slope of the Blue Ridge for 12 miles, from Trayfoot Mountain southeast of Grottoes northwestward almost to Elkton. The emperor was John A. Alexander—"Alexander the Great"; his address, State Prison.

When the Virginia State Commission on Conservation and Development published its intent to condemn this land, Alexander replied through his agent and attorney. He said he had acquired the property in 1914, and "by virtue of certain suits, confirmatory deeds, etc., the title . . . has been completely cleared up, quieted and settled." The land was "underlaid with valuable minerals, contains valuable timber, and considerable areas are fitted for agriculture." Though Alexander had clung to the land for years as if it were gold, he wasn't fighting the take-over now. From prison he merely insisted that "the land yield its full value for application upon the outstanding liens."

John A. Alexander was born November 25, 1864, on the family's farm near Weyers Cave. He was educated at Augusta Military Academy and Washington and Lee University and in 1890 was admitted to the bar. He soon had one of the best offices in Lawyer's Row, Staunton. By age 50 he was respected as one of Virginia's foremost lawyers.

John A. Alexander, a prominent lawyer of Staunton—sometimes called "Alexander the Great"—owned the largest tract in the early 1930s, one-eighth of today's entire park. His address was State Prison. (Courtesy of Rudolph B. Alexander)

John A. was a large man, about 6 feet, 1 inch tall, and 215 pounds. His nephew Rudy B. Alexander, remembering, said, "Uncle John had a personality that people couldn't turn down." Though seemingly prosperous, he never had enough money to buy all the land he wanted, and he'd persuade people to sign bonds so he could take quick advantage of land bargains. He'd pay only a small amount down and make up the balance with his own or others' notes. Almost never did he sell an acre. He just bought, and he had land in half a dozen counties.

Rudy's father David C. signed a paper to enable John A., his only living brother, to grab a rare bargain in land that was sure to make them both rich. As a result, David lost his farm and home. Rudy said, "If Uncle John had gotten justice he'd be in prison yet." David died within two years, apparently from the shock and grief resulting from betrayal by his brother.

Sixteen different indictments for felonies were on the 1926 records against John A. Alexander. He was put on trial in the Court of the City of Staunton, where he'd often been a star performer. Judge A. D. Dabney of Charlottesville presided at the request of the regular judge, who was too closely acquainted with the defendant. The first indictment charged that Alexander forged a bond for $2,100 on March 10, 1925, signing it with the names Edwin C. Edmonson and S. Emmett Walters, promising they would pay Archie E. Wine the sum with interest. This bond was secured to John A. Alexander, trustee, by 79 acres of land. Alexander then forged Wine's name and assigned the bond to Dr. J. H. Thomas.

Alexander plead guilty to this charge and two other felonious forgeries and was sentenced to six years in the state penitentiary. The rest of the indictments were *nolle prosequied*; there'd probably been plea bargaining. Alexander the Great lost everything, including his expensive Staunton home, his wife, who went back to her kin in Georgia, and his reputation.

The tract in the Blue Ridge must have disappointed him if he looked into the findings of the court's appraisers. As did most tracts here, perhaps but crudely surveyed long before, it shrank on resurvey and showed but 21,400 acres. A state geologist spent weeks examining its mineral prospects and concluded they had no present commercial value. A forest appraiser cruised all the many ridges and hollows and found little value left in timber or other forest products. The tract brought less than half what Alexander had claimed, less actually than the $62,500 he had agreed to pay for it—but never really had.

Lewis Willis, a park resident who owned 229 acres west of Marys Rock, descended from once-leading gentry. He was educated at the University of Virginia, and his wife, Ida, at Smith College in Massachusetts. About 60 of Willis's acres qualified for top price, $50 an acre—the homesite with a neat frame house, flower and vegetable gardens, barn, hen house, hog pen, meat house, and orchard. There were also 50 acres of bluegrass pasture, several small-grain fields, and a lot of forest. Willis was a "mountaineer" by choice. He'd always raised corn, potatoes, vegetables, cattle, and hogs, but there's no report he made moonshine. For many years he was a tanbark broker between mountain producers and the tanneries.

In 1929 Willis initiated the Landowners' Protective Association, which, though not believed to have elected officers and directors, employed a lawyer to help fight "the unconstitutional ejectment" of Blue Ridge families. The association helped support Thomas Jackson Rudacille in his court actions, had several large meetings to persuade members of the public, wrote letters to the editors, and seemed to have a chance to stop the park. Yet the park residents and diverse landowners outside the park were so scattered and uncohesive that full mobilization could not be achieved. The propark movement convinced a majority of active citizens. The circuit court decided for condemnation and against Rudacille. More money was raised, and Virginia's highest court took a lot of time considering Rudacille's appeal, then confirmed the decision. The condemnation was approved.

Willis fought on, though hurt and disappointed that the owners of the big bluegrass pastures, who could have afforded the very best and most thorough legal services and could have also influenced state and federal politics, failed to put up a strong battle. It isn't true, as some people have said, that the farmer-grazers didn't care. Many of them cared so much and

The comfortable home of Lewis Willis, beneath Marys Rock, less than half a mile off U.S. 211. Willis was a mountain man educated at University of Virginia. His home was half filled with books, magazines, and letters. He fought condemnation of the park-land. Even after he lost, he lived here two more decades—until blind and near death—having been put on the special lifetime list by the secretary of the interior. (NPS)

felt so bitter about the condemnation that they, like some of the mountain residents, at least imagined violence. Bernard Spitler, Jr.—who must have been remembering talk by his rancher-father and associates—commented to me that if somebody had shot Harry Byrd, Will Carson, Pollock, and Hoover there'd never have been a park. Bernard still thinks the Virginia action for the park was unconstitutional, and he describes the park to this day as "federally occupied territory." Quite a few of the farmer-grazers bitterly called Lee Long—one of the park pasture owners with holdings of greatest value (966 acres in the Big Meadows area, for which he was paid $34,840)—a turncoat because he succumbed to Will Carson's urging and accepted membership on the state conservation commission that condemned the park-land. Some say Lee Long got special grazing privileges by joining the commission and supporting its policies, but I've been unable to find any evidence to support this accusation.

Leading farmer-grazers were caught in an economic puzzle. They had invested heavily in valley land as well as in mountain land, and also in valley businesses. Some had mortgaged home farms to buy grain land near the Shenandoah River during World War I, to take advantage of soaring prices for wheat. Now with demand slackening after the stock market crash, and with the depression worsening, they had to scratch to meet mortgage payments. They needed prosperity in the valley and believed the park might help bring it; they needed to save their home bases no matter how deep the depression. The condemnation checks could prove to be a godsend to save their central farms.

Willis was knowledgeable enough to understand, but he regretted the ambiguity and tried to dissuade the federal government from accepting the state's actions—and the land. His letters to President Hoover and Secretary of the Interior Wilbur pointed accurately to flaws in the project: For a national park, the area should be, and it was claimed to be, "virginal"—but it was not. The forest had been cut many times and the land used heavily in varied ways. The national goal of preserving a splendid example of primeval Appalachia was being achieved at Great Smoky; Shenandoah was redundant. The park bills had gone through state and national legislative halls on greased tracks, with no opportunity for landowners to mobilize for effective opposition. Willis concluded his letter to Hoover: "We are unwilling to part with our homes to help a small part of our population to get their hands into tourists' pockets."

Willis was 70 when the park was established. He was soon put on the secretary of the interior's list of several dozen elderly residents authorized to keep their homes in the park as long as they lived. His wife died before he turned 80, and he clung to the mountains alone, his house almost filled with the books and papers he kept studying, trying to understand why things happened as they did.

In 1951 the park's chief ranger reported Willis was still there, though now 85 and almost blind. The mailman bought his groceries for him, the dirt road being negotiable by car. The house was deteriorating, and forest saplings grew in the yard. Willis had no children. Two different nephews had invited him to come and live with them, but he had refused to leave his mountain home. When R. Taylor Hoskins, who'd known Willis (as I had also) since 1936, returned here as park superintendent in 1958, Willis had just died. Hoskins went to the old house and walked along the aisles between stacks of books. "There was a watch," Hoskins told me, "that had been in the Willis family since Napoleon's day. We kept it in the park safe for a while. It was picked up by a nephew who was postmaster at Colonial Heights near Petersburg."

Nearly all the park residents and landowners had reacted negatively when they first learned of the proposal to acquire these mountains to make a national park. They didn't want to sell or move out. Few of them changed and welcomed the taking, but through the years, for a variety of reasons, most of them recognized the combination of forces moving toward the park and readied themselves to accept, more or less good-naturedly, whatever had to happen. Some recognized the potential value of the park and came to favor it. Many of the mountain people weren't

Martin Buracker of Madison County was on the lifetime list, authorizing him to keep his old cabin-home in the park as long as he lived, but he and other Madison County people lost their battle to save the cabin forever as a historic structure. Some evidence suggested it was built in the 1700s, maybe before the Revolution, as a squatter's home, but no funds to maintain it could be obtained. (NPS)

as averse to finding new homes as they were to being pushed around or belittled and downgraded so as to reduce the onus of their removal on the consciences of those strange outsiders who wanted their land. (Owners who sold their land voluntarily for park purposes are listed in Appendix 4.) The park proposal moved slowly, and some put it out of their minds, while others longed for the blow to fall and not keep hanging over them.

When President and Mrs. Hoover personally established the mountain school, they hired a top-notch teacher, Christine Vest, who helped prepare some of the people for a different life. Miriam Sizer, a teacher and social worker, also tried to help the people. She envisioned government-sponsored relocation communities short distances outside the park, but most of the involved state and federal leaders promptly said relocation communities would be unnecessary and more trouble than they were worth, even to that strange mountain "culture" itself. Sizer studied five mountain hollows—Nicholson, Corbin, Weakley, Dark, Richards (along Rose River where it flows out of the park)—and found in 1932 that, of

132 families, 27 didn't believe the park would ever exist, 17 were indifferent to the prospect, 4 were hostile, 10 showed anxiety, 9 wanted to remain in the park, and 65 felt positive about moving out. Another question revealed that 93 families had no plans at all to leave, 3 had definite plans, and 36 had indefinite plans. These five hollows near Skyland had more than one-fourth of all the families living inside the park boundary.

Many strange rumors about the park circulated among mountain residents and lowland neighbors. One horror story said the dead as well as the living would be evicted. Mountain cemeteries would be emptied and the remains reburied in the lowlands. Townspeople imagined their neat cemeteries inundated with Blue Ridge bones and protested. The story circulated widely—without the slightest basis in fact that has ever been discovered. Cemeteries in the park have remained where they were. Families who wished to do so have maintained them neatly, and additional burials have been made alongside kinfolk. (See Appendix 1 for details.)

Some outsiders seemed more worried about the mountain people than were these people themselves—or the governmental bodies. Elizabeth Winn, who'd been an army reconstruction aide in World War I, then taught industrial and fine arts in Baltimore, tried to teach the five-hollows people a way to make a living outside the park "without succumbing to the grind and uncertainty of factory work." In 1931 she founded the Mountain Neighbors industrial center at Old Rag, where she taught old-time homecrafts with donated looms and other equipment. She exhibited the products, recruited allies, and began developing regular markets in major urban areas. Winn and her friends admired the Blue Ridge people, many of whom resembled Lewis Willis in their preference for place and way of life, though they lacked advanced education. To some extent Winn and other helpers were able to imitate the direct method of living abundantly on the land with almost no money.

One Blue Ridge person Winn especially admired was "old Barbara Nicholson . . . who lived in a faraway, lonely spot . . . and could sing, 'Lord Ronald and the Brown Girl,' 'Barbara Allen,' and 'The Little Mohee',' which came down orally from long ago. Another was "Uncle" John Dyer, who'd been blind from youth, yet made excellent ax handles, chairs, and stools. By feel he could select the right wood for his purpose.

Few of the young and middle-aged mountain people doubted their own ability to survive in the world, and they became more and more convinced they'd have to try living out there. Work on the Skyline Drive advanced, and some mountain men got jobs with the contractors. The mountain people didn't feel they were worse off than millions of others during the depression; they'd get by somehow.

The farmer-grazers would get by, too—somehow—but they'd lose a lot of production, so a lot of profit; in some cases there'd be sizable losses and no profit left. They'd have to abandon a lot of plans and dreams. But yes, they'd get by. So would the owners of timber land and mineral land—somehow.

Then suddenly in 1934, when the park seemed to be on the very threshold of solid success, the suppressed hopes of park-land residents and owners broke out and lived again, tentatively. A man named Via came out of nowhere and challenged the land condemnation—in the federal courts—effectively enough to lock up the National Park Service appropriation. There wouldn't be any national park here in 1934, maybe not in 1935, or ever. The battle opened in the U.S. District Court for the Western District of Virginia in Harrisonburg, on November 10, 1934, and would end in the U.S. Supreme Court, Washington, D.C. Most briefly, the case was *Via* v. *Va.* Officially, it was *Robert H. Via* v. *The State Commission on Conservation and Development of the State of Virginia.*

Federal courts, including the U.S. Supreme Court, listened for a year when Robert H. Via told them Virginia's condemnation of the park-land was unconstitutional. Here's the modest title page of the inch-thick records the Supreme Court preserved on this important case. (U.S. Supreme Court Library)

IN THE

Supreme Court of the United States

October Term, 1935.

No. 58.

Robert H. Via, *Appellant,*

v.

The State Commission on Conservation and Development of the State of Virginia, *Appellee.*

On Appeal from the District Court of the United States for the Western District of Virginia.

BRIEF FOR APPELLANT.

William E. Leahy,
William J. Hughes, Jr.,
Investment Building,
Washington, D. C.
Attorneys for Appellant.

Press of Byron S. Adams, Washington, D. C.

Lewis Willis didn't know this Via; no Via was associated with the Landowners' Protective Association; nobody had noticed any around during the two trials of the Rudacille case. Robert Via gave his address as Hershey, Pennsylvania. Yet he had been very much a man of the parkland mountains and wanted urgently to continue being so. His French-Huguenot ancestor Amer Via had come to Virginia and settled at Manakintown about 1685. Amer's son William moved to what would be Albemarle County about 1730. Two generations later there were William III and Micajah Via with plantations in the edge of the Blue Ridge. The descendants moved up the mountain via Doyle River and Jones Run. As slavery was being eliminated, Christopher Columbus Via was extending his holdings over the pass that's now on the maps as Via Gap, near lofty Cedar Mountain. Christopher Columbus was the father of Robert H. Via, born in 1883, so 51 years old when he took Virginia into federal court.

While Robert was growing up, Christopher prospered in his secluded Shangri-La, producing livestock and lumber and soon apples and brandy. Because sugar to make brandy and whiskey was "always" being hauled up Moormans River, the north fork became known as Sugar Hollow all the way to Via Gap. Robert grew up fast and far. Though not the oldest of the children, he tended to take over as soon as Christopher began to weaken. He expanded the orchard and the distillery and livestock. Christopher died in 1906. Robert H.—soon mostly "Bob-Vi" with those who talked about him and his bold doings—became the boss or King of Sugar Hollow.

Bob-Vi had a big orchard of Albemarle Pippin apples, the older trees planted by Christopher, two thousand more planted later. Several of Bob-Vi's sisters—big women—helped in the orchard and the packinghouse. Brothers and other kin and several tenants helped there, too, and with the farming and livestock raising and timbering. The best apples were shipped to England. A second cousin remembers that Bob-Vi got a Model-A Ford truck to haul packed apples over the Black Rock Gap road to Harriston railroad station in the valley. Lower-grade apples were made into cider, which was fermented in large wooden tubs and, after about two weeks of warm weather, distilled into brandy—legally, under license.

Bob-Vi is remembered as 6 feet 3 inches tall, about 250 pounds in middle age, around 190 when 80 years old. He had a button nose, kinfolk say. Though physically powerful, he was a manager, not a physical worker, and he used his time and energy to organize and get his way with others. He was a schemer, often domineering, able to turn a profit and gain power in many different ways. He operated a commissary supplying his kinfolk and others. Though he'd accept cash, many of his customers worked for him and were credited for time.

A major supporter of the Via case against the park was the brother of Via's wife. This John H. Mace had a home and a famous spring in the park-land near Madison Run and sold the water in both Virginia and Pennsylvania. The manner of his eviction from the park gave rise to popular tales. (Courtesy of Herbert Via)

The Via family intertwined across the Blue Ridge from piedmont to valley. Some remember Bob-Vi as not so all-dominating but just typical of Via men, with maybe a bit of extra initiative. Bob-Vi's brother William Edward Via operated their father's old sawmill; he had probably inherited it. Their father Christopher had contributed land for the Via school in Sugar Hollow and for the first church there, a Brethren church. Bob-Vi and William are said to have built the schoolhouse. Bob-Vi may have hired and paid the teacher, Miss Lottie Maupin. She first commuted daily on horseback over Pasture Fence Mountain; later she lodged with the Oscar Via family part of the time and with the William King Via family. William King, son of William Edward, resembled Bob-Vi physically, being strong enough to lift a 50-gallon barrel of brandy and, so jokes his son, who's provided some of my information, "could drink that much in a week also." He was known as "Shake" Via; he carried mail on horseback between Black Rock Springs and Grottoes.

It's evident that Bob-Vi, though independent of the more northern land-protective group, had somewhat widespread support of his own. He was married to Elizabeth Mace; her brother John H. Mace, with land and a valuable spring in Madison Run canyon of the park-land, was a major supporter of *Via v. Va.*, maybe even coinstigator. Bob and Elizabeth had about a dozen children. So even the kinfolk group was sizable, and many who weren't kin were also on Via's side.

When park establishment threatened in 1928, Bob-Vi found another place to live. He bought farmland at Palmyra, near Hershey, Pennsylvania, and was soon making money there, while continuing to make money here—$2,000 net per year, a lot then, on his orchard alone. He was late going to court. The condemnation had happened, but he still had possession. He's said to have spent "everything" on the court case. Will Carson hinted that Bob-Vi's lawyers solicited support from park-land owners generally. Maybe so. The first statement in the petition Bob-Vi filed in November 1934 said he "brings this suit in his own right and for the benefit of all others similarly situated."

The lawyers, William J. Hughes, Jr., and William E. Leahy of Washington, D.C., justified action in federal court instead of state court by claiming Pennsylvania as Via's residence and by claiming that Virginia's condemnation of lands violated the U.S. Constitution. They said the taking of 154 acres of Via's land was "deprivation of due process of law and the equal protection of the laws within the meaning of the 14th Amendment." They also argued that the state had "no power to condemn property within the state for the purpose of making a gift of it to the United States." The Via petition asked the court to declare Virginia's park-condemnation law unconstitutional and to order the conservation commission to restore the park-land to the owners.

The state commission responded with lengthy language, showing the complexity of the park-land problem and the need for special legislation. It denied that it had "deprived the petitioner of his lands without . . . due process of law." It cited the decision of Virginia's highest court in the Rudacille case and decisions in almost similar cases around the nation.

In addition to the case in federal district court, Via filed a petition in the Supreme Court of the District of Columbia, asking an injunction against Secretary Ickes to prevent him from accepting the deeds Virginia had delivered to him. Settlement of this case would depend on the main decision.

Via v. *Va.* came before three judges of the U.S. District Court at Harrisonburg on December 10, 1934. These judges were John Paul, John J. Parker, and William C. Coleman. The commission's lawyer, A. C. Carson—brother of conservation commission chairman Will Carson— called witnesses in an effort to prove Via still "lived" in Virginia—and so the case belonged in state, not federal, court. The testimony placed Via at his orchard shortly before the condemnation; but, though he was frequently there, his post office address, immediate family, and personal belongings were not. Lawyer Carson's ploy changed nothing.

People who lived in the park believed by 1936, at least, that they'd have to leave. They were prohibited from clearing new and more fertile ground for crops or pastures, from cutting live trees, and from killing wild creatures. Many pulled back into the fewest possible rooms to save heat and energy. They planted gardens again but didn't always have the "heart" now to fight the weeds. Notice characteristic mountaineer-made ladder against cabin. The three-stone-chimney complex was still the home of Teeny Atkins and her brother, Frank "Dido" Atkins, authorized to stay lifelong here in Rappahannock County above Sperryville. (NPS)

The true problem was interpreting the Constitution, and the three judges went deeply into past decisions that might have set a pattern. On January 12, 1935, the opinion of the court was rendered. Written by John Paul—who, ten years before, had been tricounty chairman in the park-land financial campaign—it was endorsed by the other two judges. It considered Via's strongest point to be that a state can't condemn lands just to give them away. Paul recognized this question as of "far reaching importance" affecting the existence, immediately, of Shenandoah, Great Smoky, and Mammoth Cave national parks and possibly other enterprises.

The precedent decisions that came closest to the situation here were partly on Via's side. *Twombley* v. *Humphrey* went against a condemnation of private land by Michigan, to be given to the United States for a lighthouse. The three judges declared, though, that "this overlooks the true principles . . . of eminent domain." They argued that this power exists in a state for "the furtherance of the health, pleasure and recreational facilities of its people" as well as for what was more strictly called public necessity. They concluded thus: "Is the state in the performance of a legitimate function forbidden to accomplish it through such means or agency it chooses? We think not."

The national park had been closer to defeat than almost anyone realized. Now hope wavered and sank among landowners and residents, and park advocates breathed again. Yet big, tough, clever Bob-Vi was far from knocked out. He appealed to the U.S. Supreme Court. The Commonwealth of Virginia proper, through its attorney general Abram P. Staples, took over the defense from the Carson commission. Staples's first argument was that the case was a state matter and federal courts had no jurisdiction. In June the Supreme Court "noted probable jurisdiction," encouraging Via, and set the case for the October 1935 term.

The Via appeal reiterated that the state couldn't condemn land just to give it away to the federal government and that the "right to condemn exists only in case of necessity." Staples argued that the park was a legitimate public use and that Virginians would benefit from it whether it was operated by the state or the United States. The case was argued in Washington, D.C., on November 19. After numerous questions with answers by Via's attorney, William J. Hughes, Chief Justice Charles Evans Hughes ended the discussion.

On November 25 the U.S. Supreme Court dismissed Via's appeal, affirming the three-judge decision "on the ground that appellant has an adequate remedy at law." Presumably this meant that Via could fight the take-over in state court, as had Rudacille, but Via knew this route was useless. The state had the power of eminent domain and could decide its own necessity. Its procedures, of course, must be in accord with the Constitution, and they had been.

Bob-Vi saw no use in fighting further. He moved—"lock, stock, and barrel"—to Pennsylvania and buried his loss in the swirl of remaking his fortune on his dairy and hog farms there. His flair for managing people and circumstances still functioned. His relatives I've talked with said he was "comfortable" financially when he died "in his late 80s." One used the word "rich."

Robert Henry "Bob" Via and his wife Mary Elizabeth Mace "Lizzie" Via a few years after the U.S. Supreme Court had decided against them and their Blue Ridge land had become part of the park. They had moved to a farm they had acquired near Hershey, Pennsylvania. (Courtesy of son Paul C. Via)

CHAPTER XVIII

Refugees and Rangers

Not until 1934, when the boundary for an expected park of approximately 180,000 acres was embodied in deeds delivered to Secretary of the Interior Ickes in Washington, D.C., could there be an accurate view of the population involved and its relation to the land. A detailed census, taken then to consider planning for resettlement, found 465 families living inside the boundary. The family heads were asked to sign a temporary occupancy permit, presigned by Will Carson for the state, the new owner.

In that period of the Great Depression, cash income of park-land residents was usually less than $200 a year per family. About 30 percent of the families received some welfare aid. Conditions of housing, home furnishings, and clothing were rated, in social workers' judgment, mostly between fair and poor, while food was rated mostly between fair and good. The houses averaged 3.9 rooms, and the families, 5.1 persons. About 80 percent of the people were in good health; the rest, fair or poor.

Only 197 of the 465 families owned their homes or any of the park-land at all. Their tracts were almost all little, though a few of the resident families owned two hundred or more acres. Total ownership by year-around residents (mountain people) was only about 7 percent of the park acreage. Of the 1,088 tracts the state was deeding to the United States to make the park, 891 were owned by people who lived outside the park, and these tracts averaged larger, so outsiders owned about 93 percent of the park-land.

The typical park-land resident was described as a "share renter, cultivating less than 5 acres and looking after landowner's cattle." I haven't found the term "share renter" exactly right—they didn't share crops—but neither is the word "tenant" quite fitting (see Chapter 11). The census found 268 resident families with "no equity" in real estate and said they were "tenants most often and 'squatters' in some cases." From hints in the census plus information from other sources, I estimate approximately half the mountain families (233, say) were "tenants," which

Two "Park Offices" were situated on Main Street, Luray, before the park was actually established. On the left near the mules' heads was Shenandoah Park Homesteads and on the right behind the lady in the buckboard was the Shenandoah Park project office (Emergency Conservation Work-Civilian Conservation Corps-connected until it became National Park Service on March 1, 1936). (Zerkel collection, SNP archives)

leaves 35 as "squatters." At least 20 of the squatters proved successful—that is, some equity in real estate was recognized by the courts with payment to the squatter-owner resulting from the land condemnation.

President FDR, First Lady Eleanor, and Secretary Ickes—with agreement but, I gather, little encouragement by Virginia—decided parkland residents must be resettled in specially created communities. They could live in their present homes until those homesteads were ready. Yet, after thorough investigation by the Homestead Lady (Cowden) and others, only 293 families were considered homestead prospects. State welfare would somehow resettle 104 families, and 68 were put in another category, expected to relocate on their own or to be allowed to live out their lifetimes at their old homes here. The "lifetime people," mostly elderly, were soon put on a secret lifetime list by Secretary Ickes.

The Interior Department's Division of Subsistence Homesteads planned a mixture of full-time and part-time farms. Those preferring part-time farming would be expected to get supplemental work in industry or elsewhere. There was a tentative federal allotment to buy three thousand acres of farmland and build 340 homesteads, complete with dwelling houses, barns, and other outbuildings, and fences. L. Ferdinand Zerkel was to find suitable land. But confusion couldn't be dispelled. Agencies, allotments, and personnel shifted inside the government somewhat as clients did on the outside—unpredictably. Families moved out of the park without reporting; other families from "nowhere" moved into the vacated houses. People were drifting in the lowlands as well as the mountains during these depths of the Great Depression.

Another element of confusion was a Recreation Demonstration project, financed by depression-fighting funds. It came in disguise, because the park law didn't allow land buying with federal funds. The RD project bought tracts adjacent to the park—not through condemnation but sold voluntarily by the owners—and the prices negotiated were usually lower than the conservation commission's appraisals of two years before. (See Appendix 4 for names, acreages, and prices.) Soon the RD land, supposed to have been for an independent project, was transferred to the park. It totaled 10,294 acres and brought in 24 additional families needing resettlement. Almost everybody was puzzled frequently, especially the residents.

In the spring of 1934, Emmet Lam, for instance, wrote in to see if he could plant crops as he had the year before. Engineer-in-charge Lassiter gave permission and added that "all persons must move out of the Park Area by November 1st, 1934, and it is hoped that the Subsistence Homesteads will be ready. . . . No person has any right to come in and squat on . . . the Park Area." Zerkel wrote to a John A. Eppard, warning against turning old sod (well-established grassland) for new cultivation. On another case, Zerkel wrote the priest in charge of a condemned mission house in Greene County that permission for Jack Samuels to move into that building was denied. Lassiter was corresponding with Will Carson about Vernon Foltz, who had "an unauthorized filling station" on the Skyline Drive near Swift Run Gap and was suspected of "hauling firewood from the Park Area to Elkton for sale." Lassiter suggested the state evict Foltz.

In June 1934, John T. Nicholson of Nicholson Hollow was writing stanza after stanza of a poem called "The Old Mountain Home," as if expressing directly the feelings of his 73-year-old father, John Russ Nicholson. John T. sent the stanzas to Lassiter. One read:

> In the old mountain home
> For six months more.
> Where then shall I go?
> Down in the valley
> To perish and to die.

John Russ was granted permission to remain his lifetime in the park; as it turned out, he died before the people were actually moved.

When families in not-so-comfortable houses saw a better house vacated by a family escaping the uncertainties of the park, they raced to be first in occupying the vacated place. In the fall of 1934, Zerkel wrote to Newton Sisk, revoking permission he'd previously given for Newt and family to move from Frazier Hollow to the D. H. Kendall house that was also in the park, near Elkwallow. Zerkel said he'd learned Jesse Bailey had

"The Old Mountain Home" of John Russ Nicholson, as it looked after his death here shortly before the exodus of mountain folk in 1937. In a long poem, John T. Nicholson celebrated this home and his elderly father, who'd long been dreading the move to the lowland. John Russ was a son of the old "King of Free-State Hollow," Aaron Nicholson. (NPS)

priority at the Kendall house and added, "You two had better forget your differences and get along."

This Newt Sisk case illustrates several complexities. His asking permission, instead of just moving quickly on his own, must have earned him favor of future value. Records show that about 1930 Newt had owned and occupied 18 acres near Hull school, on the North Fork, Thornton River, the property having a five-room house. Later the house burned. Perhaps Newt defaulted on payments after that; in subsequent records the 18 acres (considered 20 then, perhaps one case where resurvey increased the acreage) was bought by the RD project from John W. Johnson of Hagerstown, Maryland.

Newt Sisk and family, presumably with permission, did soon move into the Kendall place. Perhaps Bailey had located a still better vacancy. That Kendall home of the Sisks, near Elkwallow, was where I stayed while botanizing and otherwise working in the park region from 1935 to 1937. I enjoyed lodging with the Sisks and thrived on their meals. Newt, age 39 in 1934, with his wife Daisy and his five children, ages 4–12, was in line for a homestead in 1936 but was shifted the next year to the welfare relocation list. The family soon moved to a tiny farm obtained for them near Amissville, Virginia.

Mr. and Mrs. Melanchthon Cliser lived beside U.S. 211 about a mile west of the summit and operated a gas station there. They owned 46 acres, and the place was condemned by the state along with other land. Cliser rejected the $4,865 check. He refused to recognize the new ownership and issued a series of warnings against trespassing, especially by state or federal officials. These enemies, he said, were violating rights granted to him by Magna Carta and the U.S. Constitution. He was discussing the matter with the president by phone, he said.

When all efforts to negotiate failed, Wilbur C. Hall, who'd taken over from Carson as head of the conservation commission, initiated eviction. Judge H. W. Bertram issued the court order instructing Sheriff E. L. Lucas of Page County to perform the task. Lucas talked with Gov. George C. Peery, hoping the state would take a different course. Only after the governor told him his duty, and the judge threatened contempt of court, did Lucas tackle the job.

The sheriff and his men found Cliser, age 62, at his station near the house on October 3, 1935. Though he didn't resist bodily, he threatened in shock and anger. He was held handcuffed while deputies piled household goods beside the highway, then barred the doors and windows to keep him and his wife from getting back in. CCC men helped carry and guard household goods. They offered to haul them. The Clisers were taken to stay with kinfolk at Luray.

Cliser couldn't bring himself to use the money—a substantial amount in those years, yet far from what he thought his place was worth. The hurt and insult wouldn't heal. The Clisers' daughter, Merle Fox of Luray, who grew up at the mountain home that had been her grandfather's, too, told me in 1987 that her father hadn't been a mean man in other situations, but in this one he deeply believed the Constitution would protect him in holding on to his home. Two years after the eviction he wrote to the president, saying the sheriff and "Grover C. Miller, clerk of the court of Page County, who must have written the order of Judge Bertram to evict me," had violated the Constitution and "should be impeached." Even 12 years after the eviction Cliser wrote Rep. Burr P. Harrison, saying he was due $8–$10,000 for his property so he could buy a proper place outside the park. Officials felt sympathy but couldn't change what had been done. Cliser died the next year, age 75.

Use of physical force was rare. Most of the park residents waited for orders, hoping they'd never come, but obeying when they did come. Vernon Foltz was evicted from his business and residence at the edge of the Skyline Drive soon after the Cliser eviction—but "peacefully," the Harrisonburg paper said. The job was done by a Rockingham deputy who'd been Foltz's boyhood friend. Six truckloads of personal property, including two hundred bushels of potatoes and apples, had to be hauled. The state scheduled two more evictions, for next spring.

When park rangers came on duty, beginning March 1, 1936, their main job was with the mountain folk. R. Taylor Hoskins, the first chief ranger, worked every day of every week for months. He got better acquainted with park residents than anyone else ever did, with the possible exceptions of Zerkel and Mozelle R. Cowden, "the Homestead Lady." He liked and enjoyed the people. The rangers came to know a few troublemakers and had to make arrests for theft or arson or other crimes, but nearly all the contacts the rangers made were friendly. They had to visit every home and issue new occupancy permits. They took pictures of many families, and the people enjoyed the pictures. A lot of the residents got employment related to the park. Some worked on the Skyline Drive, beginning at the start, in 1931, and some of the same people were still working for the park or the concessioner in 1970 or later.

Hoskins accumulated anecdotes, with laughter at himself and other rangers as well as at some mountain habits and situations. He and Wallace T. Stephens, the assistant chief, patroling in a pickup, surprised three mountain men, including Jim Nicholson, with a keg. The men dropped the keg and disappeared into the forest. The rangers picked up the keg and put it on the truck as if to haul it away. Jim quickly reappeared, but limping and using a stick, and engaged them in conversation as if he'd never seen them before. He looked at the keg and asked, "What's thet you got thar?" Hoskins answered, "Whiskey, I reckon." Jim looked from rangers to keg and back and finally said, "Let's all have a drink."

The current Jack Dodson of Hazel Mountain country, according to Hoskins, told a story on himself. He was water carrier with a big crew drilling the Skyline Drive tunnel. One day, deep inside that Marys Rock side ridge, they blasted into "heaps o' snakes, them copperheads and rattlers sleeping up together." The snakes were so excited and so numerous, striking and spitting into the air: "A hundred snakes anyhow, I reckon—and thet thar venom got so thick in the air, lots o' the men got sick and went home. I got sick m'self. The air was jist per-me-ated with thet pizen!"

George Corbin, a successful moonshiner for some years, who voluntarily retired from the profession without ever getting caught, agreed one day to mind the still of a crippled friend while the friend did something elsewhere that he had to do. Two "revenooers" came hunting

A typical new homestead within sight of the mountains, with clothes on the line and the family head watching the photographer. Mountain people adapted well to lowland life, though rather few remained long in the homes First Lady Eleanor and high officials had considered ideal for them. (Zerkel collection, SNP archives)

for the still, and George took off running with those two chasing. George put on speed and got far enough ahead to cut sideways and hide along a bushy creek. Those "revenooers" came along all puffing and puzzled, one saying to the other, "If a crippled moonshiner can run like that, I'd sure hate to try catching a healthy one!" George's son Virgil tells this one to the present day and says his father in his prime was the fastest runner in the Blue Ridge.

Mountain people could outsmart rangers sometimes, too, Hoskins said. A home had been vacated across the hollow from Lee Highway west of Panorama. He and other rangers drove past there twice a day, going to and from the Skyline Drive. They were accustomed to keeping track of empty houses to prevent reoccupation or theft of doors and windows—there being a policy to save those with good lumber for possible use in building homestead houses or barns—but they saw nothing out of order at this one, which was in such plain sight. It stayed seemingly intact and vacant. When at last a ranger did chance to come near the place at a different angle, he found that house was only a false front propped up by poles cut from the forest. Everything else was gone.

Hoskins said mountain girls admired uniformed men, such as rangers. They'd ask him if he was married, and when he said yes, they'd say, "If you git a single ranger, we'd like right well to meet him." When Cliff Harriman came, Hoskins drove him down to Old Rag school. Even the very young girls gathered around the pickup when Hoskins said, "Here's a single ranger." One named Esther examined Harriman closely through the window, then said, "Ain't he purty!"

The one forcible eviction Hoskins participated in upset him deeply. The landowner Ed Brumback, years before, had told this Walker Jenkins, his tenant out from Big Meadows toward Tanners Ridge, he could go on living there forever. Jenkins wouldn't admit the land condemnation made any difference, and the elder Brumback was now dead. The state served eviction papers, but Jenkins still wouldn't leave. Rangers were asked to help the Page County sheriff and deputy.

They approached long before dawn so as to find everyone at home. The lamp was lit and all the family in bed saying they were sick. No doctor was present to disprove sickness, so they had to return another time with the CCC doctor. He examined Mrs. Jenkins first and found her well, though pregnant. She wouldn't walk, so they picked her up bodily. She started praying, but before they got her out and into the car she'd called them all kinds of names. Then they got Walker out. After him were five or six large girls who fought like cats. But there was plenty of help, and the job was done. The furniture was moved out, and the CCC crew started tearing the house down. A reporter came, and the story was dramatized widely.

People who continued to protest that they were moved out with no payment for their homes and land were mostly such "tenants." Several generations of a family line might have lived at the same tenant house, using it and the land around it as if they were owners. Many tenants felt like owners. It's ironic that squatters holding land without agreement by the landowner could be paid for "their" homeplaces, according to law and custom, while "tenants" who weren't exactly tenants, and may have used land longer than current deed holders and most squatters, could not be paid. Some tenants were originally squatters but later agreed to help the owner a bit with his cattle.

No firsthand account of the eviction of John H. Mace from his home on Madison Run is available to me now, but the truth-based legend is still being told. Mace had owned the place a long time before condemnation. His spring flowed with "Health Mineral Water" that he transported to Harrisburg, Pennsylvania, apparently both before and after the eviction, and recommended "to all suffering from Eczema, Pimples, Tetter, or other skin diseases, Stomach Trouble, Kidney Trouble, Nervousness, or Loss of Appetite." People I've talked with claim to have been cured by this water. The sheriff's officers talked Mace out of the house, so the story goes, then got his personal belongings out and stacked them at a slight distance. While Mace stood by his belongings, the officers, probably helped by a CCC crew, burned the house. Both the procedure and the lasting resentment are understandable. Many old houses were destroyed after being vacated to keep unauthorized people from moving in, but not usually when the family couldn't help seeing.

In September 1934 the resettlement project bought 343 acres at Ida, outside the park boundary just west of Hawksbill Mountain, and laid out 28 farms. Construction of houses, barns, and fences started October 28. Then the solicitor general of the Interior Department discovered that the law authorized Ickes's homesteads division to provide homes only for refugees from urban centers, not from wild or rural places. Ickes complained in his secret diary that he'd chosen the wrong executives and that Mrs. Roosevelt and Col. Louis Howe had "interfered altogether too much." The work at Ida was shut down. An effort was made to transfer the project to another agency, without success.

There were six months of confused paralysis; then the president revived the Shenandoah project through the Resettlement Administration headed by Rexford G. Tugwell. Zerkel was now project manager with full local authority. Construction began again at Ida. Other homestead communities were moving toward action. The matching of homesteads to park residents was harder than shooting a swift-flying bird. A total of

SIX GENERATIONS STARTING WITH ARCHETYPICAL
MOUNTAIN MAN, "THE KING OF FREE-STATE HOLLOW"

The castle of "King" Aaron Nicholson   >
before it began to deteriorate from neglect.
It was unique in having stone walls as well
as stone chimneys forming both ends of
the long, otherwise log structure covered
with vertical boards. (NPS)

< King Aaron, born in 1830, was reigning
strongly when young Pollock first came to
Skyland in 1886 and continued reigning
for at least another two decades. On
monthly court days at Madison, he rode
horseback to attend the sessions. There
had been an earlier Aaron, one of the first
two Nicholsons to live in this hollow,
born on the piedmont in 1772. The very
first Nicholson in Madison-Culpeper had
been the first Aaron's grandfather,
according to genealogy by Chuck and
Nan Perdue, so ten generations of
Nicholsons are known, the earliest and the
latest living outside the mountains. Family
tradition says King Aaron himself left
Nicholson Hollow about 1910—because
after he married a second time, to Alice E.
Strother of Culpeper, other Nicholson
women allegedly tried to poison this new
wife. Aaron finally believed her
suspicions. He and she left in anger, went
to live near Wolftown, and never came
back.

< Mollie Nicholson, daughter of Aaron, and
Madison Corbin, her husband, about
1880. (Courtesy of Virgil F. Corbin)

< George T. Corbin, son of Madison Corbin, married Bertie Nicholson about 1912, bought land, and built a new home in Nicholson Hollow. The family moved out of the park to Ida Homesteads in 1937, thrived quite well for years, then moved on. (Courtesy of Virgil F. Corbin)

Virgil F. Corbin, son of George T., and > his wife Rose B. Corbin celebrated their 30th wedding anniversary at the end of September 1980 with a stay at Skyland— where the city folk used to be amused at the "odd" mountain folk. Virgil was about 20 when the family moved out of the park. He worked as a painter for many years. Now, he's "a diligent Bible student," he says. He has studied with two Bible schools, reads nonsectarian Christian literature, and is interested in teaching Bible classes. (Courtesy of Virgil T. Corbin)

Scott F. Corbin, sixth-generation from > "King" Aaron Nicholson, with his grandfather Virgil and his father Clinton, at home in the town of Luray. Scott was eight in 1988. (Courtesy of Virgil F. Corbin)

< Aaron Nicholson's Castle in the 1970s, with wilderness returning around it, rock walls and the chimneys gradually crumbling. After Aaron moved away his son Gustavos "Gust" Nicholson lived here but didn't become "King."

219 families from the 1934 census were now missing and must have moved out of the park on their own initiative. Yet 336 families were still on the relocation-aid rolls; 22 were still planning to move without help; and 15 were on the secret lifetime list. Add those who had been listed in the census but were now gone to those now listed and remaining in the park and you get 592. How? If you add the 24 RD families to the 465 in the census, you get at most 489. The enumerators couldn't have failed to find as many as a hundred families that were really there, could they? New marriages could explain some new families, and an unknown number of families had certainly come into the area before the vacated cabins could be demolished, mostly relatives with names similar to previously registered families. The extras must have just drifted in. It was impossible to reconcile the figures with the shifting reality, but Zerkel did his best. He compared inward and outward drift. Overall, the net change was at the rate of 12 percent annually—outward.

Maybe only 250 homesteads would be needed. Estimated cost was now $1.5 million, including land, houses, outbuildings, water supply, even household furnishings and livestock—about $6,000 per homestead unit. Ida had 20 homes ready early, but no water system, yet coordination steadily improved. Then, just as the new communities were ready for occupancy in the fall of 1937, there was another surprise reorganization. The project was moved in Washington from the Resettlement Administration to the Farm Security Administration, and here from Zerkel as project manager, with an office in Luray, to James S. Wills, community manager, with an office at Elkton. October 18 was announced as the day.

All around the mountains women were doing last-minute laundry and hanging clothes out to dry; men were making boxes to be filled with fresh vegetables and fruit and innumerable glass jars of canned food, including apple butter. Hogs, cows, and chickens were penned ready to load, but it was hard for anybody to be sure just when—or how . . . Rangers tried to coordinate the families, the CCC trucks, and the FSA officials and workers. It was soon obvious no great number of families could be moved in one day. Could you be totally ready at any instant to move from a home where you'd "always" lived?

The general moving continued until planting time early in 1938, and there were still stragglers. Homesteads absorbed 172 families in all—out of the 465 counted in 1934, plus the 24 RD families, plus whatever the inward drift had been, minus the outward drift. There were seven communities—at Ida Valley in Page County, near Stanardsville in Greene County, near Elkton in Rockingham County, at Madison and Wolftown sites in Madison County, and at the Washington and Flint Hill sites in Rappahannock County. Virginia public welfare, with federal help, had but 71 families on its list now. Six were placed with relatives in homesteads; homes were bought for 24. Varied arrangements were made for others.

People placed in welfare-purchased houses were to pay a little rent, enough ultimately to own the places. Homestead rules called for $5 a month rent during 1938, after which the house and land could be bought at appraised value with as much as 40 years to pay. Everyone who bought paid considerably less than the government had spent to make the new home. Not many of the park people did buy. Most soon found homes they liked better. The difficulty the "mountaineers" would have adjusting to lowland living had been exaggerated. They weren't so unlike their new neighbors; in fact many had close relatives who'd "always" lived in the low country.

No part of the Greene County community was ever bought by a park family. Despite much advice against the plan, Tugwell had imposed a French-village system, in which everyone lives in the tight little village and the land is farmed cooperatively. The mountain people moved out of that system. George Corbin liked Ida well enough to live there for years; then he moved elsewhere and lived a long life, partly in a suburb of Washington, D.C. Dennis Corbin and his wife have done well in the Flint Hill homestead community; they're still living there in 1988 on land they bought and have children and grandchildren nearby. Homesteads were on the open market when former park residents no longer wanted them. Many of the homes have been added to or remodeled beyond recognition.

The Homestead Lady, who kept track of her mountain friends for some while, was proud of the Bernie Taylors, who farmed good-sized fields successfully at the Elkton site. Bernie personally taught "school" to his numerous sons, through fourth grade, as his father Delon Taylor had taught him. All the sons graduated from high school and all bought and paid for their own homes before they married. Two daughters of Fred Dodson, who took a homestead at Flint Hill, graduated from college. The transplanted people have done as well in the world as the people around them, sometimes better.

Yet those park-land mothers and fathers who are still with us, and the park-born children, too, long grown-up now, have a longing that won't quit. They remember the mountain spring, the cold water so pure and sparkling, forever flowing. They remember the nut trees and the berries, the trout in the streams, the taste of squirrel and maybe 'possum and coon and groundhog. The cabbages grew bigger up there, and the apples tastier. Though life was sometimes hard, they could do what they had to do when they felt like doing it, not when some schedule imposed upon them. The freedom was greater there, and the security was far more dependable than outsiders ever seem to have understood.

Edward A. Harris, who had a 63-acre mountain place near Browns Gap and felt pushed out when he lost ownership, expressed the feeling of the displaced mountaineer in a ballad. The sheet music and a dozen stanzas were copyrighted in 1975. Bits are used here with permission from Mrs. Roy (Virginia) Harris, Edward's daughter-in-law. The copy was furnished by grandson Arnold L. Via, who played for me a cassette of the song being sung. Harris's home was high up on the Doyle River, above the falls. There was a six-room, two-story, frame house with two nice porches, a shingle and metal roof, brick chimneys, and a solid foundation. Nearby were a springhouse, washhouse, cement cellar, hen house, hog pen, two stables, meat house, corncrib, wagon shed, and woodshed. Tillable land totaled 17 acres and grazing land 37 acres, while forest was growing again on 9 acres. There were 96 good apple trees.

Here are some words from "The Blue Ridge Mountaineer."

> I have a good spring and a spring-house combined.
> I hate to go and leave it behind.
> I have a good orchard and lots of good fruit.
> I often watch my big hogs root. . . .
>
> In came the government people with papers in their hands,
> Saying, "Old man we have taken your land.
> You must vacate by April First."
> I felt right then my heart would burst. . . .
>
> I woke up next morning at the rising of the sun.
> I cast my eyes around me while the tears began to fall.
> I wish I was back on Old Browns Gap
> Where I used to raise potatoes as big as my cap.

Knowledge gradually leaked that there was a secret list of "aged and especially meritorious" residents who would be allowed to live out their lifetimes in their old homes. Harris might have been on it if he or his friends had known it existed. The people on the list were paid for their property if they owned any, but some were tenants and several actually squatters. They weren't charged any rent. Personal situation and "merit" were deciding factors. This lifetime list had had 43 names in 1934, recommended by Will Carson and approved by Ickes. The secrecy came from fear everyone would want on. (The names are marked with an *L* in Appendix 5, Heads of Families Living on Park-land, 1935.)

By the fall of 1937 five of the 43 had died, 21 had moved out, and 17 were still living in the park. Upon recommendation from local park people who knew the situation well, Ickes finally accepted fundamental revision of the list at the end of 1937. Six names were taken off, 11 new ones added, and the secrecy was ended. It was made clear that the privilege was for the listed persons only "and at their death the remaining members of the family will have to move out." Nearly all those on the revised list lived near cross-mountain highways or just inside the park, with neighbors just outside.

In April 1940, 19 families still lived in the park—a total of 78 people. One was Barbara Nicholson, age 75, admired by many for her folk singing. George Hurt, 79, and his wife, Lucy, 77, were described as feeble. Two years later they died—just 17 days apart—at the home of their daughter and son-in-law outside the park. In 1944 Joseph Franklin Wood, 73, died of pneumonia at the home of a son-in-law to which he and Mrs. Wood had recently moved. His home was near where Robert H. Via once lived, and he'd been affectionately known as "the Mayor of Sugar Hollow."

By 1945 only nine families remained. Family heads were George Shifflett, 55, on a special use permit as dedicated caretaker of old Lam's Mill near U.S. 33; Matilda "Aunt Cassie" Breeden, 85, Swift Run; Thomas Morris, 60, Swift Run; Barbara Nicholson, 80, Weakley Hollow; William Thomas, 83, Tanners Ridge; Nebraskey "Brass" Woodward, 64, Dark Hollow; Teeny Atkins, 70, above Sperryville; Lewis Willis, 80, below Marys Rock (his wife Ida had died); and Annie Lee Bradley Shenk, 59, Shenk Hollow (her considerably older husband had died).

Annie Shenk would be the last of the long-ago people in the park. She lived about a mile up the mountain from park headquarters, a short distance north of U.S. 211, for 33 years after her husband died. She died January 14, 1979, at the age of 92.

CHAPTER XIX

Managers and Visitors

Shenandoah's most popular attraction has been the views from the Skyline Drive—the continually unrolling panoramas of Blue Ridge, Piedmont Plain, Shenandoah Valley, and distant Alleghenies. President Hoover called them "the greatest in the world." The sensation was somewhat as if you had a Grand Canyon on both sides of you as you moved easily along. Park Service officials liked the popularity but weren't entirely comfortable with the starring role of the Skyline Drive and the fact that half the scenery was located outside the park boundary. The administration and Congress had intended this park to be an example of the natural Southern Appalachians. This meant—didn't it?—that visitors should pay attention mostly to wildflowers and forest, wild creatures, wild mountains, and streams.

When James Ralph Lassiter became the first park superintendent, he and the Civilian Conservation Corps were doing their best to bring "nature" up to star status, ready to steal the show from the Skyline Drive. The whole place was scenic when President Franklin D. Roosevelt came to Big Meadows to dedicate the park on July 3, 1936. Shenandoah had won the race with Great Smoky Mountains to welcome the public in large numbers. Though Smoky had been accepted by the National Park Service in 1930 "for protection only" and in 1934 had become a full-status national park, it was years from its grand opening or dedication. There's no evidence the president noticed the dichotomy in Shenandoah that worried park officials. He saw unity: "the joint husbandry of our human resources and our natural resources." He expected both recreation and "re-creation," the second word applying, I think, to the blending of human and natural resources.

Lassiter was an engineer and proud of the Skyline Drive, but he quickly learned what national parks featuring scenes and phenomena of nature are supposed to be like. He was keeping the CCC boys busy re-creating wild nature and grading trails to get more visitors away from the drive and into the wild. Most of the visitors, comfortably motorized, were

Top: President Franklin D. Roosevelt dedicated the park in nationally broadcast ceremonies (rare that early) at Big Meadows on July 3, 1936. In this picture he's close behind the speaker's stand but hasn't moved forward. First Lady Eleanor is at the right, next to Interior Secretary Harold L. Ickes. The men who worked the longest and hardest to establish the park—Pollock, Byrd, Carson, Zerkel, Cammerer, among others—don't seem to be in sight. (Courtesy of Dr. and Mrs. Eric Rhodes) *Bottom*: The dedication crowd at Big Meadows, which obviously had much more wide-open space in the 1930s than it does now. (Courtesy of Dr. and Mrs. Eric Rhodes)

proving reluctant to leave their cars and the "greatest" views for trails curtained by shrubs and trees.

The superintendent seemed always eager to stay in the office at Luray long past quitting time to confer with the CCC project supervisors, who couldn't seem to break away earlier from their work on the mountain. Or he'd go to confer with them there and watch the CCC boys planting trees where the ground looked empty, creating camp and picnic grounds, building stone walls so people and cars wouldn't fall off parking overlooks, or maybe installing water fountains where pure spring water was found. Lassiter liked to analyze problems with technicians and foremen. He could sit on his heels—but always ready to spring up—for longer than anyone I ever knew.

The cars flowed steadily along Skyline Drive, mostly obeying the speed limit of 35 miles an hour. When the car stopped at an overlook, the driver might keep the motor running, as the stop wouldn't take long. There'd be exclamations about the view, then on the road again. But

Myron H. Avery, left, head of the Potomac Appalachian Trail Club and the overall Appalachian Trail Conference, was a major influence during the early years of the park. He fell short, however, of getting the Skyline Drive moved off the Blue Ridge crest, away from the trail, in the south district. (Courtesy of the Potomac Appalachian Trail Club) James Ralph Lassiter, right, ECW-CCC engineer-in-charge of the Shenandoah park project, 1933–36, and Shenandoah's first superintendent, had more than 1,200 men working under his management here. (NPS)

sometimes the people would get out and stretch their legs and maybe take each other's pictures, and somebody might ask a CCC boy, stationed there, a question, and he might introduce them to "the park." An occasional bold person might venture a few yards on a trail—tentatively— but the dress shoes hurt or might get scuffed. The motorized sightseers in their thousands seemed a different species from the too-scarce hikers (who were mostly, in the early years, trail club members).

A collection of old postcards mailed by early visitors, and lent to me by Dave Musichuk, has many spontaneous expressions of enthusiasm for the ever-changing panoramic views. The old pictures remind me that wide open spaces of grassland characterized the Blue Ridge when the park was new. The views were everywhere, not just from overlooks, and legends on some of the cards proclaimed, "Shenandoah smiles a hundred miles."

There was no professional naturalist, no official interpretive program, so the Shenandoah Nature Society was formed to get and spread information in the hope that, with knowledge of flowers, trees, wildlife, rocks, and the park's human history, visitors would penetrate more deeply. The society arranged lectures and radio programs and published the *Shenandoah Nature Journal*. CCC boys helped, and even sold some magazines at 10¢ each.

Lassiter faced puzzles. Potomac Appalachian Trail Club leader Myron H. Avery seriously proposed to keep the Skyline Drive off the range in the park's south district so as to leave "a wilderness area" on the peaks. Secretary Ickes delayed awarding a drive construction contract while Lassiter studied the possibility. Though Lassiter liked to joke that the only good hiking was by people other than himself, he was open to Avery's idea. But the Avery route proved 20 percent longer and much more expensive in grading and bridge construction. Ickes kept the crest route.

A crisis over secondary roads grew when Ickes ordered collection of a 25¢ fee from every car entering the park. Cross-mountain roads other than U.S. 211 and U.S. 33 were chained shut. Virginians resented paying to enter the park they'd given as a gift to Uncle Sam. Even more, they resented the blocking of roads they'd used all their lives. Virginians in Congress legislated public use of both the Madison-Page and Browns Gap "turnpikes." Lassiter warned that if even one road were opened, "in the next ten years we will open at least one road a year," there having been so many roads in use. FDR, with strong reasoning about the integrity of national parks' serving the nation, not primarily local people, vetoed the legislation.

Virginia Sky-Line Company, Inc., newly formed at Richmond, became the park concessioner in 1937. It took Skyland over from Pollock—which I feel he never thought could happen even though his real estate had been taken. NPS officials believed Pollock, too set in the old ways of entertaining, would fail to meet the challenge of serving tens of thousands of visitors instead of merely hundreds. The new company also took over businesses at Thornton and Swift Run gaps and was soon providing meals, lodging, and other commercial services to visitors at half a dozen locations near the Skyline Drive. Following Virginia custom, the concessioner planned separate facilities for "colored people." The National Park Service, here and in Washington, D.C., cooperated in this plan.

A development called Lewis Mountain, seven miles south of Big Meadows, was designated for blacks. The Park Service installed utilities and a picnic ground and was preparing a campground while the concessioner was building a lodge and cabins. In the summer of 1939 the picnic ground was being used by substantial numbers of blacks; on August 17 alone the count was 385, mostly participants in a church picnic.

Though Lewis Mountain seemed successful, a storm was just over the horizon. Interior Secretary Ickes considered himself "in advance of every other member" of FDR's cabinet in winning "real justice and opportunity for the Negro at long last" and holding Negro voters in the Democratic party. He'd insisted on equal, though separate, dining facilities in this

Racial policy caused quarrels, mostly between officials, early in the 1940s. Virginia still had separate (but equal) facilities for "colored" people. Interior Secretary Harold L. Ickes couldn't live with that, and the park superintendent got caught in the middle. (NPS)

park's restaurants and had ordered an experiment in joint use by whites and blacks at Pinnacles Picnic Grounds.

Lassiter reported in late 1939 that there'd been white complaints and some arguments at Pinnacles but "no fights . . . yet." In December 1939 Lassiter had a heart attack. While he was confined to bed, Ickes stepped in and ordered Cammerer to prohibit mention of segregation in any park pamphlets or maps or signs. Cammerer obeyed, but in June 1940 he resigned; he died unexpectedly in 1941. Meanwhile Lassiter had recovered and, on returning to work, criticized as confusing the policy of having the Lewis Mountain development for Negroes yet not letting the fact be known. Ickes sent for Lassiter and scolded him personally, focusing on an incident that happened during Lassiter's illness and absence. A ranger here had apparently marked Lewis Mountain on a map as the park's special place for Negroes, thus violating Ickes's order. If Lassiter had trained his personnel properly, this violation wouldn't have happened, Ickes said. Lassiter promised to do his best to avoid such happenings in the future.

Three modest entrance stations of the early years—North, Thornton Gap, and Swift Run Gap. The fee was 25¢ per car. Virginians protested paying at all to enter land they'd donated. Still, the visitor count climbed to astonishing heights, climaxing in colorful autumns. Panorama Tea Room was prominent at Thornton Gap (dinners 75¢). Monuments at Swift Run intersection commemorated Governor Spotswood and his "Knights of the Golden Horseshoe," who were supposed to have crossed the Blue Ridge here in 1716. (NPS)

Though racial tensions continued, they didn't erupt again until after World War II, in the next superintendent's term, but Ickes's anger didn't fade. An Interior Department order was issued transferring Lassiter to Great Smoky Mountains National Park and Supt. Ross Eakin of that park to Shenandoah. (Ickes had a separate and different quarrel with Eakin.) Before this order could be carried out, it was indefinitely postponed. Shortly before Pearl Harbor, though, another order came. Lassiter was transferred to the NPS regional office at Santa Fe, New Mexico. Virginia newspapers protested. Ickes again called Lassiter to Washington, D.C., and verbally attacked him for "making political trouble," though Lassiter had had nothing to do with the editorials. In New Mexico, out of Ickes's sight, Lassiter advanced to a higher salary as regional engineer than he'd have had as superintendent of Shenandoah. Yet the wounds of Ickes's anger never really healed. Lassiter died in Santa Fe at age 59.

Shenandoah's boundary has had unending zags and zigs, but the deep orientation of development and heavy use along the top-middle and little or no use near the boundary have stayed surprisingly constant. One question that would sleep, then leap awake and howl, then sleep again, has been whether the park could succeed in its decreed purpose with its acreage so drastically reduced from the original concept and its boundary so terribly crooked—"like a fish skeleton."

This "Skyline Drive v. Nature Park" conflict has many facets. The Avery proposal was part of the "top-middle development v. boundary-area development" facet. Top-middle—development along the range crest in the middle of the park rather than along the park's boundary— proposed by Cammerer years before the park became official, has proved strongest, with only one significant exception so far: Park headquarters, with main offices, warehouses and shops, and employee residences, had been planned at Big Meadows, then at Thornton Gap; toward the end of Lassiter's term, it was finally located along U.S. 211 at the west foot of the mountains near Luray. Among other facets of "Drive v. Park" have been distant views v. wilderness or views v. nature study, motoring v. hiking, boulevard v. Appalachian Trail, artificial recreation v. natural recreation, interpretation through signs at overlooks v. personally conducted nature walks into the wild. You'll see even a hiking pattern that reverses the arrangement of the typical national park. In Shenandoah, "civilization" and trail entrances are in the middle of the park, while "backcountry" is out toward the boundary. And the boundary, instead of providing access, is seen as a no-man's-land, with crossings by either park visitors or park neighbors not encouraged.

Marys Rock Tunnel brought exclamations of pleasure, though it was unlined then, always dripping in warm weather, spawning giant icicles in winter. You're looking northward at Pass Mountain. (NPS)

Some puzzles have pertained to time rather than space. There's been re-creation of nature v. preservation of old structures and other man-made remnants such as clearings. Related is interpreting wild nature v. interpreting human doings in the mountains—natural history v. human history. There's also vista clearing on the drive and some trail viewpoints v. the sacredness of flowers and trees in a national park. You'll notice, I think, that as regrowth made nature look stronger and stronger here, the NPS compulsion to erase all signs of the human past began to weaken. You may even notice NPS pride in the fact that only here, after centuries of diverse human exploitation, has there been such a large-scale return to wilderness—on purpose. Since this reversing of the supposedly inevitable trend of civilization resulted from human decisions and actions, the creation of this park is beginning to be seen as, in itself, a significant event in world history.

Shenandoah's second superintendent, Edward D. Freeland, came on January 1, 1942, just after the bombing of Pearl Harbor. The CCC was abolished, and hundreds of men from Shenandoah went into military service. Similarly the NPS staff, confronted for the first time with the whole weight of park work, was severely diminished as members left for war-connected duties. Manpower here dropped to one-twentieth of former strength. Worse yet, travel stopped; millions of friends who'd regularly enjoyed the park and bolstered the personnel's morale were absent.

Edward D. Freeland, Shenandoah's second
superintendent, suffered loss of most of his
help and nearly all the park's visitors
because of World War II. (NPS)

Under the circumstances, Freeland was worried about what would
happen if, say, there were a bad forest fire. Moreover he was in strange
territory. His work experience had been mostly in the great western
parks, and he was a longtime admirer of the first NPS director, Stephen
T. Mather. To promote goodwill among neighbors who may have never
liked the park, Freeland staged the first big open house at park
headquarters, especially inviting people of the eight park counties. He
arranged for articles about the park to be published in local newspapers.
He sent top-notch rangers into nearby schools to educate children, and
through them their parents, about the long-range plan of the park: to let
nature re-create forest and wildlife where soil and vegetation had been
heavily used. The rangers explained how this re-creation would help the
bordering lowlands. The citizens responded well.

In a 1978 interview Freeland told me that his first day on the job he
heard a woman answer the telephone with, "Skyline Drive." I hadn't
supposed Lassiter had been letting that happen, but people generally
knew the Skyline Drive better than they knew the Shenandoah National
Park. Many, in fact, knew the Skyline Drive but never heard of the park.
State highway signs said—*Skyline Drive,*—and just about everyone with
key concern for the park had tried to persuade the state to use *Shenandoah
National Park* instead. State men said the words were too long and the
location "indefinite."

Crusading for the park as more important than its Skyline Drive
became part of Freeland's personality. During World War II automobiles
along the drive were scarce—averaging three or four a day—for gasoline
and tires were rationed. Freeland promoted hiking, trout fishing, and
horseback riding. Hikers came from Washington, D.C., to Thornton Gap

Some military forces trained in the park during World War II. The Engineers'
Replacement Center at Big Meadows "processed" thousands of men, sometimes in
conditions that would pass for Arctic. (NPS)

on a daily bus; they could spend most of a weekend on the trails. Freeland
encouraged a pack- and saddle-horse service operating over park trails
beginning at or near Front Royal. Overnight pack trips, exclusive of
meals, were only $6 a person in parties of four. Freeland made gains, but
for one reason or another horses have never held the high place in
Shenandoah that Pollock and other early promoters expected.

When the Smithsonian Institution sought wartime storage away from
Washington, D.C., for irreplaceable items in its collection, Freeland made
room at the headquarters warehouse for 12 truckloads of historical
artifacts and scientific specimens. He remembered the "original Old
Glory" and the "first automobile ever built." The Smithsonian chief Dr.
Alexander Wetmore spent time in the park, studying birds and investigating reports of panther. He was certain, he said in 1944, that the park
had more than one live panther. Wetmore and Freeland became personal
friends, and together they observed that nature was now restoring the
landscape much faster and better than 1,200 CCC boys could ever have
done.

As the war ended and revived motor travel was anticipated, Freeland
was aware that visitors on the Skyline Drive felt as if they were "driving
through a green tunnel." His love of trees notwithstanding, he couldn't
let the views for which the park was famous be curtained off. He
consulted Washington; then he surveyed the whole drive and put together
a detailed program of "vista clearing." There was also a decision to keep
some areas open as representing past human use; the largest of these was
Big Meadows. When vista clearing began, some conservationists

protested loudly. Freeland wanted to agree that the Park Service should never cut healthy trees, but he couldn't.

Within months after World War II, Secretary Ickes ordered all national park concessioners to eliminate segregation of races—totally! Virginia Sky-Line Company protested to Freeland and to NPS Washington, saying Ickes's order was a direct violation of the NPS-Interior agreement with the Richmond-based concessioner. If Ickes insisted on such a violation, the firm's board of directors would drop the contract to serve Shenandoah's visitors.

Ickes was adamant, but soon he got into an argument (on another subject) with President Harry Truman and resigned. The Interior Department didn't change the order but became flexible in timing enforcement. NPS gave informal assurance to the concessioner, via U.S. Sen. Harry F. Byrd, that operations of the business in the park could go on as before, at least through the summer of 1946. Superintendent Freeland remembered later: "We eased in gradually," getting whites and blacks more and more accustomed to associating with each other here. Some middle executives of Virginia Sky-Line helped greatly. The park moved just ahead of most of Virginia in desegregation. By the autumn of 1947, blacks and whites were using Lewis Mountain facilities together. Integration was becoming normal here, and the park spotlight was shifting to other concerns.

In 1947, upon the initiative of Benton MacKaye, father of the Appalachian Trail and president of the Wilderness Society (which he'd helped found largely to fight skyline drives), Shenandoah developed the first environmental nature trail, in White Oak Canyon. It told the story of soil being formed through thousands of years but sometimes, through human carelessness, being lost to erosion in a few minutes. "No soil, no plants, no food, no you!" one of the signs proclaimed. This trail foreshadowed the surge of "earthmanship" in the 1970s. The trail got nationwide publicity and soon had so much traffic it had to be closed— to avoid causing the very erosion it campaigned against.

George Pollock's fancy old dining room at Skyland burned on November 5, 1948, the park's worst building fire. Pollock had continued to spend summers at Skyland, the Park Service having rented Massanutten Cottage and Annex to him and his wife (only $120 a year, 1938–41). After she died, he lived on in the Annex when he was here, usually but a few weeks in the summer. He longed for the old Skyland instead of mass visitation and the rush of the new, but he fought away from interfering. Six months after the dining room fire, he died, just short of 80 years old. His ashes were scattered from Skyland-edge cliffs into Kettle Canyon, and an unnamed mountain was named Pollock Knob in his honor. But, like that other giant of park establishment, Will Carson, he strongly haunts the whole park.

Superintendent Freeland respected the past, but NPS policy called him to allow the burning or tearing down of most of the park's remaining old homes, now deteriorated beyond repair, and letting the forest have the sites. He succeeded in hiring Shenandoah's first park naturalist, Paul G. Favour, Jr. Favour initially saw his job as interpreting natural history— wild plants and creatures, rocks and forest—out along the trails, but he was asked so many questions about people of the park's past that he guessed human history deserved some attention. He also came around to answering questions about the beyond-the-boundary views from the Skyline Drive. Some of the views included land where U.S. presidents were born, and even Skyline drivers who admired the scenery through car windows wanted to know. In 1950, because the earlier organization had been a war casualty, Favour and Freeland formed the Shenandoah Natural History Association to aid the park's interpretive program. The new association's first publication was a bird list (188 species here) by Dr. Wetmore. Soon Wetmore became the association's president and served quite a few years.

Guy D. Edwards followed Freeland as Shenandoah's superintendent in January 1951. Like Lassiter, Edwards was an engineer. Unlike Lassiter, who'd encouraged hiking but hiked very little, Edwards enjoyed Shenandoah's trails personally and directly. Yet he had far more to do with construction than with the wild park. He worked out a long-term renewal of Virginia Sky-Line's concession contract so the company could expand overnight accommodations at Skyland and Big Meadows. He

Guy D. Edwards, Shenandoah's third superintendent, puzzled over Mission 66 plans for great expansion of park facilities. He managed to moderate his enthusiasm, and that of the Washington leaders, so future appropriations might match the amount of maintenance needed. (NPS)

was in charge when the new Skyland dining room, replacing Pollock's, was completed and brought shocked protests, particularly from the National Parks Association. Skyland had always been rustic but this dining room was "modern," and it didn't fit in with its surroundings, the association said. Edwards agreed, and from that time on he watched every plan to prevent the "modern."

Mission 66, a high-pressure program to upgrade visitor facilities before the Park Service's 50th anniversary year—1966—was planned for Shenandoah under Edwards. The park had 1.5 million visitors in 1955, and 2.4 million were expected in 1966. Edwards, though vigorous, was nearing mandatory retirement. He worried about the wisdom of constructing more facilities during this surge of enthusiasm than could be properly maintained with funds likely to be appropriated after the enthusiasm faded. Increasing campsites from 83 to 450 and picnic sites from 203 to 500, and building employee housing at eight different locations, seemed to him excessive, though he did favor building structures that would carry the often-heavy Skyline Drive traffic over highways U.S. 211 and U.S. 33. Edwards tried to trim the ambitious prospectus, but nearly all the projects were approved by NPS Director Conrad L. Wirth, the main generator of the enthusiasm. Eventually time reinstated much of Edwards's trimming.

There was a quintessential Park Service battle here, a commercial invasion. Atlantic Seaboard Corporation of Charleston, West Virginia, wanted to put a new 24-inch gas pipeline across six miles of the park, coming near the South River Picnic Grounds. Edwards quickly and strongly rejected the plan, saying it would "impair the scenery and destroy natural values" while not doing anything "for the benefit and enjoyment of visitors." The battle surged back and forth. NPS Washington supported Edwards. Soon, though, word came down (but not in writing ever filed in park headquarters) that the secretary of the interior, and maybe someone higher yet, insisted the gas line go through.

Edwards was angry, but he fought for special provisions to hide the damage. He insisted that many large trees in the swath be left undisturbed and whole screens of vegetation be left at the park boundary line and the crossings of Skyline Drive and U.S. 33. He then retired in August 1958.

Former chief ranger R. Taylor Hoskins returned as superintendent that September. He'd been superintendent at Mammoth Cave, then Carlsbad Caverns, and hadn't seen Shenandoah in 20 years. The dense wildness of the forest astonished him. So did the prevalence of deer and the presence of beaver, wild turkey, and bear. When the national wilderness preservation movement got going, he'd be ready to involve

R. Taylor Hoskins, Shenandoah's fourth superintendent, had been the park's first chief ranger. Returning after 20 years, he was astonished at the recycling forest now covering all the open spaces, complete with deer everywhere—and even bears! (NPS)

Shenandoah—with a good case that the park really was a superb example of the wild and natural Southern Appalachians.

Hoskins was seeing significance in Shenandoah beyond what he'd suspected. He encouraged a proposal by the regional naturalist, M. E. Beatty, to research and write a geographical history of this park. "Probably no other area," Beatty had written in the proposal, "so well portrays drastic ecological change." As the park "slowly returns to a near-natural state, much of the evidence of former extensive use becomes lost. For future planning, development and interpretation . . . these studies are of primary importance." Unfortunately, the thousands of dollars the geographical history would cost never became available.

Hoskins regretted there'd never been funds, either, to save buildings representing the park's human past. Even structures at Camp Hoover had been scheduled for prompt demolition. Was he too late to save them? He moved swiftly and managed to get enough support to save the president's cottage and two others from the Hoover years. From that time on, the human past of Shenandoah has been recognized along with its natural history. The interpretive program developed by park naturalists C. Kenny Dale and E. Ray Schaffner consolidated the two meanings. They led toward responsible environmentalism and creation of the main visitor center around the theme of "Man and the Mountains." The center, at Big Meadows, was named for Harry Flood Byrd, the Virginia governor who'd helped raise funds to purchase the park, recruited Carson to acquire park-land, and donated money for the construction of several hikers' shelters—called, appropriately, Byrd's Nests.

The return of the black bear to places once heavily used and marked by humankind—see old stone wall—was a phenomenon that kept impressing park officials, visitors, park neighbors, and scientists. The park's population may have grown to, or a bit beyond, six hundred bears.

An effort to correct costly difficulties stemming from the incredibly irregular boundary interested Hoskins, and he pushed it vigorously. He felt that the countless zigzags, sawtoothed by Carson but expected to be temporary, were hurting the park deeply by preventing efficient management and protection and damaging relations with neighbors. He convinced other NPS executives and Senator Byrd that the boundary must be straightened and made to conform with geographic features, like roads, creeks, and ridgetops.

In 1963 and 1964 the park staff and the NPS land specialists in Washington worked out a program to acquire 25,346 new acres, trade off 5,233, and set the maximum acreage for Shenandoah at 225,000, thus eliminating the neighbors' long-held fear that the park would expand to the old 327,000-acre Cammerer Line. Byrd wanted the maximum acreage held to 212,000—about 13,300 above the existing acreage—and the NPS compromised. The bill was introduced in both Senate and House. Hoskins said that, if passed and funded, it would be "the most important step taken to further the park . . . since the . . . original legislation."

There were potent protests from a few landowners. The program cost had climbed to $1,748,000 and was still rising. The sorest points were ameliorated, and enactment looked possible. But Byrd was not well, and he lacked the energy to push his bill. In 1966 he stepped down under an arrangement that brought the appointment of his son, Harry F. Byrd, Jr., to succeed him in the Senate. The elder Byrd died in October, after 40 years as a major supporter of Shenandoah. The park staff made a funeral wreath of fall foliage from Old Rag Mountain, Byrd's favorite place in the park. Young Byrd tried, but conditions never came right for the boundary improvement program to get through Congress.

Upon retirement in mid-1972, Hoskins moved to tidewater Virginia, where he'd grown up. The distance wasn't far, and he came back to Shenandoah a few times, but at longer and longer intervals. I looked for him at Big Meadows when the park celebrated the 50th anniversary of its original dedication. Hoskins and I had been there in 1936, and I thought he'd come to the rededication if he could. Later that summer an evening dispatcher at park headquarters heard a sound at the locked front door. He opened it, and Hoskins came in. They talked a while. Hoskins asked if it would be all right if he looked around the building a little. He seemed well, but his movements were slow. He went to the open door of the superintendent's office. He didn't go in but stood against the door frame. After some minutes he turned and said good night and walked out to his car in the parking lot.

In 1972 Robert R. Jacobsen became Shenandoah's fifth superintendent. He'd come up through the ranger ranks, had been superintendent of NPS areas in different parts of the country, and since 1967 had been in the Washington office working with legislation—including that intended to improve Shenandoah's boundary. He lived this park with intensity—officially on week days and as a visitor on weekends, hiking the trails with his family or bicycling on the Skyline Drive. Through concentrated effort, illustrative of his approach to problems, he'd taught himself the unusual skill of riding a unicycle, and sometimes he tuned up for a day's work by riding it to the office from his nearby house.

Jacobsen had inherited both the boundary problem and the wilderness question from Hoskins. Two such puzzles at the same time were not politically feasible. Interest in backpack hiking with backcountry camping was growing fast, giving long-sought proof that this park is vastly more than its Skyline Drive. Pressure on the 39 designated backcountry campsites was damaging vegetation and reducing possibilities for solitude. Jacobsen asked himself on a plane flight one day, why not let backpackers camp almost anywhere in the park, after getting a free permit and agreeing upon a general hike plan so rangers would know where they were? The idea survived heavy discussion. The new program, with a minimum of rules, went into effect early in 1974, and so many people took advantage of it that Shenandoah became a backcountry leader—as far as a park could get from the old Skyline Drive dominance when the trails were so lonely.

By 1973, after numerous studies and discussions with acreages under

Environmental education, with training especially for teachers of schools within 50 or so miles of the park, thrived here in the 1970s. Shenandoah was recognized as extraordinarily suitable for this effort because its history includes so many forms of resource exploitation over long periods; yet wilderness has returned, strongly demonstrating the healing "miracle" of nature. (NPS)

consideration gradually increasing, the Park Service was recommending that 80,000 acres of Shenandoah—about two-fifths of the park—be added to the National Wilderness Preservation System. Opposition had increased, especially in Madison County, where leaders thought the wilderness designation might finally kill their hope, held since the Carson-Hoover days, for a public entrance into the park and up to the Skyline Drive. Jacobsen went everywhere he was invited to discuss the facts of wilderness designation under the 1964 law. At times both advocates and opponents of wilderness were criticizing him. There was a wave of fear that the wilderness designation would rule out access for coping with emergencies, and Senator Byrd, Jr., amended his bill to leave narrow "corridors" of nonwilderness for emergency roads.

The bill cleared the Senate early in 1976, then almost died during the October rush toward adjournment in the House. But it did pass, and at last Shenandoah had 123 square miles of the "vast wilderness" that George Pollock and others so enthusiastically insisted it contained in the 1920s.

Robert R. Jacobsen, Shenandoah's fifth superintendent, saw Shenandoah wilderness recognized by Congress in 1976 and inaugurated an innovative backcountry camping program that made Shenandoah the leading park in overnights per square mile. He also started the annual Shenandoah Research Symposiums, which have increased and coordinated scientific research in the park. (NPS)

In that time of wilderness recognition, visitors were coming at the fastest rate ever, about three million a year. Though the diversity of interests and origins had increased, the basic pattern continued. Still the most numerous were sightseers who drove along the Skyline Drive, seldom getting out of their cars. Yet the proportion who hiked had gone up, and most visitors were wearing shoes they could at least stroll in. Groups of day-hikers shepherded by leaders from different trail clubs had become common. Hikers also came as individuals, couples, and in family groups, and there was a surge of assorted backcountry campers as well. Bicyclists and motorcyclists had definitely increased, and there were birders, wildflower enthusiasts, observers of ecology and the environment, fishermen, horseback riders, sunbathers, rock climbers, and seekers of old home sites or cemeteries and legends of people who roamed or dwelt here—spear hunters, pottery makers, tobacco growers, timber cutters, cowboys, moonshiners.

The greatest number of visitors usually come in October—for autumn colors—the majority on one-day trips from cities less than four hours away. About three-fourths of the visitors each year consistently come from the eastern states, Virginia in the lead, with midwestern states also showing strong. Some visitors do come, of course, from every state and from every part of the world.

Jacobsen used scientific findings in management decisions. He inaugurated the Shenandoah Research Symposium, held every spring for more than a decade now. A biological project in the 1980s came up with strong evidence that Shenandoah has about six hundred black bears in its three hundred square miles, nearly twice the expected number. Partly because of a giant brewery being built beside the park, Jacobsen became a well-informed battler against air pollution and acid rain. He said air pollution was obscuring the views that justified construction of the Skyline Drive. Jacobsen retired from the Park Service in January 1986.

This book ends with the rededication at Big Meadows on July 3, 1986, exactly half a century after the dedication by President FDR. The park, of course, goes on. The next half century seems unlikely to bring drastic surprises. Blue Ridge rock has lasted a billion years and will remain. The returned forest will have bigger trees, more seeing space under the canopy, and a gradually changing proportion of species. It may suffer from insects, fires, or fungal blights, such as the chestnut blight in the 1920s and the gypsy moth threat of the 1980s, but its ability to regenerate has been amply proved. Humans have used these mountains for thousands of years and will, I feel, continue.

People who lived here, or their children, are beginning to come back in larger numbers, the old resentment over the taking of the land either fading or changing enough to let them feel proud of their personal connection with these mountains that so many other people also love. The hope that buildings of plantation folk and mountain folk and cattlemen could be preserved has been mostly disappointed, yet traces remain and can be interpreted. Even in the wilderness we might find a massive stone wall or a stone chimney still standing, lichen covered. In the silences of the forest there are artifacts speaking from the human past. To those of us who pause in the wild places, quiet and receptive, the haunts sometimes come, and getting to know them can be good.

Appendix 1: Cemeteries in the Park

Human graves are history engraved on the land. Some cemeteries can be read in detail. Others are relatively mute. Yet all say with feeling that people were experiencing joys and sorrows here long before we came along.

More than a hundred cemeteries in the park are known to some extent. Most are small plots utilized by one or several families. A few may have had a hundred or more burials each. Some are active with burials of close kin continuing, perhaps until the plot enclosed at park establishment time is filled. More are maintained neatly by descendants of those buried or by helpful friends. Others are overgrown, yet still visited occasionally by people wishing to know origins and to honor ancestors. Still others are lost, yet may be rediscovered at intervals by either kinfolk or strangers.

Cemetery seeking in this recycling park has been described as an exercise of high skill and empathy, a way of touching eternal realities of nature and humanity. But few of the graveyards are easy to find in this vast returned wilderness that camouflages, yet doesn't eliminate, human traces.

The ideal list might tell how to find each cemetery and identify at least the oldest and latest burials. But the ideal has proved impossible, because the information isn't on the stones or because no one has had the almost-endless time the task would require. Many of the rediscoveries were accidental or hurried, and the information recorded, a mere clue to where and what. Initials at the end of each entry represent the reporting finders. The persons or teams providing the most recent or complete information are credited first, as they're likely to be most helpful to seekers of any particular cemetery. We give known basics and invite calls that might help interested persons locate a cemetery or bring future lists nearer the ideal. (Names and phone numbers are given at the end of this appendix.)

This listing is by counties from north to south and, within each county, by cemeteries from north to south. Tract numbers findable on park-land acquisition maps in the court houses of the eight park counties are given in some cases, along with names of the last private owners. This information can often help but is rarely a full solution to the complex search. The same is true of the milepost clues sometimes given; the Skyline Drive has mileposts numbered from north to south—0 at the Front Royal entrance, 105 at Rockfish Gap.

Warren County

BUCK/FOX slave cemetery: Perhaps .5 mi. north and a bit west of old Thomas Fox homesite on Fox Hollow Trail, about 3 mi. south of Front Royal, exact spot unknown. Samuel George "Buddy" Fox, born in Fox Hollow in 1892, said, "There was a graveyard up there where they buried the old slaves." It wasn't "too far off from our cemetery, but I can't remember just where it was."—Interview by Patricia Armel Fox Brinklow, 1977.

FOX: Cross Skyline Drive from Dickey Ridge Visitor Center and go along the self-guiding Fox Hollow Trail, which makes a round-trip circuit of 1.3 mi. Cemetery enclosed by a stone wall. Four or more burials. Oldest: Thomas Fox, d. 1873, age 68; latest: illegible wooden marker with white writing (1930s?)—LB, JCR, EDL.

MILLS: On west boundary below Dickey Ridge Picnic Ground. Drive about 4 mi. south from Front Royal on state route 649 toward Browntown. Find Dry Run and walk about 100 yd. up inside park boundary. Small area enclosed by wire fence attached to trees. Fieldstone markers, no inscriptions. Two or more burials. Among them: Henry Mills.—SNP working files.

CLATTERBUCK: In hollow below Gimlet Ridge Overlook, about 1 mi. west of Skyline Drive Milepost 18+. Near cabin site, off abandoned road. About 30 burials. Some carved monuments, lovely rock walls.—JCR.

Rappahannock County

CLARK/KELLY: On flat above Range View Cabin, park-land tract 59, the J. T. Kelly "Goat Farm," 798 acres. Stone wall enclosure lost during Skyline Drive construction; exact site now unknown. Tradition says 5 or more burials, the latest around Civil War time.—NPS.

JENKINS/KEYSER: Near Keyser Run Fire Road, park boundary, and Little Devil Stairs on park-land tract bought through negotiation, not condemnation (from Golden Jenkins, 69 acres?). No information from any visit on ground, but graveyard status was involved in land negotiations.—JRJ.

BAILEY/CLATTERBUCK: Walking down Keyser Run Fire Road northeastward from Jinny Gray Flats, find first tiny stream crossing. Go upstream about 150 yd. On rise to left, old clearings and rubble of house and barn. Cemetery about 75 ft. above house site with boulder-strewn spring and stream head visible. Six burials, latest a brother of Mrs. Ambrose Bailey in 1930s.—JCR, EDL, JRJ.

BOLEN: On Jinny Gray Flats where Keyser Run Fire Road makes a 90-degree turn and Hull School Trail begins. Cleared and neat, 60- by 90-ft. area surrounded by stone wall with wrought-iron gate, Norway maples. Fifty or more burials, with 21 engraved tombstones and a dozen fieldstone markers. Oldest: Frankline, son of John H. and Mary F. Bolen, 1854-77. Most burials early 1900s. Among them: John H. Bolen, 1831-1914.—JCR, EDL, DCL, NPS.

BEAHM: Often called George Washington Beahm. On Pignut Mountain, southeast side toward Pickerel Ridge, short distance inside park boundary. Reached by following old road up ridge from Piney River. Stone wall with iron gate. Oldest: Nancy E. Bolen Beahm, 1829-1915; latest: Alfred S. Baker, d. 1929.—LB from Galloways, JRJ, NPS.

DWYER: About 100 ft. from junction of Piney Ridge and Fork Mountain trails. Recent maintenance, remains of wire fence. Eleven engraved tombstones, 12-15 fieldstone markers, 2 metal markers. Among them: Miles J. Dwyer, 1826-1915; Alfred Dwyer, 1831-1919; Mary Dwyer, 1843-1927.—JCR, DCL, JRJ, NPS.

BOWEN: Sometimes called William Bowen, sometimes Bowen/Waters, but definitely different from the Bowen/Waters also called John Henry Waters, below. Near junction of Piney Branch and Hull School trails, about .25 mi. west of Piney River, up steep "roat cut" and about 100 ft. north of Hull trail on flattish hillock. Six engraved tombstones, 11 fieldstone markers. Oldest: Sarah M., wife of S. G. Waters, 1809-78, and Stanfield G. Waters, 1800-1880. Among others: John T. Bowen, d. 1890; Lucy

M. Bowen, 1840-1914, William F. Bowen, 1824-1912.—DCL, JCR, JRJ, EDL, NPS.

BOWEN slave cemetery: About 500 ft. northwest of Bowen cemetery at "edge of a nearly extinct wagon road." Some reports say about 100 burials, all from before Civil War. Pattern of native stones confusing, maybe a dozen gravesites still findable but uncertain.—JCR, JRJ, NPS, EDL.

BOWEN/WATERS: Sometimes called John Henry Waters. On flat east of Thornton Hollow Overlook, Skyline Drive. Start from Beahms Gap; walk east .2 mi. on Hull School Trail, then left on old roadbed trace above a stream. After about 1 mi. there's "a marsh and the old cabin site" the Reeders call "Well House, where there's still an open well (watch your step!)." Cemetery in brush-sapling thicket beyond old homesite. Victorian wrought-iron fence 30 by 20 ft. at northeast corner of larger plot, well cared for. Seven engraved tombstones, 20 or more fieldstone markers, 2 wood markers. Older burials: Joe C. Bowen, d. 1847; J. N. Bowen, d. 1867; John Henry Waters, 1833-1904; Mary J. Bowen Waters 1822-1907; latest: Frank Gip, "colored," about 1930.—JCR, DCL, JRJ, NPS.

ARMENTROUT: About 200 ft. north of Hull School Trail, more than halfway from Beahms Gap to North Fork, Thornton River. Overgrown, a few old fence posts. About 15 graves, with fieldstone markers and 3 granite tombstones. Among them: D. B. Armentrout, 1871-1916; Mrs. L. E. Armentrout, 1836-1912.—DCL, NPS.

JENKINS: Near Thornton Hollow Trail about .5 mi. below junction with Hull School Trail on park-land tract 129, Frank Jenkins, which is almost all south of the river. About 6 burials. Grave markers gone?—JRJ, NPS.

PULLEN: Also called Joe Billy Bowen or Mary Frazier. Up Frazier Hollow from North Fork, Thornton River, about 1 mi., then up right branch of fork about .5 mi. Cemetery 200 yd. north of stream. Overgrown, woven wire fence mostly lost. Thirty or more burials, 4 granite tombstones. Among them: Mrs. Peggy Pullen, 1794-1879; her husband, Thomas E. Pullen, 1789-1834; Margaret E. Pullen, wife of Joe C. Bowen, d. 1862, age 34.—DCL, JRJ, NPS.

MENEFEE: Between headwaters of Frazier Hollow and Butterwood Branch. Start at Turn Bridge, sharpest hairpin curve, about 3 mi. east of Skyline Drive on U.S. 211. Go .5 mi. up Pass Mountain Trail and find Clark cemetery (see below), where abandoned Oventop trail takes off eastward. Continue about .3 mi. on Pass Mountain Trail, around swing to right, but where it then veers left (west), find old road trace and follow it northwest about 1 mi. Cemetery is in old apple orchard about 150 ft. west of chimney and house ruins, the Ben Menefee place. About 25-30 burials, several sunken graves. Native rock markers and 1 engraved granite tombstone, for Catherine Frazier Menefee, wife of B.F.M., d. 1900.—JCR, DCL, JRJ.

DARNELL: About 1 mi. up Butterwood Branch from North Fork, Thornton River, quite near the stream. No estimate of graves as site was plowed.—JRJ, NPS.

BROWN: Between upper forks of Butterwood Branch stream, about 200 yd. west of what used to be Butterwood trail, about 75 ft. uphill from foundation of old Joseph Huffman house. Estimates of burials range as high as 300—maybe slaves. In 1976 Lyne found only 8 noninscribed stones, along with remains of a picket gate and a few posts.—DCL, JRJ, NPS.

BRUCE: Almost 1 mi. eastward from Brown, on north side of Oventop Mountain. Coming down abandoned Butterwood trail from Pass Mountain Trail, take an old fork northeastward. Three native stones in middle of path. About 6-10 burials.—JCR, NPS.

CLARK: Just northwest of junction of Pass Mountain Trail with abandoned Oventop trail on ridgetop known locally as Kibbin Hill, near ruins of Clark house with three chimneys. About 15-20 burials. Some "hidden" native stone markers, a few depressions. Site shown to Lyne in 1976 by Leo Bowen, who said some burials moved long ago to other cemeteries.—JCR, DCL, NPS.

CLISER: About .25 mi. south of Pass Mountain Hut (and Pass Mountain Trail) and about .75 mi. north of Thornton Gap. Trace of old service road parallels old rock wall just below Cliser cabin site; east of trace "is a large cistern and south of cistern is the cemetery, hard to see unless you stand on top of it." Remains of woven wire fence. One engraved headstone: S. D. Cliser, 1833-1912. About 20 other burials marked with rough native stones, no inscriptions.—JCR, JRJ, CR, EDL.

WILLIS/PULLEN/MENEFEE: Near the hairpin curve on U.S. 211 (Turn Bridge) between Sperryville and Thornton Gap. The cemetery-sleuthing Reeders say, "We enjoy the forsythia every spring at the site of this old home on the sharp curve. Uphill and south of the cabin site about 200 feet is the family plot. Native stone, about 10 sites."—JCR.

ATKINS/DODSON: About 100 ft. north of U.S. 211, coming from Sperryville, where the highway becomes 3 lanes. Cemetery maintained by mowing and brush clearing. Seven inscribed granite or marble stones, 6 inscribed fieldstones, 60 noninscribed fieldstones. Oldest: K.R.A., 1894; latest: Cora A. Dodson, wife of J.W., 1855-1933.— JCR, DCL, LB from Galloways, EDL, CR.

ATKINS: Above Beech Spring Church, just inside park boundary from direction of Sperryville, 450 yd. north of U.S. 211 and 15 yd. south of power line. Cemetery is 60 by 30 ft. with a 10- by 20-ft. stone wall enclosure in northwest corner, all overgrown, no markers left inside stone wall. Outside, 5 inscribed fieldstone markers, 20 noninscribed. Among them: a daughter of J. M. Atkins, 1844-85; F. L. Atkins, d. 1892.—DCL.

DODSON/HAZEL: Vegetation and terrain indicate cemetery about .5 mi. up abandoned old Hazel Road southwest from Beech Spring Church on U.S. 211. Adjoins small stream bed. Depressions but no stone markers found. Runyon says Hill Atkins of Sperryville knows this site. Another source indicates grandfather of Donna Dodson buried here.—JCR, CR.

JENKINS/ATKINS/WHARTON: In northeast corner of park's central section, south of U.S. 211, close to Sperryville, by Jenkins Hollow. Bridle path from Sperryville nearby. More than 20 noninscribed fieldstones. Among persons buried, Bill and Sissy Wharton, Emma Jenkins, children of Emma and Wade Jenkins, dates not known.— DCL, JCR.

ATKINS/DODSON/HAZEL: Starting from Skyline Drive Milepost 33+, go 1.6 mi. down Hazel Mountain Trail to junction of White Rocks Horse Trail. Go north on White Rocks Horse Trail .25 mi. Explore damp area on west for old home site and find cemetery beyond. Overgrown with greenbrier. About 35 burials. Native stones, many inscribed.—JCR, CR.

Page County

FORSYTH: Up Overall Run Trail about 500 yd. above junction with Thompson Big Blue Trail, cross stream, and climb steep slope 150 yd. to plateau with brushy forest, part of old homeplace. Traces of clearing remain not far away but cemetery mostly hidden in dying pines on "shelf" of ridge. Wrought-iron fence encloses bed-size space with 2 graves, 1 stone marked: DLIA FORESYT he died August 16, 1849, aged 45 years. Other burials outside iron fence. Among them: Rev. Hezekiah Freeman, d. 1820, age 60.—EDL, NPS.

MORGAN: On hill above Jeremys Run just inside park boundary, park-land tract 44, bought by David L. Kibler from Morgan heirs. Three or more burials, graves of John Morgan family.—EDL, JRJ, NPS.

BAILEY: In the second clearing up Jeremys Run, 2 mi. from park boundary, on east side of stream, upstream from abandoned old Wise Road, where stream makes first big curve. Eight to 12 burials.—NPS.

WATERS: About .1 mi. west of Skyline Drive just north of Milepost 30, on park-land tract 119, S. B. Waters. Unfenced. One row of 6 burials but possibly more close by. Oldest: Sallie Waters (Sarah E.) 1872–76; latest: Elbert J. Waters, 1894–1905.—LB, JCR, EDL.

JUDD/SHENK: South of state route 658 by park headquarters, lower Shenks Hollow. Was inside park, but due to land exchange now on private property.—EDL, JRJ.

SANFORD: Shenks Hollow, at upper end of state route 658, on left. Four or more burials. Oldest: "Infant Daughter Sandford, d. Nov. 20, 1871, age 8 days"; latest: Sarah C. Sanford, 1841–1912.—LB from Galloways, JRJ.

FOX: Shenks Hollow, state route 658 at edge of park (believed all barely outside boundary). Eight or more burials. Oldest: Jonas A. Fox, d. 1854, age 7+; latest, Isaac Fox, d. 1921, age 84+.—LB from Galloways, JRJ.

SHENK: Shenks Hollow, upper state route 658, old continuation in park. Some stones broken or illegible. At least 12 burials. Oldest: S. S., 1781; latest: S. M. [or W?] Shenk, 1856–1882.—LB from Galloways, JRJ.

BEAHM: North of U.S. 211, west of Skyline Drive, above abandoned old Shenk Mill Road. Four or more burials. Oldest: Jacob M. Beahm, d. 1897, age 74+; latest: Benjamin Franklin Beahm, 1843–1914.—LB from Galloways. I seem to recall it on old road trace running down Gravel Ridge.—CR

BARBEE: Thornton Gap, barely east of Skyline Drive, north of U.S. 211, was just behind old Panorama Tea Room, site covered with fill for drive overpass about 1960. William Randolph Barbee, internationally known sculptor, died at The Bower in the park in 1868 and was buried in this family graveyard at Thornton Gap. Others buried here from 1790 or so into 1900s. The famous Barbee was moved to Green Hill, Luray, perhaps in 1908 upon the death of his longtime widow Mary Jane McKay Barbee (see Chapter 8).—EDL, JCR.

INDIAN MOUND: Gerard Fowke, in Smithsonian Institution, Bureau of American Ethnology, Bulletin 23, 1894, reported: "On John S. Printz's land, on Dry Run," now in park below Stony Man Mountain, "is a small stone heap from which, it is claimed, human bones and fragments of pottery have been taken." We looked for the mound briefly about 1970 without finding it.—EDL.

SKYLAND: About .25 mi. west of Conference Hall and .25 mi. north of Bushytop at head of steep (dangerous) Kettle Canyon.—Scheel map.

BURACKER: Below Crescent Rock Overlook on Skyline Drive, about 1.5 mi., in Timber Hollow, about one-third of the way from park boundary to Crescent Rock.—NPS.

BIG MEADOWS: Along road between Skyline Drive and lodge-picnic-campground, near junction with road to maintenance shops (exact location now unknown?).—Scheel map.

THOMAS/MEADOWS: At junction of Tanners Ridge Road and Appalachian Trail, .3 mi. from Skyline Drive. Large, well maintained, and still used. More than 70 burials.

A "see-through" cross carved out in full relief from the stone (now broken). Oldest: R. C. Taylor, d. 1898, age 3+. Some fieldstone markers without inscriptions may represent burials earlier than 1898.—LB, JCR, EDL, NPS.

GRAY: About 1 mi. down Tanners Ridge Road from Skyline Drive, south side of road. Oscar S. Gray, 1883-1913, buried where he was killed, the remains later moved elsewhere but stone left here as memorial.—LB, JCR.

BLOSE: Steam Hollow, Fultz Run, in park near where state route 609 reaches boundary. Wash Blose, pioneer, who settled in Fultz Run "several years" after valley's first pioneer, Adam Miller, settled lower down, is buried here. Also, members of four subsequent generations. Oldest inscribed marker: Jacob Coverstone, d. Aug. 1847.—EDL from WPA Va. Hist. Inventory (1936-40), LB.

SLAUGHTER: Opposite Bearfence Mountain Hut parking on Skyline Drive, take Meadow School Trail westward about 1 mi. From a "lovely cabin site (or two)," cemetery 100 yd. south, up on ridge. Burials in woods.—JCR.

Madison County

NICHOLSON: Beside Corbin Cabin Cutoff Trail, about 100 yd. north of the cabin on the uphill side. Fenced. Native stone markers, 1 inscribed: Tabitha N[icholson], Apr. 29, 1895.—JCR, LB. Another site about 300 yd. northeast below trail after crossing one stream branch just above junction of two branches.—Scheel map.

CORBIN/NICHOLSON: Near where Corbin Mountain Trail crosses Hughes River from Nicholson Hollow Trail, a large home overlooked the river (watch out for well just west of house site!). Down and west of home site, between river and trail, is grave site, a large natural stone almost perfectly shaped.—JCR.

CORBIN HOLLOW: About 100 yd. north of Brokenback Run, roughly in line between Pinnacle Peak (on Thorofare Mountain) and the peak of Robertson Mountain.—Scheel map.

DYER: Just west of Old Rag Fire Road where it skirts Robertson Mountain.—Scheel map.

WEAKLEY: Along short "road" between Old Rag Shelter (not Byrd's Nest) and Weakley Hollow Fire Road. About 15 burials, native stones.—JCR.

TAYLOR: In Hawksbill Gap about 40 ft. from Skyline Drive, north from Cedar Run Trail, around and inside bend in drive, under large hickory. Markers broken and disappearing. One metal marker: Carroll R. Taylor, 1936-37. Markers that recently disappeared: Allen R. Taylor, 1933-33; Robert G. Taylor, 1939-40.—LB, JCR, EDL.

SISK: Lower Cedar Run, inside fork of Cedar and White Oak runs (and trails) on rising ground before it gets steep, above ruins of home site and/or an old Shirley mill. Graveyard 15 by 20 ft., fenced, with locust posts and a few boards left. Three burials have stones, 2 apparently youngsters, the other: D P M b. 4/1/1898 d 6/22/1918.—CR.

SOURS: South 1 mi. on horse trail from Upper Hawksbill parking toward Rose River Fire Road (old Gordonsville-New Market Turnpike). Watch for abandoned road going left. About .1 mi. east and south is a large, man-planted stone above spring near old Sours cabin site. Former resident here, Aubrey Sisk, says it may or may not represent a grave.—JCR.

DALLAS ANDERSON: At head of Rose River on north side, near abandoned trail that crosses river heading north, then east. About .5 acre and 30 burials, native stones; some graves kept up with metal markers. Dallas Anderson could be one occupant.—JCR.

BERRY: In Berry Hollow near state route 600 north from Syria, about halfway from Cedar Run Trail exit from park and triple peak called Buzzard Rocks, up branch that comes into Robinson River from west, near cabins but up on ridge between two forks of this branch. Definitely in park despite recent boundary changes. More than a dozen burials.—JCR.

CAVE/BREEDEN/BURACKER: About .5 mi. from Fishers Gap on Skyline Drive down Rose River Fire Road (old Gordonsville-New Market Turnpike) on right side, off a still-used access road. Cemetery and road maintained with hand tools. About 30 burials, some Civil War. About 12 inscribed stones, many more graves unmarked or with fieldstones. Oldest: Effie J. Breeden, 1884–1919, latest: Lula Belle Cave, 1905–1984.—LB, JCR.

SHEDFIELD: On south slope of Haywood Mountain (now Spitler Hill) at about 2,500 ft. elevation, perhaps between old Haywood trail that skirted slope at about 2,700 ft. and Rose River Fire Road (old Gordonsville-New Market Turnpike) northward from Lower Rose Falls. Site 200 ft. west of still-observable cabin remains. Family plot, about 10 burials, native stones.—JCR.

MEADOWS/ANDERSON: At foot of Rose River Fire Road near park boundary above "real Dark Hollow bridge" on park-land tract 146, R. A. and R. S. Graves. Large cemetery. Possibly two separate graveyards; information not complete.—NPS.

ALGER/SMITH/GRAYSON: In fork of Rose River and its Dark Hollow branch.—Scheel map.

WEAKLEY: Two Weakley graveyards at south boundary of Old Rag segment of park near Robinson River.—Scheel map.

WILHOITE: North of old Hoover Road and Rapidan River at about 1,600 ft. elevation on west side of Chapman Mountain.—Scheel map.

BUSH/JENKINS: Sometimes called Bush Field. About 2 mi. up Staunton River Trail from Rapidan River at state route 662, in forest south of Staunton River near trail junction at McDaniel Hollow. Large cemetery, probably started in 1700s, fieldstone markers. Eula Lea Yowel Nichols (Mrs. Harvey Nichols) was buried here in 1912 about 50 ft. from older graves.—Tom Floyd, *Lost Trails and Forgotten People* (1981), pp. 29, 41, and 96.

JONES/TAYLOR: About .25 mi. below Jones Mountain Cabin along the trail to Staunton River. A few fieldstone markers visible. Apparently quite old, judging by the milieu.—JCR, Scheel map.

NICHOLS: About halfway in straight line between Jones Mountain Cabin and Bear Church Rock.—Scheel map.

ESTES/STANTON: Adjoining and about 100 yds. south of parking lot at start of Staunton River Trail near Rapidan River. Many sites, a few with native stone markers.—JCR, Tom Floyd, *Lost Trails and Forgotten People* (1981), Scheel map.

Greene County

BOOTEN/McDANIEL: On Conway River Road eastward from Skyline Drive at Bootens Gap just before an old, abandoned road branches off northward toward an old lumber mill site. Details of cemetery not now available.—JCR, Scheel map.

DEVILS DITCH: About 2 mi. east of Skyline Drive at Milepost 56.4 (Bearfence Mountain area), overlooking Devils Ditch. Directions and terrain difficult—Devils Ditch aptly named. Small cemetery by "road" that drops to meet "Swiss Chalet," standing old cabin of attractive design. Chalet outside park, but cemetery believed inside. A few native stone markers.—JCR.

LAM: From Skyline Drive Milepost 56.8, find Slaughter Trail east and walk down it about 1.5 mi., then on abandoned road south a few hudred feet to old cabin site—about 1 mi. straight east of Lewis Mountain Campground. Cemetery with numerous burials is near cabin site. One of the most heartrending graves we ever found, an infant's, has miniature statue of lamb lying on top of monument with the words, "A bud of love."— JCR.

LEWIS CLUSTER/ROACH: Down Slaughter Trail beyond Lam cemetery turnoff (see above) about .5 mi., the road is descending and turns sharp right. On left (2–2.5 mi. from Skyline Drive), see the first of a cluster of cabins. Cemetery a bit west behind nearest cabin, surrounded by large, nonindigenous shrubbery (probably boxwood). About 10 burials.—JCR.

SHILOH: On knoll just inside park boundary above old Shiloh Church off state route 667 near branch of Conway (Middle) River. Cemetery small and inactive.—NPS.

SHILOH/LAM: On Conway River Road near old church site. Could be same as foregoing but NPS report (1954) distinguishes them as on different park-land tracts. Inactive.—NPS.

POCOSIN: On big flat, once a chestnut orchard, under Skyline Drive at Pocosin Hollow. Large, inactive. NPS. Cemetery originally called Chestnut Grove. About .1 mi. south of Pocosin Hollow Trail where it crosses stream and turns in creek basin. Before this creek you walk parallel to an old fence that once surrounded cemetery. Cemetery on low flat hill, about 2 acres in size. About 75 burials, all with native head- and footstones, none legibly marked, except 1 stone with the letter W at the base.—JCR.

POCOSIN MISSION: From Skyline Drive Milepost 59.5, walk down Pocosin Fire Road 1 mi. to junction with Pocosin Trail. Cemetery about 50 ft. west of ruins of old Upper Pocosin Mission. Evidence of 6 burials with fieldstones.—JCR.

MEADOWS/SOUTH RIVER: From Skyline Drive Milepost 62.7, on South River Fire Road 2.2 mi., left on horse trail .1 mi. to T intersection then right about .1 mi. Can be reached also on Pocosin Trail from old mission site. Cemetery enclosed with fence and gate, overgrown but with circular path maintained. Twelve to 25 burials. Oldest: Mary Meadows, 1837–1888; latest: Gibbon Taylor, d. 1972 (?) age 88+ (?). One large stone for five members of Meadows family. Rosa Lam burial of 1951, reported by NPS in 1954, not found in 1981.—LB, JCR.

SOUTH RIVER: About 100 yd. west of (inside) park boundary, north of South River Falls Trail, along an abandoned road.—JCR.

DEAN/MEADOWS: Across from old quarry road near site of old CCC Camp NP-3 (Baldface Mountain vicinity), a few hundred feet west of Skyline Drive, Milepost 61+. County line swings westward, so cemetery definitely in Greene, on park-land tract 67, L. Gruver Meadows. Among the few interments: Thornton Dean, 1844–88; Roda Catherine Dean, 1874–90; Michael Mitchell Dean, 1876-1920.—JCR, GD, FRB.

COLLIER/SHIFFLETT/WATSON: From South River Picnic Grounds, follow Appalachian Trail southward about 1 mi. and find on left Saddleback Mountain westward rise to 3,296-ft. elevation (PATC map 10). Down small incline to right is old home site on park-land tract 77, S. B. and C. F. Collier. Cross rise northeastward. Ahead is a flat, an old road, wagon hubs, a large multiple tree arrow-carved, and the cemetery with a giant oak. About 75 burials, a joining of what were once separate cemeteries, Watson and Shifflett.—FRB, GD, NPS.

HANEY/SHIFFLETT: Sometimes called Fern Hill. About .3 mi. north of Swift Run Gap and about .1 mi. east of Appalachian Trail. Maintenance with hand tools. Old fence poor; small section enclosed by good chain-link fence. At least 35 burials. Oldest:

Josie A. Dean, 1856–1917; latest: Lizzie J. Knighton, 1886–1945. Three Shifflett family burials inside chain-link fence, all 1932.—LB. Or park at first (unnamed) overlook north of U.S. 33. Across from parking place, eastward, follow footpath that will cross the Appalachian Trail and continue to cemetery.—JCR.

LAM'S MILL: Sometimes called Willie Lam cemetery. On old Spotswood trail close to Lam's Mill site, about 200 yd. southwest of Bench Mark 1417, just above Lydia on U.S. 33. Overgrown with pines and briers. Five or more burials.—NPS.

CALVIN MORRIS: On southeast part of Hightop Mountain, above Mutton Hollow in what is locally called Goose Pond Hollow, approached by state route 623. Cemetery 30 by 30 ft., enclosed and cleared. Twenty-three or more graves, latest 1945.—NPS.

MORRIS: On southwest slope of Flattop Mountain. Follow old road northeast from Simmons Gap Ranger Station. Posts of cemetery fence remain. Latest burial: Margie Crawford, 1933.—NPS.

SIMMONS GRAVE: About .2 mi. east of Simmons Gap on Skyline Drive, on edge of Simmons Gap road near garden plot used by occupants of ranger station. One burial believed to be that of the man (or a member of his family) for whom the gap is named, grave marked by native stone slabs.—NPS, JCR.

SIMMONS GAP 2: East on Simmons Gap Road about .5 mi., on the left, up an embankment. Wire fence deteriorating. About 10 burials.—JCR.

SIMMONS GAP 3: On south (right) side of Simmons Gap Road just inside east boundary of park, about 1 mi. from Skyline Drive.—JCR.

Rockingham County

DEAN: About .1 mi. west of Skyline Drive at Milepost 63.2, on dirt road, near South River Picnic Grounds. Cemetery currently used, well maintained. About 100 burials. Oldest: James Dean, 1797–1862.—LB, JCR, GD.

JEREMIAH DEAN: About 50 ft. south of old Dean Mountain Road, very near the park boundary as road egresses toward Cedar Falls. Cemetery on knoll about 200 ft. west of massive standing chimney. A few stones. One or more graves may be "Shiplets."— JCR, GD.

HENSLEY: Some Hensleys who lived in what's now park (Hensley Hollow north of U.S. 33) were buried in family cemetery, still private property, near state route 662, up on a ridge about .25 mi. from Hensley Hollow part of park. These include: Ben. Hensley, 1822–1908; Rebecca Hensley, 1824–1905.—FRB, EDL.

SHIPP/BAUGHER: North of U.S. 33, above Elkton, .2 mi. east of state route 628, just inside park boundary near site of famous old Mountain Hotel (Shipp Tavern?). About 20 graves, including row of 7 Shipp children under age 20. Oldest: Fannie E. Shipp, 1869-80; latest: Irene S. Frye, 1913–73; Carrie L. Baugher, 1890–1973.—LB, JCR, FRB.

LEE: Map reflecting unfinished cemetery study by NPS has cross on Lee Run about .5 mi. northeast of Shipp cross, but Lee Run cemetery not yet confirmed.—EDL.

NANGUS SHIFLETT: From roadside table on U.S. 33, Swift Run Gap, climb south bank to old Spotswood Trail and go about .5 mi. downhill (west). Cemetery on right slope, fenced (every post with inverted tin can on top to help prevent rot), no gate, some maintenance by hand tools. About 8–25 burials. Oldest: Selena V. Shiflet, 1883-84; latest: Myrtle L. Shifflett 1903–1903. Cemetery probably named for Vernangus (Angus, Nanges) Shiflett Shiflet Lam buried here.—LB, JCR, FRB.

MAIDEN: From U.S. 33 at park boundary east of Elkton, take state route 628 south to first bend, then dirt road .5 mi. Cemetery currently in use and maintained. About 150 burials. Oldest: George W. Baugher, 1786–1847. Burials started, according to legend, when a Mr. Maiden, riding horseback, was killed by lightning that melted his watch chain, and he was buried here under a cedar tree where he fell. According to Billie Jo Monger, who has done much historical and genealogical research, William David Maiden (1799–1875) and his wife Sarah Harris Gardner Maiden (1798–1886) are credited with starting the cemetery.—LB, FRB, EDL, NPS.

BAUGHER: Foot of Sandy Bottom, junction of state routes 626 and 628, on 20-acre park-land tract 115 bought by J. L. Maiden from George Baugher about 1920 and bought by Virginia for the park in 1934.—NPS, FRB.

LAWRENCE WILLIAMS: Sandy Bottom, park-land tract 189, S. G. Morris, along boundary behind house occupied (1954) by George E. Conley. Growth hiding wire fence. Thirty or more burials, with native stone and metal markers.—NPS.

LINSEY WILLIAMS: On park-land tract 188, A. E. Williams, in hollow locally called Punch Bowl, about 1.25 mi. southeast of Swift Run Post Office. Ten or more burials, overgrown.—NPS.

SLAVE BURIALS: In Gap Run on knoll near old house where foot trail comes down from Rocky Mount, on park-land tract 166, A. L. and J. F. Moubray. Burials said to be two slaves.—NPS.

MORRIS/SHIFFLETT: Far up Sandy Bottom "under Swift Run Overlook on Skyline Drive," park-land tract 221, Samuel Morris, or park-land tract 132a, John Henry Shifflett. Overgrown. Five or more burials. Latest: Josie Shifflett, 1945, age 48.—NPS.

SMITH ROACH: From Skyline Drive Milepost 68.45, Smith Roach Gap. Follow old road northwest toward Sandy Bottom about .2 mi. Watch for stone wall and remains of wire fence, on left, overgrown. About 45 burials. Oldest: Arch Roach, d. 1857; latest: 1911, no name. Inscriptions hand-carved on fieldstones.—LB, JCR, NPS.

OTHER ROACH: A separate "Arch Roach" cemetery listed by The Daughters of the American Revolution and Harrisonburg-Rockingham Historical Society as "located in the mountains in Sandy Bottom, State Road 626." It's not the same as Smith Roach; inscriptions are different. May be in park, may not.—LB. Reeders report 2 burial sites down westward on abandoned road opposite parking area in Smith Roach Gap: one about .7 mi., the other farther south and closer to Skyline Drive. No details.—JCR.

HENSLEY/SHIFFLETT/POWELL: Sometimes called Turner Shifflett or Hill Shifflett (for Turner's son Hilary). On west side of Roundtop Mountain, quite far down, about 200 ft. short of (behind) old house site, on park-land tract 47a, Soloman J. Hensley. Cemetery 50 by 50 ft., overgrown. Fifty or more burials. Native stone markers, and a marble headstone for Angus J. Shifflett. Or find from Powell Gap, starting northward on the Appalachian Trail, then following old wagon road that diverges, about 1 mi. to house site. Inscriptions as far back as 1850. Honorias Powell, who owned a thousand acres nearby (and for whom gap probably named) was buried here, according to Billie Jo Monger. Turner Shifflett was a grandson of Powell.—NPS, JCR, LB, EDL.

GEORGE SHIFFLETT: High in Beldor Hollow on south side of old Simmons road near lower park gate, on park-land tract 182, George Minor Shifflett. Overgrown, old wire fence 12 by 40 ft. Ten or more burials, with metal and slate markers.—NPS.

HAM SHIFFLETT: On small knoll north of state route 628, which becomes park fire road, near lower gate northwest of Simmons Gap, on park-land tract 178, Ambrose W. Shifflett. Now forest. Four or more burials.—NPS, JCR.

HERRING: Two cemeteries, separate but adjacent, called George Herring and Mandy Herring. Listed by rangers as at "upper end of Beldor Hollow on east side of Hawksbill

Creek and former hollow road about one mile south of Roadside School," on park-land tract 181, Charles Davis. Overgrown, decayed rail fence, metal grave markers.—NPS.

JAMES WILLIAMS: In Big Run canyon near old house site, on park-land tract 327, James Williams and Levi Sipe. About 1 mi. from park boundary. Obscure, overgrown, few graves seen.—NPS.

Albemarle County

HOWARD: About .4 mi. east of Skyline Drive on Browns Gap Fire Road, above north bank of road, on vast park-land tract 326, John A. Alexander. Single burial with marble stone marker: William H. Howard of Louisa County, Co. F, 44 Va. Inf., C.S.A.—EDL, JCR, LB, NPS.

VIA: Indications of cemeteries near Via Gap (this gap between headwaters of Jones Run and North Fork, Moormans River, near lofty Cedar Mountain off eastward, elevation 3,330 ft). We did find one, right at park border along abandoned road.—JCR. Herbert Via of Harriston says one old Via family cemetery is just outside park line above remains of big house built in 1800s by Christopher Columbus Via, father of Robert H. Via of U.S. Supreme Court case fame, and lived in by Robert and large family for decades.—EDL.

MOORMAN/TURK: Map and notes of some while ago indicate cemetery on Moormans River abandoned road (now a trail) near, and south of, intersection with Turk Branch Trail.—JCR.

McCRAIG: From Jarman Gap on Skyline Drive. Milepost 96.8, walk along road northeast toward South Fork, Moormans River. At about .5 mi. cemetery is on left, park-land tract 5, Carrie A. Walton. Overgrown (poison ivy!); fence poor. At least 25 burials. In 1954 the oldest known grave was marked by a nice headstone dated 1832, but that stone not found in 1984. Most markers native stone without inscriptions. Latest inscribed burial: S. McC., d. 1935, age 19.—LB, NPS.

Augusta County

INDIAN MOUNDS: Three burial mounds, now jumbles of rock about 35 ft. across and up to 4 ft. high, are in the park within 2 mi. of Jarman Gap. Thomas Jefferson knew about them in 1785, relating them to Woods Gap (the first designation of Jarman). He reported they had "been opened and found to contain human bones." We visited them with NPS personnel about 1970.—EDL.

Sources

Persons needing more information, or able to correct or improve information here, are invited to discuss cemeteries with searchers whose initials follow the entries above:

LB: Lois B. Bowman (703) 434-8208; parts of her information, as labeled, came to her quite complete from Dorothy and James Galloway of Ohio.

FRB: Fonda and Roy Breeden (703) 298-8292.

GD: Gloria Dean (703) 298-8661.

JRJ: James R. "Bob"Johnson (703) 743-5687.

EDL: Eileen and Darwin Lambert (703) 743-7246.

DCL: David C. Lyne, a graduate student at the University of Virginia in mid-1970s. Additional facts in his "Preliminary Survey of the Cemeteries in the Rappahannock

Portion of Shenandoah National Park," in Michael A. Hoffman, "Man in the Blue Ridge," pp. 354–89, SNP archives, Luray.

NPS: "Information on Known Cemeteries within Shenandoah National Park," 14-p. report issued by Duane Jacobs, Chief Ranger, Jan. 27, 1954,SNP ranger files, Luray.

JCR: Jack and Carolyn Reeder (202) 244–3224.

CR: Clinton Runyon (703) 743–4116; might be able to help with any cemetery in north and central districts.

Scheel map: Madison County map (with some fringe areas beyond county line). Remarkably complete and legible detail. Surveyed and drawn by Eugene M. Scheel. Issued in cooperation with Second National Bank and Madison County, 1984.

Appendix 2: Groups Formed to Work toward Park Establishment

Southern Appalachian National Park Committee (later Commission) (1924), appointed by U.S. Secretary of the Interior Hubert Work

Henry W. Temple (chairman), congressman from Pa.; Glenn S. Smith, engineer, U.S. Geological Survey; William A. Welch, manager, Palisades Interstate Park. N.Y.-N.J.; Harlan P. Kelsey, botanist, Appalachian Mountain Club leader, Salem, Mass.; and William C. Gregg, pack-train enthusiast, manufacturer, Hackensack, N.J.

Shenandoah Valley, Inc. (1924)

Frank L. Sublett, Harrisonburg, president; Maj. C. S. Roller, Fort Defiance, vice-president; Claude N. Hoover, New Market, treasurer; and Daniel P. Wine, Harrisonburg, secretary.

Directors: Jefferson County, W.Va.: William F. Alexander, Charles Town, and Henry T. McDonald, Harpers Ferry; Berkeley County, W.Va.: A. C. Nadenbousch and J. R. Poland, Martinsburg; Clarke County: A. M. Kerfoot, Berryville, and George H. Burwell, Jr., Millwood; Warren County, Hugh E. Naylor and Aubrey G. Weaver, Front Royal; Frederick County: Andrew Bell and L. Marshall Baker, Winchester; Page County, L. Ferdinand Zerkel, Luray, and V. C. Griffith, Shenandoah; Shenandoah County: C. N. Hoover, New Market, and Col. H. J. Benchoff, Woodstock; Rockingham County: R. Ray Brown, Harrisonburg, and Dr. Paul Bowman, Bridgewater; Augusta County: Col. H. L. Opie, Staunton, and Maj. C. S. Roller, Fort Defiance; Rockbridge County: J. W. Bell, Goshen, and M. W. Paxton, Lexington; Bath County: H. H. Byrd, Warm Springs, and J. T. McAllister, Hot Springs; Allegheny County: William D. McAllister and O. J. Payne, Covington; Highland County, E. B. Jones, Monterey, and S. W. Wilson, Head Waters.

Northern Virginia Park Association (1924)

L. Ferdinand Zerkel, Luray, chairman, board of directors; George Freeman Pollock, Skyland, president; George H. Judd, Washington, D.C., first vice-president; Harold Allen, Washington, D.C., second five president; Daniel P. Wine, Harrisonburg, secretary; and Floyd W. Weaver, Luray, treasurer.

Directors: Thomas W. Harrison, Winchester; Thomas Keith and R. Walton Moore, Fairfax; P. W. Drewry, Petersburg; Dr. Thomas Fell, Annapolis, Md.; Charles H.

Landram, Thomas Deford, W. C. Lauck, S. G. Sherman, and J. O. Bailey, Luray; A. M. Kerfoot, Berryville; Hugh E. Naylor, Front Royal; M. E. Roudabush, Stanley; W. T. Koontz, Shenandoah; R. J. Snapp, Elkton; J. Frank Littell, Grottoes; Col. H. J. Benchoff, Woodstock; John R. Crown, Harrisonburg; Maj. C. S. Roller, Fort Defiance; Col. H. L. Opie, Staunton; G. W. Brenaman, Waynesboro; Judge A. D. Dabney, Charlottesville; George L. Browning, Orange; Nat. D. Early and John S. Chapman, Stanardsville; J. L. Fray, Culpeper; William Meade Fletcher, Sperryville; Wade H. Massie, Washington; J. Don Richards and C. E. Tiffany, Warrenton; W. B. Hibbs and E. B. White, Leesburg; C. Bascom Slemp, Judge James Hay, Merritt W. Ireland, Lt.-Col. C. O. Sherrill, Col. H. P. Birmingham, Ernest N. Smith, M. O. Eldridge, Isaac Gans, E. H. Droop, and Harry F. Allmond, Washington, D.C.

Shenandoah National Park Association, Inc. (1925)

Col. Howard J. Benchoff, Woodstock, president; Thomas B. McAdams, Richmond, vice-president; Homer Ferguson, Newport News, vice-president; Frank Buchanan, Marion, vice-president; Hollis Rinehart, Charlottesville, treasurer; Daniel P. Wine, Harrisonburg, secretary; L. Ferdinand Zerkel, Luray, executive secretary (full-time); and Harry Flood Byrd, chairman of advisory council.

Directors: R. H. Angell, Roanoke; H. H. Harris, Lynchburg; Claude N. Hoover, New Market; Lee Long, Dante (also Page and Rockingham counties); Hugh E. Naylor, Front Royal; Col. H. L. Opie, Staunton; W. A. Ryan, Winchester; Dr. Joseph H. Smith, Petersburg; Thomas S. Southgate, Norfolk; and Julian Y. Williams, Alexandria.

Virginia State Commission on Conservation and Development (1926), appointed by Gov. Harry Flood Byrd

William E. Carson, Riverton, chairman; Coleman Wortham, Richmond, vice-chairman; Junius P. Fishburn, Roanoke; E. Griffith Dodson, Norfolk; Rufus Roberts, Culpeper; Thomas L. Farrar, Charlottesville; and Lee Long, Dante. Elmer O. Fippin was treasurer and executive secretary (full-time) and Alexander Stuart was the first supervisor of the national park division (also full-time).

Appendix 3: Park-land Owners with Acres Condemned

Much can be read from the facts of park-land acquisition. There had never been a shortage of mountain land here, so the price per acre had never been high since private ownership was inaugurated by immigrants from Europe. The earliest owners, nearly all English planters, might profit most by promoting settlement. Almost anyone willing to work a few acres and establish a home could acquire the land—by easy arrangements with the owner or even by simply occupying the place, developing and using it, regardless of the owner. There were homesteaders, sometimes called squatters, thus acquiring landowner-ship in these mountains even in the present century. Perhaps as many as two dozen persons had their ownership officially recognized for the first time even as it was being taken from them, with compensation, of course, to become national park.

President Herbert Hoover bought beautiful mountain land here in 1929 for $5 an acre. Rocky ridges with forest could be bought for $1 an acre, sometimes even less. Land suitable for cultivation might cost $8 to $12 an acre. The park-land was bought during the Great Depression, when the dollar value of just about anything was incredibly low. A loaf of bread could be bought for a nickel; a habitable house could be bought for a few hundred dollars. In the mountains and in some rural lowlands a house could be built for almost nothing from trees existing on the land. Sawmills would saw lumber on shares. Neighbors might assemble to help put up logs and roofs.

After working over the following lists, I see it's possible from these names, acreages, and payment amounts alone to envision the kind of place represented. The English planters who operated plantations alongside and inside the Blue Ridge had been mostly replaced by farmer-owners with German names. Three hundred acres or more and a price of $8,000 or more nearly always means bluegrass sod with cattle in summer, an owner with a German or Swiss or, rarely, Scotch-Irish name who also has a large farm on nearby lowland, one or more year-round tenants on the mountain place, quite possibly a summer home for the owning family, also extensive forest on the tract in addition to pasture. An acreage between 5 and 150, with a price of several hundred dollars to a bit over a thousand, almost certainly means an owner-resident's homeplace, whether or not the owner's family was living there when the park was established. Any size acreage with a total price equalling $1 an acre or no more than $5 an acre is likely to mean a tract held for growth of timber or with a far-out hope of mineral production at some future time; it usually means also an owner in the lowland or, rarely, in a faraway city who seldom visits the land and quite possibly has never become familiar with it. Perhaps it also means squatters, some of whom may have used small tracts long enough to get ownership rights. Most of the mountain residents—owners, tenants, and squatters—have English names. A fair number have German names. A very few are of Scotch-Irish descent.

The information has been compiled from park-land tract maps on file at park headquarters and in the court houses of eight park counties and from deeply stored, cobwebby card files and accounts that came to park headquarters about 1936 from Virginia State Commission on Conservation and Development. The diverse records (in SNP archives) are puzzling in places, and, if any names are spelled wrong or other errors found here, I hope to be forgiven—and corrected.

Albemarle County

John A. Alexander, 48 a., $102
Bank of Weyers Cave, 154 a., $1,700
Black Rock School, 1 a., $175
Sally R. Brown, 123 a., $216
Browns Gap School Board, .5 a., $10
John M. Craig, 515 a., $2,274
C. S. and R. S. Craun, 303 a., $4,192
Crawford and Fulton, 603 a., $9,749
The Deford Co., 1,270 a., $2,635
J. L. and I. Driver, 166 a., $1,830
W. R. and R.T.W. Duke estate, 1,571 a., $2,982
J. G. Fulton, Jr., 105 a., $2,250
Jonathan Garrison, 94 a., $927
Miletus Garrison, 53 a., $900
John T. Hansberger, 44 a., $660
E. A. Harris, 63 a., $2,280
David Hawkins, 318 a., $3,626
J. T. Hoy, 530 a., $1,644
Huffman, Miller and Wampler, 570 a., $5,264
Jackson-Frazier estate, 6 a., $60
Jacob Kyger, 356 a., $2,982

M. F. and James Marshall, 81 a., $1,452
Geo. McAllister, 67 a., $255
S. D. Miller, 60 a., $1,800
D. H. and H. G. Patterson, 1,045 a., $14,922
H. G. and A. B. Patterson, 394 a., $4,199
H. G., D. H., and H. H. Patterson, 125 a., $2,690
W. Frank Patterson, 421 a., $2,611
R. E. Rohleder, 1,029 a., $2,301
T. J. and C. S. Roller, 1,724 a., $4,877
D. D. Royer, 115 a., $1,550
Amanda and Julie Sandridge, 429 a., $1,863
Vacant [no owner ever claimed, property of the state], 295 a., $1,491
Robert H. Via, 152 a., $3,230
Carrie A. Walton, 74 a., $884
Weast and Wonderly, 288 a., $2,262
Western and Williams, 109 a., $725
E. A. Wine, 54 a., $540
Wright and Early, 190 a., $3,595

Augusta County

John A. Alexander, 802 a., $3,115
W. C. Archer, 54 a., $500
Barnhart and Ham, 296 a., $296
G. G., N. G., and F. M. Barnhart, 805 a., $805
H. G. Barnhart, 393 a., $393
Jas. S. Beard, lot, $15
A. H. Berry, 67 a., $1,806
Black Rock Springs Co., 96 a., $143
G. C. Bruce, 162 a., $202
Clayton and Zirkle, 125 a., $125
J. M. and Lydia Cline estate, lot etc., $215
John M. Craig, 104 a., $104
J. W. Crawford estate, 1,264 a., $1,214

S. T. East estate, 810 a., $810
W. P. Eppard, 26 a., $182
Fretwell and Wright, 3 a., $45
Fulton-Crawford estate, lot etc., $105
J. G. Fulton, 1,480 a., $1,480
A. M. Hamrick, lot, $15
Janet Harnsberger, lot, $15
K. B. Koiner, 808 a., $808
K. K. Koiner and G. E. Layman, lot, $15
George Layman, 59 a., $543
Lloyd K. Layman, 99 a., $928
A. H. Lehmecke and John Sinclair, 924 a., $924
Geo. W. McCullough estate, 928 a., $928

R. T. Miller, 60 a., $190
Mattie Mowry estate, lot, $15
J. W. Palmer estate, 210 a., $420
Emma Patterson, lot, $15
H. H., D. H., and Louisa Patterson, lot, $15
Wm. Plummer, 4 a., $510

W. S. Ross, 15 a., $165
John W. Spitler, lot, $15
Lucy Stout, lot etc., $150
John Wampler heirs, lots, $45
John West estate (colored), 812 a., $812
John Wine estate, 895 a., $895

Greene County

S. E. B. Adams, 1,817 a., $11,749
John A. Alexander, 807 a., $2,264
C. E. Armentrout, 182 a., $2,859
J. C. Armstrong, 135 a., $3,890
C. C. Baugher, 261 a., $2,281
J. M. Beasley, 68 a., $1,735
Annie R. Begoon, 29 a., $2,045
Ella Breeden, 44 a., $711
John W. Breeden, 42 a., $385
Nancy Breeden, 42 a., $300
Reuben Breeden, 296 a., $2,648
W. M. and Marcellus Breeden, 53 a., $1,001
C. J. and R. M., Burke, 56 a., $1,344
S. V. and B. B. Burke, 37 a., $465
Elijah Catterton, 80 a., $3,595
Clarence Collier, 34 a., $1,000
Martha Collier estate, 64 a., $1,531
Millie C. Collier estate, 31 a., $752
S. B. Collier, 167 a., $1,525
S. B. and C. F. Collier, 159 a., $3,441
Annie May Comer, 91 a., $621
G. W. Conley, 172 a., $2,236
Jack Crawford estate, 84 a., $599
Moses Crawford, 92 a., $1,282
Davis and Miller, 118 a., $1,495
Minnie Davis, .5 a., $50
A. and H. Deane, 6 a., $265
C. P. Deane and E. Marshall, 15 a., $203
D. C. Deane, 26 a., $525
G. R. Deane, 166 a., $3,846
J. Frank Deane, 202 a., $3,770
L. N. Deane, 160 a., $1,985
Mathew Deane, 36 a., $575
The Deford Co., 799 a., $6,363
A. T. Dulaney, 13 a., $82
H. R. and F. D. Eiler, 47 a., $1,439
Howard Eiler, 110 a., $4,317
Episcopal Church (Simmons Gap), 10 a., $8,525

Episcopal Church (Pocosin), 2 a., $4,455
Jackson Frazier estate, 46 a., $920
J. M. and Effie Funkhauser, 84 a., $1,154
John P. Guilford, 54 a., $135
Basil Haney, 147 a., $891
J. A. Haney, 213 a., $7,060
J. K. Haney, 41 a., $1,760
P. H. Haney, 184 a., $2,728
J. P. Harner, 215 a., $2,600
Malcolm Harner, 124 a., $2,033
J. T. Heard, 319 a., $1,650
C. L. and J. C. Hedrick, 45 a., $3,000
J. T. Helbert, 159 a., $3,441
G. R Herring, 26 a., $1,800
Hightop Christ Church, .5 a., $13
J. W. Hinkle, 65 a., $480
James and Davis, 3 a., $135
H. C. Jarrell and D. A. Jenkins, 198 a., $1,188
Harry Jarrell, 20 a., $322
G. Luther Kite, 24 a., $102
Sally and Luther Kite, 448 a., $3,678
Elmer Lam, 78 a., $1,670
Mathew Lam, 88 a., $970
A. T. Lamb, 50 a., $1,340
C. H. Lamb, 64 a., $1,734
Charles Lamb, 11 a., $605
J. W. Lamb, 68 a., $1,664
James Lamb, 28 a., $490
Silas Lamb, 44 a., $561
W. and E. Lamb, 114 a., $1,683
W. J. Lamb estate, 124 a., $2,980
Willie Lamb, 129 a., $1,191
G. S. Lough, 82 a., $2,509
R. A. Malone, 4 a., $440
Harvey McDaniel, 64 a., $626
John W. McDaniel, 8 a., $430
J. W. Meadows, 93 a., $2,080
John P. Meadows, 105 a., $744
L. G. Meadows, 453 a., $3,500

Eleanora Morris, 40 a., $675
Elizabeth Morris estate, .25 a., $10
Emanuel Morris, 3 a., $352
Houston Morris, 40 a., $914
J. T. Morris estate, 1 a., $125
Mitchell and Ben Morris, 20 a., $224
Raleigh Morris, 24 a., $645
S. G. Morris, 17 a., $51
Smith Morris, 39 a., $550
W. L. Morris, 152 a., $2,075
Myrtle Reynolds, 7 a., $137
Andrew Roach, 78 a., $1,536
Cora V. Roach, 244 a., $3,008
Michael Roach, 50 a., $636
John E. Roller estate, 434 a., $3,777
Cicero Samuels, .25 a., $10
Wm. and Ed. Sellers, 15 a., $600
H. K. and T. M. Shelton, 231 a., $990
Bessie and Earman Shiflett, 31 a., $504
Earman Shiflett, 7 a., $570
G. W. Shiflett estate, 24 a., $248
Hosea Shiflett, 41 a., $923
J. D. Shiflett, 52 a., $5,075
J. J. Shiflett, 18 a., $682
L. N. Shiflett, 62 a., $2,040

Russell Shiflett, 62 a., $900
Shiloh Church of the Brethren, 1 a., $260
Mittie Lee Shoals, 27 a., $195
Columbia Smith, 63 a., $936
J. Al Snow, 3 a., $15
Wm. Sullivan, 33 a., $624
Swift Run Gap School, 1 a., $400
Chas. J. Taylor, 25 a., $404
Claude Taylor, 42 a., $3,085
Mrs. Columbia Taylor, 95 a., $722
Gibbon Taylor, 104 a., $1,535
Hiram Taylor, 94 a., $1,404
Minnie Taylor, 234 a., $1,358
Robert L. Taylor, 190 a., $2,442
Thomas Taylor, 242 a., $1,754
Zachariah Taylor estate, 50 a., $580
Vacant, 15 a., $59
M. W. Walker, 72 a., $1,000
James Weaver, 25 a., $862
W. P. R. Weaver estate, 430 a., $5,700
E. W. Webster and W. S. Shaver, 245 a.,
    $2,231
Lutie B. White, 48 a., $192
H. W. Zetty, 259 a., $1,800

Madison County

Mrs. S. E. B. Adams, 25 a., $85
S. R. and H. L. Aleshire, 88 a., $1,077
Martin Alger, 38 a., $956
Nancy Alger, 6 a., $250
W. D. Anderson, 18 a., $253
Sarah E. Benninghoff, 382 a., $2,214
Chadwell Berry estate, 30 a., $135
Howard Berry, 110 a., $1,660
Walker J. Berry, 105 a., $1,720
Blue Ridge Copper Co., 100 a., $310
Bowman and Goodall, 486 a., $1,648
D. H. Breeden, 354 a., $3,570
D. L. Breeden, 380 a., $7,610
Z. Thomas Breeden, 30 a., $315
A. Hamp Brown, 41 a., $855
Dewey Brown, 2 a., $448
Ira H. Brown, 8 a., $20
O. P. Brown, 140 a., $306
W. A. Brown, 36 a., $1,065
Jas. M. Broyles, 20 a., $470
John Butler, 122 a., $1,307
James Campbell, 25 a., $503

Wash Carpenter, 18 a., $166
Ashby Cave, 74 a., $625
Geo. W. Cave, 1 a., $350
Gordon A. "Gurd" Cave, 16 a., [includes
    church building], $755
Ralph Cave, 14 a., $250
Miley H. "Click" Cave, 8 a., $185
T. W. Cave, 20 a., $170
Christadora heirs, 2,779 a., $15,541
T. B. Clore, 249 a., $2,098
Fred I. Coates, 1 a., $5
Robert C. Coates, 340 a., $2,044
W. E. Coates, 2 a., $5
Ambrose P. Corbin, 165 a., $3,460
Chas. W. Corbin, 56 a., $845
Finnel Corbin, 19 a., $530
Geo. T. Corbin, 4 a. , $576
J. E. Corbin, 81 a., $1,182
Madison Corbin, 34 a., $768
Wesley Corbin, 24 a., $311
Ernest Dodson, 9 a., $90
Mrs. J. A. Dodson, 30 a., $199

Lester Dodson, 19 a., $555
Mary S. Dodson, 3 a., $235
N. C. Dodson, 56 a., $405
Odie Dodson, 5 a., $300
Robert Dodson, 5 a., $50
Schuyler Dodson, 58 a., $231
W. A. Dodson, 61 a., $231
Chas. E. Dyer, 64 a., $717
Elmer Dyer, 44 a., $847
George W. Dyer, 100 a., $2,092
Herbert Dyer, 16 a., $233
Jas. N. Dyer, 13 a., $338
John C. Dyer, 312 a., $1,613
W. E. Dyer estate, 28 a., $478
Waverly T. Dyer, 225 a., $1,130
J. B. Early et al., 4 a., $230
A. B. Fincham, 46 a., $271
Amanda Fincham, 21 a., $1,045
B. W. Fincham, 99 a., $2,000
Ray Finchum, 16 a., $296
Fray and Green, 456 a., $3,155
Fray and Miller, 1,780 a., $8,638
J. D. Fray, 3,034 a., $6,847
J. D. and G. B. Fray, 1,013 a., $2,482
J. D. and H. B. Fray and Mrs. W. R.
   Rose, 764 a., $8,384
M. V. Gander estate, 30 a., $534
J. P. and Annie Goodall, 112 a., $798
R. A. and R. S. Graves, 679 a., $7,491
R. S. Graves and Bros., 829 a., $13,085
J. G. Grove, 210 a., $3,571
Annie V. Hawkins, 152 a., $1,371
C. E. Hawkins, 177 a., $1,844
Highlands Baptist Church, .4 a., $100
Herbert C. Hoover, 166 a., $0 (donated)
Mrs. H. H. Hudson, 432 a., $2,514
Huffman and Spitler, 320 a., $4,380
G. W. Hurt, 16 a., $420
G. C. and D. A. Jenkins, 292 a., $2,633
J. Elliott Jenkins, 44 a., $601
J. M. Jenkins, 392 a., $3,008
J. Noah Jenkins, 16 a., $44
J. Noah and R. A. Jenkins, 387 a., $1,122
C. E. Kite, 133 a., $1,562
W. L. Knighton, 2 a., $10
Chas. G. Koontz estate, 1,091 a., $12,975
Fanny Lamb, 163 a., $6,980
C. S. Landrum, 967 a., $5,632

Lariloba Mining-Development Co., 859 a.,
   $2,285
H. M. Lillard estate, 172 a., $2,980
Ida Lillard, 64 a., $1,236
Arthur W. Long, 309 a., $3,074
I. N. Long, 210 a., $5,102
Lee Long, 524 a., $13,740
P. P., W. M., G. E., and R. B. Long, 8 a.,
   $400
Madison Timber Co., 67 a., $396
McDaniel and Shifflett, 264 a., $2,503
Nethers Baptist Church, 2 a., $4
J. W. Nethers, 151 a., $1,318
P. L. Nichols, 5 a., $550
Bailey Nicholson, 25 a., $910
Chas. Nicholson, 1 a., $60
Eddie Nicholson, 2 a., $185
Edw. Nicholson, 42 a., $747
Effie B. Nicholson, 158 a., $1,758
Mrs. Ella Nicholson, 52 a., $821
E. N. and V. E. Nicholson, 75 a., $1,001
Ephraim B. Nicholson, 97 a., $1,951
H. W. Nicholson and Children, 75 a.,
   $1,055
Ida E. Nicholson, 31 a., $78
Ida Lee Nicholson, 62 a., $1,042
J. Daniel Nicholson, 70 a., $1,669
J. Russ Nicholson, 130 a., $1,638
Jack Nicholson, 32 a., $400
Lewis K. Nicholson, 3 a., $55
Neda Nicholson, 125 a., $1,494
Newton Nicholson, 3 a., $30
Oscar Nicholson, 7 a., $510
Paul Nicholson, 77 a., $2,416
Peter B. Nicholson, 197 a., $732
R. V. Nicholson, 31 a., $530
Rast Nicholson, 37 a., $615
Thomas Nicholson, 28 a., $102
Tiny Nicholson, 14 a., $600
V. E. Nicholson, 110 a., $1,532
Walter Nicholson, 73 a., $867
Wheeler Nicholson, 56 a., $167
Wm. B. Nicholson, 21 a., $976
Old Rag Church (United Brethren), .25 a.,
   $250
Old Rag School, .5 a., $400
Geo. F. Pollock, 2,005 a., $8,591
Pollock and Fox, 35 a., $116

Pollock and Homer Fox, 300 a., $908
E. L. Price, 130 a., $825
Henry Quaintance estate, 272 a., $569
A. Cameron Richards, 59 a., $1,192
B. P. and Henry Richards, 42 a., $201
Benton P. Richards, 100 a., $621
Henry Richards, 26 a., $428
H. S. Rider, 76 a., $450
J. W. Rider, .5 a., $2
John L. Rivercomb, 28 a., $83
J. M. Rowson, 6 a., $20
Wm. Saunders, 60 a., $834
Chas. E. Seal, 55 a., $984
Ernest Seal, 14 a., $467
J. Parker Seal, 82 a., $969
W. T. Shifflett, 155 a., $3,276
O. N. Shiflett, 275 a., $3,240
Dr. Chas. H. Shivers, 31 a., $562
C. O. Simms estate, 64 a., $910
Fenton Sisk, 92 a., $2,084
J. O. Sisk estate, 169 a., $2,000
Kemper Sisk, 31 a., $533
Newman Sisk, 24 a., $154
Wade Sisk, 34 a., $1,113
Wesley C. Sisk, 56 a., $1,306
A. F. Smith and H. Lillard heirs, 22 a., $79
F. P. Smith, 186 a., $1,117
Jas. E. Smith, 115 a., $477
M. T. Smith, 12 a., $529
Mrs. Mollie Smith, 4 a., $27

O. B. and G. W. Smith, 277 a., $712
J. C. Smoot, 515 a., $2,092
C. G. Southards, 16 a., $84
John Henry Sowers, 54 a., $610
B. N. Spitler, 3 a., $9
Carroll M. Spitler, 1,245 a., $7,963
Jacob Spitler, 229 a., $5,153
S. H. and B. H. Spitler, 110 a., $3,469
Bernie Taylor, 60 a., $234
W. Delon Taylor, 62 a., $810
Davie A. Twyman, 10 a., $25
R. D. Twyman estate, 34 a., $81
W. B. Twyman estate, 260 a., $3,386
B. S. Utz, 5 a., $40
B. S. Utz, trustee, 19 a., $529
State of Virginia, .5 a., $1,600
C. M. and R. E. Wayland, 286 a., $1,064
Arthur Weakley, 25 a., $658
E. H. Weakley, 23 a., $149
Geo. Weakley, 17 a., $630
J. K. Weakley, 439 a., $1,339
Jemima Weakley, 90 a., $1,294
Tera Weakley, 1 a., $416
Will N. Weakley, 37 a., $582
Chas. S. Woodward, 10 a., $335
Marion S. Woodward, 21 a., $500
Mollie Woodward, 18 a., $61
W. A. Woodward, 154 a., $2,117
Wm. A. Woodward, 275 a., $780
Mrs. Judie Yowell, 2 a., $25

Page County

M. E. Alger, 15 a., $297
Allegheny Ore and Iron Co., 1,434 a., $2,833
Fred T. Amiss, 3 a., $200
Anita M. Atkins, 23 a., $2,330
Clifford Atkins, 2 a., $1,250
A. G. Bailey, 653 a., $1,555
Gilbert E. Bailey, 334 a., $1,864
Mrs. M. O. Bailey, 68 a., $2,588
Sam Bailey, 30 a., $335
O. and G. B. Baldwin, 26 a., $78
Lura Barnhart, 26 a., $150
S. L. and P. S. Batman, 158 a., $720
C. L. Beahm, 81 a., $1,475
J. M. and G. A. Beahm, .3 a., $2,150
J. W. Beahm, 16 a., $2,365
R. R. Beahm, 109 a., $5,240

W. T. Beahm, 24 a., $4,395
J. W. Beaver, 413 a., $5,026
Blue Ridge Land Corp., 246 a., $9,080
J. G. Bradley, 69 a., $2,457
J. R. Breeden and M. R. Burgess, 370 a., $3,895
W. C. Breeden estate, 219 a., $3,851
L. and W. T. Brubaker, 600 a., $4,005
Sarah Brubaker, 102 a., $4,386
E. G. Brumback, 412 a., $4,048
J. B. Brumback, 61 a., $1,205
J. W. and L. Brumback, 617 a., $21,170
James Gilbert Buracker, 31 a., $503
Nancy and J. H. Buracker, 66 a., $1,033
T. L. Buracker, 20 a., $668
W. P. Buracker, 109 a., $4,048
Ellen Burrill, 3,660 a., $8,590

Mattie L. and Geo. P. Clark, 430 a., $3,050

H. M. [Melanchthon] Cliser, 46 a., $4,865

W. D. Collier estate, 452 a., $4,295

Comer and Hoak, 452 a., $3,098

Geo. N. Conrad, 206 a., $554

W. W. Corbin, 177 a., $1,080

W. M. Cullers, 8 a., $80

Angeline Deavers, 68 a., $206

Frank Deavers, 7 a., $76

John A. Eppard, 172 a., $2,074

Fitzhugh and Bryan, 518 a., $1,036

David and Edith Foltz, 78 a., $2,460

W. V. Ford, 8 a., $96

E. B., P. G, and B. C. Fox, 106 a., $1,319

Homer C. Fox, 69 a., $3,140

M. H. Fox, 13 a., $65

Noah Fox estate, 33 a., $190

Fray and Miller, 742 a., $2,248

Gander Bros., 36 a., $708

M. J. Gander estate, 292 a., $3,978

B. T. Grandstaff, 91 a., $7,270

S. L. Grandstaff, 52 a., $1,992

J. G. Grove, 46 a., $808

Mabel Grove, 38 a., $139

Mrs. A. P. Hammer, 2 a., $900

Susan J. Heiskell and Roy Heiskell's heirs, 134 a., $168

J. J. Heiston, 584 a., $6,526

Mrs. Victoria Hensley, 215 a., $2,630

E. N. Hershberger, 511 a., $12,975

W. P. Herschberger, 24 a., $3,712

E. L. and H. S. Hite, 637 a., $6,725

Joe Hite, 88 a., $2,575

A. B. Hockman, 363 a., $1,481

Huffman and Yates, 267 a., $2,803

David Huffan estate, 756 a., $1,379

Buddy Jewell, 93 a., $1,436

Ann P. Jolliffe heirs, 2,700 a., $8,318

C. S. Jones et al., .7 a., $150

B. Roberta Judd, 173 a., $7,225

Bernard S. Judd, 14 a., $710

G. H. and M. A. Judd, 14 a., $17,583

L. L. Judd, 17 a., $815

J. W. Kendall, 13 a., $33

Mrs. Bessie Keyser, 102 a., $335

C. P. Keyser, 37 a., $240

H. H. and S. B. Keyser, 160 a., $1,795

John T. and Chas. P. Keyser, 119 a., $772

David L. Kibler, 33 a., $370

H. and A. L. Kleinhaus, 10 a., $120

Wm. H. Knight, 98 a., $362

V. B. Knight, 5 a., $180

C. G. Koontz, 60 a., $1,035

F. L. and G. C. Koontz, 660 a., $14,965

Bessie Lam, 8 a., $750

Fannie Lamb, 8 a., $320

D. K. Lambeth, 8 a., $765

Lariloba Copper Co., 33 a., $87

I. W. Lehew, 48 a., $275

Alice Long, 12 a., $135

Isaac Long, 624 a., $11,144

Lee Long, 442 a., $21,100

P. P. and W. M. Long, 500 a., $6,115

P. P., W. M., G. C., and F. S. Long, 364 a., $18,020

Luray Water Supply, 12 a., $480

Madeira Hill and Co., 1,099 a., $4,003

Mrs. Lizzie H. Massie, .5 a., $125

A. T. Meadows, 97 a., $1,694

Arthur Meadows, 10 a., $128

J. W. Meadows, 331 a., $1,889

Ulysses Meadows, 127 a., $1,555

Menefee, Keyser, and Walton, 252 a., $1,217

Dan Miller, 10 a., $48

E. K. and Susan Miller, 41 a., $148

Emmanuel Miller heirs, 86 a., $545

John M. Miller, 618 a., $4,826

R. Mims, 4 a., $2,000

R. T. Mims, 30 a., $2,035

Bassett W. Mitchell, 431 a., $1,072

C. E. and V. C. Musselman, 31 a., $1,550

M. W. Nichols, 49 a., $438

Overall-Heiskell, 80 a., $160

Isaac Overall heirs, 173 a., $411

Wm. C. Overall heirs, 944 a., $2,646

Chas. W. Payne, 56 a., $1,619

Geo. F. Pollock, 1,672 a., $8,139

Presgraves and Bumgardner, 1 a., $200

E. Luther Price, 92 a., $879

Geo. Price estate, 13 a., $199

Rebecca J. Price, 5 a., $72

Charles Printz, 338 a., $3,025

Chas. H. Printz, 162 a., $747

Daniel J. Printz, 14 a., $56

Julia and M. O. Printz, 44 a., $234

J. I. and E. K. Rice, 103 a., $552

B. E. Rickard, 41 a., $205
B. E. and C. W. Rickard, 122 a., $968
John E. Roller, 320 a., $3,260
B. F. Shenk estate, 427 a., $906
Gabriella V. Shenk, 27 a., $363
R. A. Shenk, .4 a., $140
Shenk School, 1 a., $500
Thos. W. Shenk, 8 a., $400
Abram Smeltzer, 49 a., $1,404
J. B. Smith, 26 a., $3,705
M. Snider, 61 a., $2,895
Geo. W. Somers, 52 a., $934
Julius Somers, 250 a., $3,341
N. R. Somers, 101 a., $429
Bernard Sours estate, 125 a., $859
Bertha V. Sours, 307 a., $1,893
Betty S. Sours, 136 a., $450
C. W. Sours et al., 125 a., $2,437
David C. and Wm. Sours, 80 a., $160
Ernest C. Sours, 12 a., $129
Fred Sours estate, 20 a., $196
J. S. Sours and Samuel Miller, 19 a., $106
Jacob S. Sours, 56 a., $229
James L. and Nellie M. Sours, 103 a., $494
John W. Sours, 49 a., $1,375
P. J. Sours, 18 a., $82
Sola K. Sours, 317 a., $5,876
B. N. Spitler, 694 a., $22,072

C. M. Spitler, 16 a., $16
Lloyd K. Spitler, 2 a., $200
S. H. and B. H. Spitler, 204 a., $4,520
Mrs. A. M. Stombock, 6 a., $510
A. V. Strickler, 30 a., $340
B. C. Strickler, 48 a., $1,200
B. F. and Annie V. Strickler, 494 a.,
    $1,970
Jas. H. Strickler, 176 a., $1,320
John A. Strickler, 49 a., $430
Dolly Taylor, .6 a., $300
Sylvanus Taylor, 622 a., $4,597
W. Delon Taylor, 22 a., $87
Thornton Gap School, 1 a., $450
A. J. Triplett, 35 a., $409
J. W. Walter, 29 a., $208
S. B. Waters, 185 a., $6,070
Wm. Weaver, 19 a., $726
Williams, Taylor, Cheatham, and Priest,
    94 a., $16,957
Chellie Williams, 14 a., $93
Mrs. I. G. Willis, 6 a., $388
L. and M. Willis, 3 a., $400
Lewis Willis, 229 a., $6,890
Mrs. Elizabeth Yancey, 6 a., $650
A. J. Yowell, 107 a., $787
L. F. Zerkel, .25 a., $125
E. J. Zirkle, 17 a., $224

Rappahannock County

A. Jack Atkins, 248 a., $1,631
Ashby G. Atkins, 3 a., $500
Britten L. Atkins, 148 a., $2,250
Burkett Atkins, 82 a., $1,421
Homer C. Atkins, 22 a., $117
J. B. Atkins, 2 a., $10
J. W. Atkins, 71 a., $4,203
J. W. Atkins and J. W. Ramey, 30 a., $120
James A. Atkins, 40 a., $160
Jeremiah Atkins, 310 a., $8,406
Jeremiah and Caroline Atkins, 70 a., $275
John Atkins, 84 a., $800
Jonas M. Atkins, 41 a., $1,592
Jos. B. Atkins, 13 a., $144
Martha Atkins, 13 a., $715
Mrs. Sally Atkins, 23 a., $223
Clifton Ayler, 146 a., $1,709
A. G. Bailey, 20 a., $28

J. O. Bailey, 76 a., $777
Jas. Bailey, 91 a., $595
Bank of Warren, 52 a., $1,897
Welton Beaty, 55 a., $420
Blue Ridge Land Corp., 14 a., $1,050
J. Bernard Bolen, 633 a., $12,994
H. E. Boyer, 464 a., $4,703
C. C. Bray, 3 a., $150
J. E. Broy, trustee, 140 a., $722
E. G. Brumback, 105 a., $1,095
J. B. Brumback, 44 a., $1,110
Ellen Burrill, 192 a., $4,253
A. J. and Susan Campbell, 8 a., $600
Shirley Carter, 710 a., $11,393
Church of the Brethren, 1 a., $800
Addie F. Clark, 10 a., $1,310
Andrew J. Clark, 490 a., $4,675
Mathias Clark, 93 a., $1,058

Nina H. Clark, 452 a., $5,508
Joe Clatterbuck, 92 a., $1,028
Isaac Claytor, 21 a., $234
Mary M. Claytor, 17 a., $103
A. T. Compton, 118 a., $723
Frank Cox, 112 a., $2,107
E. L. Crane, 128 a., $273
H. M. and D. H. DeJarnette, 52 a., $1,187
Alice Dodson, 140 a., $1,841
Booten Dodson, 129 a., $532
F. F. Dodson, 31 a., $143
F. W. Dodson, 90 a., $1,150
J. B. Dodson, Sr., 72 a., $1,405
J. B. Dodson, Jr., 52 a., $1,094
J. F. Dodson, 48 a., $193
Lily Dodson, 48 a., $203
W. B. Dodson, 153 a., $629
Alfred Dwyer estate, 82 a., $994
M. J. Dwyer heirs, 285 a., $4,235
R. M. Dwyer, 52 a., $75
S. Jacob Dwyer, 116 a., $949
Thomas B. Dwyer, 1 a., $10
Jas. A. Estes estate, 281 a., $1,367
James H. Fletcher, 565 a., $1,589
E. B. and M. H. Fox, 387 a., $5,333
Amos Frazier, 86 a., $270
Jeff T. Frazier, 240 a., $1,650
Emma J. Fry, 48 a., $602
James Fry, 10 a., $131
Samuel Fry, 3 a., $467
Gander Bros., 34 a., $718
Grove and Spitler, 160 a., $5,642
J. J. Heiston, 350 a., $4,129
D. H. and D. B. Hershberger, 320 a.,
 $5,622
Joseph A. Huffman, .1 a., $50
E. H. Jenkins, 3 a., $420
Nathan Jenkins, 283 a., $1,106
Ann P. Jolliffe heirs, 50 a., $698
Dr. C. E. Johnson, 88 a., $361
R. A. Jones, 112 a., $112
Mrs. Kate Judd, 2 a., $635
J. T. Kelley, 1,310 a., $6,814
David Kendall, 148 a., $1,795
J. W. Kendall, 503 a., $2,135
John A. Keyser, 184 a., $2,227
John Major, 48 a., $445
J. K. Marlow, 137 a., $2,072

Alberta V. Menefee, 65 a., $1,503
H. R. Millar, 8 a., $8
Miller, Taylor, Spitler, and Huffman,
 128 a., $936
B. F., C. E., and H. W. Miller heirs, 355 a.,
 $2,182
C. J. and Louise Miller and W. T. Taylor,
 905 a., $3,094
E. T. and G. T. Miller, 398 a., $5,974
Ellis Miller, 177 a., $1,535
J. J. Miller estate, 3,565 a., $22,617
Lewis Nicholson, 12 a., $120
Lippie Nicholson, 40 a., $213
Newton Nicholson, 101 a., $510
R. H. O'Bannion, 35 a., $105
Julia Overall heirs, 146 a., $674
Wm. C. Overall heirs, 180 a., $1,073
Pomeroy estate, 165 a., $597
A. M. and Jessie Priest, 3 a., $300
Bernie O. Pullen, 60 a., $359
Dudley Pullen, 5 a., $250
Elmira Pullen, 59 a., $646
J. P. Pullen, 20 a., $139
Robinson Pullen, 25 a., $896
S. B. and Mary L. Pullen, 71 a., $1,235
J. W. Ramey, 198 a., $10,516
Rappahannock School Board, 1 a., $325
Mary Ann Overall Roy heirs, 56 a., $140
W. J. Rutherford, 305 a., $1,738
Julia M. Settle, 148 a., $6,385
Thos. H. Settle, 1,145 a., $4,425
Virginia R. Smith, 156 a., $2,391
W. M. Stuart, 13 a., $80
Mrs. L. F. Swindler, 206 a., $853
Taylor, Cheatham, Priest, and Williams,
 178 a., $17,119
Dolly Taylor, 2 a., $150
Vacant (Oventop), 36 a., $90
W. M., J. G., and James A. Varner, and
 Isaac Spitler, 321 a., $4,990
B. M. Willis, 104 a., $543
F. D. Wood, 650 a., $2,286
Ben Woodward, 22 a., $122
Wm. H. Woodward estate, 9 a., $55
Elizabeth Yancey, 99 a., $2,055
C. W. Yates, trustee for L. Berry, 299 a.,
 $1,092
Thomas Young, 13 a., $57

Rockingham County

John A. Alexander, 19,665 a., $46,374
Allegheny Ore and Iron Co., 16 a., $24
J. C. Armstrong, 29 a., $1,815
Annie L. Baugher, 821 a., $2,731
Elsie B. Baugher, 62 a., $2,220
G. Scott Baugher, 14 a., $305
Geo. B. Baugher, 980 a., $9,923
J. W. Baugher, 8 a., $1,935
W. D. Baugher, 49 a., $1,945
Wesley H. Baugher, 127 a., $3,801
J. M. Beazley, 7 a., $210
Chas. Begoon, 89 a., $2,878
Doctor Breeden, 1 a., $25
Wesley and Amanda C. Breeden, 75 a.,
     $3,012
Robert M. and G. J. Burke, 132 a., $4,730
S. V. and B. B. Burke, 254 a., $4,163
Elijah Catterton, 50 a., $2,700
Ashby J. Collier, 120 a., $1,277
Geo. N. Conrad, 1,030 a., $1,757
Crawford and Fulton, 23 a., $690
Chas. Davis, 115 a., $4,222
Dean Mountain School, 1 a., $915
Edgar Dean, 175 a., $2,998
Sarah A. Dean, 20 a., $188
Thos. L. Dean, 214 a., $7,870
W. F. Dean, Jr., 48 a., $990
Wesley A. Dean, 75 a., $920
W. J. Downs, 353 a., $3,663
H. R. and F. D. Eiler, 138 a., $4,600
Howard Eiler, 10 a., $480
J. W. Eutsler, 10 a., $60
Fern Hill W. B. Church, .5 a., $1,200
Vernon Foltz, 143 a., $4,880
J. M. and Effie Funkhauser, 132 a., $4,459
Emma V. Gibbons et al., 120 a., $3,685
J. K. Haney, 74 a., $5,065
J. J. Heard, 228 a., $1,665
J. T. and W. B. Helbert, 39 a., $1,340
N. W. Hensley, 138 a., $10,410
S. J. Hensley, 313 a., $3,190
Sarah E. Hensley, 56 a., $1,413
Stephen Hensley, 7 a., $35
Thos. B. Hensley, 220 a., $6,360
Mrs. Victoria Hensley, 28 a., $86
Ellie Herring, 36 a., $2,285
Ella F. Hickle, 98 a., $1,367
J. W. Hinkle, 76 a., $660

F. H. Hughes, 10 a., $100
Carrie James and H. C. Davis, 195 a.,
     $8,237
M. M. Jarman, 74 a., $1,920
G. Luther Kite, 376 a., $2,184
Sallie Kite, 60 a., $270
Mrs. John Knighting, 52 a., $1,053
E. C. Lam, .1 a., $1,300
E. C. and E. E. Lam, .12 a., $1,500
Elmer Lam, 13 a., $265
Harvey Lam, 41 a., $1,548
Rosa E. Lawson, 22 a., $2,005
Lydia H. LeBaume, 59 a., $384
M. D. Longley, 154 a., $1,429
G. S. Lough, 24 a., $750
John H. Mace, 381 a., $2,296
J. Luther Maiden, 80 a., $7,180
Chas. S. McDaniel, 167 a., $4,770
E. S. Meadows, 386 a., $3,160
L. C. Meadows, 109 a., $9,650
L. G. Meadows, 701 a., $3,350
L. W. Meadows, 240 a., $4,787
R. T. Miller, 507 a., $4,744
Salem Mishelleny, 2 a., $10
Millie E. Moore, 88 a., $1,590
Annie H. Morris, 12 a., $24
Raleigh Morris, 37 a., $905
S. G. Morris, 168 a., $4,585
Samuel Morris, 28 a., $14,295
Wm. Morris, 8 a., $303
A. L. and J. F. Moubray, 101 a., $523
R. L. Moubray, 3 a., $320
E. M. Mundy, 3 a., $5,100
Patterson and Harner, 5 a., $125
D. H. and H. G. Patterson, 415 a., $9,675
H. G., D. H., and H. H. Patterson, 73 a.,
     $2,095
Ida Phelps, 205 a., $389
Robert Roach, 37 a., $548
W. W. and E. B. Sellers, 188 a., $5,573
Ambrose Shiflett [Shifflett], 325 a., $7,166
Bernard Shiflett, 2 a., $10
Daniel Shiflett, 232 a., $3,053
Geo. E. Shiflett, 52 a., $1,268
G. M. Shiflett [Shifflett], 81 a., $1,504
Hosea Shiflett, 86 a., $2,830
J. Henry Shiflett, 63 a., $1,634
L. N. Shiflett, 28 a., $1,785

Moses Shiflett estate, 21 a., $113
Warren Shiflett, 24 a., $1,519
Wilmer Shiflett, 30 a., $825
Shipp estate, 80 a., $6,314
Maude M. Shipp, 19 a., $2,300
Frank Sipe, 65 a., $354
John and Catherine Smart, 5 a., $30
W. B. and Ida C. Smart, 10 a., $65
Q. E. Smith, 309 a., $11,616
Mable T. Stever, 5 a., $30
Sunny Side School, 2 a., $350

Swift Run W. B. Church, .5 a., $1,000
Webster and Shover, 8 a., $250
A. E. Williams, 113 a., $2,375
A. J. Williams, 67 a., $2,371
H. E. and C. Williams, 43 a., $3,580
Jas. Williams and Levi Sipe, 132 a., $680
Lizzie E. Williams, 13 a., $1,895
H. W. Wyant, .5 a., $440
T. L. Yancey, 106 a., $2,180
Jacob Yost, trustee, 4,217 a., $8,123

Warren County

Jennie D. Anderson, 6 a., $501
Noah W. Aleshire, 2 a., $200
A. G. Bailey, 717 a., $1,301
Geo. Bailey, 63 a., $350
Lura Barnhart, 59 a., $456
H. W. Beaty estate, 288 a., $2,208
James W. Beaty, 30 a., $269
Paul Beaty, 186 a., $1,662
Welton Beaty, 64 a., $213
B. J. Borden, 694 a., $1,500
H. E. Boyer, 196 a., $542
O. K. Brown estate, 63 a., $350
W. O. Carter, 31 a., $253
H. H. Clatterbuck, 73 a., $1,605
H. T. Compton, 20 a., $40
Z. T. Compton estate, 68 a., $166
Mary F. Cook, 35 a., $193
A. C. Corbin, 49 a., $1,123
Dr. R. B. Cullers estate, 37 a., $369
Buddy Fox, 92 a., $1,062
Elsie Fox, 17 a., $170
Henry Fox, 98 a., $893
Winfield Fox, 127 a., $3,290
Fristoe and Lockhart, 854 a., $3,892
Earl Fristoe, 34 a., $127
M. M. Hartley, 268 a., $1,530
Lizzie Heflin, 20 a., $190
B. W. and J. E. Hickerson, 57 a., $2,770
C. D. Hickerson estate, 35 a., $208
Dan Hickerson, 70 a., $636
Ella V. Hickerson, 150 a., $3,729
B. J. Hillidge, 77 a., $142
S. A. Johnson, 128 a., $1,329
Lewis Granville Jones, 80 a., $609
Joseph W. Kenner, 220 a., $1,686
Richard Lewis, 10 a., $2,991

Virgie C. Lockhart, 100 a., $5,500
J. Milton Manuel, 71 a., $431
J. K. Marlow, 42 a., $690
Levi Marlow, 135 a., $1,560
W. A. Marlow, 41 a., $507
Annie Matthews, 132 a., $713
James M. Matthews estate, 32 a., $493
Chas. L. Melton and/or Edgar Merchant,
    90 a., $3,920
H. R. Millar, 450 a., $1,005
S. R. Millar, 100 a., $770
J. J. Miller estate, 2,438 a., $5,824
Jacob Mills, 122 a., $682
H. G. Morrison, 55 a., $275
J. J. Morrison, 254 a., $5,408
R. T. Morrison, 9 a., $40
W. J. Morrison, 77 a., $835
New York Life Ins. Co., 81 a., $3,500
Harriet and W. C. Overall heirs, 404 a.,
    $1,642
Wm. C. Overall, 702 a., $2,227
Myra Lew Partlow, 55 a., $220
F. D. Poe, 8 a., $24
K. S. Poe, 5 a., $15
Pomeroy and Wines, 144 a., $6,344
William Pomeroy estate, 180 a., $799
B. H. Potts, 15 a., $6,125
B. H. and Eva M. Potts, 10 a., $7,502
Eva M. Potts, 4 a., $1,000
Edith Rudacille, 96 a., $327
T. J. and W. F. Rudacille, 662 a., $1,756
W. E. Rudacille, 1 a., $200
Julia M. Settle, 52 a., $1,100
Geo. Lee Sheppard, 4 a., $1,025
Wm. Sheppard, 4 a., $272
Ed Smelzer, 19 a., $38

Ernest Thompson, 127 a., $1,063
S. B. Thornhill, 3 a., $6
J. Randolph Updike, 40 a., $700
U.S. Army Quartermaster, 37 a., $1
Robert W. Vaught, 53 a., $645
Mrs. W. E. Vaught, 6 a., $37
Clifton Walters, 15 a., $295

Eliza Walters, 5 a., $20
John H. Walters, 11 a., $294
Warren County road, 1 a., $1
A. G. Weaver, 70 a., $7,488

Appendix 4: Park-land Owners Selling Voluntarily

Most of these tracts were bought in a federal Recreation Demonstration project designed to fight the Great Depression. It was independent of the park project, but the land was later added to the park, and quite a few of its residents were accepted into the resettlement or homestead project designed for park residents. Some officials were surprised that land in the park area could be bought quite easily by negotiation, often land less rocky than the park average and at prices lower than the appraisals and the payments ordered by the courts in the condemnation cases. Real estate values must have been falling in the prolonged depression.

The information is from the 50-year-old Shenandoah Land Program file (FERA Recreation Demonstration Project VA R-4), a few file folders that were found representing individual sellers of tracts, and a diversity of other papers in SNP archives.

Albemarle County

Edgar Ballard, 281 a., $2,320
Charlottesville City, 147 a., $3,696
Wright and Driver, 327 a., $5,295

Page County

S. L. and P. S. Batman, 8 a., $736
Naomi B. Beahm, 25 a., $510
E. H. Breeden, 92 a., $1,697
I. Casper Judd, 67 a, $8,045
J. S. Judd, 26 a., $750
Lena Judd, 12 a., $1,071
Roy Judd, 25 a., $1,940
W. Lee Judd, 3 a., $990
Fannie Lamb, 6 a., $3,400
Mary I. Shomo, 43 a., $1,790
Annie L. Sours, 27 a., $2,865
Arthur C. Sours, 18 a., $625

Rappahannock County

Mrs. Ben Armentrout, 102 a., $2,571
J. P. Atkins, 15 a., $585
A. Bailey, 215 a., $1,791
A. S. Baker, 88 a., $1,327
Wm. Baker, 91 a., $624
Oscar Baldwin, 57 a., $715
Bank of Warren, 72 a., $532
John W. Bennett estate, 190 a., $1,600
Ruby Bolen, 101 a., $1,065
Anna V. Bowen heirs, 153 a., $3,867
C. H. Bowen, 410 a., $10,000
Oklahoma Bowen, 77 a., $600
H. A. Brown, 437 a., $4,844
W. W. Brown estate, 362 a., $1,876
Jas. A. Burke, 80 a., $380
Joshua Burke, 49 a., $779
Robert Burke, 98 a., $900
W. M. Burke estate, 22 a., $540

James Campbell, 48 a., $1,057
Judith M. Carter, 83 a., $653
Alpheus Clark, 50 a., $967
W. Moses Clark, 55 a., $400
F. Compton, 127 a., $1,000
Culpeper National Bank, 119 a., $1,304
Joe Darnell, 54 a., $1,500
Booten Dodson, 27 a., $403
C. Brook Dodson, 245 a., $1,500
Jack and Hunter Dodson, 55 a., $678
Jonnie Dodson, 27 a., $511
Jos. S. Dodson, 96 a., $500
Nathan Dodson, 197 a., $1,500
Wayman Dodson, 35 a., $350
David Dwyer, 49 a., $497
J. T. Dwyer, 125 a., $1,500
Nina B. Dwyer, 213 a., $1,560
R. M. Dwyer, 67 a., $314
S. Jacob Dwyer, 29 a., $87
Thos. B. Dwyer, 159 a., $2,229
Jas. P. Fincham estate, .5 a., $10
J. R. Finchum, 230 a., $2,119
W. M. Fletcher, 27 a., $381
C. F. Frazier, 80 a., $312
Mrs. James H. Frazier, 31 a., $275
Lee Frazier, 191 a, $1,800
Mrs. Mortimer Hawkins, 143 a., $1,350
Mrs. Savilla Herrell, 164 a., $1,300
H. H. Hudson, 278 a., $8,500
Joseph A. Huffman, 216 a., $7,000
A. H. Jenkins, 420 a., $5,729
A. K. Jenkins, 43 a., $298
Delia B. and Chas. I. Jenkins, 122 a., $798
Della B. Jenkins, 70 a., $139
Fannie E. Jenkins, 44 a., $950
Frank Jenkins, 39 a., $275
Golden Jenkins, 69 a., $496

Hattie M. Jenkins, 43 a., $339
Hubert C. Jenkins, 53 a., $775
J. Boot Jenkins, 97 a., $781
J. W. Jenkins, 61 a., $911
Johanas Jenkins, 10 a., $216
Linsay Jenkins, 34 a., $700
McLane Jenkins, 140 a., $1,055
Silas Jenkins, 29 a., $575
H. L. Johnson, 212 a., $1,456
J. A. and J. O. Jones, 77 a., $555
R. A. Jones, 112 a., $1,550
J. T. Kelly, 91 a., $1,300
Ben Menefee estate, 173 a., $1,386
Mt. Olive Baptist Church, .5 a., $300
Chas. Mundy, 2 a., $21
J. W. Nethers, 29 a., $86
Ida E. Nicholson, 48 a., $550
Inez V. Nicholson, 133 a., $761
J. M. Nicholson, 232 a., $2,149
R. L. Nicholson, 40 a., $300
Thos. Nicholson, 277 a., $3,121
Clarence Pullen, 70 a., $1,253
Rappahannock School Board, 5 a., $280
Mrs. Izza Rector, 18 a., $215
Newton Sisk [or John W. Johnson, legal
    owner?], 20 a., $600
Smith, Jenkins and H. A. Brown, 50 a.,
    $494
Vacant [no owner claimed, property of the
    state] (Pignut Mountain), 123 a., $260
Eva Weakley, 53 a., $350
J. Amos Weakley, 24 a., $464
F. W. Weaver and W. L. Hudson, 79 a.,
    $5,000
Martha B. Wharton, 32 a., $251
Mrs. Mollie Woodward, 272 a., $1,579

Rockingham County

Daniel T. Dean, 101 a., $2,800
E. Dyche Dean, 96 a., $2,161
J. B. Dean, 161 a., $3,475

N. Lester Dean, 91 a., $2,580
Stephen Hensley, 23 a., $800

Warren County

Henry Fox, 90 a., $2,000

Potts Farm, 70 a., $16,000

Appendix 5: Heads of Families Living on Park-Land, 1935

The resident situation was fluid while the park was being established, partly because of the state and federal actions but also because of the severe depression and drought. Families now averaged around seven members, including the "heads," so resident population was about two thousand in 1935. Many resident families, of course, had been owners until acquisition of the park-land by Virginia, but the Supreme Court case had caused a year's delay in park establishment. Perhaps 20 percent of the residents moved out during that year, but other families quickly occupied the houses, many of them without permission from either the former owners or the new owner, so the accuracy of records lagged behind the changes.

My sampling indicates that fewer than one-third of the residents in December 1935 had been the owners. Some resident family heads could have been children or other kin of the recent owners. In any event, a large proportion of the residents of these mountains had always been tenants or other nonowners. Earliest actual statistics show that about 40 percent of residents owned the land they lived on.

The information is from continually changing lists of park residents compiled and used from 1934 to 1936 by personnel of the Homesteads Division, a federal unit that repeatedly shifted supervising agencies in Washington, D.C., separate from but cooperating with National Park Service offices. These working lists were often scribbled with corrections. Additions or corrections for improving the list for any future publication will be welcomed. The symbol (L) after a name here indicates lifetime list—residents authorized by the Secretary of the Interior to live in their old homes for the rest of their lifetimes (mostly because of advanced age).

Albemarle County

James Henry Blackwell
Delia Bowen
John Bowen
Robert Bowen
Drucilla (Mrs. Laird) Garrison

Edward A. Harris
Jesse Rossen
Russell Rossen
Willie Rossen
Joseph F. Wood (L)

Augusta County

Lionel C. Fisher

Greene County

Addie Breeden
George Breeden
Jack Breeden
Marcellus Breeden (L)
Matilda "Aunt Cassie" Breeden (L)
Missie Martha Breeden
Addie Collier
Charlie F. Collier
Clarence Collier
George W. Conley
Lloyd Conley
Lonnie Conley
Grover Crawford (L)
Moses Crawford
Elijah Dean
Gilbert Dean
H. Scott Dean
Herman Dean
Alex Dunnivan
Andrew Dunnivan
Herbert Dunnivan
Donald B. Hensley
Ervin Hensley
Luther G. Kite
Ardiste Lamb
Davis Lamb
Edgar Lamb
Elijah Lamb
James Lamb
Arthur McDaniel
Harvey McDaniel

Tommie McDaniel
Mary S. Meadows (L)
Cutie Morris
Eleanora Morris (L)
John Wesley Morris
Mrs. Leedie Morris
Lou Ella Morris
Luther Morris
Manuel Morris
Melvin Morris
Thomas Morris (L)
E. H. Mundy
Andrew Roach
Mrs. Cora V. Roach
Jack Rossen
Jack Samuels
Sewel Samuels
Andrew Shifflett
Bell Shifflett
George F. Shifflett
Russell Shifflett
Thomas Shifflett
Harvey Sholes (Shoals)
Jesse Sims
Johnny Snow
Baldwin Taylor
John L. Taylor
Lacey Taylor
Roy Taylor
Thomas S. Taylor
Whit Taylor

Madison County

Nacy Alger (L)
John Beahm (L)
Harry E. Berry
Minnie "Mittie" Breeden
Tom Breeden
Ira H. Brown
James Broyles
George Buracker
Martin Buracker (L)
James R. Campbell
Douglas Cave
G. A. Cave
Lester R. Cave
Mylie W. "Click" Cave
Ralph Cave

Walter Cave
Charles W. Corbin
Dennis Corbin
Finnel Corbin (L)
George Luther Corbin
George T. Corbin
James Corbin (L)
James Luther Corbin
Marvin Woodie Corbin
Oddie W. Corbin
Stanley Corbin
Buck Dodson
Ernest Dodson
Oddie W. Dodson
Robert D. Dodson

Schuyler E. Dodson
Seldon M. Dodson
Wilbur Dodson
Willie Dodson
Charles E. Dyer
Davis Louis Dyer
James H. Dyer
John C. Dyer (L)
Vander Dyer
Festus Fincham
Justus Fincham
George W. Hurt (L)
Albert Nicholson
Barbara Nicholson (L)
Charlie Nicholson
Edward H. Nicholson
Ephraim B. Nicholson
Ernest A. Nicholson
Haywood Nicholson
Hillton Nicholson
Mrs. J. R. (Carrie E.) Nicholson
John Russ Nicholson (L)
John T. Nicholson
Louis K. Nicholson
Oscar Nicholson
Peter C. Nicholson
R. Velt Nicholson
Rast Nicholson
Mrs. W. Nicholson

Walter Nicholson
Wm. Buddy Nicholson
George F. Parks
A. C. Richards
J. Parker Seal
Benny O. Sisk
Eldon Sisk
Kemper Sisk (L)
Wade Sisk
West Sisk (L)
Charlie Smith
Fred Sours
Mrs. Mary Sours (L)
Bernie Taylor
Delon Taylor
Arthur M. Weakley
Fannie Weakley (L)
June "R. J." Weakley
William N. Weakley (L)
Andrew J. Woodward
Ashby Woodward
Charlie Woodward
John "Jim" Woodward (L)
Lloyd J. Woodward
Marion Woodward
Nebraskey "Brass" Woodward (L)
Roy Woodward
Willie M. Woodward

Page County

Charles Franklin Bailey
Elmer W. Bates
John W. Beahm
Frank Berry
Rebecca Breeden (L)
Emmett Buracker
Ozzie Buracker
Reuben Buracker
Cletus Cave
H. Melanchthon Cliser
Oliver Jett Cliser
Cletus O. Deavers
Willie Deavers
John C. Ellis
Walker Jenkins
Henry Jewell
Emmett Lamb
Hezekiah Lamb (L)

Raymond D. Lamb
Walter A. Lamb
Alfred Meadows
Ben Meadows
Robert Meadows
Ulysses E. Meadows
Charles W. Payne (L)
David L. Richard
Fred L. Seal
Raymond H. Seal
Thos. W. Shenk and wife, Annie
    Bradley Shenk (L)
Ivan D. Taylor
S. Clark Taylor
Ernest Thomas
James G. Thomas
William Henry Thomas (L)
Willie Weaver (L)
Lewis Willis (L)

Rappahannock County

J. H. Armentrout (L)
Ashby G. Atkins
Britton L. Atkins (L)
Burnam Atkins
Emerson Atkins
Frank "Dido" Atkins (L)
George W. Atkins (L)
Grover Atkins
Herbert Atkins
James P. Atkins
John A. Atkins
John H. Atkins (L)
Jonas Atkins (L)
Levi Atkins
Lloyd Atkins
Olden Atkins
Oliver J. Atkins
Teeny Atkins (L)
Ambrose Bailey (L)
Archie D. Bailey
Jesse Bailey
George D. Baker
Ira Baker
William Baker
Oscar Baldwin
John B. Bolen
Charlie C. Bowen
Elton Burke
John A. Burke
Joshua Burke
A. J. Clark (L)
Albert Clark
Andrew Clark
Charlie Clark
Eddie J. Clark
Rasby Clark
Rosser Clark
Howard Clatterbuck
D. P. Curtis (L)
John Morris Curtis
Boot Dodson (L)
Clarence L. Dodson
Ellis B. Dodson
Fred Dodson
Hensel Dodson
Hunter Dodson
Mrs. J. B. (Maude A.) Dodson, Jr.
Jack Dodson

John Frank Dodson
Nathan Dodson
William Dodson
J. T. Dwyer
Jacob Dwyer (L)
Jeff Dwyer
Richard M. Dwyer (L)
Thomas Booten Dwyer
Ellis L. Frazier
Herman Frazier
Ira Frazier
James I. Frazier
Jos. Ira Frazier
Martha Frazier (L)
Samuel Jackson Fry
Savilla Harrel
Amiss Jenkins
Henry Peyton Jenkins
Herbert Jenkins
Hubert C. Jenkins
Jas. Henry Jenkins
Lindsay Jenkins
Silas Jenkins
Wade Jenkins
Herman Leach
B. William Menefee
Carroll B. Menefee
Floyd Menefee
Andrew Nicholson
Ather Nicholson
James M. Nicholson
John. R. Nicholson
Newton Nicholson (L)
Otis W. Nicholson
Ben O. Pullen
Clarence Pullen
Clarence M. Pullen
Dudley W. Pullen
Elmer Pullen
Lloyd Pullen
Mary A. Pullen
Robinson Pullen
James W. Ramey
Floyd Seal
Eddie Sisk
Newton Sisk
Thurman Woodward

Rockingham County

Ben F. Atkins
Gid Baugher
Jos. W. Baugher
Lloyd Baugher
Albert Beasley
R. Howard Beasley
Doc Breeden
E. H. Breeden
Ward Breeden
Laura Bruce
Berlin Louis Collier
Charlie Conley
Charles Davis (L)
Otis L. Davis
A. N. Dean
Anna Eliza Dean (L)
Emory Dean
Ennis Dean
Henry Dean
J. W. Dean
Jacob R. Dean
Ollie Dean
Vernon Foltz
C. E. Haney
Dewey Haney
J. K. Haney
Dewey Hansborough
A. D. Hensley
Alex Hensley
Elmer Hensley
Ralph Hensley
Sarah Hensley
Mittie Keyton
Henry Knighton

Mrs. Z. J. Knighton
Z. K. Knighton (L)
Emmett Lam
Ernest R. Lam
Harvey L. Lam
J. W. Lawson
John H. Mace
Howard L. Maiden
Harold Meadows
Hubert Meadows
Nelson Meadows
Richard McDaniel
Wesley McDaniel
Alec Morris
John Morris
Norman Morris
Thomas Morris (L)
A. C. Moubray
H. R. Osbourne
Bennie Roach
Luther Roach
Clark Shifflett
George M. Shifflett (L)
J. Clyde Shifflett
Joseph Shifflett
Oscar Shifflett
Sam Shifflett
Fred Smith
James Snow
A. J. Williams
J. E. Williams
Walter W. Williams
Gordon Wood
J. F. Wyant

Warren County

W. C. Campbell
James H. Clatterbuck
C. A. Corbin (L)
Cleva Deavers
Everet Fox

R. C. Fox
S. G. "Buddy" Fox
John Jewell
Robert Mathews
Kate Walters (L)

Sources and Helpers

In 1985 the Shenandoah Natural History Association (SNHA) encouraged me to renew my research into the park's human past. For half a century I'd been watching the story unfold and, at intervals, doing active research and writing articles, a book or two for general readers, and an administrative history of 464 typed pages for governmental policy makers.

A research grant from the association, plus fresh ideas from several friends, helped me immediately into channels beyond those I'd explored in previous projects. The launching friends were Dennis Carter, then chief park naturalist; Robert R. Jacobsen, just retiring as park superintendent; W. Dean Cocking of James Madison University, president of SNHA; Chuck Anibal, assistant chief park naturalist; Ray Schaffner, former chief park naturalist, and his wife, Vera; Lynne Overman of Richmond, a director of SNHA and publications committee member; Dee Houston, twice president of SNHA; Charles Foster, retired professor of English literature, and his wife, Doris; and Don Larson, a former naturalist in western parks, now researcher-writer in the nation's capital and frequent Shenandoah hiker. My wife Eileen, fellow free-lance writer, has been a reliable tester of ideas old and new, a companion in many interviews and excursions, first and last adviser on manuscript drafts, and continual bolsterer of morale.

The 1988 SNHA publications committee, helpfully overseeing completion of the project with the professional aid of editor Ann Hofstra Grogg, is as follows: James R. "Bob" Johnson (chair), Clark P. Baker, Deborah Bloxom, Tessy Shirakawa, Terry Lindsay, Warren Bielenberg (chief park naturalist), Greta Miller (SNHA business manager), and Lynne Overman, now SNHA president.

Footnote identification of the thousand or more sources of information is impractical and inappropriate for a book intended for a general audience. I'll try, however, to pick out and list the main sources, and I invite anyone urgently needing more precise pinpointing to phone me: (703) 743-7246.

Our great treasure trove of 20th-century facts is the park headquarters complex beside U.S. 211 (Post Office address: Luray). Some of the most valuable records in the SNP archives date back to the 1920s, when citizen organizations were pushing recognition of this site, and to the first half of the 1930s, when the Commonwealth of Virginia was struggling to acquire the park-land. The slight gaps here have been filled from National Archives, Library of Congress, and the Supreme Court Library in Washington, D.C., and from Virginia State Library in Richmond.

Official records of human doings here since white people took control have been kept in the county court houses and partly published in local newspapers, along with unofficial chronicles of life. Court records, deed books, and will books are basic though time-consuming sources; to speed the task I've found concentrations of pertinent information elsewhere and used the county records directly in the few cases where authenticity was in doubt or additional details were necessary.

All eight counties with significant acreages of park-land are represented by published books that focus the main lines of settlements and other historic events. These counties also have voluntary organizations linked to a generally rising interest in genealogy and other aspects of the human past. The following have helped me find key facts and/or supplied photocopies of meaningful documents: Harrisonburg-Rockingham, Madison County, Rappahannock, Albemarle County, Greene County, and Augusta historical societies; Page County Heritage Association; and Warren Heritage Society. Records of importance have been brought forth by families of the park region. Public libraries in county seats have also helped, and I've drawn significantly from Carrier Library at James Madison University, Harrisonburg, especially for professional journals relating to the human past before Europeans settled. Thunderbird archeological site beside the park has been in the forefront of discoveries revealing the early people; its professional personnel provided much information, and exhibits at Thunderbird Museum made the long-ago life three dimensional. NPS research inside the national park has also been extensive in its penetration of the human past.

I'm grateful to all institutions and persons who have helped. Of course no one but me is to blame for any errors that might have crept in.

Main Sources by Chapters

The documents, including taped interviews, that I've used most directly in this book—maybe one-fourth of those that have helped me in one way or another but with at least three-fourths of the information—are identified below in one word when possible. More complete references are in the alphabetical list of documents that follows this section.

The persons listed for each chapter by family names are further identified in a separate alphabetical list that follows the list of documents. On one or more occasions between 1935 and 1988 these persons have helped me interconnect facts and trace their meanings into real life. They've found and lent family documents or pictures. They've included helpful hints in personal correspondence and informal conversation. Quite a few have read or discussed manuscript drafts and thus contributed to the final version. More formal and concentrated letters or conversations, sometimes involving the same persons, are on record and listed among the documents. Where the same name appears on both lists, the document author has given me additional help in person.

Many people who've helped me substantially are gone now. Among those who have died since I started writing on this project in 1986 are Frances Heiskell, R. Taylor Hoskins, William "Bill" McHenry, Paul Broyles, and Laura Virginia Hale.

Chapter 1, Spear Hunters
Documents: Brennan, Carbone, Eastern, Farb, D. Fisher, J. Gardner, W. Gardner, Griffin, both Hoffman, Holland 1960, Inashima letters, Kopper, McCord and Hranicky, Painter, Shipman, Walker, Wayland's Rockingham, Wilkison. Also numerous articles of the 1980s (mostly not listed individually) in *Natural History, Paleobiology, Chesopiean, Nature* (London), *Quaternary Research, Archeology of Eastern North America, National Geographic,* and other magazines dealing scientifically or popularly with the early people in America.
Persons: Anibal, Holland, McCord, Rodgers, R. Smith, Walker.

Chapter 2, The Last Indians
Documents: Adair, Amiss 1940, Brennan, Erichsen-Brown, Ewan, Farb, D. Fisher, Fowke, W. Gardner, Griffin, Harrington, both Hoffman, all Holland, all Inashima, Jefferson, Judy, Kercheval, Kopper, Lederer, McCord, Painter, J. Smith, Sullivan, both Swanton, Walker, Wilkison, Wills, both Yowell.
Persons: F. Amiss, Anibal, Davis, Firth, M. Hoffman, Holland, McCord, Rodgers, R. Smith, Sullivan, Yowell.

Chapter 3, Fur Trader-Explorers
Documents: Adair, Carpenter, Fontaine, Gray, Hatch, Lederer, Morrison, J. Smith, Slaughter, Strickler, all Wayland, both Yowell.
Persons: Davis, Firth, Monger, Pawlett, Wilson, Yowell.

Chapter 4, The Powdered Wigs
Documents: Bailyn, Bean, S. Brown, Davis, Dickinson, L. Fisher, Floyd, Hale 1969, Haley, Hite, E. Johnson, Kercheval, Miller, Moody, Nugent, Overall, Poe, Scott, Slaughter, SNP archives with numerous land patents of 1700s (also on record in the counties), Stewart, Strickler, all Wayland, White, J. Woods, both WPA, both Yowell.
Persons: Brooks, Bushman, T. Fristoe, Geisler, Good, Hale, Heiskell, Hoak, the Hubbards, A. Miller, Monnington, Morris, Pawlett, Pearson, Stephenson, Strickler, Volchansky, Yowell.

Chapter 5, Nonestablishment Settlers
Documents: Bailyn, Bauserman, Bean, Cowell, Davis, Dean, Fishback, L. Fisher, Floyd, Hale 1969, both Hoffman, Hutton, Kercheval, Miller, R. Mitchell, both Monger, Moody, Nugent, Perdue, Peyton, Pitman, both Steere, Strickler, Via, Waddell, all Wayland, Wilson, both Yowell.
Persons: F. Amiss, the Breedens, Bushman, Firth, Fishback, Fisher, the Fosters, the Galloways, Geisler, Hale, Hoak, S. Hoffman, Holschuh, Jenkins, the McHenrys, A. Miller, Monger, Pawlett, Turk, A. Via, H. Via, Volchansky, Wilson, Yowell.

Chapter 6, Planters and Laborers
Documents: Bean, C. Brown, Davis, Floyd, Gray, Hite, Jefferson, E. Johnson, Miller, Newlon, Poe, Slaughter, Via, all Wayland, Wilson, Wright, both Yowell.
Persons: Brooks, Davis, Firth, Fisher, Holschuh, the Hubbards, A. Miller, Pawlett, Pearson, Sheridan, R. Smith, Wilson.

Chapter 7, Miners and Charcoal Makers
Documents: Allen 1967, Bauserman, Comstock, Fishback, Grimsley, Hack, Hutton, E. Johnson, Kiblinger, King, McGill, Overall, Pollock 1960, SNP archives, both Steere, Stose, Strickler, USGS, Waddell, Watson, all Wayland.
Persons: Black, Davis, Fishback, Hale, Heiskell, Hutton, Keys, Kiblinger, Mills, N. Smith, Sullivan, Sweitzer, Wilson.

Chapter 8, Roadmen and Boatmen
Documents: Bauserman, Boggs, Davis, E. Johnson, Jones, Kiblinger, Millar, Miller, Moon, Newlon, both Steere, Strickler, Sullivan, Waddell, all Wayland, Waynesboro, Weaver, White.

Persons: Berry, Davis, T. and F. Fristoe, Hoak, the Johnsons, Kiblinger, Lowe, A. Miller, Mills, Overman, Pawlett.

Chapter 9, Warriors and Watchers
Documents: Beaty, Laurance Buck, Lucy Buck, M. Buck, both Hale, Haley, Moon, Overall, Quad, Selby, Steere 1935, Strickler, Sullivan, Waddell, all Wayland, Waynesboro.
Persons: Brinkow, Hale, Heiskell, Morris, Pearson, Sullivan, Wilson.

Chapter 10, Dynasty
Documents: Lucy Buck, Burrill, Overall, Pitman, Poe, Rappahannock, Steere 1935, Strickler, Taylor, all Wayland, WPA 1936-40.
Persons: Black, the Fosters, R. Fristoe, T. and F. Fristoe, Hale, Heiskell, Hutton, Keys, N. Smith.

Chapter 11, Farmer-Grazers and Tenants
Documents: C. Corbin, Gray, E. Johnson, L. Long, R. Long, Meadows, J. Smith, SNP archives including land records, Spitler, Steere 1935, Strickler, USDA, H. Varner, J. Varner, Waddell.
Persons: C. Corbin, Cullers, Gander, Hoagg, Huffman, Long, Mills, Moore, Musselman, all listed Spitlers.

Chapter 12, Millers, Townsmen, and Railroaders
Documents: both Atlases, Beaty, Boggs, G. Corbin, Davis, Gray, Haley, Hutchinson, Hutton, E. Johnson, Millar, Miller, R. Mitchell, Newlon, Poe, Showacre, SNP archives, Waddell, all Wayland, White, J. Woods, WPA 1936-40.
Persons: Beaty, G. Corbin, V. Corbin, Good, A. Miller, Mills, Morris, Overman, Pawlett, Price, the Reeders, N. and D. Sisk, A. Via, Winn.

Chapter 13, Lumbermen and Barkers
Documents: both Atlases, Bert, D. Campbell, Carbone, Edmonds, Floyd, Gray, Haley, Hall, E. Johnson, Knight, R. Mitchell, Poe, Roosevelt, SNP archives, Spitler.
Persons: Bert, Broyles, Cook, Davis, Fray, Heiskell, Kite, Moore, Nicholson, Nollert, D. Smith, Janie Spitler, Willis.

Chapter 14, The Mountain Folk Image
Documents: both Atlases and dozens of other old maps (in the Library of Congress and Virginia State Library) dating back to 1700s but mostly of Civil War time, Bailyn, Bean, Beaty, Lucy Buck, Chase, C. Corbin, G. Corbin, both Cowden, Davis, Dean, Ellis, Erichsen-Brown, Floyd, Gray, Heatwole, Hoskins, Humrickhouse, Hutchinson, E. Johnson, J. Johnson, Kephart, Kercheval, Knight, Lumpkin, Marsh, Meadows, Millar, Monger, Neve, J. Nicholson, M. Nicholson, Perdue, Poe, all Pollock, Reeder, Schaffner, Schairer, Sexton, Sherman, Sizer, D. Smith, SNP archives, Spitler, both Steere, Sullivan, Waddell, Wayland 1912, Wilhelm, Witcofski, all Zerkel.
Persons: Anibal, Beaty, the Breedens, Brinklow, Chase, Cook, all listed Corbins, Cowden, Dean, Firth, Hoagg, Holschuh, Hoskins, the Johnsons, Kiblinger, the McHenrys, Monger, Nicholson, Pollock, Price, the Reeders, Sherman, all listed Sisks, Sours, Sparks, Stephens, Sullivan, Taylor, A. Via, H. Via, E. Walker, Whittle, Willis, Winn, Yowell, Zerkel.

Chapter 15, National Park Dreamers
Documents: All Albright, Amiss 1935, Benchoff, Davis, Dodd, Floyd, Hall, Jefferson, Lambert 1979 with 819 footnotes pinpointing sources, Mather, Naylor, Northern, all Pollock, Schairer, Simmons, SNP archives, both Shenandoah National Park Association, Spitler, Steere, Wayland 1957, Zerkel 1940 and Additional.
Persons: Benchoff, Byrd, Harnsberger, Lassiter, Pollock, Price, Sours, Janie Spitler, Stephenson, A. Via, E. Walker, Zerkel.

Chapter 16, Conservation-Developers
Documents: Abernethy, all Albright, Amiss 1935, Benchoff, Boone, Burrill, Cammerer, Carson, Dabney, Governors', Horan, Kiblinger, Lambert 1971 and 1979, MacKaye, Marsh, McLandon, Naylor, Poe, Pollock 1960, Potomac, Simmons, Sizer, Witcofski, all Zerkel—plus park-land maps, deeds, and other details in Albemarle, Augusta, Greene, Madison, Page, Rappahannock, Rockingham, and Warren county court houses, most of which exist also in the SNP archives papers representing the land-acquisition work of the Virginia State Commission on Conservation and Development.
Persons: Both Amiss, Avery, Benchoff, Bert, Boone, Byrd, Cashion, Coffman, Fray, Gochenour, Hale, Harriman, Hoak, Jenkins, Kiblinger, Lassiter, Lowe, Moore, Noyes, Pollock, Speake, Zerkel.

Chapter 17, Embattled Owners
Documents: Alexander, Cammerer, D. Campbell, C. Corbin, G. Corbin, Hoskins, Lambert 1971 and 1979, McGill, Sizer, Staunton, U.S. Supreme, Virginia, Warren, Zerkel 1934 and Additional.
Persons: Alexander, Bert, Blackwell, all listed Corbins, Cowden, Gander, Hoskins, Lassiter, Long, Mills, Musselman, Sheridan, all listed Sisks, all listed Spitlers, Taylor, A. Via, H. Via, Willis, Winn.

Chapter 18, Refugees and Rangers
Documents: Bert, Carson, C. Corbin, G. Corbin, both Cowden, Governors', Harris, Hoskins, Humrickhouse, Ickes, Lambert 1979, J. Nicholson, Shenandoah Land Program, D. Smith, SNP archives including files and many newspaper clippings 1937–38, both Steere, Zerkel Additional (files on homesteads).
Persons: Bert, D. Corbin, G. Corbin, V. Corbin, Cowden, Fox, Harriman, Hoskins, N. Sisk, Sours, Stephens, Taylor, A. Via, Willis, Wills, Zerkel.

Chapter 19, Managers and Visitors
Documents: All Albright, Borman, J. Campbell, Favour, Freeland, Hoskins, Ickes, Jacobsen, J. Johnson, Lambert 1979, Mrs. Lassiter, Liles, MacKaye 1932 and 1947, V. Mitchell, Potomac, Reeve, Schaffner, both Shenandoah Nature, SNP archives including dedication speech by President Franklin D. Roosevelt and many files reflecting park situations and actions 1935–86.
Persons: Avery, Bielenberg, Butcher, Campbell, Carter, Edwards, Freeland, Hoskins, Jacobsen, Jarvis, J. Johnson, Lassiter, Lowe, Moore, Musichuk, Overman, Packard, the Reeders, Schaffner, A. Smith, E. Walker, Wetmore, Zerkel.

Documents

Abernethy, Paul G. Camp Hoover. Interview by author, 1967. Tape. SNP archives, Luray.

Adair, James. *History of the American Indians.* 1930. New ed. Edited by Samuel Cole Williams. New York: Promontory Press, 1986.

Albright, Horace M. Past of Shenandoah park. Interview by R. Taylor Hoskins, E. Ray Schaffner, and Bruce McHenry, 1969. Tape. SNP archives, Luray.

———. Past of Shenandoah park. Letter to author, Sept. 27, 1976. Author's files.

———. Shenandoah park's 50th anniversary. Letter to superintendent, Apr. 3, 1986. SNP working files, Luray.

Alexander, Rudolph B. About park-land's largest tract and its owner. Interview by author, 1986. Tape. Author's files.

Allen, Rhesa M., Jr. *Geology and Mineral Resources of Greene and Madison Counties.* Charlottesville: Virginia Division of Mineral Resources, 1963.

———. *Geology and Mineral Resources of Page County.* Charlottesville: Virginia Division of Mineral Resources, 1967.

Amiss, Fred T. "A Sketch of the Early History of the Shenandoah National Park." Apr.–May 1935. Handwritten original, 41 pp. SNP archives, Luray.

———. Letter to park superintendent about Medicine Man of Stony Face, Apr. 29, 1940. SNP archives, Luray.

Atlas of Page and Shenandoah Counties, Va. Philadelphia: D. J. Lake and Co., 1885.

Atlas of Rockingham County, Va. Philadelphia: D. J. Lake and Co., 1885.

Author's files. Two-foot file drawer of papers, notes, and tapes concentrated to produce Administrative History (see Lambert 1979), plus scattered assortment of books, pamphlets, notes, and other materials, including 15-inch file concentrated to produce the present book. Home in Shaver Hollow beside park. Post Office address: Luray.

Bailyn, Bernard. *The Peopling of British North America: An Introduction.* New York: Alfred A. Knopf, 1986.

Bauserman, Gary, and others. *Page, The County of Plenty.* Luray: Page County Bicentennial Commission, 1976.

Bean, R. Bennett. *The Peopling of Virginia.* Boston: Chapman and Grimes, 1938.

Beaty, Richard Edward. *The Mountain Angels: Trials of the Mountaineers of the Blue Ridge and Shenandoah Valley.* Front Royal: R. E. Beaty, 1928.

Benchoff, H. J. "Report to Arno B. Cammerer . . ." Park project history. 22-p. booklet. Woodstock: Printed privately, Aug. 1934. Author's files.

Bert, C. V. CCC Camp projects and resettlement of mountain folk. Interview by author, 1969. Tape. SNP archives, Luray.

Boggs, Mary Jane. "Rambles among the Virginia Mountains" [1851 journal], edited by Andrew Boni. *Virginia Magazine of History and Biography,* Jan. 1969.

Boone, Joel T. Camp Hoover. Interviews by the author and E. Ray Schaffner. Tape, SNP archives, Luray; some notes, author's files.

Borman, Ralph E. "Proposed Boundary Revisions of SNP." June 30, 1967. 2 vols., 116 p. and 280 p. SNP files, Luray.

Brennan, Louis A. "The Definable Reality of a Prehistoric Middle Atlantic Region Culture Province." *Chesopiean* 19, no. 5–6 (Oct.–Dec. 1981): 89–104.

Brown, Dr. Charles. "Reminiscences of Early Albemarle." *Papers of the Albemarle County Historical Society* 8 (1947–48): 55–70.

Brown, Stuart E. *The Virginia Baron* [Lord Fairfax]. [Berryville]: Chesapeake Book Co., 1965.

Buck, Laurance M. Letter and enclosures to Supt. J. R. Lassiter about Belmont plantation, May 31, 1940. SNP archives, Luray.

Buck, Lucy Rebecca. *Sad Earth, Sweet Heaven: Diary, 1861-1865* [Bel Air Plantation, Front Royal]. Edited by William P. Buck. Birmingham, Ala.: Cornerstone, ca. 1950.

Buck, Marcus Blakemore. Diary written at his home—Belmont on Dickey Ridge—before, during, and after the Civil War. Alderman Library, Univ. of Va., Charlottesville.

Burrill, Edna. Neighbor Mountain 4,000-acre tract. Interview by author, 1986. Tape. Author's files.

Cammerer, Arno B. "Report and Map on Shenandoah of Mr. Cammerer to the Secretary of the Interior." Dec. 8, 1927. NPS Washington. National Archives, Washington, D.C.

Campbell, Donald. "Report on John A. Alexander Tract, 22,000 Acres." Timber appraisal for State Commission on Conservation and Development, 1931. Typescript, SNP archives, Luray.

Campbell, June, James R. "Bob" Johnson, and Miriam Reeve. Interview by author, 1977. Tape. Author's files.

Carbone, Victor A. "Environment and Prehistory in the Shenandoah Valley." Ph.D. diss., Catholic Univ., Washington, D.C., 1976.

Carpenter, Delma R. "The Route Followed by Governor Spotswood in 1716 across the Blue Ridge Mountains." *Virginia Magazine of History and Biography* 73 (1965): 405-12.

Carson, William E. *Conserving and Developing Virginia.* Published report by the chairman, State Commission on Conservation and Development, for the period 1926-34. Richmond: Commonwealth of Virginia, 1935. SNP archives, Luray.

Chase, Richard. *The Grandfather Tales.* Boston: Houghton Mifflin, 1948.

Comstock, H. E. "The Redwell Ironworks." *Journal of Early Southern Decorative Arts,* May 1981. Reprinted in *Shenandoah Heritage,* Summer 1985.

Corbin, Charlie "Buck." Interview by author and E. Ray Schaffner, 1969. Tape. SNP archives, Luray.

Corbin, George T. Interview by Ed Garvey, 1966. Copy of typescript in SNP archives, Luray.

Cowden, Mozelle R. [later Brown]. Mountain folk resettled. Interview by author and wife, Sept. 15, 1976. Tape. Author's files.

———. "What Are They Like?" [Park residents]. *Shenandoah Nature Journal* 1, no. 2 (Winter 1936-37): 14-19. SNP archives, Luray, and author's files.

Cowell, M. W. "Thomas Lewis's Will, 1789." *Rockingham Recorder* 3, no. 3 (Apr. 1985): 15-30.

Dabney, Virginius. *Virginia: The New Dominion.* New York: Doubleday, 1971.

Davis, Margaret G. *Madison County, Virginia: A Revised History.* Madison: County Board of Supervisors, 1977.

Dean, Gloria. *The Dean Mountain Story.* Washington, D.C.: Potomac Appalachian Trail Club, 1982.

Dickinson, Josiah Look. *The Fairfax Proprietary.* Front Royal: Warren Press, 1959.

Dodd, John Bruce, and Cherry Dodd. "Massanutten Lodge-Skyland." Historic Structure Report for NPS, 1977. SNP archives, Luray. Much about Addie and George Pollock.

Eastern States Archeological Association. "Fluted Point Survey." *Archeology of Eastern North America* 11 (Fall 1983): 1-97. Thick issue devoted almost entirely to Clovis points in the East.

ECW-CCC-NPS. Category of old papers and pictures originating in park-land mostly between 1933 and 1936 but some as late as 1942. SNP archives and NPS photo files, Luray. Park-type projects were financed by Civilian Conservation Corps allotments and carried out by CCC "boys" supervised by Emergency Conservation Work administrators, technicians, and foremen, also CCC-paid while generally directed by the National Park Service.

Edmonds, C. T. "Affidavit of . . . dated August 25, 1933, re Warren County J. J. Miller Tract." Prepared for Virginia Commission on Conservation and Development. SNP archives, Luray.

Ellis, Rev. J. R. "The Episcopal Church in East Rockingham." 1912. Copy of *Rockingham Supplement* clipping, sent by Lewis F. Fisher, a descendant of Thomas Lewis. Author's files.

Erichsen-Brown, Charlotte. *Use of Plants: For the Past 500 Years.* Aurora, Ont., Can.: Breezy Creeks Press, 1979.

Ewan, Joseph, and Nesta Ewan. *John Banister and His Natural History of Virginia, 1678–1692.* Chicago: Univ. of Ill. Press, 1970.

Farb, Peter. *Man's Rise to Civilization: As Shown by the Indians of North America . . .* New York: Dutton, 1968.

Favour, Paul G., Jr. Letters to author, Jan. 5, Feb. 11, 1953, Nov. 3, 1976. Author's files.

Fishback, John. Account book, ca. 1820–31. Raymond Fishback papers, Madison.

Fisher, Daniel C. "Mastodon Butchery by North American Indians." *Nature* (London) 308, no. 5956 (1984): 271–72.

Fisher, Lewis F., Irwin Frazier, and Mark W. Cowell, Jr. *The Family of John Lewis, Pioneer.* San Antonio, Tex.: Fisher Publications, 1985.

Floyd, Tom. *Lost Trails and Forgotten People: The Story of Jones Mountain.* Washington, D.C.: Potomac Appalachian Trail Club, 1981.

Fontaine, John. *Journal of John Fontaine* [Spotswood expedition]. Edited by Edward Porter Alexander. Williamsburg: Colonial Williamsburg Foundation, 1972.

Fowke, Gerard. *Archeology Investigations in the James and Potomac Valleys.* Smithsonian Institution, Bureau of American Ethnology, Bulletin 23. Washington, D.C.: GPO, 1894.

Freeland, Edward D. Interview by author, May 14, 1978. Tape. Author's files.

Gardner, Joseph L. [project editor] and editorial staff. *Mysteries of the Ancient Americas.* Pleasantville, N.Y.: Reader's Digest Association, 1986.

Gardner, William M. *Lost Arrowheads and Broken Pottery: Traces of Indians in the Shenandoah Valley.* Front Royal: Thunderbird Museum, 1986.

Governors' Papers. 1926–38. Archives Division, Virginia State Library, Richmond.

Gray, Lewis Cecil. *History of Agriculture in the Southern United States to 1860.* 2 vols. Washington, D.C.: Carnegie Institution of Washington, 1933. More than a thousand-pages rich in source notes.

Griffin, J. B., ed. *Archeology of Eastern United States.* Chicago: Univ. of Chicago Press, 1952.

Grimsley, G. P. *Iron Ores, Salt and Sandstones.* Vol. 4, *West Virginia Geological Survey.* State of West Virginia: Geological Survey Comm., 1909.

Hack, John T. *Geomorphology of the Shenandoah Valley . . .* U.S. Geological Survey, Paper 484, 1965.

Hale, Laura Virginia. *Four Valiant Years in the Lower Shenandoah Valley.* Strasburg: Shenandoah Publishing House, 1968.

———. Inteview by author and E. Ray Schaffner, 1969. Tape. SNP archives, Luray.

Haley, Elliott Clarke, and others. *An Economic and Social Survey of Warren County.* Charlottesville: Univ. of Va., 1943.

Hall, R. Clifford. "Report on the Reconnaissance of the Blue Ridge in Virginia between

Simmons and Manassas Gaps." U.S. Forest Service, Department of Agriculture, R.E.C. Report 1, Sept. 1914. National Archives, Washington, D.C.

Harrington, M. R. *Indians of New Jersey; or Dickon among the Lenapes.* 1938. Reprint. New Brunswick, N.J.: Rutgers Univ. Press, 1966.

Harris, Edward A. "The Blue Ridge Mountaineer" [song of a dozen stanzas]. Copyright 1975 by Mrs. Roy (Virginia) Harris. Parts quoted by permission through Arnold L. Via. Photocophy of sheet music. Author's files.

Hatch, Charles E., Jr. *Alexander Spotswood Crosses the Blue Ridge.* NPS, U.S. Department of the Interior, Washington, D.C., 1968. History, maps, and pictorial illustrations.

Heatwole, Henry. *Guide to Skyline Drive and Shenandoah National Park.* 3d ed. Luray: Shenandoah Natural History Association, 1985.

Hite, Mary Elizabeth. *My Rappahannock Story Book.* Richmond: Dietz, 1950.

Hoffman, Michael A. "Man in the Blue Ridge: The Cultural Resources of the Shenandoah National Park—A Multidisciplinary Approach." Anthropology Dept., Univ. of Va., 1976. Copy in SNP archives, Luray. Includes contributions by Douglas McLearen, James Miller, Charles L. Perdue, Nancy J. Martin-Perdue, Robert Vernon, David Lyne, and Robert Foss.

———. "Patterns in Time: Human Adaptation in the Blue Ridge from 7000 B.C. to 1930 A.D." Report for NPS, 1979. SNP archives, Luray. Includes contributions on prehistory by Robert Foss, on history by John R. Van Atta, and on social anthropology by Robert Vernon.

Holland, C. G. "Madison Run Rock Shelter in the Shenandoah National Park," with preface by J. C. Harrington. *Bulletin of the Archeological Society of Virginia* 7, no. 4 (June 1953).

———. "Migration in a Late Archaic Horizon." *Bulletin of the Archeological Society of Virginia* (Mar. 1965).

———. *Preceramic and Ceramic Cultural Patterns in Northwest Virginia.* Smithsonian Institution, Anthropological Papers 57. Washington, D.C.: GPO, 1960.

Horan, John F., Jr. "Will Carson and the Virginia Conservation Commission 1926–1934." *Virginia Magazine of History and Biography* 92, no. 4 (Oct. 1984): 391–415.

Hoskins, R. Taylor. Interview by author, 1969. Tape. SNP archives, Luray.

Humrickhouse, Mabel B. "They Can't Buy a Homestead." *Shenandoah Nature Journal* 1, no. 3 (Spring 1937): 11–23. SNP archives, Luray. Park residents helped by Virginia Welfare.

Hutchinson, Daphne, and Theresa Reynolds, comps. *On the Morning Side of the Blue Ridge.* Washington: Rappahannock News, 1983.

Hutton, R. B., and H. V. Langley. *The History of Elkton.* Elkton: Commemorative Committee, 1976.

Ickes, Harold L. *The Secret Diary of Harold L. Ickes.* Vol. 1. New York: Simon and Schuster, 1953.

Inashima, Paul Y. "Archeological Survey Reports." 14th report in this series, Apr. 1, 1988. SNP files, Luray. For the Skyline Drive rehabilitation project, beginning in 1983. The file now 14+ inches thick; investigations continuing.

———. Letter to Charles Anibal, with enclosed analysis of residues on projectile points, up to 10,000 years old, found in park, Apr. 4, 1986. SNP interpretive division files, Luray.

———. Letter to author, Mar. 16, 1987. Author's files.

Jacobs, Duane. "Information on Known Cemeteries within Shenandoah National Park." Jan. 27, 1954. 14 p. SNP ranger files, Luray.

Jacobsen, Robert R. Interview by author, 1977. Tape. Author's files.

———. Voluminous looseleaf books on wilderness designation, SNP, 1972-76. SNP archives, Luray.

Jefferson, Thomas. *Notes on the State of Virginia.* Paris, 1785. New ed. Chapel Hill, N.C.: Univ. of N.C. Press, 1955.

Johnson, Elizabeth B., and C. E. Johnson, Jr. *Rappahannock County, Virginia: A History.* Salem, W.Va.: Walsworth Publishing Co., Don Mills, Inc., 1981.

Johnson, James R. "Bob." See with June Campbell.

Jones, Katie Barbee. Letter to NPS director Arno B. Cammerer about her childhood home, The Bower, in the park, Aug. 11, 1936. SNP archives, Luray.

Judy, Frank O. "Indians of Shenandoah National Park." *Shenandoah Nature Journal* 1, no. 2 (Winter 1936-37): 4-7. SNP archives, Luray, and author's files.

Kephart, Horace. *Our Southern Highlanders.* New York: Macmillan, 1913. Paperback reprint. Macmillan, 1963.

Kercheval, Samuel. *A History of the Valley of Virginia.* 4th ed. Strasburg: Shenandoah Publishing House, 1925.

Kiblinger, Frank. Interviews by author, 1967-68. Notes. Author's files. Tape of interview by author and E. Ray Schaffner. Ca. 1965. SNP archives, Luray.

King, Philip B. *Geology of the Elkton Area, Va.* U.S. Geological Survey, Professional Paper 230, 1950.

Knight, Clyde. *Pathways to Remember.* Stanardsville: Clyde H. Knight, 1986.

Kopper, Philip, and others. *The Smithsonian Book of North American Indians before the Coming of the Europeans.* Washington, D.C.: Smithsonian Books, 1986.

Lambert, Darwin. *Herbert Hoover's Hideaway.* Luray: Shenandoah Natural History Association, 1971.

———. Shenandoah historical papers. Author's files.

———. "Shenandoah National Park Administrative History, 1924-1976." NPS Mid-Atlantic Region and Shenandoah Natural History Association, 1979. Photocopies in NPS office, Luray; NPS regional office, Philadelphia; and NPS Washington, D.C., office.

Lassiter, Mrs. J. R. Interview by author, 1976. Tape. Author's files.

Lederer, John. *The Discoveries of John Lederer.* London, 1671. New ed. Edited by William P. Cumming. Charlottesville: Univ. Press of Va., 1958.

Liles, Granville. Interview by author, 1977. Tape. Author's files.

Long, Louise Varner. Interview by author and wife, 1986. Tape. Author's files.

Long, Reuben. Account book, ca. 1831-73. Louise Long papers, Stony Man-Luray.

Lumpkin, Bill, Jr. "Mountain Man Lives in Memory," "A Mountain Man Remembered," and other articles. *Greene County Record,* 1983-85.

MacKaye, Benton. "The Appalachian Trail: A Guide to the Study of Nature." *Scientific Monthly,* April 1932. Reprint with MacKaye essay-letter (below) in SNP archives, Luray.

———. "An Appalachian Trail—A Project in Regional Planning." *Journal of the American Institute of Architects,* Oct. 1921. Reprinted in *PATC Bulletin,* July 1942.

———. Essay-letter to Supt. E. D. Freeland, May 13, 1947, proposing and philosophically justifying an environmental, self-guiding nature trail. SNP archives, Luray.

Marsh, S. H. "Shenandoah National Park: Solving Virginia's Greatest Jigsaw Puzzle." *Commonwealth,* May 1934.

Mather, Stephen T. *NPS Annual Report* [Fiscal year 1923]. Washington, D.C.: Department of the Interior, 1924.

McCord, Howard A. Interview by author and E. Ray Schaffner, 1961. Tape. SNP archives, Luray.

———, and William Jack Hranicky. *A Basic Guide to Virginia Prehistoric Projectile Points.* Archeological Society of Virginia, Publication 6, 1979.

McGill, William M. "Mineral Prospects on the John A. Alexander Property (#326) in Rockingham County." Report to State Commission on Conservation and Development, Nov. 25, 1931. Copy in SNP archives, Luray.

McLandon, William Porter. "Economic Aspects of the Shenandoah Park Project." M.A. thesis, Univ. of Va., 1930.

Meadows, Lila. Tenants on Cattle Pasture. Interview by author, 1986. Author's files.

Millar, S. R. Excerps from Diary, Front Royal, 1865-1929. Edited by Alvin Dohme, 1977. Photocopy, 28 pp. Samuels Public Library, Front Royal.

Miller, Ann Brush. *Orange County Road Orders, 1734-1749.* Charlottesville: Virginia Highway and Transportation Research Council, 1984.

Mitchell, Robert D. *Commercialism and Frontier: Perspectives on the Early Shenandoah Valley.* Charlottesville: Univ. Press of Va., 1977.

Mitchell, Virginia. Lassiter's transfer, etc. Interview by author, 1976. Author's files.

Monger, Billie Jo. *Elkton Diamond Jubilee.* Elkton: Community Commemorative Book, 1983.

———. *The Mongers: A Family of Old Virginia.* Elkton: By the author, 1980.

Moody, Minnie Hite. *Long Meadows.* New York: Macmillan, 1941.

Moon, W. A. Series on "Historical Significance of Browns Gap in the War Between the States." *Waynesboro News-Virginian,* Jan. 1937.

Morrison, A. J. "The Virginia Indian Trade to 1673." *William and Mary Quarterly,* 2d ser., 1, no. 4 (Oct. 1921): 217-36.

Naylor, Hugh E. "A Brief History of the Movement for a National Park in Northern Virginia." Front Royal: privately printed, 1934.

Neve, Archdeacon F. A. "Fifty Years of Mountain Work." *Southern Churchman,* May 21, 1938. Episcopal missions and schools in park region.

Newlon, Howard, Jr., and Nathaniel Mason Pawlett. *Backsights.* Charlottesville: Virginia Highway and Transportation Research Council, 1985. Historical articles with illustrations.

Nicholson, John T. "The Old Mountain Home" [poem of about 30 stanzas]. *Madison Eagle,* June 1, 1934. SNP archives, Luray.

Nicholson, Murphy. Letter to Thomas Y. Crowell Co., 1975, refuting information and conclusions of 1933 book *Hollow Folk* by Sherman and Henry. Copy in SNP archives, Luray, and other park files.

Northern Virginia Park Association. "A National Park Near the Nation's Capital" [pamphlet]. Skyland: NVPA, Nov. 1924. SNP archives, Luray.

Nugent, Nell Marion. *Cavaliers and Pioneers.* Richmond: Virginia State Library, 1979.

Overall papers. Hundreds of old pages dating as far back as the 1700s, including genealogy by A. S. Furcron, mineral reports, pictures, and Ann P. Overall Jolliffe drawings and religious pamphlets. Saved by Sue Heiskell, Frances Heiskell, and other family members. Present contact Thelma Fristoe, Front Royal.

Page, Thomas Nelson. *Social Life in Old Virginia,* with drawings by Edith V. Cowles and M. Cowles. New York: Charles Scribner's Sons, 1897.

Painter, Floyd. "Two Basic Paleo-Indian Lithic Traditions Evolving from a Southeastern Hearth." *Archeology of Eastern North America* 11 (Fall 1983): 65-79.

Perdue, Charles, and Nancy Martin-Perdue. "Appalachian Fables and Facts: A Case

Study of the Shenandoah National Park Removals." *Appalachian Journal* 7, nos. 1–2 (Autumn–Winter 1979–80): 84–104.

Peyton, J. Lewis. *History of Augusta County, Virginia.* 1882. Bridgewater edition, 1953. Reprint. Harrisonburg: Harrisonburg-Rockingham Historical Society, 1985.

Pitman, Levi. Diary written at Mt. Olive, Shenandoah County, Virginia, 1845–92. 17 vols. Manuscripts Division, Alderman Library, Univ. of Va., Charlottesville.

Poe, Rebecca. Series on history of Warren County communities. *Warren Sentinel*, 1985.

Pollock, George Freeman. Assorted promotional pamphlets, booklets, and "newspapers" of early Skyland, unsorted. SNP archives, Luray.

——. *Skyland: The Heart of Shenandoah National Park.* Edited by Stuart E. Brown, Jr. Berryville: Chesapeake Book Co., 1960.

——. "Why Skyland? Beginnings of Shenandoah National Park." *PATC Bulletin*, Oct. 1935–Oct. 1937.

Potomac Appalachian Trail Club *Guide to Trails in the Shenandoah National Park* and *Trail Maps.* Revisions at intervals for more than half a century.

——. Photo archives. David M. Bates, Arlington.

Quad, M. *Field, Fort and Fleet.* Detroit: Detroit Free Press, 1885. On the Civil War, with numerous drawings.

Rappahannock County Circuit Court. *Keyser* v. *Pitman's Executrix,* or *John A. Keyser* v. *Mary C. Pitman et als.,* 1898 to jury verdict Nov. 21, 1902.

Reeder, Carolyn, and Jack Reeder. *Shenandoah Heritage: The Story of the People before the Park.* Washington, D.C.: Potomac Appalachian Trail Club, 1978.

Reeve, Miriam. See with June Campbell.

Roosevelt, Theodore. *Message from the President.* Washington, D.C.: GPO, 1902. Regarding danger of drastic deterioration of Southern Appalachian forests.

Rothstein, Arthur. Photographs in Farm Security Administration collection, Virginia State Library, Richmond.

Schaffner, E. Ray. Interview by author, 1977. Tape. Author's files.

Schairer, Frank. "Reminiscences at Fortieth Anniversary of Potomac Appalachian Trail Club." Tape. SNP archives.

Scheel, Eugene M. *Map of Madison County.* Madison: Second National Bank and Madison County Supervisors, 1984.

Scott, W. W. *A History of Orange County, Virginia.* Richmond: Everett Waddey Company, 1907. Reprint. Berryville: Chesapeake Book Company, 1962.

Selby, John. *Stonewall Jackson as Military Commander.* New York: Batsford/Van Nostrand, 1968.

Sexton, Dr. Roy Lyman. "The Forgotten People of the Shenandoah." *American Civic Annual,* 1930.

Shenandoah Land Program. Federal Emergency Relief Administration, Recreational Demonstration Project, FERA-RDP VA R-4. SNP archives, Luray. Old file long kept in SNP safe. Records of voluntary land deals, acreages now in park, as early as Feb. 1935.

Shenandoah National Park Association, Inc. Original minute book, typed record by Daniel P. Wine, secretary, June 2, 1925–Apr. 1928. 67 pp. SNP archives, Luray.

——. "Virginia's Proposed National Park" [pamphlet]. Luray: SNPA Inc., 1925. SNP archives, Luray.

Shenandoah Nature Society. Original minute book, handwritten or typed by secretaries James R. Sigler and Gladys R. Homer, 1936–37. Author's files.

——. *Shenandoah Nature Journal,* quarterly 1936–37. Continued as *Shenandoah Magazine* and *Travel Lore* by the Lambert Company into 1942. Some in SNP archives, Luray; some in author's files. Only known complete set (1979) in Virginia State Library, Richmond.

Sherman, Mandel, and Thomas R. Henry. *Hollow Folk*. New York: Crowell, 1933. Facsimile. Berryville: Virginia Book Company, 1973.

Shipman, P., D. C. Fisher, and J. J. Rose. "Mastodon Butchery: Microscopic Evidence of Carcass Processing and Bone Tool Use." *Paleobiology* 10, no. 3 (1984): 358-65.

Showacre, Charles. Letter to George Shifflett, Sept. 24, 1938. SNP archives, Luray.

Simmons, D. E. "The Creation of Shenandoah National Park and the Skyline Drive, 1924-1936." Ph.D. diss., Univ. of Va., 1978. Copy in SNP archives.

Sizer, Miriam M. "Investigations, 1926-32, Five Mountain Hollows." Report for NPS, 1932. National Archives, Washington, D.C. Study of park-land residents and attitudes.

Slaughter, Philip. *A History of St. Mark's Parish*. Baltimore: Innes and Co., 1877. Revised by T. W. Green as *Notes on Culpeper County and Slaughter's History of St. Mark's Parish*. Culpeper: Culpeper Exponent, 1903. Second revision, by Raleigh Travers Green, author-comp., as *Culpeper County, Virginia*. Baltimore: Regional Publishing Company, 1978.

Smith, Dorothy Noble. "Shenandoah National Park Oral History." 1976-80. Tapes and many typed transcriptions. SNP archives, Luray. About 140 interviews with people remembering their pasts in park-land mountains ca. 1900-37.

Smith, John. *The True Travels, Adventures and Observations*. Vol. 1. London, 1629. New ed. Richmond: Franklin Press, 1819. Includes maps and sketches.

SNP archives. Large quantity and variety of old papers and pictures at Shenandoah National Park headquarters on U.S. 211, west foot of Blue Ridge, Post Office address: Luray.

Spitler, Janie Bailey Mauck. Prepark Skyland, timber, cattle, tenants. Interview by author and wife, 1986. Tape. Author's files.

Staunton Corporation Court. Trial of John A. Alexander, 1926. City Hall, Staunton.

Steere, Edward. "Report on Preservation of Structures." June 1, 1936. SNP archives, Luray. Usually spoken of, with below, as "the Steere Report."

———. "The Shenandoah National Park: Its Possibility as an Historical Development." Dec. 1935. 62 pp. typescript, plus photos. SNP archives, Luray.

Stewart, George R. *Names on the Land*. Boston: Houghton Mifflin-Riverside, 1958.

Stose, G. W., and others. "Manganese Deposits of the West Foot of the Blue Ridge, Virginia." Univ. of Va., 1919. Technical study.

Strickler, Harry M. *A Short History of Page County*. Richmond: Dietz, 1952.

Sullivan, Roy. Interview by author and E. Ray Schaffner, 1969. Tape. SNP archives, Luray.

Swanton, John R. *The Indians of the Southeastern United States*. Smithsonian Institution, Bureau of American Ethnology, Bulletin 137. Washington, D.C.: GPO, 1946.

———. *Indian Tribes of North America*. Smithsonian Institution, Bureau of American Ethnology, Bulletin 145, Washington, D.C.: GPO, 1952.

Taylor, Richard C. "Explorations of Copper Veins in Warren and Page Counties, Virginia." 37 handwritten pp. Overall papers. Thelma Fristoe, Front Royal.

U.S. Department of Agriculture. *Wintering Beef Cattle in the Appalachian Region*. USDA Pamphlet 408. Washington, D.C., May 1927.

U.S. Geological Survey. *21st Annual Report*. Washington, D.C.: GPO, 1901. Including Crimora Mine.

U.S. Supreme Court. *Robert H. Via* v. *The State Commission on Conservation and*

Development of the State of Virginia. Oct. term 1934. *Via v. Commonwealth of Virginia.* Oct. term 1935, including complete record of hearing before three federal judges at U.S. District Court, Harrisonburg, Dec. 10, 1934, and opinion rendered Jan. 12, 1935. Printed record of U.S. Supreme Court, Supreme Court Library, Washington, D.C.; photocopy, author's files.

Varner, Hamilton. Account book, ca. 1861–89. Louise Long papers, Stony Man–Luray.

Varner, James. Account book, ca. 1883–1908. Louise Long papers, Stony Man–Luray.

Via, Vera. "Headquarters" [Brown family]. *Charlottesville Daily Progress,* Sept. 16, 1954.

Virginia Supreme Court of Appeals. *Thomas Jackson Rudacille v. State Commission on Conservation and Development.* Decision at Richmond, 1931.

Waddell, Joseph A. *Annals of Augusta County, Virginia, 1726–1871.* 2d ed. 1902. Reprint. Harrisonburg: C. J. Carrier Co., 1979.

Walker, Joan M. "Fundamentals of Archeology with Focus on Shenandoah Region." Oct.–Nov. 1986. Thunderbird Museum, Limeton-Front Royal. Lecture course with handling of artifacts representing Paleo-Indians and later Indians until about 1700 A.D.

Warren County Circuit Court. *Thomas Jackson Rudacille v. State Commission on Conservation and Developement.* 23 pp. Decision at Front Royal, Oct. 1929.

Watson, Thomas Leonard. "Crimora Mines." Univ. of Va., 1907. Technical study of economic geology.

Wayland, John W. *A History of Rockingham County, Virginia.* 1912. Reprint. Harrisonburg: Harrisonburg-Rockingham Historical Society, 1980.

———. *A History of Shenandoah County, Virginia.* Strasburg: Shenandoah Publishing House, 1927.

———. *Twenty-Five Chapters on the Shenandoah Valley.* Strasburg: Shenandoah Publishing House, 1957.

Waynesboro Historical Commission. Series on "Days of Yore." *News-Virginian,* 1986.

Weaver, Delmar, F., M.D. Series on turnpikes. *Madison Eagle,* 1985–86.

White, Rita Rothgeb. *Papa's Diary.* Luray: R. R. White, 1961.

Wilhelm, Eugene J., Jr. "Folk Geography of the Blue Ridge Mountains." *Pioneer America* 2, no. 1 (Jan. 1970): 29–40. Includes photos of Nicholson Hollow houses.

Wilkison, Elizabeth, M. "A Complex of Paleo-Indian Quarry-Workshop and Habitation Sites in the Flint Run Area of the Shenandoah Valley of Virginia." *Chesopiean* 24, no. 3 (Summer 1986). Virtually the entire issue devoted to early studies of Flint Run archeology, including site later called Thunderbird.

Wills, J. W. "Indians of Northern Piedmont Virginia." *Shenandoah Nature Journal* 1, no. 4 (Summer 1937): 13–19.

Wilson, Howard McKnight. *The Tinkling Spring: Headwater of Freedom.* The Tinkling Spring and Heritage Presbyterian Churches, 1954.

Witcofski, Christine Vest, and Lou K. Witcofski. Camp Hoover and Hoover School. Interview by author and E. Ray Schaffner, 1967. Tape. SNP archives, Luray.

Woods, Rev. Edgar. *History of Albemarle County in Virginia.* 1932. Reprint. Harrisonburg: Harrisonburg-Rockingham Historical Society, 1982.

Woods, Jack, and Mary Ellen Loftin, co-chairmen. *Warren County Sesquicentennial.* Front Royal, 1986.

WPA Virginia Historical Inventory, 1936–40. Microfilm. Virginia State Library, Richmond.

WPA Writers Program. *Virginia: A Guide to the Old Dominion.* New York: Oxford Univ. Press, 1946.

Wright, Lewis B. *The First Gentlemen of Virginia.* Charlottesville: Dominion Books, 1964.

Yowell, Claude Lindsay. *A History of Madison County, Virginia.* Strasburg: Shenandoah
  Publishing House, 1926.

——. Interview by author and others, 1969. Tape. SNP archives, Luray.

Zerkel, L. Ferdinand. "Brief History of SNP Movement and Related Projects 1924-36."
  Report for Supt. James Ralph Lassiter. 1940. SNP archives, Luray.

——. "Virginia CWA Project, Shenandoah National Park Evacuation and Subsistence
  Homesteads Survey." 1934. Summary in SNP archives, Luray. Original with detailed
  data about each family found on park-land probably lost; the author and others have
  searched for two decades without success.

——. Additional materials concerning the park, largely from 1920s and 1930s,
  representing Northern Virginia Park Association, Shenandoah National Park
  Association, Inc., the park-land residents, and the "homesteads," including many
  photographs by Harry Staley of Harrisonburg and others. Four-drawer file cabinet.
  SNP archives, Luray.

In-Person Helpers

Rudolph B. Alexander, Mt. Crawford, nephew of John A. Alexander; Fred T. Amiss,
chief civil engineer in Virginia's acquisition of park-land; Mrs. F. Thomas Amiss,
daughter-in-law of Fred T. Amiss; Charles "Chuck" Anibal, assistant chief park naturalist
(historian); Myron Avery, early leader of Potomac Appalachian Trail Club and
Appalachian Trail Conference.

Clark P. Baker of SNHA, botanist; Richard E. Beaty, Blue Ridge boy, author, seller
of books at north end of park; Col. H. J. Benchoff, Woodstock, park project leader;
Margaret Berry, Luray, Barbee contact, newspaperwoman in park's early years; C. V.
Bert, CCC camp project superintendent; Warren Bielenberg, chief park naturalist; Vivian
Black, Page County research unpublished, including papers in WPA Virginia Historical
Inventory; Jim Henry Blackwell, Sr., kin of Supreme Court plaintiff Robert H. Via;
Deborah Bloxom of SNHA, photographer; Dr. Joel T. Boone, personal physician to
President Hoover; Fonda and Roy Breeden, Elkton, descendants of park families, seekers
of old cemeteries; Patricia Armel Fox Brinklow, Winchester, Fox Hollow family history
interviews; Jeanette Brooks, Texas, descendant of Kirtleys who owned plantations in
park; Paul Broyles, Luray, park region generalist for many decades; Mrs. William
Bushman, Staunton, Augusta County family histories; Devereux Butcher, executive
secretary, National Parks Association; former U.S. senator Harry Flood Byrd, Jr., lifelong
involvement with old Skyland and the park since establishment.

June Campbell, secretary of park superintendents; Dennis Carter, former chief park
naturalist; L. L. Cashion, secretary, Annual Reunion (54th in Sept. 1987) CCC Camp
Fechner, Big Meadows; Richard Chase, collector of folk tales and songs; W. Dean
Cocking, James Madison University, former SNHA president; Dave Coffman, project
superintendent, CCC camp at Big Meadows; Lucy Cook, maker of white-oak baskets
since age 14; Charlie "Buck" Corbin, tenant on mountain pastureland; Dennis Corbin,
park family head, still living at Flint Hill "homestead"; George T. Corbin, owner-builder
of log house in Nicholson Hollow that's now Corbin Cabin used by hikers; Virgil F.
Corbin, Luray, former park resident, son of George T.; Mozelle R. Cowden (later
Brown) "Homestead Lady" when park established; Louisa Brubaker Cullers, Page
County, mountain-and-valley cattle growing.

Dorothy Popham Cox Davis, former mayor town of Washington, glimpses deep into
past via elderly kin; Gloria Dean, researcher-author in Blue Ridge family history.

Guy D. Edwards, third superintendent of park.

Grace Firth, researcher-writer dealing with old ways of cooking, etc.; Raymond Fishback, genealogy and other glimpses of German settlers; Lewis F. Fisher, well-informed descendant of Thomas Lewis; Charles H. Foster, retired professor of English, and his wife, Doris Foster, perceptive critics and generators of ideas; Merle Cliser Fox, Luray, daughter of the Melanchthon Clisers, evicted by force from their Blue Ridge home in 1935; J. D. Fray, longtime Madison County leader who owned large park-land acreages; Edward D. Freeland, second superintendent of park; Raymond Fristoe who grew up near old Overall place knowing descendants of Isaac; Thelma Fristoe, Front Royal, descendant of Isaac Overall, keeper of Overall papers, and her husband, Forrest, who helped Raymond and me find cemeteries.

Dorothy and James Galloway, Ohio, Florida, etc., who keep digging into Beahm family history; James E. Gander, Page County, ridge-and-valley cattle; Mary Geisler, Harrisonburg-Rockingham Historical Society; Rebecca Good, Front Royal genealogist-historian; civil engineer Bob Gochenour, park-land records; Ann Hofstra Grogg, Winchester, editor for SNHA.

Laura Virginia Hale, for decades a most helpful historian of Warren County and Shenandoah part of War Between the States; Bob Harnsberger, Skyland and Pollock long before and after park establishment; C. J. Harriman, early park ranger, land officer in NPS Washington; Frances Heiskel, Compton (P.O. address: Rileyville), who discussed the Overall story with me until it illuminated the park-land past; Don Hoagg, Tanners Ridge-Stanley, seeing Blue Ridge people and doings with fresh vividness; civil engineer Dale Hoak, who guided me into park-land records and their meanings; archeologist Michael A. Hoffman, discussions of park's millenniums-long human past; Steve Hoffman, Madison County Historical Society, German pioneers; C. G. Holland, Charlottesville, medical doctor become archeologist; Helen L. Holschuh, Rappahannock Historical Society; R. Taylor Hoskins, park's first chief ranger and fourth superintendent; Dee Houston, former president of SNHA; Robert M. and Frances Johnson Hubbard, Albemarle County Historical Society; Ray W. Huffman, mountain-and-lowland cattle, tenants, squatters; Elza Hutton, Luray, Overall family.

Robert R. Jacobsen, fifth superintendent of park; Destry Jarvis, National Parks and Conservation Association; Don Jenkins, park-land records and Jenkins families; James R. "Bob" Johnson, born in park-land, longtime district ranger, and his wife, Stella Johnson.

Robert Keys, Front Royal, Overall family; Frank Kiblinger, Stanley, who grew up involved in park-land and people and worked decades in park; Luther Kite, Greene County, steam sawmill, timber industry.

Eileen Lambert, wife of author, former president SNHA, photographer-researcher-writer; Don Larson, researcher-writer in Department of Agriculture, leader of group hikes in park; James Ralph Lassiter, engineer-in-charge during prepark years of ECW-CCC, first superintendent of park; Terry Lindsay, NPS interpreter, SNHA committee; Louise Varner Long, mountain-and-valley cattle, landowners and tenants; Rodney Lowe, the park's chief of engineering and maintenance; Bill Lumpkin, Jr., Greene County, interviewer-writer.

Archeologist Howard A. McCord, Sr., digs in Shenandoah region; William "Bill" and Violet McHenry, Shenandoah town, Page County Heritage Association; Ann Brush Miller, research historian-author, Orange County Historical Society; Greta Miller, coordinator, business manager of SNHA; Joseph P. Mills, Shenandoah town, mines, railroads, river flatboats; Billie Jo Monger, Elkton, ethnohistorian-genealogist-author; Mrs. E. Keith Monnington, Front Royal, present owner of Happy Creek House site; Robert B. Moore, forester with ECW-CCC, later chief ranger; Mary T. Morris, Warren

Heritage Society; Dave Musichuk, collector of Shenandoah postcards of 1930s on; Dorothy Varner Musselman; mountain-and-valley cattle people.

Eddie Nicholson, park resident, longtime crafter of white-oak baskets; August Nollert, manager of Virginia Oak Tannery, Luray, which used to buy chestnut-oak tanbark; E. M. Noyes, CCC camp project superintendent.

Lynne Overman, hiking club leader, delver into old papers and illustrations, president of SNHA.

Fred Packard, executive secretary of National Parks Association; Floyd Painter, Norfolk, editor of archeological magazine *Chesopiean*; Nathaniel Mason Pawlett, Charlottesville, faculty research historian, Virginia Highway and Transportation Research Council; Mary Pearson, Luray, long-ago people and customs of Virginia, sketch of Stonewall Jackson believed to be one of only two portraits of Jackson actually drawn from life; George Freeman Pollock, much discussion 1935–42 about old Skyland, mountain folk, and the park; Jessie Ann Price, Luray, daughter of Miller E. Roudabush, early 1900s recreation in park-land.

Jack and Carolyn Reeder, Washington, D.C., and Potomac Appalachian Trail Club, researchers, writers, editors, searchers of old ways, companions on Blue Ridge hikes; Miriam Reeve, secretary in ranger division; Dr. and Mrs. Eric Rhodes, Luray, photo collection including work by Wallace Rhodes; Thunderbird archeologist C. Lanier Rodgers.

E. Ray Schaffner, former chief park naturalist and SNHA leader, and his wife, Vera Schaffner, both deeply informed and widely acquainted with others having stores of useful facts; Phil Sheridan, Mountfair, Albemarle County, long-ago Browns and Via families; Mandel Sherman, psychologist, co-author of *Hollow Folk*, returned from Los Angeles in 1960s seeking people who had to leave the park in the 1930s; Tessy Shirakawa, NPS interpreter, SNHA committee; Charlie D. Sisk, mountain man and stone mason; Newt and Daisy Sisk and their children Winfield, Marie, Coty, Athey, and Annie, park-land residents; Anthony Wayne Smith, National Parks and Conservation Association; Dorothy Noble Smith, oral history interviewer; Norma Smith, Luray, Overall family; Ruth Smith, botanist exploring use of wild plants by Indians and whites, and her husband, Ed Smith; Mattie Taylor Bates Sours, Hawksbill Gap, then Skyland; Lee Sparks, great-granddaughter of Mary Catherine Cave Thomas, park-land resident who lived a century-plus; C. A. Speake, CCC camp project superintendent; Bernard H. Spitler, Jr., Page County, mountain-and-lowland cattle ranching; Charles Spitler, Jr., Page County, mountain-and-lowland cattle; Janie Bailey Mauck Spitler, Luray, prepark Skyland, timber and cattle industries; Joe Spitler, Arizona, descendant of Blue Ridge cattleman; Wallace T. Stephens, first assistant chief ranger, later chief; Jean Stephenson, researcher-writer, Appalachian Trail clubs and conference; Harry M. Strickler, valley region historian-author; Roy Sullivan, park ranger born near Simmons Gap, noted for number of times struck by lightning; A. J. "Bud" Sweitzer, Rileyville, mines and mining.

Delon Taylor, Hawksbill Gap resident, Skyland worker, early gatekeeper on Skyline Drive; professor Robert A. Turk, Florida, delvings into long-ago Turk family of Turk Mountain area.

Arnold L. Via, Via family and other park history; Herbert Via, life in Sugar Hollow including Robert H. Via family; Jane C. Volchansky, Madison High School teacher exploring the region's past.

Egbert H. Walker, botanist, PATC trail map chairman for many years; Joan Walker, Thunderbird Museum director-archeologist-teacher; Alexander Wetmore, secretary of Smithsonian Institution, longtime president of SNHA; Rev. Dennis Whittle, Blue Ridge missions; Lewis Willis, park-land resident, defender of landowners' rights; James S. Wills, manager of resettlement homesteads, student of Indian life; John W. "Bill" Wilson, Port Republic, Harrisonburg-Rockingham Historical Society; Elizabeth Winn, Mountain Neighbors, crafts organizer-teacher-distributor; Christine Vest Witcofski, Hoover School teacher, and her husband, Lou K. Witcofski, Marine detachment for Camp Hoover protection.

Claude L. Yowell, Madison County historian, collector of Indian relics.

L. Ferdinand Zerkel, prominent in park's genesis and resettlement of mountain folk, U.S. magistrate for park, enthusiastic answerer of questions.

Index

agriculture: in park-land, 67–68
Albright, Horace M., 208, 220
Alexander, John A., 227–229
Alexander, Rudy B., 228
"Alexander the Great." *See* Alexander, John A.
Allen, Harold, 196–197, 215
American Revolution: episodes in park-land, 99–101
Amiss, Fred T., 22, 212
Appalachian Trail movement, 214
Atkins, Teeny, 255
Avery, Myron H., 215, 258

backcountry camping in SNP, 271
Bailey, James O., 194
Bailey, Jesse, 243–244
Banks, N. P. (Union general), 102
Barbee, Andrew Russell, 86, 88–89
Barbee, Herbert, 90–91
Barbee, William Randolph, 89–90
Barbour, James, 43–44, 116
bears, black, in SNP, 273
Beatty, M. E., 269
Beaty, Richard E., 177. *See also The Mountain Angels*
Benchoff, Colonel, 204, 210
Berkeley, William, 25
Beverley, Robert, 30, 32, 38
Beverly, William, 58–59
Black Rock Springs, forest fires around, 219–220
Black Rock Springs Hotel, 190–191
"The Blue Ridge Mountaineer" (ballad), 254
"Bob-Vi." *See* Via, Robert
Boehm, Jacob, family, 57–58
Bower, The (Barbee house), 89, 90
Bradley Shenk, Annie Lee. *See* Shenk, Annie Lee Bradley
Breeden, Dave L., 147
Breeden, Matilda "Aunt Cassie," 255
Brown, B., family, 62–64
Brown, Mozelle. *See* Cowden, Mozelle R.
Brumback, Ed, 248
Buck, Lucy Rebecca, Civil War diary of, 109–110, 112–113, 171. *See also* Buck, Marcus Blakemore, Civil War diary of
Buck, Marcus Blakemore, 172; Civil War diary of, 108 109, 110, 111 112, 113. *See also* Buck, Lucy Rebecca, Civil War diary of
Buracker, George, 178
Buracker, Ray, 194, 219
Byrd, Harry F., Jr. (senator), 270, 272
Byrd, Harry F., Sr. (senator), 266

Byrd, Harry Flood (governor), 204, 205, 208, 210, 211, 269
Byrd, Colonel William, 37

Cammerer, Arno B., 212, 216, 260
Cammerer Line, 212, 214, 216, 270
Carson, A. C., 216, 237
Carson, William E., 208–212, 217; professional background of, 208; Fred T. Amiss commissioned by, 212; national historical park alternative considered by, 214; money for topographic map advanced by, 216; Herbert Hoover's support gained by, 218–219; Skyline Drive construction advocated by, 220–221; CCC camps in park-land aided by, 222; FDR support given to, 224; deeds to form SNP delivered by, 225; blizzard on Skyline Drive, caught in, 226; death of, 226; *Via v. Va.,* involvement in, 237; lifetime list names recommended by, 254. *See also* Carson commission
Carson commission: topographical map commissioned by, 215–216. *See also* Carson, William E.
cash crops. *See* agriculture in park-land
Catlett, Colonel John, 28
Cave, Gordon A. "Gurd," 178–179
Cave, Mary Catherine. *See* Thomas, Mary Catherine Cave
Centre Mills. *See* Overall village
charcoal blast furnace, design of, 75–77
charcoal-making, process of, 78–79
Chester, Captain Thomas, 39
city people: attitudes toward mountain people, 184
Civilian Conservation Corps (CCC): work in SNP, 223–224
Civil War: episodes in park-land, 101–107; battle in park-land, 111. *See also* Buck, Marcus Blakemore, Civil War diary of; Buck, Lucy Rebecca, Civil War diary of
Cliser, Melancthon, 245–246
"colored people." *See* desegregation in SNP; segregation in SNP
Conley family, 176–177
Coolidge, Calvin, 207
copper mining. *See* mining: copper
Corbin, George, 185, 247–248, 253
Corbin, Warren, 178
Cover Brothers Tannery, 164–165
Cover brothers, 164–165
Cowden, Mozelle R. (The Homestead Lady), 186–187, 242, 246, 253
Craig, John, 59